The Collected Works of J. Krishnamurti

Volume X

1956–1957

A Light to Yourself

COLLECTED WORKS VOLUME 10

Photo: J. Krishnamurti, ca 1955

P.O Box 1560, Ojai, CA 93024

Website: www.kfa.org

Printed in the United States of America

ISBN 13: 9781934989432
ISBN: 1934989436

Contents

Preface vii

Talks in Stockholm, Sweden 1

First Talk, May 14, 1956 1
Second Talk, May 15, 1956 6
Third Talk, May 21, 1956 10
Fourth Talk, May 22, 1956 16
Fifth Talk, May 24, 1956 20
Sixth Talk, May 25, 1956 25

Talks in Brussels, Belgium 31

First Talk, June 16, 1956 31
Second Talk, June 17, 1956 37
Third Talk, June 18, 1956 43
Fourth Talk, June 23, 1956 49
Fifth Talk, June 24, 1956 56
Sixth Talk, June 25, 1956 61

Talks in Hamburg, Germany 69

First Talk, September 5, 1956 69
Second Talk, September 6, 1956 74
Third Talk, September 9, 1956 79
Fourth Talk, September 14, 1956 85
Fifth Talk, September 15, 1956 92
Sixth Talk, September 16, 1956 98

Talks in Athens, Greece 107

First Talk, September 24, 1956 107
Second Talk, September 26, 1956 112
Third Talk, September 30, 1956 116

Talks in New Delhi, India 121

First Talk, October 10, 1956 121
Second Talk, October 17, 1956 128
Third Talk, October 21, 1956 135
Fourth Talk, October 24, 1956 141
Fifth Talk, October 28, 1956 148
Sixth Talk, October 31, 1956 155

Talks in Madras, India 163

First Talk, December 12, 1956 163
Second Talk, December 16, 1956 169
Third Talk, December 19, 1956 176
Fourth Talk, December 23, 1956 183
Fifth Talk, December 26, 1956 191

Talks in Colombo, Ceylon 197

First Talk, January 13, 1957 197
Second Talk, January 16, 1957 203
Third Talk, January 20, 1957 210
Fourth Talk, January 23, 1957 216
Fifth Talk, January 27, 1957 223

Talks in Bombay, India 231

First Talk, February 6, 1957 231
Second Talk, February 10, 1957 238
Third Talk, February 17, 1957 245
Fourth Talk, February 20, 1957 252
Fifth Talk, February 24, 1957 259
Sixth Talk, March 3, 1957 266

Questions 273
Index 281

Preface

Jiddu Krishnamurti was born in 1895 of Brahmin parents in south India. At the age of fourteen he was proclaimed the coming World Teacher by Annie Besant, then president of the Theosophical Society, an international organization that emphasized the unity of world religions. Mrs. Besant adopted the boy and took him to England, where he was educated and prepared for his coming role. In 1911 a new worldwide organization was formed with Krishnamurti as its head, solely to prepare its members for his advent as World Teacher. In 1929, after many years of questioning himself and the destiny imposed upon him, Krishnamurti disbanded this organization, saying:

Truth is a pathless land, and you cannot approach it by any path whatsoever, by any religion, by any sect. Truth, being limitless, unconditioned, unapproachable by any path whatsoever, cannot be organized; nor should any organization be forced to lead or to coerce people along any particular path. My only concern is to set men absolutely, unconditionally free.

Until the end of his life at the age of ninety, Krishnamurti traveled the world speaking as a private person. The rejection of all spiritual and psychological authority, including his own, is a fundamental theme. A major concern is the social structure and how it conditions the individual. The emphasis in his talks and writings is on the psychological barriers that prevent clarity of perception. In the mirror of relationship, each of us can come to understand the content of his own consciousness, which is common to all humanity. We can do this, not analytically, but directly in a manner Krishnamurti describes at length. In observing this content we discover within ourselves the division of the observer and what is observed. He points out that this division, which prevents direct perception, is the root of human conflict.

His central vision did not waver after 1929, but Krishnamurti strove for the rest of his life to make his language even more simple and clear. There is a development in his exposition. From year to year he used new terms and new approaches to his subject, with different nuances.

Because his subject is all-embracing, the *Collected Works* are of compelling interest. Within his talks in any one year, Krishnamurti was not able to cover the whole range of his vision, but broad applications of particular themes are found throughout these volumes. In them he lays the foundations of many of the concepts he used in later years.

The *Collected Works* contain Krishnamurti's previously published talks, discussions, answers to specific questions, and writings for the years 1933 through 1967. They are an authentic record of his teachings, taken from transcripts of verbatim shorthand reports and tape recordings.

The Krishnamurti Foundation of America, a California charitable trust, has among its purposes the publication and distribution of Krishnamurti books, videocassettes, films and tape recordings. The production of the *Collected Works* is one of these activities.

Stockholm, Sweden, 1956

First Talk in Stockholm

I think it is important to understand the relationship between the speaker and the audience, between you and me, because I do not represent India at all, or Indian philosophy, nor am I going to speak of the ideals and teachings of the East. I think our human problems, whether we are of the East or the West, are similar. We may each have different customs, different habits, different values and thoughts, but fundamentally I think we all have the same problems.

We have many problems, have we not?—social, economic, and more especially, perhaps, religious problems—and at present we all approach these problems differently. We approach them only partially, either as a Christian, a Hindu, a communist, or what you will, or we separate them as problems which are Oriental or Occidental. And because we approach our problems partially, through all these various forms of conditioning, it seems to me that we are thereby not understanding them. I feel that the approach to any problem is of much more significance than the problem itself, and that if we could approach our many difficulties without any particular form of conditioning or prejudice, then perhaps we would come to a fundamental understanding of them.

So I would suggest that it is very important that we should each discover for ourselves in what way we are at present approaching the many human problems which beset us, because unless we are very clear about this, then however much we may struggle to understand the complex issues of life and all the confusion and contradiction in which we are caught, I feel we shall not be able to do so. That is why I think it would be really worthwhile if we could go into the beliefs, prejudices, dogmas, and ideas which in various forms are at present corrupting the mind and preventing it from being free to discover what is truth, reality, God, or what you will. And I assure you, it needs extraordinary earnestness to do this: to uncover as we go along the many hindrances to understanding and to see how the mind—which is, after all, the only instrument of discovery we have—is blunted by the many thoughts, emotions, fears, habits, and conditionings of which it is made up.

To do this, I think it is essential not to listen to what is being said as if it were merely a lecture or a discourse—which it is not—but rather to follow as we go along, each one of us, the reactions and responses of our own minds. For what is important, surely, is to understand the actual working of one's own mind. Mere agreement or opposition does not create understanding; it only creates confusion and contradiction, does it not? Whereas, if we can follow patiently and intelligently what is being said—without judging, without comparing, without agreeing or opposing—so that we see the functioning of our own minds, then perhaps we shall discover for ourselves how to approach our many problems.

Our thinking has become dependent on our surroundings because we are caught in so many prejudices—nationalistic, ideological, religious, and all the rest of it. We are ever looking for security, for some means of self-confidence, both inwardly and outwardly, are we not? And it seems to me that so long as we are caught in this pursuit of security, in this search for self-confidence and certainty, we are not free to examine our problems and to find out if there is a lasting solution. Surely it is only in understanding ourselves, in watching the process of our own minds—which is, after all, self-knowledge—that there is a possibility of discovering for ourselves what is true, what is reality. For this no teacher, no guide, no textbook, or other authority is necessary. To follow and comprehend the ways of our own thinking and feeling is to be able to dissolve our own problems, which are the problems of society also.

But it is very difficult for us not to think in a particular fashion, according to a particular set of values, dogmas, beliefs, or theories. We are so eager to arrive at a solution or an answer to our problems that we never stop to consider whether the instrument we are using, which is the mind—my mind and your mind—is really free to investigate. A mind which is burdened with knowledge, beliefs, theories, is obviously not free to investigate and find out what is true. Whereas, if we can understand and dissolve the conditioning, the prejudices, and dogmas which cloud and twist our minds, then perhaps the mind will be free to discover, so that the truth itself can operate on the problem, rather than the mind struggling to come to a solution through its own conditioning—which does not lead anywhere.

That is why I feel it is so important to know how to listen. Very few of us really listen; very few of us hear or see anything really clearly because what we are observing or listening to is immediately interpreted, translated by our own minds in terms of our particular ideas and idiosyncrasies. We think we are understanding, but surely we are not. We are so distracted by our own opinions and knowledge, by approval or disapproval, that we never see the problem as it is. But if we can put aside our own particular points of view, and by listening and following the operation of our own minds, see what is actually the fact, then I think we shall find that quite a different process is taking place which will enable us to look at our problems freely and clearly.

That is why I feel that one should listen totally. At present we listen with only a part of the mind, and it is very difficult for us to give complete attention—not only to what is being said now, but to all that is happening to us in our lives. We have so many problems, religious, social, and economic, as well as the problems of life, of survival, of death; and the very process of our own thinking is, it seems to me, increasing these problems. The way of our own thinking, which is the mind, yours and mine, is conditioned, is it not? It is conditioned by the religion we have been brought up in, by our nationality, political outlook, economic circumstances, and by innumerable other influences. All of these have shaped, molded our minds in a certain way; and if we would be free of this pressure and influence, it is surely useless merely to discard any particular form of authority in order to seek some new form, some new method, some new belief. Yet this is what we are always doing. Surely it is only the mind that is completely free from all conscious or unconscious authority that is able to discover if there is any reality beyond the mere conceptions of the mind. The free mind is the mind that is empty of all belief, of all patterns of thought—the unconscious as well as the conscious, the hidden as well as the obvious. At present, all our thinking is the result of our particular conditioning; it comes from our accumulated experiences, memories, fears, hopes. Such a mind is obviously not free. There is freedom only when the entire thought process is understood and transcended, and only then is it possible for a new mind, a fresh mind, to come into being.

So, can the mind free itself from its own conditioning and look at its problems anew? Can the mind be free?—not as a Christian, a Hindu, a Swede, a communist, or what you will, nor merely in the sense of giving up some particular ideal, belief, or habit, but free to discover—which means going beyond all the influences and contradictions of the mind and of society.

Now, how does the mind respond to all this? To respond with agreement or disagreement is surely vain, for such response is obviously the product of our own background, our own accumulated knowledge and belief. But to experiment with oneself is, it seems to me, really worthwhile. So can we investigate intelligently, patiently, and find out if it is at all possible to free one's own mind from all particularity, from all influence and authority, so that it is able to go beyond its own activities? Otherwise our lives will be very shallow, empty—and perhaps that is the case with most of us. We have masses of information, knowledge, innumerable beliefs, creeds, dogmas, but really we are very shallow and unhappy. Although in some countries they have established outward, economic security, nevertheless inwardly, psychologically, the individual remains uncertain, unsure. And the outward, physical security which all human beings want and need, whatever their nationality, is made impossible for us all because of our demand for inward, psychological security. The very demand for inward security prevents understanding. It is only when the mind is no longer acquisitive, no longer seeking or demanding anything, that it is free to find out what is true, what is God.

That is why it is very important to understand ourselves—not analytically, with one part of the mind analyzing another part, which merely leads to further confusion, but actually to be aware, without judgment or condemnation, of the way we act, the words we use, of all our various emotions, our hidden thoughts. If we can look at ourselves dispassionately so that the hidden emotions are not pressed back but invited forth and understood, then the mind becomes really quiet, and only then there is the possibility of leading a full life.

These are the things which I think we should explore together. We can help each other to find the door to reality, but each one must open that door for himself, and this, it seems to me, is the only positive action.

So there must be in each one of us an inward, religious revolution, for it is only this inward, religious revolution which will totally change the way of our thinking. And to bring about this revolution, there must be the silent observation of the responses of the mind, without judgment, condemnation, or comparison. At present the mind is uncreative in the true sense of that word, is it not? It is a made-up thing, put together through the accumulations of memory. As long as there is envy, ambition, self-seeking, there can be no creativeness. So it seems to me that all we can do is to understand ourselves, the ways of our own mind, and this process of understanding is an enormous task. It is not to be done casually, later on, tomorrow, but rather every day, every moment, all the time. To understand ourselves is to be aware spontaneously, naturally, of the ways of our own thinking so that we begin to see all the hidden motives and intentions which lie behind our thoughts, and thereby bring about the liberation of the mind from its own binding and limiting processes. Then the mind is still, and in that stillness something which is not of the mind can come into being of its own accord.

There are some questions, and I think it would be worthwhile to find out what we mean by "asking a question" and what we mean by "getting an answer." After all, to any of the big, fundamental questions—of love, of life, of death and the hereafter—are there any answers? We ask questions only when we are confused, do we not, and therefore the answers must also be confused. That is why it is very important not to look to others for answers but rather to look directly at the problem for ourselves. So the difficulty is not in asking a question or receiving an answer; it is to see the problem clearly. And when there is clarity, there are no questions and no answers.

Question: We Swedes do not as a rule like to tackle the problems of life only with the mind, leaving the emotions aside. Is it possible to solve any problem only with the mind, or only by the emotions?

KRISHNAMURTI: Do you think you can so easily divide the emotions from the mind? Or do we mean not emotion but sentiment? We are all sentimental, are we not, and we would all like to get answers which give us a sense of satisfaction, security—which is surely a very superficial approach. To understand any problem, there must be keenness of mind; and when it is blunted by opinions, judgments, tradition, fears, the mind is not keen. It is not with the mind alone, or with the emotions alone, that we look at anything fully; it is with the totality of our whole being. And that is a very difficult thing to do—to look at something totally, fully, and freely. It is very difficult to look at the problem of death, of love, of sex, and so on with one's whole being because all the time one is building up an answer, a belief, or a theory. If the answer is pleasant to us, we accept it; if it is unpleasant, we reject it. And we can never look at a problem totally so long as the mind is merely demanding an answer, seeking a way of living, an inward security.

Most of us are trying to understand our problems with a mind that is confused, and we are confused, though most of us do not admit it. When a man is confused, whatever his actions may be, they will only lead to further confusion and misery. So if we are concerned with clearing up the confusion in the world, we must first discover and acknowledge to ourselves that we are confused—completely. But when we do realize that we are confused, most of us want to act immediately on that confusion, to do something about it, to reform, to alter ourselves—which only accentuates the confusion—and it is very difficult to stop all this fruitless activity, which is merely a running away from the actual, from *what is.* Only when one stops running away and faces the fact of one's confusion with the totality of one's being is there the possibility of dissolving that confusion. No one can do this for us; we must do it ourselves.

Question: Juvenile delinquency is increasing. What is the reason and what is the remedy?

KRISHNAMURTI: Are not the roots of this problem buried in the whole structure of modern society? And is not society the outcome of what we are? We are at war with each other, are we not, because we all want to be somebody in this society; we are all trying to achieve success, to get somewhere, to acquire virtue and become something.

Politically, economically, socially, and religiously, we want to arrive, to have the best or to be the best, and in this process there is fear, envy, greed, ambition, ruthlessness. Our whole society is based on this process. And we want our children to fit into society, to be like ourselves, to conform to the pattern of so-called culture. But within this pattern there is revolt among the children as among the grown-ups.

The problem is even more complex when we consider the whole system of education. We have to find out what we mean by education. What is the purpose of education? Is it to make us conform, to fit into society?—which is what we are doing now with our children. Or does education consist in helping the child, the student, to be aware of all the conditioning influences—nationalistic, religious, and so on—and be free of them? If we are serious about this—and we should be serious—we will really study the child, will we not? We will not subject him to some particular influence or authority and thereby mold him into a pattern, but will help him to be aware of all influences so that he can grow in freedom. We will observe him constantly and carefully—be aware of the books he reads, with their glorified heroes, watch him in his work, in his play, in his rest—and will help him to be unconditioned and free.

To help the child to be aware of all the nationalistic tendencies, the prejudices, and religious beliefs which condition the mind really means, does it not, that we must be aware first of our own ways of thinking. After all, we grown-ups do not know how to live together; we are everlastingly battling with each other and within ourselves. This battle, this struggle, projects itself into society, and into that society we want to fit the child. We cannot change society; only the individual can change. But we are not individuals, are we? We are caught up in the mass, in society, and so long as we do not understand ourselves and free the mind from its self-imposed limitations, how can we help the child?

Question: Can one live in the world without ambition? Does it not isolate us to be without ambition?

KRISHNAMURTI: I think this is a fundamental question. We can see what ambition makes of the world. Everybody wants to be something. The artist wants to be famous, the schoolboy wants to become the president, the priest wants to be the bishop, and so on. Everyone throughout the world is trying, struggling, forcing himself, in order to be important. Even in our education, the boy who is not clever is compared with the boy who is clever—which is utterly stupid. And we see the result of this ambition projected in the world. Each nation is seeking to maintain itself at all costs.

Now, the questioner wants to know whether we can be free from this ambition, and if so, whether we shall not be isolated from society. Why is there this fear of being free from ambition, this fear of being alone? Can ambition and love go together? The mind that is seeking all the time to be something, to become great, surely does not know what love is. So long as we are pursuing ambition, we are isolated. We are isolated already, are we not? But, you see, we accept ambition. Whether a man lives in a small village far away or in a crowded city, if he can call himself something—a Swede, a Hindu, a Dane, or anything else—then he feels that he is someone. To be respectable, to be known, to have power, position, money, virtue—all these things give us a sense of importance. So it is very difficult not to be ambitious.

The man who is as nothing is without fear, without ambition; he is alone, but not isolated. To free oneself from ambition requires a great deal of insight, intelligence, and love; but such a man, who is as nothing, is not isolated.

May 14, 1956

Second Talk in Stockholm

I think it would be worthwhile this evening if we could attempt something which might be rather difficult but perhaps important to go into. I wonder if we can discover what it is that most of us are seeking and whether what we are seeking has any validity, any real basis. Perhaps we are seeking something which we cannot properly articulate to ourselves. Or we may hope to find something that will be deeply satisfactory, that will give us some measure of happiness or certainty. Until we have discovered what it is that we are seeking, I think our lives must be uncertain, chaotic, and contradictory. It is really very difficult to find out what we are seeking because we do not know for ourselves the motives, the urges, the drives that are forcing us to seek at all. Obviously, as you have all come here to listen, you are seeking something. But to know what it is we are seeking, we must find out, must we not, what the drive is behind our search.

Most of us are well settled in life; we have homes, families, responsibilities, some position, a job, and so on. But our lives are generally humdrum, routine; there is boredom, a sense of frustration, and we want something more than mere logical conclusions, religious beliefs, and ideologies. So I think it would be worthwhile if we could spend this evening trying to find out what it is we are groping after. What is the urge behind this search? Can we put our finger on it? Can we know what it is, this urge? We are concerned, not only with the more superficial urges, compulsions, and fears, but we want to know, do we not, what it is we are seeking with our whole life, our total existence. And can we intelligently find out? Surely, without understanding this seeking, and the pressure, the compulsion behind it, our search may be utterly vain and have no meaning.

So, how can one find out for oneself what it is one is after? If we are old, we want peace, security, comfort, and if we are young, we want pleasure, excitement, success. And if we cannot have success, then we want some kind of self-assertion. So each one of us is groping for something, and what is it? Are we moved by the desire to find out what is true, or whether there is any permanency? Or is it worldly satisfaction we are seeking, a better position in our various environments?

I wish we could really go into this matter, because I think that when the urges within one have become very clear to oneself, then life has quite a different meaning. When the mind is free from the compulsion, the drive, the confusion which now exists, there may be no search at all, but something entirely different—the sense of being free. So, can we find out for ourselves what is the drive that is making us seek, that has made us come here to listen? Or are there so many different urges, so many pleasures, that we cannot separate them to find out which is the primary urge? I think it is important to discover the primary urge; otherwise, our search has no meaning.

Many people are everlastingly talking about seeking God, seeking truth, seeking immortality, virtue, and all the rest of it, but this search has very little meaning; it becomes just a fad. I think it is significant that so few of us who seek have so far discovered for ourselves anything that has real depth and significance. Is it happiness that we are seeking, a sense of self-fulfillment? If we seek without understanding what is behind this urge, our lives remain shallow, for self-fulfillment becomes very important, and to self-fulfillment there is no end. The moment you fulfill yourself, there is always something more in which to be fulfilled.

Our urges are so strong, and unless we understand the whole significance of this inward compulsion, it seems to me that mere search has no meaning at all. To find out what we are after, and what is the motive behind it, is surely essential. Being uncertain, confused, afraid, perhaps we want to escape into some kind of fancy that we call reality, some kind of hope, some kind of belief. If we could understand for ourselves why the mind is always seeking security, then we might have not security but a new kind of confidence. That is why I think it is important to go into all this.

After all, it is a function of society and of government to help to bring about outward security. But the difficulty is that we also want to be secure psychologically, inwardly, and therefore we identify ourselves with the nation, with a religion, an ideology, a belief. We never question whether there is such a thing as inward security at all, but we are always seeking it, and the very search for inward, psychological security actually prevents outward security, does it not? Obviously that is what is happening throughout the world. In our search to be psychologically secure through nationalism, through a leader, through an ideology, physical security is destroyed. So, can the mind which is seeking permanency in everything—in "my country," "my religion," through innumerable dogmas, beliefs, ideas—discover for itself whether there actually is such a thing as permanency, inward security?

We have never questioned whether there can ever be security inwardly, and perhaps there is no such thing. It may be this very desire to seek security, permanency, for ourselves, both inwardly and outwardly, which is conditioning the mind and preventing the understanding of what is true. So, can the mind free itself from this urge to be secure? It can do so, surely, only when it is completely uncertain—not uncertain in opposition to security, but when it is in a state of not-knowing and not-seeking. After all, one can never find anything new so long as one's mind is burdened with the old, with all the beliefs, fears, and hidden compulsions which bring about this search for security. So long as we are seeking security in any form, inward or outward, there must be chaos and misery. And if we observe ourselves, that is what we are doing all the time. Through property, through money, through virtue, position, fame, we are constantly trying to bring about a sense of permanency for ourselves. And is it not important to find out whether the mind can be free of that whole process? Can we actually experience for ourselves the significance of the compulsion behind the urge to be secure? Can we experience it directly, not later on, at another time, but now, as we are discussing? Can we look at this urge to be secure and find out if it has any validity and from what source it springs?

And when we do look, what happens? We feel, do we not, that if we were not inwardly secure, if we did not identify ourselves with innumerable ideals, ideologies, beliefs, nationalisms, we would be nothing, we would be empty, we would be of no account. So our immediate response is to escape from that sense of emptiness by seeking some form of inward richness, some sense of fulfillment, and we set up leaders to follow, we look for teachings and authorities which we can obey. But the misery, the inward poverty continues; there is everlasting struggle, and we never experience directly, actually, that state of inward insufficiency, inward emptiness. But if we could look at it, experience it directly, which means not running away from it by picking up a book, turning on the radio—you know the innumerable things we do in order to escape—if we could experience completely what it is, then I think we would find that that emptiness has quite a different significance. But all the time we try to escape, do we not?—through the church, through patriotism, through an ideology or a belief. Whereas, if we could understand the futility of running away from this sense of inward poverty and would look at it, examine it patiently, without any condemnation, then perhaps it would reveal something totally different.

But it is very difficult, is it not, to be free of the desire to escape from this sense of emptiness and to be free of fear, ambition, envy. At present we are forever trying to establish our own security through identifying ourselves with something greater, whether it be a person or an idea. But if one is really serious in the endeavor to find truth, reality, or God, one must first of all totally free oneself from all conditioning. This means that one must be able to stand completely alone and look at the truth of *what is* without seeking any escape. If you will experiment with this, you will find that the mind which is willing to go into this whole problem of the search for security, which is willing to look at its own emptiness completely, totally, without any desire to escape—that such a mind becomes very quiet, alone, free, creative. This creativeness is not the outcome of struggle, of effort, of search; it is a state in which the mind, seeing the truth about its own fears and envies, is completely alert and silent. That state may be, and I think it is, the real.

Question: Does suffering ultimately lead one to inward peace and awareness?

KRISHNAMURTI: I am afraid not. We think suffering is a means to something else—to heaven, to the attainment of peace, and so on—and hence we have made suffering into a virtue. But what do we mean by suffering? How does suffering arise? Suffering is a sense of disturbance, is it not?—an inward, psychological disturbance. I am not now talking of physical suffering, which has its own significance, but what we are talking about is the psychological suffering which comes when we are frustrated, when we are lonely, when we do not understand the process of our own being, the complexity of our own thinking.

What happens when we suffer? We try to use it as a means to something else, do we not?—we say it makes us more intelligent, that it leads to peace, to awareness; or we immediately seek to escape from it through ideas, through amusements, through every form of distraction. Suffering comes, does it not, when there is ignorance, when there is a lack of knowledge of the workings of one's own mind, when the mind is torn by contradictory desires, by loneliness, by comparison, by envy. But when we understand the whole process of ignorance, of envy, when we look at it, face it totally, without any desire to escape or condemn it, then perhaps we shall see that there is no necessity for suffering at all. Peace cannot be found through suffering or through anything else. It comes only when there is understanding of the workings of one's own mind and when, through that understanding, the thought process comes to an end.

Question: Why do you go about the world giving talks? Is it for self-fulfillment, or is it because you think you can help people in that way?

KRISHNAMURTI: If I went about talking in order to help people, you would all become followers, would you not? Is that not what is happening throughout the world today? We are all seeking leaders, teachers, to help us out of our confusion, and the only result is that we get more confused, more chaotic. I do not believe in such help; I only believe in total understanding. We all want to be helped, we all want guides, leaders, someone to follow politically, socially, and religiously; that is what we want. And that leads to exploitation, does it not? It leads to the totalitarian spirit—the leader and the led. So long as we depend upon another for inward peace, we shall not find it, for dependence only breeds fear. It is not for that reason I am talking. And is it for self-fulfillment, to have the feeling that one is doing something for others, to feel gratified, popular, and so on? I say it is not. Then why is one talking? I do not think there is any answer to that question, any more than there is an answer if one asks of a flower, "Why do you grow in the sunshine?"

If I were trying to help you or trying to fulfill myself, it would put me in the position of being the one who knows and you in the position of not knowing, so I would be using you, and you would be using me. Whereas, I think that the moment one is conscious that one knows, one does not know. When a person is aware of his virtue, his humility, or what you will, he is no longer virtuous. What we are trying to do here is to understand ourselves, for self-knowledge alone brings reality. We are not trying to discover who knows, who can help, and who does not know. After all, what is it that we really know? Very little, I think. We may have a lot of technical knowledge, we may know how to build a bridge, how to paint, and so on, but we know very little about ourselves, about the ways of the mind and the urge of ambition, envy. Only the mind that is aware that it does not know, that is totally aware of its own ignorance—only such a mind can be at peace. The mind that has merely gathered experience, accumulated knowledge, or acquired a lot of technical information is everlastingly in conflict.

When the mind is no longer burdened with the memory of the things it has learned, when it is willing to die to all the knowledge it has accumulated, only then can it know what it is to have peace. I think this is a state which most of us have experienced occasionally, a state when the self is entirely absent. But we are so occupied most of the time with superficialities that the real things of life pass us by.

Question: I have read an American book which certainly seems to prove through hypnosis that reincarnation is a fact. What comment will you make on this?

KRISHNAMURTI: This is rather a complex question, and I think one has to go into it fairly deeply. We all know that there is death. The physical organism will come to an end because it has been used up and is finished, and we want to know if there is continuity after death. The things that we have known and experienced will all come to an end, and so we ask what will happen to us then. This is a problem all over the world. In the East reincarnation is accepted as a belief, and the questioner says a book has been written which proves, through hypnotism, that a person has lived before, and we want to know whether reincarnation is a fact. I do not know if you have ever felt that thought is independent of the body, independent of the physical organism. We have the organism, the nervous responses, and thought; and so we ask if thought continues after death.

Now, what happens when we ask that question? The fact is that we want to continue, do we not?—or else we say we would like to put an end to everything. In both cases the mind is selecting a theory which suits it. Whether you believe or disbelieve in reincarnation has little significance, but can we discover the truth of the matter, the truth about death? We all like to think that there is a soul which exists everlastingly, and we accept various beliefs which tell us that the soul is a spiritual entity beyond the physical organism. But belief in an idea, however comforting, however reassuring, does not give us the full understanding of what death is. Surely, death is something totally unknown; it is something completely new, and however anxiously we inquire, we cannot find an answer that will satisfy. All that we know is within the field of time, and all that we are is the accumulation of past memories and experiences. We have established our own identity through memory, as "my house," "my name," "my family," "my knowledge," "my country," and we want this 'me' to continue in the future. Or else we say, "Death is the end of everything," which is no solution either.

So, can we discover what is the truth about death? We know that we seek the continuity of the 'me'. Thought is ever seeking permanency, and hence we say that there must be some form of continuity. Thought is continuous, is it not, and so long as there is the desire to continue, we give strength to the idea of the 'me' and "my importance." Thought may continue, it may take another shape and form, which is called reincarnation, but does that which continues ever know the immeasurable, the timeless? Can it ever be creative? Surely, God, or truth, or what you will is not to be found in the field of time. It must be entirely new, not something out of the past, not something created out of our own hopes and fears. And yet the mind wants permanency, does it not? And so it says, "God is permanent," and "I shall continue hereafter."

So you see, the problem is not whether or not there is reincarnation, but the fact that we are all seeking permanency, security, here and hereafter. So long as the mind is seeking security in any direction, whether it be through name, family, position, virtue, or what you will, suffering must continue. Only the mind which dies from day to day, from moment to moment, to all that it has accumulated, can know what the truth is. And then perhaps we shall discover that there is no division between life and death, but only a totally different state in which time, as we know it, does not exist.

May 15, 1956

Third Talk in Stockholm

To those of us who are serious, it must be a real problem to find out how to bring about a fundamental change in ourselves. It is obvious that such a change is necessary, and not merely a change forced by circumstances, which is no change at all. The pressure of circumstances may bring about a change, but such change invariably leads to further conflict and stagnation. But if one is concerned with a fundamental change, how is it to be brought about?

One sees in the world a great deal of misery, not only physical, but psychological—the limitations of the conditioned mind, the constant threat of war, the national and racial divisions, as well as those which the organized religions create with their dogmatism and vain, repeated rituals—we all know of these things. And seeing all this, it must surely be a matter of serious concern for each individual to find out for himself how he can bring about a fundamental, radical change within himself, a change that will set free the mind from the constant pressure of conflict, suffering, and limitation. It is obvious that there must be a change, but the difficulty with most of us is, I think, that we do not know how to change.

Now, what I mean by change is not merely conforming to a new pattern of thinking, to a new ideology, but a change that is brought about without any form of compulsion or pressure, without influence, and even without motive. Because if one has a motive in bringing about a change, one is back in the old pattern of achievement, ambition. So it must be our concern, I think, to inquire into this question and find out for ourselves how a deep, inward transformation can be brought about.

I am going to talk as usual this evening for about twenty or thirty minutes, and then I suggest that we discuss together. You ask me questions, and there will be an exchange between us so that you and I will get to know what we actually feel and think about this problem. I hope you will agree to this.

We think ideals are necessary to bring about this change, do we not? Being violent, we say that the ideal of nonviolence will help us to put away that which is violent; we seek to replace violence by what we call nonviolence, to replace greed by generosity, and so on. But to me, ideals do not bring about a change; on the contrary, ideals are impediments to a fundamental, radical change. Ideals are merely a means of postponing, an excuse to avoid bringing about a real change. So long as we have an ideal, there is always a conflict between *what is* and 'what should be', and we spend a great deal of energy in this inward conflict, through which we hope to bring about a fundamental change. If we are envious, we set up the ideal of nonenvy, hoping thereby to free the mind from envy. But if you examine closely this whole process, you will see that the ideal actually prevents the understanding of *what is,* which is envy. So the ideal is not important, it is an impediment, a thing to be put away completely.

Now, what is it that will bring about a change? Can the mind which has been conditioned in a particular pattern bring about a change? Or does such a mind merely modify the pattern of its thinking and imagine that it has thereby radically changed? Does not a fundamental change come about only in understanding the whole background in which one has been brought up? Surely, so long as the mind operates within the pattern of a particular society or a particular religion, there can be no change. However much we may struggle within the pattern, however much we may suffer, a change is not possible so long as we do not understand the pattern in which we live and in which our whole being is caught. The desire to change within the pattern only creates further complications. We spend our time in ceaseless struggle, making vain efforts to change, and there is constant friction between *what is* and 'what should be', which is the ideal.

So it seems to me that if we are to bring about a fundamental change, it is first necessary to understand the background in which we have been brought up, the pattern in which the mind operates. If we do not understand that pattern, if we are not familiar with our own conditioning, if the whole trend of our education, in which the mind is caught, is not understood, then we merely follow a tradition, which invariably leads to mediocrity. Tradition inevitably cripples and dulls the mind. So it is imperative, surely, to bring about a fundamental change within ourselves because, though we may be very clever and know a great deal, most of us are very mediocre, empty, shallow, inwardly insufficient, are we not? And to bring about such a change, it is necessary to understand the totality of our background. Until we understand that background, however much we may struggle to change ourselves, it will lead us nowhere.

What do we mean by the background? The background is made up of the traditions, the influences in which we have been raised, and the education, the theories, the formulas, the conclusion that we have acquired. If we are not free of all that, which is mere occupation with ideas, any effort to change ourselves must invariably lead to the same kind of respectability or mediocrity; and this struggle, in which we are all caught, can only bring about noncreative thinking.

It is only the free mind, surely, that can find out what is true, not the mind that is conditioned by beliefs, ideals, and compulsions. If we want to find out if there is a reality beyond the limitations and projections of thought, surely the mind must first be free of all the beliefs, dogmas, and traditions, of all the patterns in which it is caught. For it is only the free mind that can discover, and not the mind that is constantly struggling to adjust itself to a particular pattern or ideal, whether imposed upon it by society or by the mind itself.

It seems to me that one of our main difficulties is that we really want to live casual, sluggish, dull lives, with perhaps a little excitement now and then. Our pattern of existence is very shallow, and we are everlastingly struggling in a superficial way to deepen this shallowness through various formulas. I think this shallowness, this emptiness within ourselves, is brought about by not understanding the whole background in which we live, the habitual ways of our thinking; we are not aware of that at all. We are not aware of our thoughts, we do not see from whence they come, what their significance is, what values we are giving to them, and how the mind is caught in dead dreaming, in competition, in ambition, in trying to be something, in adjusting to all the narrow formulas of society.

Therefore it is really important, if one would bring about a fundamental change, to be totally free of society. And that is the real revolution—the revolution which comes when we begin to understand the whole pattern of society, of which we are a part. We are not different from society, we are the result of social influences, and we cannot be free from the stamp of social influences so long as we do not understand the whole composition of society. The composition of society is a mixture of greed, envy, ambition, and of all those conditioning beliefs based on fear, which are called religion. So it is only the man who steps out of society, who is free from the compulsion of neighbors and tradition, as well as from his own inward envy and ambition—it is only such a man who is really revolutionary, really religious, and only he can find out if there is a reality beyond the projections of our petty, little minds.

I think this is a very important problem, especially in our world today, which is facing such great crises. Science and so-called civilization may bring about a change, but any such change is invariably superficial; it is merely a yielding to the pressure of circumstances, and so it is no real change at all. Therefore there is no creative release but merely the pursuit of a routine which is called virtue. But if we can go very deeply into this problem, as we should, then I think we shall be able to understand the background of which we form a part. The background is not different from ourselves because we are the background. Our minds are a result of the past, with all its traditions, beliefs, and dogmas, both conscious and unconscious. And can such a mind ever be free? It can be free only when it begins to understand the whole structure of this background, of the society in which we live. Then only is it possible for the mind to be truly religious, and therefore truly revolutionary.

To go into this a little more, verbally at least—and nonverbally also—perhaps we can try discussing it together. What I have said may be contradictory to what you think, and it might be profitable if we could discuss it easily, naturally, and in a friendly manner, so as to find out more about this problem. But to discuss it is going to be quite difficult. We must all stick to the point and not bring in various issues which are irrelevant. And obviously, to discuss wisely we must not make long speeches.

Question: Can we reach an understanding of ourselves other than by conscious effort?

KRISHNAMURTI: Do we understand anything through effort? If I make an effort to understand what you say, do you think I shall understand? All my attention is given to making the effort, is it not? But if one can listen effortlessly, then perhaps there is a possibility of understanding.

In the same way, how am I to understand myself? First of all, surely, I must not assume anything about myself, I must not have a mental picture of myself. I must look at my thoughts, at the way I talk, at my gestures, at my beliefs, as easily as I look at my face in a mirror—just watch them, be aware of them without condemnation, because the moment I condemn, there is no furthering of understanding. If I want to understand, I must look, and I cannot look if I condemn. If I want to understand a child, it is no good comparing him with his older brother, or condemning him. I must watch him when he is playing, crying, eating; and I can watch him only if I have no sense of condemnation or evaluation. In the same way, I can watch myself—not little bits of myself, but the totality of myself—only when there is an awareness in which there is no choice, no condemnation, no comparison.

Question: Is it possible for any of us, who are living in this particular society, to bring about the change of which you are talking?

KRISHNAMURTI: If we as individuals do not bring about this change, how is it to be done? If you and I, living in this society, do not do it, who will? The powerful, the millionaires, the people of great possessions are not going to do it. It must surely be done by ordinary people like you and me—and I am not saying this rhetorically, stupidly. If you and I see the importance of this change, then it is not courage but the very perception of the importance of change which will bring it about. A man may have the courage to stand against the dictates of society, but it is the man who understands the complex problem of change, who understands the whole structure of society—which is himself—it is he alone who becomes an individual and is not merely a representative of the collective. Only the individual who is not caught in society can fundamentally affect society. You think that courage, strength, conviction, is necessary to understand and withstand society. I think that is entirely false. If one deeply feels it is important to effect a real change, that very feeling brings about such a change within oneself.

Question: A man has a right to go his own way, and if he does so, will not this change come about?

KRISHNAMURTI: Are you suggesting, sir, that there can be change through an action of will? Most of us are accustomed to the idea that through will we can bring about a change. Now, what do we mean by will? We generally mean, do we not, making an effort in one particular direction, suppressing *what is* in order to reach something else. We exercise will in order to achieve or to bring about a certain desired change. Will is another word for desire, is it not? Each one of us has many contradictory desires, and when one desire dominates other desires, this domination of one desire over the others we call will. But it is still the domination of one desire over other desires, so there is contradiction, suppression, a ceaseless conflict going on between the dominant desire, which we call will, and the other desires.

Now, this conflict can never bring about a change—which is psychologically obvious. So long as I am in conflict within myself, there can be no change. There can be a change, not by one desire dominating other desires, but only when I understand the whole structure of desire. That is why it is important to understand the background, the values, the influences, the motives in which the mind is caught.

Question: You say that in order to bring about a change we must understand the background. Do you mean by this that we must understand reincarnation and karma?

KRISHNAMURTI: Karma is a Sanskrit word which means action. And reincarnation—you know what that means!

I think it is fairly clear that a mind that believes in anything, that adheres to any psychological wish or hope—which comes from fear—lives always within the pattern of that belief, and to struggle within the pattern of any belief is no change at all. A man who merely believes in reincarnation has not understood the whole problem of death and sorrow, and when he believes in that particular theory, he is trying to escape from the fact of death.

The word karma has many problems involved in it. One has to understand the motives of one's actions—the influences, the compulsions, the causes which have brought about the action. Surely, all this is part of the background which must be understood, and belief in reincarnation is also part of the background. The mind that believes is not capable of understanding because belief is obviously an escape from reality.

Question: I think it is rather important to know what we mean by seeing and watching. You have said that there is no motive or center, but only a process. How can a process watch another process?

KRISHNAMURTI: This is like a cross-examination! Surely you are not trying to trap me, and I am not trying to answer cleverly. What we are trying to do is to understand the problem, which is very complex, and one or two questions and responses are not going to solve it. But what we can do is to approach it from different directions and look at it as patiently as possible.

So the question is this: If there is only a process, and not a center which observes the process, then how can a process observe itself? The process is active, moving, changing, all the time in motion, and how can that process watch itself if there is no center? I hope the question is clear to you; otherwise, what I am going to say will have no meaning.

If the whole of life is a movement, a flux, then how can it be watched unless there is a watcher? Now, we are conditioned to believe, and we feel we know, that there is a watcher as well as a movement, a process, so we think we are separate from the process. To most of us there is the thinker and the thought, the experiencer and the experience. For us that is so; we accept it as a matter of fact. But is it so? Is there a thinker, an observer, a watcher apart from thought, apart from thinking, apart from experience? Is there a thinker, a center without thought? If you remove thought, is there a center? If you have no thought at all, no struggle, no urge to acquire, no effort to become something, is there a center? Or is the center created by thought, which feels itself to be insecure, impermanent, in a state of flux? If you observe, you will find that it is the thought process that has created the center, which is still within the field of thinking. And is it possible—this is the point—to watch, to be aware of this process, without the watcher? Can the mind, which is the process, be aware of itself?

Please, this requires a great deal of insight, meditation, and penetration because most of us assume that there is a thinker apart from thinking. But if you go into it a little more closely, you will see that thought has created the thinker. The thinker who is directing, who is the center, the judge, is the outcome of our thoughts. This is a fact, as you will see if you are really looking at it. Most people are conditioned to believe that the thinker is separate from thought, and they give to the thinker the quality of eternality, but that which is beyond time comes into being only when we understand the whole process of thinking.

Now, can the mind be aware of itself in action, in movement, without a center? I think it can. It is possible when there is only an awareness of thinking, and not the thinker who is thinking. You know, it is quite an experience to realize that there is only thinking. And it is very difficult to experience that because the thinker is habitually there, evaluating, judging, condemning, comparing, identifying. If the thinker ceases to identify, evaluate, judge, then there is only thinking without the center.

What is the center? The center is the 'me'—the 'me' that wants to be a great person, that has so many conclusions, fears, motives. From that center we think, but that center has been created by the reaction of thinking. So, can the mind be aware of thinking without the center—just observe it? You will find how extraordinarily difficult it is just to look at a flower without naming it, without comparing it with other flowers, without evaluating it out of like or dislike. Experiment with this and you will see how really difficult it is to observe something without bringing in all your prejudices, all your emotions, and evaluations. But however difficult, you will find that the mind can be aware of itself without the center watching the movement of the mind.

Question: If anyone wishes to find freedom along the lines you have spoken of, is it not also necessary for that person to renounce the church or whatever other religious organizations he is taking an interest in?

KRISHNAMURTI: If one wishes to free oneself, should one give up, renounce, or set aside organizations that demand belief? Obviously. If one belongs to an organization which demands belief, which is based on fear, on dogma, then the mind is a slave to that organization and cannot be free. Only the mind that is free—and this is an extraordinarily complex and difficult problem— can find out if there is reality, if there is God, not the mind that believes in God.

Now, why do we cling to the dogmas, beliefs, and rituals which religions introduce? When we understand that, then they will drop away like leaves in the autumn, without any effort.

Why do you belong to any particular religious organization? We must obviously have organizations to deliver letters, milk, and so on, but why does the mind cling to dogmas? Does it not cling because in dogma, in belief, it finds security, something to rely on? Being uncertain, fearful, insecure, it projects a belief or clings to a dogma that some church or other organization offers. The mind clings to dogma, to belief, as an escape from its own uncertainty, its inward poverty, insufficiency. It tries to fill that emptiness with dogmas, beliefs, superstitions, rituals. You may renounce a belief and put aside a dogma, but so long as you have not understood this inward poverty, insufficiency, so long as the mind has not understood its own emptiness, merely relinquishing organized religion has no meaning. It will have meaning only when you understand the inward nature that forces you to cling to a conclusion, a belief. That is why it is very important to have knowledge of oneself, to know why one believes, rejects, renounces. It is only through self-knowledge that there is wisdom—not in beliefs, not in books, but in understanding the whole structure of the mind. Only the free mind can understand that which is beyond time.

May 21, 1956

Fourth Talk in Stockholm

I think it is important to consider the negativeness of experience because our whole life is a series of accumulated experiences, and a false center forms around these accumulations. Whether experience is destructive or so-called creative, what is it that nevertheless makes the mind insensitive and brings about deterioration? Does experience liberate the mind from the deteriorating factor? Or must there be freedom from this craving for experience, from the accumulative process of experience? We take experience as a necessary factor for the enrichment of life, and I think it is, at one level. But experience nearly always forms a hardened center in the mind, as the self, which is a deteriorating factor. Most of us are seeking experience. We may be tired of the worldly experiences of fame, notoriety, wealth, sex, and so on, but we all want greater, wider experience of some kind, especially those of us who are attempting to reach a so-called spiritual state. Being tired of worldly things, we want a more extensive, a wider, deeper experience; and to arrive at such an experience, we suppress, we control, we dominate ourselves, hoping thereby to achieve a full realization of God, or what you will. We think the pursuit of experience is the right way of life in order to attain greater vision, and I question whether that is so. Does this search for experience, which is really a demand for greater, fuller sensation, lead to reality? Or is it a factor which cripples the mind?

In our search for sensation, which we call experience, we do various things, do we not? We practice so-called spiritual disciplines; we control, suppress, put ourselves through various forms of religious exercise—all in order to arrive at a greater experience. Some of us have actually done all this, while others only play with the idea. But through it all, the fundamental desire is for greater sensation—to have the sensation of pleasure extended, made high and permanent, as opposed to the suffering, the dullness, the routine and loneliness of our daily lives. So the mind is ever seeking experience, and that experience hardens into a center, and from this center we act. We live and have our being in this center, in this accumulated, hardened experience of the past. And is it possible to live without forming this center of experience and sensation? Because it seems to me that life will then have a significance quite different from that which we now give it. At present we are all concerned, are we not, with the extension of the center, recruiting greater and wider experience which ever strengthens the self, and I think this invariably limits the mind.

So, is it possible to live in this world without forming this center? I think it is possible only when there is a full awareness of life—an awareness in which there is no motive or choice, but simple observation. I think you will find, if you will experiment with this and think about it a little deeply, that such awareness does not form a center around which experience and the reactions to experience can accumulate. Then the mind becomes astonishingly alive, creative—and I do not mean writing poems or painting pictures, but a creativeness in which the self is totally absent. I think this is what most of us are really seeking—a state in which there is no conflict, a state of peace and serenity of mind. But this is not possible so long as the mind is the instrument of sensation and is ever demanding further sensation.

After all, most of our memory is based on sensation, either pleasurable or painful; from the painful we try to escape, and to the pleasurable we cling; the one we suppress or seek to avoid, and the other we grope after, hold on to, and think about. So the center of our experience is essentially based on pleasure and pain, which are sensations, and we are always pursuing experiences which we hope will be permanently satisfying. That is what we are after all the time, and hence there is everlasting conflict. Conflict is never creative; on the contrary, conflict is a most destructive factor, both within the mind itself and in our relationship with the world around us, which is society. If we can understand this really deeply—that a mind which seeks experience limits itself and is its own source of misery—then perhaps we can find out what it is to be aware.

Being aware does not mean learning and accumulating lessons from life; on the contrary, to be aware is to be without the scars of accumulated experience. After all, when the mind merely gathers experience according to its own wishes, it remains very shallow, superficial. A mind which is deeply observant does not get caught up in self-centered activities, and the mind is not observant if there is any action of condemnation or comparison. Comparison and condemnation do not bring understanding, rather they block understanding. To be aware is to observe—just to observe—without any self-identifying process. Such a mind is free of that hard core which is formed by self-centered activities.

I think it is very important to experience this state of awareness for oneself, and not merely to know about it through any description which another may give. Awareness comes into being naturally, easily, spontaneously, when we understand the center which is everlastingly seeking experience, sensation. A mind which seeks sensation through experience becomes insensitive, incapable of swift movement, and therefore it is never free. But in understanding its own self-centered activities, the mind comes upon this state of awareness which is choiceless, and such a mind is then capable of complete silence, stillness.

The capacity of the mind to be still, which is so essential, is not of the Occident or the Orient, though in the Orient some people may talk about it more. Without this extraordinary stillness of the mind which is not seeking further experience, all our activities will merely add to the dead center of accumulation.

Only when the mind is completely still can it know its own movement—and then its movement is immense, incalculable, immeasurable. Then it is possible to have that feeling of something which is beyond time. Then life has quite a different significance, a significance which is not to be found through capacities, gifts, or intellectual gymnastics.

Creative stillness is not the end result of a calculating, disciplined, and widely-informed mind. It comes into being only when we understand the falsity of the whole process of endlessly seeking sensation through experience. Without that inward stillness, all our speculations about reality, all the philosophies, the systems of ethics, the religions, have very little significance. It is only the still mind which can know infinity.

Question: Can you tell us more clearly what it is you mean by consciousness?

KRISHNAMURTI: What is consciousness? Is it not everything that we think and everything that we have thought in the past? Is it not the past which we project through the present into the future? Are not both the conscious and the unconscious mind within the field of time? Consciousness is made up, is it not, of the responses of the past propelled into the present through memory, as the 'I', as the mind, which then seeks further forms of fulfillment in the future. The whole of that is consciousness, is it not? It is the result of inherited ideas, of accumulated experiences, of fears, inspirations, motives, beliefs, hopes, and innumerable other influences. All that is what we are. We may divide ourselves into the 'I' and the 'not-I', into the lower self and the higher self, but this whole field of consciousness, you will find, is made up of reactions, of the past, of conditioned thinking, and is therefore obviously limited.

After all, it is only because we are forever thinking about something, pursuing something, or running away from something that we know we are alive. We search for reality, for permanence, and because we want it, we say we know of it. But our search is merely the outcome of desire, is it not? It is conditioned, limited, a product of time. All this is part of consciousness.

So the question is: Can the mind, being conditioned, limited, free itself from the past, from its own center of experience which is based on like and dislike? You cannot answer yes or no. You can only find out for yourself whether the mind can be free. But to find out, you must first know that you are conditioned; you must first be aware of the compulsions, the fears, the beliefs, and traditions which now corrupt the mind. This means, does it not, that one must watch oneself in relationship—not merely with people, but also in one's relationship with things and with ideas. Then you will understand, if you really observe it, the whole process of conditioning, and can perhaps be free of it forever.

Question: Is it possible for the ordinary person to come to this freedom without special training and knowledge?

KRISHNAMURTI: What does special training imply? It implies, does it not, continually conditioning the mind to a certain practice, to a certain discipline, to various forms of conformity and compulsion. When you say that special training is necessary to achieve this freedom, what is implied is the practice of a method, and can any method bring about freedom? Or is the practice of a method the very denial of freedom? Surely, when you practice a method, you become a slave to that method, to a technique, and therefore there is no freedom. The practice produces a result, but the result is not freedom.

We think that by careful training of the mind, by certain practices, by observing certain rules, we will come to freedom, but the only result is to make ourselves prisoners of the method. Freedom is in the beginning, not at the end. We think that inner freedom is to be achieved only at the end because from the very beginning we have denied ourselves freedom. We do not see that only from the very beginning can freedom be realized. Anyone with enough intelligence, diligence, and patience can be free. Freedom comes to all of us if we give our time to it, if we dedicate ourselves to seeking out and understanding our own conditioning. But if one relies on a method, on training, one becomes a follower, one needs a teacher, and therefore one becomes a slave to that teacher. By becoming a follower, one has denied the whole experience of freedom.

Question: One finds that one makes the same mistakes repeatedly. Are there those who have been able to break this pattern?

KRISHNAMURTI: I wonder why we ask if there is anybody else who has broken the pattern of habit. Why? Is it because if others have broken the pattern, it may help and encourage us? Or are we asking a vain question which has no meaning at all? Surely what has importance is not whether X or Y has broken the pattern but whether we can break it, you and I. And that means, first of all, being aware of the pattern, of the prison in which the mind is held, knowing it for oneself—the racial prejudices, the educational ignorance, the religious limitations, the hopes, the fears, and all the rest of it. Then we will find out for ourselves whether we can break the pattern or not; we will not have to look to anybody else. Then we will know what it is to be free, to live, to be creative.

Question: Would you kindly explain what you mean by negative thinking?

KRISHNAMURTI: Before we inquire into the problem of positive and negative thinking, let us ask ourselves, what is thinking? When I put you a question with which you are familiar, the response is immediate; you do not have to think. For example, if I ask you where you live, you reply without having to think about it. But if a more complicated question is asked, there is hesitation, which indicates that you are looking for an answer; the mind is then seeking an answer in the cupboard of memory. That is what we call thinking. I do not know, but I am trying to find an answer in all the memories, the knowledge that I have accumulated, and finding it, I verbally respond. This response, which is a reaction of memory, is what we call positive thinking, is it not? We are always thinking from our background of knowledge and experience, so our thinking is very limited, and such thinking can never be free. In that process there is no freedom of thought, in the fundamental sense of the word. You may change your opinions, your conclusions, but so long as you draw upon knowledge, which is what we are accustomed to doing, you are not really thinking at all. In that there is no freedom of thought because memory and knowledge have already conditioned your thinking. Negative thinking may be, and probably is, freedom from knowledge as conclusions. After all, everything we know is of the past. The moment we say, "I know," knowledge has already moved away from the present and established itself in memory, in the past.

So, can the mind be in a state of not-knowing? Because only then can the mind inquire, not when it says, "I know." Only the mind which is capable of being in a state of not-knowing—not merely as a verbal assertion, but as an actual fact—is free to discover reality. But to be in that state is difficult, for we are ashamed of not-knowing. Knowledge gives us strength, importance, a center around which the ego can be active. The mind which is not calling upon knowledge, which is not living in memory, which is totally emptying itself of the past, dying to every form of accumulation from moment to moment—it is only such a mind that can be in a state of not-knowing, which is the highest form of thinking, and then thinking has a different meaning altogether. It may not be thinking at all, as we know it, but a state of being which is not merely the opposite of not-being.

Question: Would you please give us some practical way of getting free from our conditioned minds? You say that any particular training, such as yoga or other spiritual exercises, only makes us slaves, but I still think we have to use some kind of method. You say that to have this freedom, we must devote our lives to it, but how are we to do this without a method or a system?

KRISHNAMURTI: This is rather a complex question, and I hope you will listen with attention to what is being said. By attention I do not mean waiting in your mind for the answer you wish to receive—which is, is it not, the assurance that some kind of help, some kind of discipline or practice is necessary if we would be free. We are used to the idea of getting results through practice and moving from results to further results. But there is a limit to what can be known by the mind through practice, through discipline; and we are now trying to find out, are we not, what is truth, what is reality, what is God. To do that, the mind must first be made limitless, capable of receiving the unknown. The mind cannot go to truth, it cannot invite truth into its enclosure. Truth is immeasurable, it is too immense to be captured by any amount of practicing on the part of the limited mind.

And is it not true that your motive in asking this question is to gain something, to attain or capture truth? But truth must come to you; the mind cannot go to meet it. You think that if you practice overcoming your passions, it is going to lead you to reality; and so for you the method is very important; but such a mind, which is always hoping, inviting, expecting, can never under any circumstances reach that which is beyond the mind. There is no path, no yoga, no discipline which will lead you to it. All that the mind can do is to know itself. It must know its own limitations—the motives, the feelings, the passions, the cruelties, the lack of love—and be aware of all its many activities. One must see all that and remain silent, not asking, not begging, not putting out a hand to receive something. If you stretch out your hand, you will remain empty-handed forever. But to know yourself, the unconscious as well as the conscious, is the beginning of wisdom; and knowing yourself in that sense brings freedom—which is not freedom for you to experience reality. The man who is free is not free for something or from something; he is just free, and then if that state of reality wishes to come, it will come. But for you to go seeking it is like a blind man seeking light; you will never find it. The man who understands himself seeks nothing; his mind is limitless, undesirous, and for such a mind the immeasurable can come into being.

May 22, 1956

Fifth Talk in Stockholm

It might be profitable this evening if we could spend the time really discussing. By this I do not mean that you should merely ask questions and wait for my answer, but let us exchange ideas and think things out together. Perhaps it will be worthwhile, in a smaller group like this one, to try to go more deeply into what we have been talking about during the last four meetings.

We have been talking about how important it is that individual creativity should somehow come out of the chaos and confusion which exists in us and in the world today. And we have seen how essential it is, in this connection, to understand the background in which the mind is caught—the background which conditions us and limits our thinking. For it seems to me that, however much capacity we may have, the mind is nevertheless caught in the background, in the traditions, the experiences which it has stored up. It is fairly obvious that all experience tends to condition the mind, and I think it would be worthwhile to find out if it is possible for the mind not to be conditioned, not to build up a center out of experience from which every judgment, every act then takes place because that center is inevitably self-enclosing, limited, and narrow. If one thinks about it deeply, that is fairly clear.

Several questions have been asked as to why experience is a limitation, and I thought we might try to go into this matter rather thoroughly this evening. So, instead of my just talking about it, or our discussing merely as a verbal exchange, let us see if we can feel out this problem together.

Most of us think that experience is necessary, for our lives are full of experiences, both pleasant and unpleasant. One's memory is crowded with the residue of experience, and according to this accumulated experience, we judge or evaluate life. Such evaluation, judgment, is invariably limited. The mind is bound by centuries of slavery to experience, and the question is: Can it free itself? Can it be in that state of awareness which is entirely different from the state of accumulation? Can it be free of all accumulations so that it never deteriorates but is fresh and, in that sense, innocent? For I think only such a mind can discover—not a mind that is loaded with experience.

So, can we go into this matter? Is it possible for us to find out together whether the mind can break through all this accumulation, which we call knowledge, experience? Can the mind also be free of the urge for further experience, which is really the pursuit of sensation, and thereby make itself new, fresh? Surely it is only the fresh, uncontaminated mind that is free to observe and discover for itself if there is something beyond its own creations.

In discussing all this, please do not treat me as an authority. You are not asking, and I am not telling you, which would be absurd, because that kind of exchange can only lead to authority and the crippling of the mind. What we are trying to do is to go seriously into this whole matter without verbally blocking each other or asking irrelevant questions, but really sticking to the point. Can we do that this evening?

Audience: Yes.

Comment: To observe is to be free already, and to understand is also to be free—if I have understood you rightly. So it seems to be a real problem to know how to begin.

KRISHNAMURTI: Let us bear in mind that you are not just asking questions for me to reply to. We are putting our minds together to try to find out whether experience helps man to be free from the limitations he has imposed upon himself. And it has been suggested that to understand is to be free, to observe is the beginning of freedom.

Now, what is our problem? What is actually happening with each one of us? Please examine your own mind and see what is happening to you. We have had very many experiences, both pleasant and unpleasant. To some we cling, while others we reject, but they are all held in our consciousness; we cannot build a wall and shut out any of them. They are there, whether we like it or not. And do these experiences help man or hinder him? Will they bring freedom, or do they prevent freedom from taking place? This is really an important question because psychologists say that every experience is retained by the mind. The death of a son leaves a mark—the hurts, the insults to our vanity—it is all held there in the mind. And what we are actually discussing is: Can the mind free itself? If it can, then what is it that sets going this movement of freedom? Can you and I discover it for ourselves? Is it possible for the mind to break through its limitations and find true freedom? And is this to be done through observation? Is it to be done through some analytical process, or through confession, introspection, and so on?

Question: Experience which is in the deepest conformity with our innermost wishes will, I think, help us to free our minds. I personally have found that fasting and the vegetarian way of living are helping me to free my mind. When the stomach is empty, the mind is set free. Should one give up such experience?

KRISHNAMURTI: What do we mean when we say that vegetarianism, or certain other practices, will help us to be free? And what do we mean by "being free"? We say that some things free us and some things bind us. When there is suffering, pain, we want to be free of it, but we do not want to be free of pleasure, do we? Our minds are only concerned with directing our activities in accordance with the pattern of satisfaction which the 'I' has established.

We are not talking merely about vegetarianism or yoga, and whether those practices bring freedom; we are inquiring to find out whether it is possible to be free from all experience. For example, the mind which is conditioned by Christianity, Hinduism, or what you will may have visions, and the visions will be according to its particular background. All experience is both conditioned and conditioning, is it not? And we are discussing whether or not experience is helping us to be fundamentally free.

Comment: Such things are not helpful.

KRISHNAMURTI: Please do not agree with me. I do not mean this sarcastically or ironically, but the problem is much too fundamental for us merely to agree or disagree. We must go into it.

Comment: I think that, living in this world of time and space, it is impossible to escape from experience. If we fight against our experiences, or cling to them, then they leave a hardened residue in the mind. But I think it is possible to go through experiences and still keep oneself absolutely free. I have done something like this myself. If one does not fix one's position in an experience but just allows it to pass over one like a wave, then something happens—one will be changed and one will be free.

KRISHNAMURTI: But you see, sir, when we say, "If I do this, then something else will happen," all discussion stops. Surely, suppositional thinking is not thinking at all. What we are trying to go into is this: When there is some accident in life, a death or a hurt, it leaves a mark on the mind, and is it possible not to have that mark from an experience? Experience is going on all the time. Our whole life is a series of experiences, conscious or unconscious. The mind is like a sieve; some things we let go through it, and some are held. If you will observe your own mind you will see this as an obvious fact. So the experiences of yesterday condition the experiences of today—which is again a fact, surely. And can the mind be free of experience so that experience does not leave a mark upon it which gives a bias to the oncoming experiences?

Comment: But you can never get away from it!

KRISHNAMURTI: If we say that, then all discussion ceases. Can we remove the "never" and go into the problem more deeply? After all, a mind which has conclusions and thinks only from those conclusions is thinking no longer; it has stopped thinking.

Comment: It seems fairly clear that when we are caught in a certain experience, the mind is not free. But when we live, as it were, in the dance of experience, then experience brings us to a point where we look at things differently and the mind has a chance to be free.

KRISHNAMURTI: We all have conclusions, have we not?

Audience: No.

KRISHNAMURTI: You mean to say you have no conclusions?—that there is life after death, that you are Swedish, that your friends are like this or like that, that experience has led you to a certain point, that there is a God, or no God, and so on? We are a mass of conclusions, are we not? And from this background we judge, we look at and evaluate life. Your conclusions are based on your experiences and on the conventions of society which the collective has impressed upon you, and you are thinking from these conclusions. Now, someone comes along and points out that when you are thinking from conclusions, from past experiences, you are not thinking at all. And is it possible for the mind not to think from conclusions and yet to act, to live, to function, to think? Because only such a mind is capable of looking, observing very keenly.

Comment: I can follow you to the extent of seeing that it is a hindrance to accumulate knowledge for the sake of knowledge, and I also see the futility of disciplines, methods, and of striving for more and more sensation. But I cannot understand why you say we must not collect any experiences. You yourself must have had many experiences, for you have traveled and given lectures for over thirty years. You say we should free ourselves from religions, dogmas, and conventional biases. To do that we must know the structure of society, and we cannot get to know that structure without a great deal of penetrating personal experience, such as you certainly have had.

KRISHNAMURTI: I do not think we are quite understanding what the problem is. The gentleman says that I have had lots of experience and implies that it must have left a great deal of knowledge and many impressions; the cupboard must be full of riches. I do not think so. What we are talking about is this: All of us have a center, either a solid kernel or a fluidic one, but still a center—a center of hurts, fears, of wanting something, of pettiness, frustration, lack of love, and so on. This center is the result of our experiences, and it is always accumulating through further experiences. It is alive with memories, with various hopes and fears, and the mind is acting from this center. And we are trying to find out whether the mind can ever be free from this center, which is a vast bundle of experiences.

My son is dead. That leaves a tremendous wound, does it not? War is a terrible experience, and it leaves a scar, a mark on the mind. These marks direct all our thinking, do they not? They determine our attitude, our way of thinking and living, and they shape our future experiences. If I believe in Christ, in Buddha, or in some other person, that belief is an experience which will govern other experiences.

So, do we know, all of us, that we have such a center? And is it possible to break it down, or does it have to go on?—which may be the process of life; we are going to find out. Is it inevitable that the process of life should form a center, which then governs and directs further experience? Or is there something else, something entirely different, which will break down this center of accumulation?

That is, acting from your center, you are ambitious—you want to be a great architect, a painter, a poet. There is always something we want to be, either positively or negatively, and this center invites future experience according to its conditioning. Am I making it clear?

Audience: Yes.

Question: But without a center which accumulates memories, I would be lost; I would not even know where I lived. Surely it is right to remember and store up memories; otherwise, how can I live?

KRISHNAMURTI: That is the whole problem, is it not? If I forget where I live, there is something wrong with me mentally. At one level there must obviously be the retention of certain experiences, but they will be only those experiences which do not condition my thinking and feeling. Whereas, if I have been brought up as a Hindu or a Catholic, that background is surely going to condition my whole outlook. Living in a particular society and conforming to its sanctions, I am conditioned in that particular way, and I look at everything from a certain fixed point of view.

So, we are talking about the possibility of removing its conditioning from the mind—the conditioning which causes conflict, which perverts the mind and makes it really insane. When I call myself a Hindu, a communist, a Catholic, or what you will, it is not sanity; that is insanity because it divides human beings and sets man against man. Naturally it would be absurd to forget where I live, or if I am, say, a physicist, to forget what I know. We are not talking about that. But a physicist who calls himself an American, a Russian, or a Swede and uses his knowledge from that center perverts life, does he not? That is the kind of thing we are talking about.

So let us proceed to investigate whether you and I have in fact got these accumulated experiences, these conclusions which are perverting thought. We obviously have got them, so the question is how to deal with them. How is the mind, which has certain dominant beliefs, to be free of them? I do not know if you have ever thought about this problem, but it is surely important. The mind has a background of belief, of conclusion, of experience, both pleasurable and painful, and this background is so strong, so corroding. How is the mind to be free of it? Or is this not a problem to you?

Comment: I do not think we can do anything except let it pass away.

KRISHNAMURTI: No, sir, we cannot do that.

Comment: But we do not have to dwell on it.

KRISHNAMURTI: But we do! I do not think we are meeting the problem. You have had certain experiences, and you have certain beliefs, conclusions, have you not? These conclusions, beliefs, and experiences direct your life, and according to them you have further experiences. You may have visions of Christ or visions of a future utopia, of this or of that. And we are trying to find out whether the mind is not very harmful, very destructive, when its thoughts spring from conclusions, beliefs. If I believe in nationalism—which is one of the causes of war—if I feel myself to be an Englishman, an Indian, a Russian, and so on, from that crystallized thinking, I will inevitably create war. So, can the mind be free from conclusions—that is my problem. Is it not yours also? I am sure it is. I am not pushing you into a corner, but you will have to face it. As long as you have any conclusions, you are one of the causes of war. If you realize this, then how are you to be free from conclusions?

Question: If we can reason freely, we may be able to find a way of freeing our minds from the conclusions which lead us in the wrong direction. The fact that we have flags shows that we are on the wrong path; we think as Swedes instead of as human beings. Perhaps it will free us if we can ask: Will this deed, which is the result of my thinking, benefit those among whom I live, or will it not?

KRISHNAMURTI: I am afraid the problem is not quite so simple. If I merely say, "I am going to live by what I think is good," where does it lead? A dictator, a tyrant, thinks he is doing good, so do the exploiter and the imperialist. "Doing good" cannot be the criterion by which the mind can free itself. If it were as simple as that, it would be very easy. I have to know myself first, do I not? I have to know all my hidden motives, my desires, my tendencies, the totality of myself. Whether I am doing good or doing harm depends, surely, on whether I know and understand myself.

And how am I to know myself? Can I know myself on the basis of a conclusion—the conclusion that there is in me a divine spark or that I am only the result of environmental influences or any other conclusion? To know myself, surely, I must have no preconceptions, no assumptions. I must see those hopes and fears which are dictating my thoughts about myself; I must know the conclusions, the fixed points to which the mind clings—and the very knowing of them may be the action of breaking them down. The moment I know I am talking as a Hindu, and understand the significance of it, the thought that I am a Hindu has lost its influence; but if I profit by it, if I find security in it, then I will cling to it.

We have to know the total content of our being, and we cannot know it if we start from any fixed point. If we have a fixed point built up through fear, through hope, through dogma, then when we try to look at ourselves, that fixed point is always coloring, distorting what we see.

Comment: All that I can do with a conclusion is to become aware of it, to question it; and when I do that, I find that I do not know.

KRISHNAMURTI: We are touching now upon a very complex problem, and it has taken one and a half hours to come to this point. The problem is whether we can find out how our thinking is actually conditioned, and whether to go beyond that conditioning will take time.

To know for oneself very clearly in what way one is conditioned, to what beliefs the mind is clinging, and of what one is afraid—to know all this and then discover how to go much deeper needs patient inquiry, and perhaps we can go further into it tomorrow. The brain will not take more than a certain amount.

May 24, 1956

Sixth Talk in Stockholm

I think we should continue with what we were talking about yesterday. I do not know whether it is a problem for each one of us, this question of experience. Life is a continuous series of experiences; it is an endless process of challenge and response, and there is always a conflict when our response is inadequate to the challenge. Invariably this conflict, this inadequacy of response, is the result of the background, of tradition, of the previous experiences we have had. Following tradition inevitably leads to mediocrity, and most of our minds, it seems to me, fall into habits, into reactions based on tradition. We dwell in our past experiences, and we use the present as a means to the future. Few of us live to break out of this circle of unrealities and ghosts; and our future is merely the result of projections from the past.

I feel that if we can approach this inquiry with a mind that is not conditioned, that is not held, bound by the past, then there is a possibility of understanding, of seeing and feeling something which is not merely the outcome of the conditioned center. But most of us live and work from that center, which is the residue of all human experience, both individual and collective, and therefore all new experience is bound to condition our thinking further. The mind never goes beyond its own conditioning, and that is why it is never free.

So the question is: Can the mind be free from its own self-centered activity? Is it possible for the mind not to be self-centered? And what is such a state of mind?

After all, we can see that we are the result of our education, of our particular society, of the religion in which we have been brought up, and of the many other influences bearing upon us. Whether we are atheists or believers, we repeat what we have learned, what we have been taught, what we have accepted. A man who believes does not necessarily know more of the reality of God than a nonbeliever because both are conditioned—which is fairly obvious. So the question is: Can the mind free itself from all these influences, from all this accumulated experience? That is what we are trying to find out. There are those who maintain that such a thing is impossible and who think that all we need do is to find a better form of conditioning, so they turn from worshiping the dictates of a church to worshiping the dictates of a state, a party, or a government. But if we would seriously inquire into whether it is possible to free the mind from all conditioning, how are we to set about it? Can we discuss and go further into this problem?

Comment: I think one must begin by discovering a means.

KRISHNAMURTI: Can we not dispose of all the means which the mind invents in order to free itself? One means is the will—using the action of will to break down our conditioning. Another means is analysis. You go to an analyst or analyze yourself; you try to interpret your dreams, you carefully investigate each layer of memory, you examine every reaction, and so on. That is not the way, surely. And when we try to break down our conditioning through the action of will, what happens? One desire becomes dominant and resists the various other desires—which means that there is always the whole problem of suppression, resistance, and so-called sublimation. Does any of this free the mind from conditioning?

I wonder if we fully understand the implication of using the will to get rid of something or to become something. What is will? Surely will is, in itself, a way of conditioning the mind, is it not? In the action of will, one dominant desire is imposing itself upon other desires, one wish is overriding other motives and urges. This process obviously creates inward opposition, and hence there is ever conflict. So will cannot help us to free the mind.

Probably you have not thought about all this before and are therefore finding it rather difficult. But let us take a simple example and go into it, and we shall see.

Supposing I am violent or envious, how is the mind to be free of that—totally free, not just in little bits? Will the exercise of will free the mind from anything? If I am envious and, feeling that envy is wrong, I resist it, push it away, does that get rid of it? It does not, does it? And if the will does not help me, then how is the mind to be totally free from envy or anything else? It is really a very interesting problem. We are all consumed with something, whether it be envy, fear, ambition, or what you will; and can the mind be totally free of these things, or must we go on chopping at them little by little until we die and still not be free at the end of it all?

If we see that will does not free the mind from envy, then what is the next thing to try? Will analyzing oneself, introspection, get rid of envy? In analysis there is always the possibility of misinterpretation, and the question of whether the analyzer himself is free.

We saw yesterday that each one of us is a bundle of experiences, of reactions, and we asked ourselves: How is one to be free from this complex center? I am now trying to take one thing out of that bundle and look at it. It is an experience which we all have—envy. By what process can this experience be totally rooted out, eradicated? Is this a problem to everyone?

Audience: Yes.

KRISHNAMURTI: Then how would you tackle it?

Comment: One can learn to accept oneself.

KRISHNAMURTI: But one is still envious!

Comment: Truth will make us free.

KRISHNAMURTI: That is perfectly true. But to see what is true, and not merely repeat phrases, the mind must be very alert, vivid, sensitive—it must be in a state to see the truth.

Comment: We must be able to conquer envy by some sort of feeling of brotherhood.

KRISHNAMURTI: The problem is much more complicated than that. Conquering does not solve it. It is like putting a bandage over a wound. The wound is still there.

Comment: If we understand our envy, we see how it inhibits us.

KRISHNAMURTI: But do we? Most of us know the experience of envy, and we have created a society in which envy is very dominant, have we not? Our education, our religious ambitions, our whole lives are based on it—"You know, I do not; I must also know." This process breeds a competitive, ruthless society. Envy is an extraordinarily strong feeling, and having it, we function from that center. If there were no envy at all, what would be the state of the mind? And would it not then be possible to create quite a different society, quite a different kind of education? As individual human beings, is it not important that we should understand this problem and find out for ourselves if it is possible for the mind to be free of envy in its entirety?

Comment: If we stop wishing, stop desiring. . . .

KRISHNAMURTI: How is one to stop desire? By will? By tearing it to pieces? By discipline? By resisting, suppressing it? If you do any of these things, there is a conflict.

Comment: By studying it in all its forms.

KRISHNAMURTI: You can intellectually study all the various forms of envy and still suffer from it.

Comment: We must try to look at envy very calmly when it comes into our minds, and not hope too much to get rid of it.

KRISHNAMURTI: If I am envious, how am I to look at it?

Comment: Very calmly, I said.

Comment: Is this not the main difficulty, that we never really meet envy? We are envious, but we do not see our envy, actually.

Comment:: We can help our children to be free of it.

KRISHNAMURTI: To help the children, the educator himself must first be free. That seems fairly clear. But as the other gentleman said, "Do we really know what envy is?" Do we know envy as a living thing or merely as a word, a verbal statement? Do we know it as an intimate fact?

Comment: I am afraid most of us know it only as a word, and not as a fact.

KRISHNAMURTI: Of what significance is the word unrelated to the feeling?

Question: How would it be if one studied one's needs and tried to reduce them?

KRISHNAMURTI: I may become a monk, but I am still envious of another hermit who is holier or more clever than I am.

Comment: I think we must accept envy and give it its right place in our lives. If we can see, without condemning it, that envy does not lead anywhere, we shall get rid of it.

Comment: Perhaps envy is based on fear. If we could believe in ourselves as individuals, then we would not have to be envious.

KRISHNAMURTI: To say one must accept envy, or that envy is based on fear, does not help us. The cause of envy we know, but I am talking of the totality of it, the cause and the effect. After all, I know why I am envious; I am not as beautiful or as clever as you are; I compare myself with you, and I am envious. But is it possible to be free from that whole complex process?

Comment: If I dwell in the self, it is not possible. But by meditating every day, I can find out that the self has no value, and be free from envy.

Comment: If we could live in the now, we should not be attracted by what happened yesterday or what will happen tomorrow.

Comment: We must know that we are envious and live with it, feel it in every cell, and then this envy will absorb itself and something will suddenly happen.

KRISHNAMURTI: Surely we are all merely advising each other what to do, which is rather unfortunate because we shall never find out that way. If you are telling me how to live, what to do, I shall never discover anything, shall I?

Question: Who are we that we should think we can get rid of envy? After all, life has made us envious. We can try to be a little less envious, but even if we do not achieve that aim, life will still go on for many more years.

KRISHNAMURTI: Those for whom envy is not a real problem can chop away at it slowly, but that will never resolve our struggle and sorrow. I am afraid we are not really meeting each other. The problem needs a lot of penetration, and we are just putting out words and ideas. One knows one is envious, and that one's life is based on envy to a very large extent. From childhood we are brought up in envy, encouraged in it, consciously or unconsciously. On the surface I may be able to brush it aside, but deep inside, envy is still biting and burning. How is that fire to be completely quenched? You are just telling me what to do, you are not following the problem in yourselves. Can we not think it out together?

Question: When you speak of the mind being free, what do you mean by "mind"?

KRISHNAMURTI: I thought we made this whole problem clear yesterday. We have discussed for more than an hour, and unfortunately we have not really touched the subject at all. We can define our terms and so perhaps make verbal communication better, but this problem is not a matter of mere verbal communication or the further definition of terms. Also we have been talking of what to do and what not to do, and that may not be the question at all. It may be that we have to look at the problem in an entirely different manner. To find out, we must think out the problem together.

Question: If I know I am envious and I look at it without any condemnation, would that not be a way to be free of it?

Question: We tried to find out yesterday how to be free of experience and of conclusions. Can we leave envy for a moment and go into the question of what it is to be free? If there is a center, what is it? Is it a spark of God? And is not God free? What does it mean to be free?

KRISHNAMURTI: Has it never happened to you that you have been very angry and wanted to be free from it? Have you never asked yourself whether you can be free from envy, from this everlasting drive after something? When this happens to you, what is your response? You try discipline, suppression, and various other ways to get rid of that feeling, but still it obsesses you wherever you go. So what are you to do? How are you to look at it? What kind of action or nonaction must take place? So long as you are fighting it, one part of the mind resisting another part, envy will continue, will it not?

Audience: Yes.

KRISHNAMURTI: It is not a question of agreeing; you have to see it for yourself. So long as there is conflict, one part of the mind dominating another part, there can be no freedom. Do you see that fact?

Audience: Yes.

KRISHNAMURTI: I wonder if you do. You like this, do you not, because I am doing all the talking and you are just listening.

The problem is this: I am envious, and I see that mere resistance, suppression, bringing the will into action, only creates conflict. So my problem is conflict, not envy. My problem is not envy at all, but the fact that I am always striving in order to arrive somewhere. This striving is the very process of envy. What am I striving after? I am discontented, and I am striving to reach contentment. I think that if I can go to some place or reach some end, I shall be content. So I strive. I am unhappy, I am envious, always wanting more, more, more. My whole outlook on life is based on accumulation because in myself I am discontented, unhappy, lonely, empty. Being empty, I want somehow to enrich myself. I try various activities—painting, writing, worshiping, and many other avenues of self-expression—hoping to cover up this sense of emptiness. Is this not a fact?

Audience: Yes.

KRISHNAMURTI: But can this emptiness ever be filled? Can I enlarge myself inwardly? Please listen. When I try to be like Jesus, like Buddha, or like anybody else, it is because in myself I am nothing, and I am envious. So my problem is: Can I fill this emptiness? Surely, the moment I try to fill my emptiness, there is again the whole problem of struggle, of how to make myself richer. Then I look around to see who is richer, more beautiful, more talented than I am, and immediately I am caught in the field of comparison and struggle.

What then? I know there is an inner insufficiency, and can I look at it without any sense of wanting to enrich myself, without any desire to run away from it? Because the moment I try to escape from it, I enter into all sorts of false pursuits and stupidities through envy and comparison.

So now we are no longer concerned with the question of envy; we are considering the question of emptiness. How do I know that I am empty? Is it a mere verbal recognition, or is it an actual experience? Is the mind really aware of its emptiness? When I am not escaping from it, when I am no longer trying to enrich myself, when the mind is no longer caught in the mere verbal statement that it is empty, then there is only emptiness, the sense of insufficiency, of being inwardly poor. To recognize that fact, to be fully aware of it is what is important—not the question of what to do about it. When I ask what to do about it, I am again in the field of envy. But when one is aware of the simple fact that the totality of one's being is empty, and that one is constantly trying to find various ways of running away, all of which involve envy, then one no longer seeks to escape from this emptiness.

So, can the mind be aware of the fact of its emptiness without trying to alter it? I think that is the real issue. If the mind is only concerned with the fact that it is empty, then it no longer cares who is more beautiful or more intelligent. But we seem incapable of looking at that fact as it is. We are always translating it; we have opinions about it. We condemn it; we seek to escape from it; we are constantly trying to operate in some way on the fact, and so the fact is prevented from operating of itself. When the fact operates, it is the truth that operates. But we are so afraid of this emptiness that we try to do something about it all the time and thereby create a hindrance between ourselves and the fact.

If the mind can be completely still in front of the fact of emptiness, loneliness, violence, envy, if it does not translate that fact or wish it were different, then the fact operates. But so long as we operate upon the fact, we cannot be free. The man who is conscious that he is free, is not free, any more than the man who is conscious that he is humble, is humble. But to be silently aware of the fact without condemnation, without wanting a result, reveals the truth, which is freedom.

May 25, 1956

Brussels, Belgium, 1956

First Talk in Brussels

It seems to me that it would be wise if we could put away from our minds the various forms of prejudice that we have built up, especially the idea which many of us have that wisdom lies with those people who come from the Orient. That is really quite an absurd idea because human beings all the world over have essentially the same problems, whether they happen to live in the Orient or in the Occident. The Orient, from where I happen to come, is no different fundamentally from the Occident. The people over there have problems similar to ours—the same economic and social struggles, and the same problems of the spirit, of the mind, of the heart. We are all alike in our suffering, in our search, in our loneliness, and in the things which give the mind the power to create its own delusions.

It is surely important from the very beginning for you to understand not only what is being said but your own reaction to it, and to know why you have come here. After all, most of us come to these talks with the hope of finding something, do we not? We are all groping, seeking a better attitude or way of life, a more realistic evaluation of the things that matter. We are seeking something which we feel is very essential. So I think it would be good if we could go into this problem, to the very heart of it, and find out what it is that each one of us is earnestly seeking. We spend our days and our years in struggling to find out what life is all about. And it seems to me that our problem is not to find some satisfactory explanation of what life is about but rather to understand life directly for ourselves.

Our problems, which are many, cannot be translated either in terms of the Occident or the Orient. Many of us think that if we can follow a particular system of philosophy or some method, the more mystical the better, it will lead us to a higher form of happiness or to a greater depth of understanding. So we read, we search, we go to lectures, we follow teachers, we join religious organizations with their creeds and dogmas—but unfortunately we never find what we are looking for because we do not know exactly what it is we want. Within ourselves we want so many things; we are confused. Therefore it is obviously very important to spend some time, energy, and thought in inquiring into what it is that each one of us is seeking.

First of all, is it possible to find out what it is we are seeking? Our minds are so conditioned by the collective; we are either Christians, Hindus, Buddhists, or we are trying to follow some other system. Our minds are so shaped, so controlled, so conditioned by the particular society in which we live—economically, socially, and religiously—that we only seek whatever is promised by that particular tradition or system of thought. So we are always conditioned in our search. And I think it is very important to understand this conditioning. Because so long as our minds are conditioned as Christians, as Buddhists, as Hindus, or what you will, our search is of no avail. So long as the mind is limited, shaped by a particular belief or dogma, our search can only lead to whatever that dogma or belief promises. Only the mind which liberates itself from dogma, from belief, will find out what is true.

Whether one comes from the East or from the West, it is extraordinarily difficult to liberate oneself, culturally as well as religiously, from the various encrustations which society has imposed so that the mind is free to inquire. Without this freedom, surely, no inquiry is possible, especially in matters appertaining to the spirit, to the mind. And I think it is most essential not merely to grope vaguely after some kind of happiness, some kind of comfort or security, which almost any form of authority can give, but rather to inquire, with a free mind, to find out if there is reality, if there is God. Only such a mind can discover, and not the mind that believes, that is held in a dogma, however venerable and apparently worthwhile. A mind caught in belief is incapable of finding out if there is reality, if there is something beyond its own projections.

But it is not easy for the mind to free itself from the ideas in which it has been brought up, especially with regard to psychological issues, because it is ever eager to be comforted, to feel secure; so it creates or accepts some form of authority which promises the comfort it wants, an illusory reality without substance.

So, if our inquiry is to be at all worthwhile, I think that with attention, with purposefulness, we must go deeply into what it is that each one of us is seeking. Most religious people assert they are seeking God, truth, peace, or what you will. But those are just words, without much substance. The believer is as the nonbeliever, for both are conditioned by the particular society in which they have grown up. And one can put aside all the beliefs, the dogmas, the prejudices one has acquired only when there is deep discontent. Surely truth, or reality, is not for the man who is seeking comfort, but rather for those who have a deep inward discontent which is not easily canalized or assuaged through any particular satisfaction or gratification, but which is steadily intensified so that the mind rejects reasonably the comforting illusions which churches, so-called religious organizations, and one's own crippling desires have projected. Only a mind sharpened by thought, by reason, by doubt, is capable of inquiry. Such a mind is aware of its own workings, of its own background, of the values it has created, of the beliefs, the illusions, the hopes to which it clings; and it is only when all these things are set aside that the mind can find out whether or not there is a reality, something beyond its own projections.

Most of us live very shallow lives; we are lonely people, and we try to enrich our poverty-stricken minds with a great deal of knowledge, information, facts. But the mind is not capable of deep inquiry if it is filled with knowledge, or if it is bound to any form of dogmatic belief. What matters is to ask ourselves whether the mind is capable of self-knowledge. That is, can I know myself, am I able to observe, to inquire into the whole movement of my mind—not with morbidity, not with despair, not with the idea that it is ugly or beautiful, but just to watch it? It seems to me that this capacity to be alertly watchful of one's own mind is of the greatest importance because it is only through self-knowledge that one can understand those things which are crippling the mind.

To know oneself is an extraordinary process because the self is never the same from moment to moment; there are so many contradictory desires, so many compulsions, so many urges. And unless we understand the totality of it all, how can the mind be free? Only the mind that is free can really experience something beyond its own limitations, beyond its conditioning beliefs and dogmas.

It seems to me that these talks will be worthwhile only if we can really listen to what is being said. Most of us never listen to another, and when we do hear what someone says, we are always interpreting it. Such interpretation is not listening. Whereas, if we can listen, not with enforced concentration, but freely giving attention to what is being said, then the deep significance of the words will penetrate the mind, and I think such listening is far more vital than merely struggling to understand through the screen of our prejudices and preconceptions. That is, if you can listen to what is being said without resisting, without intellectually projecting reasonable arguments, without opposing or accepting, then I think the very act of listening is a purgation of the mind. It is like a seed that is planted in the earth; if the seed has vitality, it will grow of itself.

But unfortunately most of us are so concerned with our own ideas, with our own beliefs and prejudices, that there is no attention. Attention is the total good, but we do not know how to attend. We never really look at anything either. I do not know if you have ever experimented with really looking at something—by which I mean looking without naming, without giving it a label, without interpreting it. Then you see much more, you see with greater intensity the clarity of the color, the beauty or ugliness of the shape, and so on. And if you are capable of listening with that kind of attention, then your mind will be the soil in which something totally new can be born. Then you will find, at the end of these talks, that I have really told you nothing at all. Because what is it that we are trying to do in these talks? You are not trying to understand me; you are trying to understand yourself. And to understand yourself, you have to look within yourself. But a mind that is authority-ridden never looks within itself; a mind that is desirous of achieving an end, a goal, cannot possibly understand itself.

So it seems to me that what is of prime importance is to understand oneself. Self-knowledge is the beginning of wisdom. But we know so little about ourselves; we do not know the unconscious as well as the conscious parts of ourselves, the totality of our whole being. And is it possible to know ourselves totally? Surely, if one is incapable of knowing oneself, the totality of one's being, then all search is without meaning. Then search becomes a contradiction, one desire against another desire. But if we can understand ourselves, if we can patiently and diligently observe the functioning of our whole being, then we shall find that the mind becomes very clear and free. Only such a mind is capable of inquiring into, searching out the eternal—and then perhaps there is no search at all, for then the mind itself is the eternal.

It is very difficult for most of us to know ourselves because we are always measuring our thoughts, our actions, our feelings. We hope that through this measurement we shall come to know ourselves; but surely a mind that is always judging, evaluating, can never know itself as it is because it has a standard, a pattern, by which it evaluates. I think this is one of our major difficulties—that we cannot observe our feelings, our thoughts, without evaluation, without approving or condemning. For most of us, judgment, comparison, approval, condemnation, is the very essence of our existence. That is why we are unable to go into the greater depths of our own thoughts and feelings, the conscious as well as the unconscious.

If we would understand a child, for instance, it is surely of no value to compare him with his brother. To understand him, we must look at him without comparison; we must observe him at different times, in all his various moods. But we are brought up, we are educated, to compare, to judge, to condemn; and we think that by comparison, by condemnation, by judgment, we shall understand. On the contrary, as long as we compare, judge, condemn, we shall never understand a thing.

In the same manner, if we would understand the totality of our being, however ugly or beautiful, transient or permanent, we must be capable of looking at ourselves in the mirror of relationship without evaluation, without comparison, and then we shall find that the totality of consciousness begins to unfold.

After all, though we are somewhat aware of the functioning of the conscious mind, most of us know very little about ourselves at the greater depths of consciousness. We never look at that part of ourselves; we have never even inquired into it, or if we inquire into it, it is only when we are troubled by some kind of neurosis, and then we have to run to somebody to help us. That is not knowing ourselves. Knowing ourselves implies self-observation at every moment of the day—in our relationships, in our speech, in our actions, in our gestures—it implies being fully aware of ourselves so that we begin to find out what we are. And we will find that we are very little. We are only that which we have been conditioned to be. We believe, or we do not believe; we repeat what we have been told. We accept because we are afraid, and religions grow out of our fear. That is why it is very important to know oneself—not theoretically or according to the psychologist's point of view, but to know for oneself what one intrinsically is. And I do not think this is very difficult if one gives one's full attention to discovering what one is in every moment of relationship.

Then you will find that religion is something entirely different from anything you already know. Religion has nothing to do with these absurd organizations which control the mind through this belief or that; it has nothing whatever to do with any so-called religious society. On the contrary, a truly religious man does not belong to any such society, to any organized religion; but to be truly religious requires immense understanding of the ways of the self, of one's own integral state. There is no essential difference between the man who believes in God and considers himself to be religious and the man who disbelieves and who thinks he is not religious. Each is conditioned by the society in which he lives, and to be free from that conditioning requires the intensification of discontent. It is only when the mind is discontented, in revolt, when it is not merely accepting or trying to find some new form of comfort—it is only then that a truly religious man comes into being.

Such a truly religious man is the true revolutionary because only he can alter, at quite a different level, the whole attitude of society. But this requires an extraordinary understanding of oneself. Self-knowledge is of prime importance; it is absolutely essential for any seeker after truth, for if I do not know myself, how can I seek truth? The instrument of search, which is my own mind, may be perverted, twisted, and it is only through self-knowledge that the mind can be straightened out. The clear, straight mind alone can inquire into that which is true—not the confused mind. A mind that is confused can only find that which is also confused.

But a confused mind cannot become unconfused by relying on another, by seeking the authority of a book, of a priest, of an analyst, or what you will. Confusion comes to an end only when the mind begins to understand itself. And out of this understanding come clarity and stillness of mind. It is only the mind which is completely still that is capable of receiving the timeless.

I have been given some questions, and I shall try to answer some of them. But before I do so, I think it would be wise to explain that the complex problems of life have no answer. None of the great issues have an answer which will be satisfactory. What we can do is to inquire into the problem itself. The mind that is seeking an answer to the problem will never understand the problem because it is concentrated on finding the answer, and invariably it is seeking an answer which will be immediately satisfying, comforting. So, if one really wants to understand a problem, one should never ask for an answer but rather inquire into the problem itself.

This, again, is very difficult for most of us because to inquire into a problem requires intelligence, patience, diligent observation—never accepting or rejecting but exploring. When we suffer, most of us want an immediate response because our only concern is to escape from that suffering. In seeking an escape, we create illusions, and those illusions can be exploited by the cunning.

So, in considering these questions, we are not seeking an answer because, as I said, there is no answer, and that is true. You may ask what love is, and perhaps someone will answer you verbally, but that answer will have very little meaning. If we would find out what it means to love, all forms of attachment must go. Attachment brings fear, and how can there be love if there is fear?

So, through these questions we are going to explore the problem. If you are merely looking for an answer, I am afraid you will be disappointed. But if together we can undertake the journey of exploration so that each one of us experiences the state of inquiry, then we shall find that the problem is resolved—not because we have actively done something about the problem, but because the problem exists only while we are not giving it complete attention. We can give complete attention to the problem only if there is no sense of condemnation, no reference to the past in order to understand the present.

Question: Is not authority helpful in this world of chaos and confusion?

KRISHNAMURTI: I think this is a good question to go into. Most of us are confused, are we not? The issues of life are many and difficult, and there are innumerable specialists, teachers, Oriental gurus, innumerable books and churches, all claiming to know the answers. Being confused, you look to those who say they know, but because you are confused, your choice of a guide will also be confused. Being anxious to find out, you invariably create authority—the authority of a book, the authority of a church, of an individual, of the collective, or of an idea. So authority exists because you create it; you create it out of your own confusion and uncertainty. The anatomy of authority is the anatomy of our own uncertainty. We want to be certain, to be gratified, and so we look to someone for an answer—to a teacher, a guru, and God knows who else. So our whole structure of thinking is based on authority.

It is an extraordinarily complex problem, and what is important, surely, is not the worship of authority, or the substitution of one authority for another, but rather to find out if the mind can free itself from its own confusion. When the mind is very clear, it needs no authority, but when it is uncertain, confused, when it is in misery, in turmoil, then it looks to another for help. And can another help? Or is there fundamentally no help at all because the misery, the turmoil, the confusion, is created by oneself, and therefore must be cleared away by oneself? Surely, whatever another can do to help is but a temporary alleviation.

But to clear up one's own confusion requires great energy, freedom to find out what is true—not rushing about asking for help. I think this is important to understand. There are wars, starvation in the East, economic problems, the hierarchical outlook on life, the divisions of class, religions, and nationalities; and we are caught in all this contradiction and turmoil, which is very confusing; and it seems to me of the utmost importance to find out, amidst all this chaos, what is true. To find out, surely, we must stop seeking. Because, how can a man seek when he is confused? His seeking and finding will only add to the confusion. I think this is such a simple fact, if only we could realize it. But if one knows how to clarify one's own confusion, then one will not look to another, one will not depend on another.

So, in order to bring about clarity, sanity in this mad world, it is important, first of all, to know for oneself what one is actually doing. Being confused, having so many contradictory desires and compulsions, we are everlastingly trying to bring out of this inward chaos one dominant desire that will control all the others—which only creates another problem. That is why it is very important, for those of us who are really serious about these matters, to understand ourselves, and not merely pursue, in our confusion, the various dogmas of the East or of the West. It requires a great deal of attention to perceive for oneself how deeply rooted one's confusion is, but most of us are unwilling even to admit that we are confused.

It seems to me that authority will exist—the authority, whether inward or external, that compels psychologically, spiritually—so long as we are seeking any form of security for ourselves or for a particular group or nation. Authority breeds exploitation, it brings darkness, brutality, in the name of God or peace or the state. That is why the man of peace has no authority, inward or outward—which does not mean that he goes about breaking the law.

To realize all this requires a great deal of penetration, insight into oneself. Self-knowledge cannot be learned from any book, nor through merely attending one or two talks or discussions. The treasure lives within oneself, and it is revealed in the mirror of our daily relationships through watchfulness, observation, which is to be aware without any choice.

Question: Will you please tell us what freedom is? Is this not an illusion which we are all pursuing?

KRISHNAMURTI: We want freedom only when we are aware of our bondage, and because we do not know how to free ourselves from bondage, we pursue freedom. But if we have the capacity to free ourselves from bondage, then there is freedom; we do not have to pursue it or inquire what freedom is—we can leave that to the philosophers and speculators. The important thing is to find out in what manner we are held, bound, for in the very understanding of that bondage, there is freedom. The moment we struggle against bondage, we create another bondage. But if we can understand the whole psychological process of bondage—not merely what binds us now, but how it has come into being—the motives, the implications, the whole background of it, both conscious and unconscious—then in that very understanding there is freedom; we do not have to "become" free.

Take fear, for example. Most of us are bound by fear in one form or another, and it is a very complex process, is it not? Do we know that we are afraid, and how fear comes into being? Or do we merely theorize about it? Fear exists, surely, only in relationship to something; it does not exist by itself. I am afraid of something—of death, of poverty, of what my neighbor might say, and so on. And can I look into this whole problem of fear? I can look only if I am not trying to do something about it.

What is this fear? Is it fear of the unknown? Or are we afraid of losing the known—of being poor, for example. Can the mind be free from this fear of being poor? And is it poverty of the mind or poverty of physical existence to which we give importance? Surely, the thoughtful man, the man who is really trying to find out, is concerned with the poverty of the mind. And can this poverty of the mind be overcome by knowledge, by reading books? Can the mind enrich itself through any form of fulfillment? And is there fulfillment at all, or merely the demand of a mind which is afraid of its own poverty and therefore seeks to fulfill itself?

So the problem of fear is not very simple, and it requires a great deal of inquiry on the part of the mind to find out in what manner it is afraid. When there is an understanding of the whole process of fear, there is freedom—not just freedom from fear, but freedom for the mind to go beyond itself. The man who is free from something knows only a limited freedom.

You see, to inquire into all this takes a great deal of energy, attention, not merely for an hour or two, but at every moment of the day—when you are in the bus, at your office, with your family, or walking by yourself. There must be this constant inquiry, a searching, a watching, so that the whole content of one's being is revealed. Then you will find, in the discovery and understanding of what one actually is, there comes the opening of the door to freedom.

June 16, 1956

Second Talk in Brussels

It seems to me that one of the most difficult things to do is to communicate rightly. If I want to say something, I must use certain words, and words naturally tend to have a somewhat different meaning or significance for each one of us who listens. Merely to sit together in silence has its own benefit, but really to communicate we must verbalize, and it is very difficult to communicate properly what one means to convey so that the other understands the full intent of it, especially when dealing with subjects which are rather complex, as we are doing now. We require a certain ease of communication so that all of us understand what it is we are talking about.

I want to deal with something which I feel is rather important—whether it is possible, living in this world, to free oneself from all conditioning so that one becomes truly individual and hence is able to find out what it means to be creative. Surely, that which may be called reality, God, truth, or what you will, is a state of constant renewal, a state of creativeness; and this creativeness cannot be realized, cannot be experienced or known without true individuality; and to come to that true individuality, there must be freedom from conditioning.

Our minds are conditioned by the society in which we live, by the books which we have read, by religion, by moral and social values, by our own fears, ambitions, envy, and so on; all these things go to create a conditioning of the mind. I think this is very obvious. And is it possible to free the mind from this conditioning—not to find a better or more noble conditioning, but to totally free the mind from all conditioning? Until we do that, surely, we are not individuals; we are merely the result of the collective—which again is very obvious, though we may not have thought about it. When we examine ourselves a little, closely, it is apparent that most of our thinking, most of the values, the experiences, the knowledge, the beliefs that we have are the result of our education, of innumerable influences—the climate we live in, the food we eat, the literature and newspapers we read, the whole environmental background—all this conditions the mind. We can see that our thinking is always according to a pattern, and that the pattern is well-established. The more highly organized a society, the more efficient and ruthless it is, the more thoroughly the pattern is cultivated and drilled into the mind. And is it possible to be free of that conditioning so that the mind does not think according to a pattern, but goes beyond all thought?—which does not mean a vague mysticism, a dreamy state; on the contrary, it is a very precise state.

So, can the mind free itself from its conditioning? I know there are those who say it is impossible because human beings are entirely the result of environmental influences. One man, being brought up as a Christian, believes in the dogmas of Christianity, while another who is brought up as a communist believes in none of those things—which again shows how the mind is influenced and set going in a pattern, in a groove, in which it continues to function.

Looking at all this, what is our response? Whether we are Christians, Hindus, Buddhists, or what you will, it must have occurred to us, if we are at all serious, that each one is shaped, conditioned by a particular pattern—not only the pattern imposed by society, by the culture, the economic influences, the religion in which one is brought up, but also by a pattern imposed from within. And we must have asked ourselves whether it is possible for the mind which habitually thinks in a certain groove to break out of it. Surely, it is only a free mind that can discover anything new. A man who merely believes or disbelieves in God is still caught in the pattern of a particular environment; through fear, through compulsion, through every form of influence, he is still part of the collective. So, is the mind thus bound capable of freeing itself?

The capacity to be free surely does not depend on another. I see that my mind is the result of innumerable experiences, that its responses are determined by an already conditioned state, and if I am interested to find out whether my mind can free itself, not partially but totally, at the unconscious as well as at the conscious level, then I do not have to ask another; I can watch myself. I may free myself from the idea of "my country," from stupid nationalism, from the beliefs in which I have been brought up; but in the very process of freeing myself, I may fall into another set of patterns. Instead of being a Hindu I may become a Christian, a Buddhist, a communist, or what you will—which is still a pattern. So, is it possible to break away from one pattern without falling into another?

If one is very alert and observant of the habit-forming process of the mind, it is possible superficially to free the mind from the formation of habits. But the problem is not so simple because there is the whole unconscious, which is also conditioned, and its conditioning is much more difficult to see. After all, through talk, through reasoning, through various forms of observation, I can free my mind from the superficial conditioning of being a Hindu or a Catholic—and this is obviously necessary. If I am to seek out what is real, I must first have a mind which is unconditioned. A conditioned mind can project its own ideas and then experience those ideas. The Christian who is very devout and heavily conditioned can experience a vision of Christ, but he is experiencing his own projection from the background in which he has been brought up, and such experience has no validity at all. But if we can go beyond all the superficial responses of the mind, then perhaps we can penetrate much more deeply into the unconscious, which is ceaselessly projecting its conditioning.

So, is it possible consciously to go into the unconscious and discover its various forms of conditioning? I do not know if you have thought about this at all. You may have opinions about it, you may assert that it is possible or impossible, but I do not think a student who is really inquiring into the whole question will ever make assertions of that kind. He must be in a state of inquiry. And he cannot inquire with regard to someone else, he can only inquire into his own mind.

Inquiry, it seems to me, must be without a motive, without a compulsion in any direction. If I have a motive for my inquiry, that motive dictates what I shall find. So real inquiry does not exist so long as there is a motive. And most of us have a motive of some kind, have we not? We want to be happy, we want to be inwardly rich, we want to find God, we want to achieve this or that. And can the mind strip itself of all motive and be in a state of inquiry? I think this is really a fundamental question, because it is only when we are free of motive that we shall be able to inquire into the totality of the unconscious.

After all, the unconscious is the repository of many motives of which we are unaware—fears, anxieties, and the racial residue. To inquire into all that, the conscious mind, at least, must be free of motive. And to cleanse even the conscious mind of motive demands a great deal of watchfulness, observation of oneself. It means being aware of the whole process of thinking—finding out how thought springs into the mind, and whether it can ever be free, or whether thought is merely the reaction of a particular background through memory, and therefore is never free. One may be able to reason very intelligently, very cleverly, but that reasoning has the background of a particular conditioning.

So, if the conscious mind is to inquire into the unconscious, where all the motives, the urges, the compulsions of centuries are stored, then the conscious mind must surely begin by being free of motives and patterns. And it is only in that inquiry, it seems to me, that we begin to dissolve the collective influences of which we are now made up. We are not individuals now; though we may have a distinctive name, a personal bank account, and all the rest of it, that does not constitute individuality. But what does bring about the true individual is this state of mind in which there is freedom from conditioning. Only then is it possible to find out whether there is a reality beyond the limitations of thought, beyond the inventions and theories of the mind.

Until we come to this state, what we believe or do not believe about God, or truth, has very little significance. Our beliefs and disbeliefs will merely be the repetitive, imitative ideas and thoughts which we have learned from some book, or from another person, or which we have projected out of our own desire for comfort. The truly religious man is not the one who clings to certain beliefs and dogmas, or who strictly practices morality, but rather the man who begins to understand the whole process cf his own thinking—the unconscious as well as the conscious. Such a man is an individual, for his mind is no longer repetitive; although there is the memory of the things it has known, they do not interfere. Such a mind becomes extraordinarily quiet, without any movement of desire, without any projection or motive. In that state there is the creativity of reality.

But this is not a thing that you can hear about and repeat, like a boy learning and repeating his lessons. To do that has no meaning at all. One has to go into oneself very deeply, pushing aside all the trivial fears, the envies, the ambitions, the desire to be secure, to be attached, to be dependent, which for most of us is very important—pushing all that stupid nonsense aside, not just temporarily, but actually being free of it. Only then is it possible to find out if there is a reality or not, if there is God, if there is something which is beyond time. Until we find that out for ourselves—not through somebody else, not through saviors or teachers, but directly experience it for ourselves—life is a very superficial thing. We may have immense riches, great influence, and be able to travel all over the world; we may have vast knowledge and be very clever in our talk, but without that direct experience, life becomes very trivial, and underneath there is always misery, struggle, pain. Then we are everlastingly trying to give life a meaning, we are forever asking what is the purpose of life, so we invent a purpose—a cynical purpose of despair, or a purpose of delight.

But if we are capable of this constant inquiry, which is really a form of meditation, then we are bound to come to the point when we realize that all our thinking is conditioned and that our beliefs and dogmas have no value at all. And when we see that they have no value, they drop away without our struggling against them. The totality of our conditioning can be broken—not bit by bit, which takes time, but immediately, by directly perceiving the truth of the matter. It is the truth that liberates, not time, or your intention to be free. That is why the mind must be extraordinarily open, receptive. For truth is not to be pursued and caught; it must come.

So it is important to inquire into this whole question of conditioning, and not merely accept another's assertion as to whether the mind can be free or not. One has to inquire and free oneself. Then I think we shall find something beyond all words, about which there can be no possible communication. The man who has realized, experienced that thing for himself, is a truly religious man, for he is no longer influenced by society—society being this structure of ambition, of acquisition, of envy, the self-centered activity of the collective.

Question: Is there such a thing as real happiness? Can anyone ever find it, or is our pursuit of it an illusion?

KRISHNAMURTI: I think if we pursue happiness, life becomes very shallow. After all, happiness is a thing that comes to you, it is a byproduct; when you go after happiness, it eludes you, does it not? If you are conscious that you are happy, you are no longer happy. When you know that you are joyous, surely at that very moment you have ceased to be joyous. I do not know if you have noticed this. It is like the man who is conscious of his humility; surely such a man is not humble.

So happiness, I think, is something that cannot be pursued, any more than you can pursue peace. If you pursue peace, your mind becomes stagnant. For peace is a living state, and to understand what peace is requires a great deal of intelligence and hard work—not merely sitting down and wishing for peace. Similarly, happiness requires immense understanding, insight, and hard work—as much hard work as you give to earning a livelihood, and far more. But if you are merely seeking happiness, then you might just as well take a drug.

To pursue happiness, it seems to me, is to pursue an illusion. In that pursuit is involved a very complex process. There is the pursuer, and the thing which he pursues. When there is a pursuer wanting something, there is always conflict; and so long as there is conflict, there is no understanding, but only a series of miseries and an endless struggle to overcome them in order to reach happiness. This is the conflict of duality, of the thinker and his thought. Only when the mind is no longer pursuing its own gratification, its own fulfillment, no longer trying to reach happiness, which is a self-centered activity—only then is there the cessation of all conflict. This state may be called happiness—but that is irrelevant.

So it is important to go into this problem of effort and conflict. I wonder if we understand anything through effort? And if we do not make an effort, what will happen? We have been brought up, educated, to make an effort; and if we do not make an effort, we think something is wrong, we fear that we shall stagnate, degenerate. But if we are at all observant of ourselves, I think we must have found that understanding comes at those moments when the mind is very quiet, and not during the period of struggle. And the mind is in a state of perpetual struggle so long as it wants to be happy, secure, or is seeking some kind of permanency.

Where there is conflict, there must be tension, misery; but to live without conflict is an immense problem. One cannot just brush it aside, saying, "I'm going to live without conflict"—that has no meaning. Nor can one meditate, do all kinds of mystical things, in order to have no conflict—which is very childish. One has to understand the psychological process of this movement which we call conflict, and we cannot possibly understand it so long as there is the motive to achieve something. So long as I want to be something—happy, good, virtuous—so long as I want to find God, or what you will, there must be conflict, and with it, misery and pain.

One has to understand totally the whole process of achieving, end-gaining, and not merely say, "If I do not make an effort, I will degenerate, I will lose my job," which is a very superficial response. To understand deeply the psychological problem, the inward nature of effort, requires a great deal of self-perception. That is why it is very important to know oneself. In the very process of self-knowledge, perhaps there will be happiness on the side—which is very unimportant.

Question: You seem to deny yoga. Do you think it has no value at all?

KRISHNAMURTI: Yoga is a particular system invented by the Hindus, by which to find, to be, to become. We think that through some such system we shall be able to achieve peace of mind. We think that by right breathing, by having the right kind of yoga, by practicing meditation, controls, discipline, we shall arrive at that state of mind in which it is possible to find out what God is, or if there is God. Many people think these systems will lead to that. But I think the whole idea of any method or system leading to God—though it may produce a particular result which is apparently practical in this world—is utterly illusory. Because, truth or God has no path, no system by which you can approach it, and I think this is fairly obvious to anyone who is not already committed to a pattern or a method. After all, merely doing a particular exercise, thinking along a fixed line, struggling to control all one's thoughts—none of this makes the mind really alert, pliable, intelligent, perceptive.

What is required is not to set the mind in a particular pattern, however fascinating, but to free the mind so that it is able to discover. How can the mind discover what is true if it is caught in a system? There are new kinds of drugs which give all the things that yoga promises. You can take these drugs and become very happy, have a mind that is very quiet, intensely aware of things, of people, of nature. But surely those are all tricks. They do not help the mind to discover what is true. By taking a drink, or one of these pills, or by doing yoga, you can have a certain temporary alleviation, satisfaction, peace; but you will have to keep on taking your drug.

Please, those of you who practice yoga, do not merely brush this aside, saying that I am prejudiced. This is a very important question—whether you can, through any trick, by taking a pill or practicing some method of making the mind quiet, bring about that state of deep comprehension of what is true. I say it cannot be done. Yoga, drugs, drink—all the various stimulants produce their own results, but they cannot possibly make the mind into that astonishing instrument of inquiry, of search and discovery.

You see, we all want methods, systems, pills, to make us immediately happy; it is the immediacy we are after. But if we are at all alert to the whole issue, we shall see that merely to go on asserting that yoga is useful indicates a very shallow mind. The problem is not whether yoga is right or wrong but whether the mind can be freed from creating a habit and living in that habit. A mind that seeks peace and establishes itself in the routine of peace is not a peaceful mind; it has merely disciplined itself, compelled itself to conform to a pattern, and such a mind is not a living mind, it is not innocent, fresh. Only the mind that is innocent, fresh, free to discover, is creative.

Question: How is it possible to live in this world without any kind of security?

KRISHNAMURTI: I do not think it is possible to live in this world without security. If you did not know where you were going to get your next meal, where you were going to sleep tonight, and so on, it would become impossible; you would not be able to think; you could not call it living. Governments and society are gradually bringing about that physical security—the welfare state and all the rest of it.

But surely that is not the real problem. The problem is that we want to be secure inwardly; psychologically we want to be secure. Therefore we invent such things as nationalism, God, this and that, in which we seek psychological security—and thereby bring about physical insecurity. After all, so long as I insist that I am a Hindu and find delight in being an Indian—making an ideal of it, or what you will, and depending on that for my inward security—I create a division between man and man, the division of nationalities, frontiers, class differences, which will invariably bring about insecurity, psychologically as well as physically.

So, is it possible for the mind not to seek security at all? Is it possible to be psychologically free of this demand to be secure, this demand for permanency? At present we are all seeking permanency in some form or other—permanency in relationship, permanency after death, permanency in our ideas, a continuity of belief—all of which indicates an inward insufficiency which makes us want psychological security. So, is it possible for the mind to be free from this urge to be secure? After all, if you observe, we are always seeking permanency in our relationships, are we not? We want permanency in our relationship with society, with a particular person, or with one or two. And if that is once established, then we want permanency in another direction—we want to become something, we want to be well-known, famous. If it is not that, then we want permanency after death, or permanent peace, a permanent state of happiness, or we want to be permanently good.

I think this is the whole problem—to understand and free the mind of this constant urge to seek a permanent state. For does not this demand for permanency lead to mediocrity? Surely it is only the mind that is uncertain, that has no continuity in the known—it is only such a mind that is capable of discovery, capable of renewing itself, not the mind that is merely moving from the known to the known. After all, that is what we are doing, is it not? What we want is the continuity of the known—the known experience, the known pleasure. And so long as the mind is seeking that state of permanency, we are bound to create division between man and man.

The problem is, then, can the mind live without seeking permanency at all? Is there a mind if there is no permanency? After all, the mind is the result of time, of the innumerable experiences it has had, and it cannot brush all that aside. The very words it is using are the result of memory, the known. But need those memories, the known, interfere and make the mind incapable of inquiring? The mind is capable of inquiring, of discovering, only when there is uncertainty, when there is freedom from the known.

All this is not a mere matter of acceptance or rejection. You have to experiment with this—that is, if you are at all seriously interested. You have to go deeply into yourself, inquire most profoundly, so that the mind becomes capable of renewing itself, of remaining innocent in spite of the innumerable experiences and accidents of life. For only the innocent mind, the fresh mind, is open to receive that which is eternal.

June 17, 1956

Third Talk in Brussels

It seems to me that it would be a waste of time and energy if one merely came to these talks as an intellectual distraction or to find new ideas with which to play. We are concerned here with something much more fundamental than mere amusement or intellectual stimulation. We are concerned with a radical change in human thought, and this requires considerable inquiry, deep questioning, and hard work.

A radical change is obviously necessary because society is in conflict within itself. Although we profess love and brotherhood, every man is against another; each one belongs to a particular religion or country, and the whole social structure of the world is based on conflict, on envy, on acquisition. Those of us who are really seriously concerned, who are at all alive to the whole human problem of existence, must be aware of the extraordinary suffering there is, both within and without. And we must also be aware of how urgent it is to bring about a fundamental change in human relationship—which is, after all, society.

At present what we call religion is principally a matter of conforming to a particular dogma or belief, and the fact that we are greedy, envious, brutal, is evidently irrelevant. But religion, surely, is something quite different; it is the process of trying to find out, to establish, the right relationship between man and man so that we do not merely conform to a particular pattern of society or to the pattern of any belief or dogma.

If we are at all serious—as we must be in a world that is full of crises—we must be concerned, not merely intellectually or sentimentally, but as individuals, as vital human beings, with how to bring about a radical change. And it seems to me that it will be utterly useless for us to go through all these talks unless you and I are willing to inquire into the whole matter very deeply, actually experiencing as we go along. We shall have to feel out for ourselves how to change deeply and fundamentally, how to approach the whole problem anew, and not merely repeat the old pattern of existence in different ways and under different labels. Surely, to bring about a radical change in the world, we need a tremendous revolution—not a communist revolution, which is no revolution at all, nor any revolution of a merely social nature, but a fundamental transformation in ourselves.

Is it possible to bring about this radical change? And what is the motive that makes us change? If there is a motive, is there a change? And what is the factor that brings this change? Is it the action of will, or the action of knowledge, or the action of mere social convenience? Or does the change come about not at any of these levels but much more radically and away from all social and environmental influences? I think this must be a very deep problem for most of us, if we have thought about it at all. Because we see an enormous amount of starvation in Asia, while in the West there is overproduction and the piling up of armaments. The whole of the West is much better off in the material sense; the people are more healthy, more vigorous, they have more to eat, and the welfare state is bringing about security for old age; whereas, in the East there is not enough food for the majority of the people; there is starvation, and the exploitation of centuries continues. And even in the West there are contradictions; they are in conflict among themselves.

Seeing this whole picture—not as Christians or communists, nor as representatives of the East or of the West, but as human beings who are struggling, who are suffering, who have love—we must surely be concerned to find out how to bring about a radical change so that we do not continue in the same old patterns of existence. And can this change, this revolution, come about through conscious effort or only through understanding the psyche, not merely intellectually, but actually? And who is the entity that is to bring about this change?

As a human being I see this extraordinary world problem, and I also see that the world problem is my problem because society is what I am. I have been educated in a particular society, as we all have; as human beings we are conditioned. And how am I to bring about this change in myself, and so in society? Am I now different from society? Must I not break away from society totally, completely, if I am to affect society? And who is to break away from it? Is there an 'I', a center, from which there can be independent action which is not controlled, dominated, shaped by society? If there is a center which is independent, uninfluenced by society, then that center, given the opportunity, will act. But is there such a center? Or is the totality of consciousness—the whole of it, not merely a segment—the result of innumerable social influences, contradictions, and urges?

Can I—when I say "I," it also includes you—can I, who am the product of society, of time, of influence—can this "I," through any action, through any desire, through any compulsion, bring about a change? Is not this "I," who wishes to bring about a change, made up of all the various elements which also compose society? And if I merely alter one or two of these elements in myself, discard one or two patterns, surely I have not broken away from society.

So it seems to me that we must first find out whether it is possible to change at all, and what is the force, what is the drive, what is the compulsion that makes me want to change? In what way is this whole structure of the 'me' related to society? Am I—the thinker, the entity who wants, desires, seeks, who is frustrated, envious, brutal, loving, and all the rest of it—am I different from society? And what do we mean by society? Society is obviously the relationship between man and man; it is a structure we have built up in our relationship with others. That relationship, which is society, is based on acquisitiveness, envy, fear, ambition, on the seeking of power, position, prestige. And these things are what each one of us also wants—only perhaps in a more tolerant, more dignified, more respectable way. The very essence of society is the seeking of wealth, and the effort to fulfill one's ambition by identifying oneself with a particular group or country. Those who seek to reform—the missionaries, the internationalists, the believers—are also within the acquisitive pattern of society, as we all are.

So, I am not different from society—which is so obvious, is it not? The whole social structure is based on this drive to be great, to fulfill one's ambition, to distract oneself, to escape from pain or pursue amusement; and it gives rise to brutality, to war, to hatred, with occasional use of the word *love*. That is the source from which all our thinking comes—and we are aware of it. Now, how are you and I, as two human beings concerned with this enormous problem—how are we to break away from society? How are we to completely free ourselves from all the things which society represents, and of which we are made up—envy, hate, ambition, greed, vanity, the search for power, for position, and so on? For only then is it possible to break away from society, not by becoming a hermit and wearing a loincloth, or going into a monastery—that is not breaking away from society because even though I may enter a monastery, I am still ambitious to become the abbot, or to be more "spiritual" than somebody else.

So how is that center, from which all my thinking and your thinking proceeds, to be changed? Can it be changed through discontent? If there is any form of change through discontent, it will produce a pattern, will it not, which will again create a structure in which the dominant factor will be the desire for satisfaction. If my change is based on discontent, then the mind is seeking contentment, satisfaction—which is exactly what society is after, so I am back again in the old pattern, only under a different name. A fundamental change cannot possibly be brought about through discontent, and I think this is very important to understand. If I change because I am dissatisfied with things as they are in the world—with the rottenness, the vanity, the snobbishness, the cruelty, the rich and the poor—if, seeing all that, I am merely discontented, and my drive to change is based on that discontent, then surely I will create a new pattern of society which will be similar to the old, only in different terms. I think one must see this very clearly. For unfortunately, most of the so-called change which is brought about in the world comes through discontent, dissatisfaction.

How is one, then, to bring about this change? I do not know if you have thought it out seriously and deeply, with real intention to find out. If one has, one can see that when any form of motive brings about change, it is no change at all. So long as I am discontented, or identify myself with a group or a belief, so long as I have a motive of any sort, noble or personal, that motive is bound to create the old pattern again in a different field. And yet I know there must be change. For unless one changes, not superficially, but radically, one is dead—even though one may have all the latest improvements, the latest gadgets and mechanical conveniences—including the electronic brain, which does some things much better than the human mind.

So, if we are at all serious, our problem is how to bring about this fundamental change. A change which is conscious is surely no change at all. The mind of each one of us is formed, shaped through motive, through drive, through urge, through desire, through time; it is educated in the pattern of society. And for such a mind, can there be a conscious, deliberate action of will which will bring about this change? Is it not rather that a change, this fundamental, radical revolution, comes only when the mind has dissociated itself from the center which is the 'me', which is society? After all, the 'me'—this center from which all our thinking takes place—is the result of social influences, of reaction between man and man; it is the result of time, and any change which is brought about from this center is still part of the center. It seems to me very important to understand this, for surely, any action based on will is no action at all because it creates contradiction, struggle, and therefore repression, defense, resistance. Similarly, action brought about by desiring to do "good" leads to innumerable contradictions and misery. How can one know what is good for the whole of man?

Furthermore, any action based on the intellectual gathering of information, which is called knowledge, again conditions the mind. Action born of knowledge is bound to be limited. And yet knowledge is the whole content of one's mind, is it not? Although one may think there is a God who is going to influence one's action, that concept is still within the field of thought.

So, being very desirous to bring about a change, what are you and I to do? Can the mind totally free itself from ambition? I am taking that as an example. Can it be completely free from envy, which is part of ambition?—the envy that is always comparing, desiring to have more knowledge, more success, more power, more money, or prestige. Can the mind—which is the result of this society based on acquisitiveness and comparative thinking—totally free itself from envy and ambition, from wanting more, more, more? If we could understand this one thing—how to free the mind from envy—then perhaps we should be able to break away from the whole structure of society.

But to understand that one thing, to really go into it, requires a great deal of attention. After all, most of us are ambitious—if not in regard to this world because here we have been frustrated, then our ambitions turn to the other world, where we want to sit next to God, we want to be spiritual entities. Here or hereafter, we want to be somebody—which does not mean we must not be anybody. But the urge, the compulsion, the thing that makes me desire to be something—can that be completely cut off? If my mind does not shake itself totally free from all that, then however much I may desire to change, I shall merely be caught in a new pattern in which the seed of ambition still exists, only in a different garb.

So, how is the mind to free itself from this problem of ambition, envy, the desire for more? How is it to free itself, not merely from wanting a better job, a bigger house, a finer car, and all that kind of thing, but from the totality of envy, right through? I see that if I resist envy, my very resistance is another form of ambition because I want to get rid of envy in order to be something else; therefore, resistance has no value. By suppressing envy, I am not free of it; it is still there, rotting and distorting one's vision, and then there is bitterness, cynicism. So I see the futility of suppression, of resistance, and also the futility of trying to escape from envy, or to find a substitute for it, or to sublimate it. That whole process implies the desire not to be this but to be something else, all of which is still within the field of envy.

We all know what envy is, and can the mind totally dissociate itself from envy? To dissociate itself from envy, the mind must first be aware that it is envious. And are we aware of it? Do we know that we are envious? Or do we only agree that we are envious because we know the word *envy?* If you care to, I think you should experiment with what I am saying—not tomorrow, or later on, but now. Let us take that word envy and actually go through the whole experience of it, fundamentally, deeply, and see if one cannot totally wipe away envy from one's whole process of thinking. When we use that word we mean not only the envy of wanting more than one has but the envy of comparison, the envy of wishing to be something different from what one is, the envy that creates the ideal and the pursuit of that ideal. The man who is free of envy has no ideal—not because he is satisfied with what he is, but because he no longer thinks in terms of the 'more' and therefore knows no discontent. It is only the demand for the 'more' that creates discontent, envy, and time in which to become something. Can the mind free itself from that whole process?

I think the mind can be totally free—not merely verbally, but it can really experience freedom. And this experiencing of freedom is not a fancy, an illusion. Envy can actually be rooted out. Then life becomes an entirely different thing. Then perhaps we shall know what love is, what peace is; we shall know what it is to be truly content without decaying.

So, do we know that we are envious? I hope you will be good enough to follow this rather closely, for then perhaps we shall be able not only to think it out together but actually to eradicate this thing—not for the moment, but finally.

We know all the various reasons why we are discontented, and we also know what envy implies, both socially and inwardly. But do we actually experience envy? Surely, there is a great difference between actually experiencing something and merely having a theory or an opinion about it—or allowing the word envy to influence us, and therefore condemning it. Do I know envy directly? Do we know anything directly, or merely through the word? The moment I use the word envy, all the sociological implications come up, and I condemn that feeling. When I use the word *love*, again I am conditioned by sociological influences, and I accept the feeling which that word represents. The one I reject, the other I accept.

So, am I aware that the word itself has an extraordinary influence on me, on the mind? And can the mind be free of the word? I think that is the first thing—to recognize the influence and to be free, if one can, of the word itself. If you will experiment with this, you will see how extraordinarily difficult it is for the mind to free itself from words. And that may be one of the fundamental reasons why the mind is never free from envy—because it is caught in words.

Now, can the mind be free from the effect of that word envy—not only nervously, neurologically, but inwardly? If the mind can be free from that word, does not the mind then look directly at the feeling which it has called envy? And in giving full attention to that feeling without naming it, is there not a cessation of the feeling?

Perhaps all this sounds a bit too complex. But surely, if one would understand the whole process of envy, one must go into it very deeply, and not merely accept or reject envy, or try to resist it and cultivate a virtue in its place. When virtue is cultivated, it is no longer virtue. A man who tries to cultivate goodness has ceased to be good. Goodness is something entirely different. If I try to free myself from envy by cultivating a state of mind in which there is no envy, I am still envious because the drive to cultivate a state of nonenvy is based on envy.

If I would eradicate the feeling called envy, I must understand this whole problem so that the mind can dissociate itself from all words, including that particular word envy. And if it does, is there envy? But merely getting rid of the word, as a clever trick in order not to be envious, does not bring about a mind that is completely still, without a word. Only the mind that is completely still, without a word, without a movement, without an image, that is no longer functioning from the center which is society—only such a mind is free from envy, and can therefore function in a totally different dimension. To me, such a mind is a religious mind. And it is only the religious man who is really revolutionary—not the man who believes, who belongs to a certain church or organization. The truly religious man has nothing to do with all that, for he is outside of society, and it is only he who can bring about a fundamental change in mankind through right education.

Question: Although what you say seems to be of the highest religious quality, you do not lay down any mode of conduct. Why don't you do this? Most of us definitely need one.

KRISHNAMURTI: Why do we want a mode of conduct? If we can be a light unto ourselves, why do we want someone else to lay down the rules of behavior? The question is not, "Why don't you lay down a mode of conduct?" which is too silly, but rather, "Can we be a light unto ourselves under all circumstances?" Though we may fail, though we may make mistakes, isn't it possible to be a light unto ourselves and not look to another, not seek authority of any kind to tell us what to do? I think this can come about only when we are not seeking comfort, when we are not stretching out a hand and begging someone to give us something by which we shall be satisfied, by which we shall know. We can be a light unto ourselves only when we understand ourselves totally and completely, right through. It is an arduous task to know oneself; it requires persistent inquiry, alertness, watchfulness. But unfortunately most of us are lazy, and we turn to somebody else to tell us what to do, to take the responsibility off our shoulders; we push it off on the priest or on God or on some specialist. That is why we ask this question. We want to be told how to act in order to arrive safely at the other shore. But there is no other shore; there is only a process of traveling, of learning, of experiencing—not something to be arrived at or achieved. One has to be both the teacher and the pupil oneself. That requires energy, attention, watchfulness; but we are lazy, and it is much easier to be told what to do. The man who tells you what to do, you set up as your authority, and you become his slave; therefore, you are never free, you are never a light unto yourself. So you invent the exploiter, and you become the exploited.

To find out how to be a light unto ourselves, how to think truly and rightly from moment to moment, requires a great deal of energy; it is really hard work. But unfortunately we want an easy way, a shortcut, so we become increasingly lazy, and old age and death await us.

We can find a mode of conduct in any religious book; they all tell us what to do—to be kind, to be loving, to be good, and all the rest of it. But surely that is not enough because we are human beings with extraordinary capacity to do good and to do evil, and without understanding for oneself the whole mechanism of the mind, the whole structure of one's own being, without knowing love, merely to have a mode of conduct seems to me utterly useless. We can always circumvent the mode of conduct, and we do. But if we begin to understand the whole content of ourselves from the very heart, then we shall not look to another. Then we shall be our own saviors, we shall be our own teachers and our own pupils.

Question: What is the fundamental difference between the materialistic and the religious concept of life?

KRISHNAMURTI: Do you think there is any fundamental difference between the materialistic and the so-called religious concept of life? Material things, made by hand or by machinery, are invented by the mind, and what we call the religious life may also be an invention of the mind—because it is the mind that invents ideas, gods, rituals, saviors. So why separate the two? The materialistic existence and the so-called spiritual existence are both a product of the mind—of the mind that is seeking position, power, wealth, comfort, whether physically or psychologically. You may not worship the things made by the hand, but to worship the things made by the mind is still materialistic, unspiritual. You may worship ideas, ideals—the idea of heaven, the ideal of goodness, of beauty—as others worship refrigerators, cars, but it is all within the field of the mind.

So the question is not, "What is the difference between the materialistic and the religious concept of life?" but whether the mind can free itself from all idealization and the worship of ideas. Can the mind cease creating images and becoming a slave to those images, both materially and in thought? It is much more difficult to be free from thought-images than it is to be free from material things. After all, you can fairly easily be detached from your coat or your car, but it is much more difficult to be free from ideas, beliefs, dogmas, nationalities, because these are your gods.

I think it is only when one is free from ideas, from images, from concepts, from conclusions, that one will find out what it is to be really spiritual. Otherwise we shall live in a phony world of spirituality, a world without any meaning beyond mere sentimentality and emotionalism.

So the man who would seek out what is true must not only be free of the idol made by the hand; he must also be free of the idea which lies behind the idol, and which is produced by the mind. Only the man who is free of the idea and the symbol, as well as of material things, can know what it is to be truly religious.

June 18, 1956

Fourth Talk in Brussels

This evening I think it would be worthwhile to go into the whole question of tradition and memory, and try to discover what is the significance of this background, and how it functions. Tradition, it seems to me, invariably leads to mediocrity. And most of us are merely following tradition—the tradition of security, the tradition which has been handed down through the churches and other so-called religious organizations, or the tradition which we ourselves have built up as experience or knowledge. I think it would be wise and significant if we could go into this whole problem of experiences which condition the mind, and find out whether there is an experiencing which never limits the mind, never creates tradition, conformity. Can the mind ever be free from habit? Or must the mind always move in what is essentially a groove of habit, however apparently significant and worthwhile? Most of our minds do function in the groove of habit, and we seem to be at a loss when for a moment habit is gone. Habit may be necessary for the mind up to a certain point, and then it may become detrimental, a blockage, a hindrance.

So it seems to me important to find out what is the function of memory, and how far the mind can free itself from the mere pattern of memory. Is the mind capable of experiencing anything new, or must it always continue in the pattern of the old, however modified?

Memory—which is, after all, tradition—has value up to a certain point; but however much information the mind may have stored up, it is incapable, through memory, of discovering something totally new. It seems to me that truth, or God, or whatever name one may like to give to that immeasurable thing, must be wholly unimaginable, not something projected from memory, something which has already been experienced; it must be totally new, something which the mind has never before experienced. A mind that is caught in tradition, that is merely the instrument of memory, living in the pattern of many yesterdays, is surely incapable of finding out what is true. And without the perfume of that reality, life becomes merely mechanical.

So it is important, I think, to go into this whole question of what is the function of memory—which means, really, what is the process of the mind? What is thinking? Can thinking ever be free of memory? All thinking—not merely specific thinking, but the totality of it—is the reaction of a background of tradition, of memory, is it not? And can the mind free itself from that background of the past, or is it incapable of being free? A mind that is merely inquiring through thought, through reason, through logic, moving from conclusion to conclusion—surely such a mind can never find out what is true and whether there is a reality. And is our whole process of inquiry into reality merely a conditioned response, an escape from our tortures, from our pain and suffering?

So, what is thinking? How do we think? Let us try to go into this, not theoretically, not philosophically or speculatively, but directly experience what we are talking about so that each one of us finds out how thought actually operates. This will perhaps help us to be aware of the total process of thinking, and then to see if the mind can go beyond thinking.

How do we think? If a question is asked which is familiar, the response is immediate, for there is no need to think. But a more complex question demands thinking—the thinking which is an inquiry, a looking into memory, the storehouse of knowledge. If a question is asked on a subject about which we know nothing, even then there is hesitation, a gap between the question and the response, which means that the mind is again looking into memory to find out if at any time it has learned something about that subject. So our thinking is always the response of memory, of association; our minds move from a fixed point in the past, from a belief or an experience which colors all our thinking. It is fairly obvious that this is the process which most of us go through, consciously or unconsciously, when we think.

Now, is it possible for the mind to go beyond that point so that when it is inquiring into a very complex, unanswerable question—such as whether there is truth, or God, what lies beyond death, and so on—the mind is in a state of 'not-knowing'? Can it look at the problem and say, "I do not know," because the thought process is entirely dissociated from the past? I think it is very important to come to that point, when all thinking ceases—thinking in the sense of responding according to the past, which is memory.

I do not know if I am making myself clear on this issue. If the totality of my thinking process is the response of my conditioning—which it is—then the mind can never discover what is true, and whether there is anything which has not already been experienced. If the mind is to discover something totally new, it must come to this point, surely, when it is in a state of 'not-knowing'. That is why it is very important to go into this whole problem of consciousness—consciousness being the totality of all experience, of all memory, the residue of the past. One must know oneself, for self-knowledge is essential if one is to find out whether the mind can ever be free of all knowledge and discover something new.

If we look into ourselves, we shall see that experience conditions the mind. Every new experience is translated in terms of the old; it is absorbed by the established pattern of mediocrity, tradition. And obviously, a mind that is caught in tradition, in mediocrity, can never find out what is true; it can never discover that which is unimaginable, which cannot be conceived of, described, or believed in.

So, can the mind free itself from tradition and conformity—not only from those imposed by environment, but from the tradition and conformity which are built up by the mind itself through experience? One can see very well that all one's thinking is the response of one's conditioning. Our reaction to a challenge is always according to the background in which we have been brought up, and so long as we do not know our own conditioning, our thinking is never free. We may be able to adjust ourselves to a new pattern, to a new way of life, to new beliefs, to new dogmas, but in that process thought never frees itself.

So one has to inquire very deeply within oneself as to the significance and purpose of memory. And is memory the totality of our consciousness? Consciousness is within the field of time, is it not? My thinking, which is the result of the past, colors the present and projects the future—and this is the process of time. So all my experience is within the field of time. Can the mind free itself from that whole process? And if it does free itself, can it discover something new?

I do not think this is so very complicated if one is at all aware of oneself. You can see it for yourself quite simply if you observe the process of your own thinking. We know how extraordinarily easy it is to fall into a groove of habit, how quickly the mind reduces everything to habit—which is sometimes called "adjustment." The mind always functions from the known to the known, and if the mind is to discover the unknowable, surely it must be free from the known. Can the mind free itself from the known? It is really a very interesting problem—not only interesting, but extraordinarily profound, if we can go into it.

All accumulated experience makes the mind conform, does it not? And can the mind free itself from the accumulation of experience? When it is free, is there such a thing as an experiencer? What is it that experiences? Surely, it is the accumulation of previous experiences and memories. The mind responds to any challenge through its previously accumulated knowledge. Either its response is adequate or inadequate. When it responds adequately, there is no conflict, no suffering; but when there is inadequacy of response, then there is suffering, there is conflict. This is obvious and superficial. To know ourselves we must inquire much more profoundly, we must understand the whole process of our consciousness, the totality of it—not merely the superficial consciousness of daily activities, but the deep unconscious, which contains the whole residue of racial conditioning, the racial memories, the hidden motives, urges, compulsions, fixations. This does not mean that we must go to a psychologist. On the contrary, we must understand ourselves through direct experience.

To have this self-knowledge, the mind must be aware of itself from moment to moment; it must see all its own movements, its urges, its motives, the operations of memory, and how, through tradition, it is caught in mediocrity. If the mind can be aware of all that within itself, then you will find there is a possibility of being free from all conditioning and discovering something totally new. Then the mind itself is made new—and perhaps that is the real, the immeasurable.

Question: How is it possible to free oneself from psychological dependence on others?

KRISHNAMURTI: I wonder if we are conscious that we do depend psychologically on others? Not that it is necessary or justifiable or wrong, psychologically, to depend on others, but are we, first of all, aware that we are dependent? Most of us are psychologically dependent, not only on people, but on property, on beliefs, on dogmas. Are we at all conscious of that fact? If we know that we do depend on something for our psychological happiness, for our inward stability, security, then we can ask ourselves why.

Why do we psychologically depend on something? Obviously, because in ourselves we are insufficient, poor, empty; in ourselves we are extraordinarily lonely, and it is this loneliness, this emptiness, this extreme inward poverty and self-enclosure that makes us depend on a person, on knowledge, on property, on opinion, and on so many other things which seem necessary to us.

Now, can the mind be fully aware of the fact that it is lonely, insufficient, empty? It is very difficult to be aware, to be fully cognizant of that fact because we are always trying to escape from it; and we do temporarily escape from it through listening to the radio, and other forms of amusement, through going to church, performing rituals, acquiring knowledge, and through dependence on people and on ideas. To know your own emptiness, you must look at it, but you cannot look at it if your mind is all the time seeking a distraction from the fact that it is empty. And that distraction takes the form of attachment to a person, to the idea of God, to a particular dogma or belief, and so on.

So, can the mind stop running away, escaping, and not merely ask how to stop running away? Because the very inquiry into how the mind is to stop escaping becomes another escape. If I know that a certain path does not lead anywhere, I do not walk on that path; there is no question of how not to walk on it. Similarly, if I know that no escape, no amount of running away will ever resolve this loneliness, this inward emptiness, then I stop running, I stop being distracted. Then the mind can look at the fact that it is lonely, and there is no fear. It is in the very process of running away from *what is* that fear arises.

So, when the mind understands the futility, the utter uselessness of trying to fill its own emptiness through dependence, through knowledge, through belief, then it is capable of looking at it without fear. And can the mind continue to look at that emptiness without any evaluation? I hope you are following this. It may sound rather complex, and probably it is, but can we not go into it very deeply? Because a superficial answer is completely meaningless.

When the mind is fully aware that it escapes, runs away from itself, when it realizes the futility of running away and sees that the very process of running away creates fear—when it realizes the truth of that, then it can face *what is*. Now, what do we mean when we say that we are facing *what is?* Are we facing it, looking at it, if we are always giving a value to it, interpreting it, if we have opinions about it? Surely opinions, values, interpretations, merely prevent the mind from looking at the fact. If you want to understand the fact, it is no good having an opinion about it.

So, can we look, without any evaluation, at the fact of our psychological emptiness, our loneliness, which breeds so many other problems? I think that is where the difficulty lies—in our incapacity to look at ourselves without judgment, without condemnation, without comparison, because we have all been trained to compare, to judge, to evaluate, to give an opinion. Only when the mind sees the futility of all that, the absurdity of it, is it capable of looking at itself. Then that which we have feared as being lonely, empty, is no longer empty. Then there is no psychological dependence on anything; then love is no longer attachment, but something entirely different, and relationship has quite another meaning.

But to find that out for oneself and not merely repeat it verbally, one must understand the process of escape. In the very understanding of escape, there is the stopping of that escape, and the mind is able to look at itself. In looking at itself, there must be no evaluation, no judgment. Then the fact is important in itself, and there is complete attention, without any desire for distraction; therefore, the mind is no longer empty. Complete attention is the good.

Question: Does awareness mean a state of freedom, or merely a process of observation?

KRISHNAMURTI: This is really quite a complex problem. Can we understand the whole significance of what it is to be aware? Do not let us jump to any conclusions. What do we mean by ordinary awareness? I see you, and in watching you, looking at you, I form opinions. You have hurt me, you have deceived me, you have been cruel to me, or you have said nice things and flattered me, and consciously or unconsciously all this remains in my mind. When I watch this process, when I observe it, that is just the beginning of awareness, is it not? I can also be aware of my motives, of my habits of thought. The mind can be aware of its limitations, of its own conditioning; and there is the inquiry as to whether the mind can ever be free from its own conditioning. Surely this is all part of awareness. To say that the mind can or cannot be free from its conditioning is still part of its conditioning, but to observe that conditioning without saying either is a furthering of awareness—awareness of the whole process of thinking.

So through awareness I begin to see myself as I actually am, the totality of myself. Being watchful from moment to moment of all its thoughts, its feelings, its reactions, unconscious as well as conscious, the mind is constantly discovering the significance of its own activities—which is self-knowledge. Whereas, if my understanding is merely accumulative, then that accumulation becomes a conditioning which prevents further understanding. So, can the mind observe itself without accumulation?

All this is still only part of awareness, is it not? A tree is not merely the leaf or the flower or the fruit; it is also the branch, the trunk—it is everything that goes to make up the whole tree. Likewise, awareness is of the total process of the mind, not just of one particular segment of that process. But the mind cannot understand the total process of itself if it condemns or justifies any part, or identifies itself with the pleasurable and rejects the painful. So long as the mind is merely accumulating experience, knowledge—which is what it is doing all the time—it is incapable of going further. That is why to discover something new, there must be a dying to every experience, and for this there must be awareness from moment to moment.

All relationship is a mirror in which the mind can discover its own operations. Relationship is between oneself and other human beings, between oneself and things or property, between oneself and ideas, and between oneself and nature; and in that mirror of relationship one can see oneself as one actually is—but only if one is capable of looking without judging, without evaluating, condemning, justifying. When one has a fixed point from which one observes, there is no understanding in one's observation.

So, being fully conscious of one's whole process of thinking, and being able to go beyond that process, is awareness. You may say it is very difficult to be so constantly aware. Of course it is very difficult—it is almost impossible. You cannot keep a mechanism working at full speed all the time; it would break up; it must slow down, have rest. Similarly, we cannot maintain total awareness all the time. How can we? To be aware from moment to moment is enough. If one is totally aware for a minute or two and then relaxes, and in that relaxation spontaneously observes the operations of one's own mind, one will discover much more in that spontaneity than in the effort to watch continuously. You can observe yourself effortlessly, easily, when you are walking, talking, reading—at every moment. Only then will you find out that the mind is capable of freeing itself from all the things it has known and experienced, and it is in freedom alone that it can discover what is true.

Question: When we dream, do we enter the collective unconscious? Are the dreams symbolic of our psychological state and therefore a useful guide?

KRISHNAMURTI: I wonder why we are so bothered about dreams? Why is it that we have so many problems, so many questions, and so many experts telling us what to do and how to think? Why has life become such an extraordinarily complex thing? Life is essentially simple, and why has the mind made it complicated? We have made even love complex. We are forever trying to find ways to love, to be compassionate, to be gentle, to be kind—and yet in that very effort we miss it all. And dreams have become still another problem.

To solve a problem is not to search for an answer, a solution. If my mind is concerned with the solution of the problem, then I have created another problem, have I not? Do you understand what I mean? Here is a problem—the problem of dreams. I do not know why we have made it into a problem, but we have. Now, if I am concerned with the solution of the whole problem of dreams, then the search for the solution becomes another problem, does it not? So instead of having just one problem, I now have two. And that is the way of our life—problem after problem. We never seem to understand the one central problem from which arise all our problems, and that is our self-centered activity and concern from morning till night. So let us inquire into this.

Is each one of us a collective entity or a separate, distinct individual? Are you and I separate individuals, totally different from one another? That is what we mean by individuality, is it not?—a mind which is not contaminated by the collective, which is not shaped by circumstance, by environment, by the past. Are you and I such individuals? Obviously not. We may think we are individuals, but actually our beliefs, our traditions, our values, our ways of life are those of the collective. You are Christians or Hindus or Buddhists or communists, which means that you have been contaminated, conditioned to be what you are, and each one is trying to brainwash the others.

Obviously, the superficial consciousness, the everyday working mind, is educated to adjust itself to the present environment, to the present society. It may have acquired a new skill or a different kind of technology, and may therefore consider itself an individual, but actually it is still conditioned by the past. To me, the totality of consciousness is the result of the past—the past being the experiences of the race, and also the impressions made on the mind during its own past and present activities.

So the mind that is trying to be an individual, the mind that has learned new techniques, new ways of speech, new adjustments, is still the totality of the collective; it still has the same hidden motives, the same pursuits, ambitions, envies, suffering. Are we aware of the collective in ourselves? Or, being indifferent to all that, do we merely cultivate the superficial?

Now, when our minds are merely being cultivated superficially, when they are occupied all day long with the things we have to do—with various jobs, with earning a livelihood, and so on—there is no opportunity to inquire into the unconscious. So when we go to sleep, the unconscious projects its movement, its activity, into the relatively quiet conscious mind in the form of symbolic dreams. Surely this is all very obvious. So our dreams may be symbols, hints, intimations from the unconscious, from the totality of the collective consciousness. Then the problem arises of what these symbols mean, what their significance is, how to get them interpreted, and all the complications begin.

So the question is: Can the mind be free from all symbols in the form of dreams? That is, can the mind be free not to dream? As we said, dreams—not the superficial ones, but the significant dreams—are obviously intimations or hints from the unconscious, of which we are not aware when the mind is absorbed, as it generally is, in earning a livelihood, and so on. And can the mind be free from all dreams so that during sleep it is able to penetrate more deeply into itself? I think this is the important question—not what dreams are, but whether the mind can be free from all unconscious urges and symbolic hints, intimations, so that it is really silent, for in that silence it can discover great depths.

Perhaps this possibility has not occurred to you, but do not make it into another problem. In considering this question, we are not trying to find out what is the significance of dreams. You can discover that for yourself if you begin to be aware, during the day, of your unconscious motives, urges, fixations, beliefs, frustrations. If you are really aware of all that during the waking consciousness, if you are watchful, alertly observant, so that your mind no longer gets caught in ambitions, in frustrations, in the fear of failure, and all the rest of it, then surely, there is no need to dream. Having been alert during the day, watchful of its reactions, the mind, when it goes to sleep, is quiet, peaceful; and then there is a possibility of touching something unknowable which, on waking, brings great clarity.

This is not superstition or mystical nonsense; we are talking of very simple, straightforward facts. So long as my mind is crowded with problems, so long as it is occupied with itself and its ambitions, its fears, its anxieties, its frustrations, obviously it is incapable of going beyond itself. And most of our days are spent in self-occupation; we are concerned with ourselves all the time. Inevitably, therefore, when we go to sleep, our dreams are the intimations of something deeper which we have not understood, and which we again translate in terms of our own self-concern. But if, during the day, we can be fully aware of and so remove all the ambitions, the frustrations, the conflicting desires, the psychological dependencies, then surely the mind is capable—not only during the day, but also during the hours when the body is at rest—of discovering something beyond the measurement of thought.

That is why it is so important to know oneself. To know yourself you need not go to any book, to any priest, to any psychologist. The whole treasure is within yourself. It demands only that you observe it—observe yourself in the mirror of relationship. But you cannot observe if you are merely concerned with absorbing and accumulating. Only when the mind is not self-concerned is there a possibility of bliss.

June 23, 1956

Fifth Talk in Brussels

One of our great difficulties is to know how to free ourselves from the complex problem of sorrow. Intellectually we try to grapple with it, but unfortunately the intellect has no solution to the problem. The best it can do is to find some verbal rationalization or invent a theory, or else it becomes cynical and bitter. But if we can very seriously examine the problem of suffering—not just verbally, but actually experience the whole process of it—then perhaps we shall discover its cause and find out whether that discovery brings about the solution of it.

Obviously, the problem of sorrow is one of the fundamental issues in our life. Most of us have some kind of sorrow, secret or open, and we are always trying to find a way to go beyond it, to be free of it. But it seems to me that unless we begin to understand for ourselves the really deep workings of the mind, sorrow will inevitably continue.

Is sorrow a thing to be got rid of through rationalization, that is, by explaining the cause of sorrow? Superficially, we all know why we suffer. I am talking particularly of psychological suffering, not merely of physical pain. If I know why I suffer, in the sense that I recognize the cause of my sorrow, will that sorrow disappear? Must I not look for a deeper issue, rather than be satisfied with one of the innumerable explanations of what it is that brings about the state which we call sorrow? And how am I to seek out the deeper issue? Most of us are very easily satisfied by superficial responses, are we not? We quickly accept the satisfactory escapes from the deep issue of suffering.

Consciously or unconsciously, verbally or actually, we all know that we suffer because we have in us the contradiction of desires, one desire trying to dominate another. These contradictory desires make for conflict, and conflict invariably leads to the state of mind which we call suffering. The whole complex of desire which creates conflict—this, it seems to me, is the source of all sorrow.

Most of us are caught up in this mass of contradictory desires, wishes, longings, hopes, fears, memories. That is, we are concerned with our achievements, our successes, our well-being, the fulfillment of our ambitions; we are concerned about ourselves. And I think this self-concern is the real source of our conflict and misery. Realizing this, we try to escape from our self-concern by throwing ourselves into various philanthropic activities or by identifying ourselves with a particular reform, or we stupidly cling to some kind of religious belief, which is not religious at all. What we are essentially concerned with is how to escape from our suffering, how to resolve it.

So it seems to me very important, if we would free ourselves from sorrow, to go into this whole complex which we call desire, this bundle of memories which we call the 'me'. Is it possible to live in the world without this complex of desire, without this entity called the 'me', from which all suffering arises? I do not know if you have thought of this problem at all. When we suffer for various reasons, most of us try to find an answer, we try to escape by identifying ourselves with one thing or another, hoping it will alleviate our suffering. Yet the suffering goes on, either consciously or underground.

Now, can the mind free itself from suffering? This must be a problem to all of us who think about these things because all of us suffer, acutely or superficially. Can there be an ending to sorrow, or is sorrow inevitable? If it is our human lot to suffer endlessly, then we must accept it and live with it. But I think merely to accept the state of sorrow would be foolish because no man wants to be in that state.

So, is it possible to end sorrow? Surely, sorrow is the result, not only of ignorance—which is lack of self-knowledge—but also of this enormous effort that everyone is continually making to be something, to acquire something, or to reject something. Can we live in this world without any effort to be or become something, without trying to achieve, to reject, to acquire? That is what we are doing all the time, is it not? We are making effort. I am not saying that there must be no effort, but I am inquiring into the whole problem of effort. I can see in myself—and it must be obvious to most of us—that so long as I desire to be successful, for example, either in this world or psychologically, spiritually, I must make effort, I must exert myself to achieve; and it seems to me that suffering is inherent in the very nature of that effort.

Please do not brush this aside. It is easy to say, "One cannot live in this world without effort. Everything in nature struggles, and if we do not make effort, there will be no life at all." That is not what I am talking about. I am inquiring into the whole process of effort; I am not saying that we should reject or sustain effort, augment or decrease it. I am asking whether effort is necessary psychologically, and whether it does not produce the seed of sorrow.

When we make an effort, it is obviously with a motive—to achieve, to be, or to become something. Where there is effort, there is the action of will, which is essentially desire—one desire opposing another, so there is a contradiction. To overcome this contradiction, we try in various ways to bring about an integration—which again involves effort. So our way of thinking, our whole way of living, is a process of ceaseless effort.

Now, this effort, surely, is centered in the 'me', the self, which is concerned with itself and its own activities. And can the mind free itself from this complex, from this bundle of desires, urges, compulsions, without effort, without a motive?

I hope I am making myself clear because this is a very complex problem. I know that my life is a series of desires; it is made up of many wants and frustrations, many hopes, longings, and aspirations; there is the cultivation of virtue, the search for moral standing, trying to conform to an ideal, and so on; and through it all there is the urge to be free. All that is the 'me', the self, which is the source of sorrow.

Surely, any move I make in order to be free of sorrow furthers sorrow, because that again involves effort. I think one must understand this fundamentally—that any effort to be or become something, to achieve success, and so on, produces sorrow. By making an effort to get rid of sorrow, I build a resistance against it, and that very resistance is a form of suppression which breeds further sorrow. If I see this, then what am I to do? How is the mind which is caught in sorrow to free itself from sorrow? Can it do anything? Because any action on its part has a motive behind it, and a motive invariably breeds conflict, which again begets sorrow.

This is the whole issue. I think I shall be happy if I make a success of my life, have plenty of things, position, power, money. So I struggle. And in the very process of struggling to achieve that which I want, there is conflict, there is pain, there is frustration; so sorrow is set going. Or, if I am not worldly-minded, I turn to so-called spiritual things. There also I try to achieve something—to realize God, truth, and all the rest of it—I cultivate virtue, obey the sanctions of the church, follow yoga or some other system to the end that my mind may be at peace. So again there is a struggle, there is conflict, suppression, resistance—which seems to me utterly futile, without meaning.

So what is the mind to do? I know the whole pattern of suffering and the causes of suffering; I also know the ways of escape, and I see that escaping from suffering is no answer. One may escape momentarily, but suffering is still there, like a lingering poison. So what is the mind to do?

How does the mind know anything? When I say, "I know the pattern of suffering," what do I mean by that? Is it merely intellectual knowledge, a verbal, rationalized understanding of this whole network of suffering? Or am I aware of it totally, inwardly? Do I know it merely as something which I have learned, which I have been taught, which I have read about and captured through a description? Or am I actually aware of suffering as a process taking place in myself, at every moment of my existence? Which is it? I think this is an important question.

How do I know that I suffer? Do I know it merely because I feel frustrated, or because I have lost someone—my son is dead? Or do I know with my whole being that suffering is the nature of all desire, of all becoming? And must I go through the process of every desire in order to find that out?

Surely, there must be suffering so long as one does not totally comprehend desire, which includes the action of will and involves contradiction, suppression, resistance, conflict. Whether we desire superficial things, or the deep, fundamental things, conflict is always involved. So, can we find out whether the mind is capable of being free from desire—from the whole psychological process of the desire to be something, to succeed, to become, to find God, to achieve? Can the mind understand all that and be free from it? Otherwise life is a process of continuous conflict, misery. You may find a panacea, a semipermanent escape, but misery awaits you. You may throw yourself into some activity, take refuge in a belief, find various ways of forgetting yourself, but conflict is still there.

So, can the mind understand the process of desire? And is this understanding a matter of effort? Or does understanding come only when the mind sees the whole process of desire—sees it, experiences it, is totally aware of it, and knowing that it cannot do anything about it, becomes silent with regard to that problem?

I think this is the fundamental issue—not how to transcend, transform, or control desire, but to know the full significance of desire, and knowing it, to be completely motionless, silent, without any action with regard to it. Because when the mind is confronted with an enormous problem like desire, any action on its part distorts that problem; any effort to grapple with it makes the problem petty, shallow. Whereas, if the mind can look at this enormous problem of desire without any movement, without any denial, without accepting or rejecting it, then I think we shall find that desire has quite a different significance, and that one can live in this world without contradiction, without struggle, without this everlasting effort to arrive, to achieve.

When the mind is thus able to look at the whole process of desire, you will find that it becomes astonishingly capable of experiencing without adding anything to itself. When the mind is no longer contaminated by desire and all the problems connected with it, then the mind itself is reality—not the mind as we know it, but a mind that is completely without the self, without desire.

Question: You talked yesterday of mediocrity. I realize my own mediocrity, but how am I to break through it?

KRISHNAMURTI: It is the mediocre mind that demands a way to break through or achieve. Therefore when you say, "I am mediocre, how am I to break through it?" you do not realize the full significance of mediocrity. The mind that wants to change or improve itself will always remain mediocre, however great its effort. And that is what we all want, is it not? We all want to change from this to that. Being stupid, I want to become clever. The stupid man who is attempting to become clever will always remain stupid. But the man who is aware that he is stupid, and realizes the full significance of stupidity, without wishing to change it—that very realization puts an end to stupidity.

So, can the mind look at the fact of what it is without trying to alter it? Can I see that I am arrogant or stupid or vain—just realize the fact—and not wish to change it? The desire to change it breeds mediocrity because then I look to someone to tell me what to do about it; I go to lectures, read books, in order to find out how to change what I am. So I am led away from facing the fact of what I am, and being led away from the fact is the cultivation of mediocrity.

Now, can I look at the fact of mediocrity without wishing to break through it? After all, the mind is mediocre—it does not matter whose mind it is. The mind is mediocre, bound by tradition, by the past; and when the mind tries to improve itself, to break through its own limitations, it remains the same mediocre mind, only it is seeking a new sensation, that is, to experience the state of not being mediocre.

So the problem is not how to break through mediocrity, for mediocrity is invariably the result of pursuing tradition, whether that tradition has been established by society or cultivated by oneself. Any effort on the part of the mind to break through mediocrity will be an activity of mediocrity; therefore, the result will still be mediocre.

This is the real issue. We do not see that the mind, however cultivated, however clever, however erudite, is essentially mediocre, and that however much it may try to break through mediocrity, it is still mediocre. When the mind sees the fact of its own mediocrity, not just the superficial part, but the totality of it, with all that it involves, and does not try to do something about it, then you will find you are no longer concerned with mediocrity or with attempting to change this into that. Then the very fact itself begins to operate.

That is, when the mind is aware of the fact of its own stupidity, mediocrity, and does not operate on that fact, then the fact begins to operate on the mind, and then you will see that the mind has undergone a fundamental change. But so long as the mind wants to change, whatever change it may bring about will be a continuation of that which it has been, only under a different cloak.

That is why it is very important to understand the whole process of thinking, and why self-knowledge is essential. But you cannot know yourself if you are merely accumulating knowledge about yourself, for then you know only that which you have accumulated—which is not to know the ways of your own self and its activities from moment to moment.

Question: How are we to put an end to man's cruelty towards animals in the form of vivisection, slaughterhouses, and so on?

KRISHNAMURTI: I do not think we will put an end to it because I do not think we know what it means to love. Why are we so concerned about animals? Not that we should not be—we must be. But why this concern about animals only? Are we not cruel to each other? Our whole social structure is based on violence, which erupts every so often into war. If you really loved your children, you would put a stop to war. But you do not love your children, so you sacrifice them to protect your property, to defend the state, or the church, or some other organization which demands of you certain things. As our society, of which we are a part, is based on acquisitive violence, we are invariably cruel to each other. The whole structure of competition, comparison, position, property, inheritance—violence is inherent in all that, and we accept it as inevitable; so we are cruel to each other, as we are cruel to animals.

The problem is not how to do away with slaughterhouses and be more kind to animals but the fact that we have lost the art of love—not sensation, not emotionalism, but the feeling of being really kind, of being really gentle, compassionate. Do we know what it is to be really compassionate—not in order to get to heaven, but compassionate in the sense of not wanting anything for oneself?

Surely, that demands quite a different psychological education. We are trained from childhood to compete, to be cruel, to fit into society. So long as we are educated to fit into society, we will invariably be cruel because society is based on violence. If we loved our children, we would educate them entirely differently so that there would be no more war, no nationalism, no rich and no poor, and the whole structure of this ugly society would be transformed.

But we are not interested in all that, which is a very complex and profound problem. We are only concerned with how to stop some aspect of cruelty. Not that we should not be concerned with stopping cruelty. The point is, we can find or join an organization for stopping cruelty, we can subscribe, write, work for it ceaselessly, we can become the secretary, the president, and all the rest of it, but that which is love will be missing. Whereas, if we can concern ourselves with finding out what it is to love without any attachment, without any demand, without the search for sensation—which is an immense problem—then perhaps we shall bring about a different relationship between human beings and with the animals.

Question: What is death, and why is there such fear of it?

KRISHNAMURTI: I think it would be worthwhile to go into this problem, not merely verbally, but actually. Why do we divide life and death? Is living separate from death? Or is death part of living? It may be that we do not know what living is, and that is why death seems such a terrible thing, something to be shunned, to be avoided, to be explained away.

Is not living part of dying? Am I living if I am constantly accumulating property, money, position, as well as knowledge and virtue, all of which I cherish and hold on to? I may call that living, but is it living? Is not that whole process merely a series of struggles, contradictions, miseries, frustrations? But we call it living, and so we want to know what death is.

We know that death is the end for all of us; the body, the physical organism, wears out and dies. Seeing this, the mind says, "I have lived, I have gathered, I have suffered, and what is to happen to me? What lies for me beyond death?" Not knowing what lies beyond, the mind is afraid of death, so it begins to invent ideas, theories—reincarnation, resurrection—or it goes back and lives in the past. If it believes in reincarnation, it tries to prove that belief through hypnosis, and so on.

That is essentially what we are all doing. Our life is overshadowed by this thing called death, and we want to know if there is any form of continuity. Or else we are so sick of life that we want to die, and we are horrified at the thought that there might be a beyond.

Now, what is the answer to all this? Why have we separated death from living, and why does the mind cling to continuity? Cannot the mind be aware of that which it calls death in the same way that it knows living? Can it not be aware of the whole significance of dying? We know what our life is—a process of gathering, enjoying, suffering, renouncing, searching, and constant anxiety. That is our existence, and in that there is a continuity. I know that I am alive because I am aware of suffering, of enjoyment; memory goes on, and my past experiences color my future experiences. There is a sense of continuity, the momentum of a series of events linked by memory. I know this process, and I call it living. But do I know what death is? Can I ever know it? We are not asking what lies beyond, which is really not very important. But can one know or experience the meaning of that which is called death while actually living? While I am conscious, physically vigorous, while my mind is clear and capable of thinking without any sentimentality or emotionalism, can I directly experience that thing which I call death? I know what living is, and can I, in the same way, with the same vigor, the same potency, know the meaning of death? If I merely die at the last moment through disease or through some accident, I shall not know.

So the problem is not what lies beyond death, or how to avoid the fear of death. You cannot avoid the fear of death so long as the mind accumulates for itself a series of events and experiences linked by memory because the ending of all that is what we actually fear.

Surely, that which has continuity is never creative. Only the mind which dies to everything from moment to moment really knows what it is to die. This is not emotionalism; it requires a great deal of insight, thought, inquiry. We can know death, as well as life, while living; while living we can enter the house of death, the unknown. But for the mind, which is the result of the known, to enter the unknown, there must be cessation of all that it has known, of all the things it has gathered—not only consciously, but much more profoundly, in the unconscious. To wipe all that away is to die, and then we shall find there is no fear.

I am not offering this as a panacea for fear, but can we know and understand the full meaning of death? That is, can the mind be completely nothing, with no residue of the past? Whether that is possible or not is something we can inquire into, search out diligently, vigorously, work hard to find out. But if the mind merely clings to what it calls living—which is suffering, this whole process of accumulation—and tries to avoid the other, then it knows neither life nor death.

So the problem is to free the mind from the known, from all the things it has gathered, acquired, experienced, so that it is made innocent and can therefore understand that which is death, the unknowable.

June 24, 1956

Sixth Talk in Brussels

I think it would be a waste of time and energy if we regarded these talks merely as an intellectual stimulation, or as an entertainment of new ideas. It would be like plowing a field everlastingly, without ever sowing.

For those who are eager to find something much more significant than the weary routine of daily existence, who want to understand the greater significance of life, it seems very difficult not to get sidetracked in their search because there are so many things in which the mind can lose itself—in work, in politics, in social activity, in the acquisition of knowledge, or in various associations and organizations. These things apparently give a great deal of satisfaction, and when we are satisfied, our lives invariably become very superficial.

But there are some, I think, who are really serious, and who do not wish to be distracted from the central issue. They want to go to the very end of their search and discover for themselves if there is something more vital than mere reason and the logical explanation of things. Such people are not easily side-tracked. They have a certain spontaneous virtue, which is not the emptiness of cultivated virtue; they have a certain quietness, gentleness, and a sense of proportion; they lead a sane, balanced life, and do not accept the extremes. But unfortunately even they seem to find it very difficult to go beyond the everyday struggles and the understanding of them, and discover for themselves if there is something really deeply significant.

Those of us who have thought about these things at all, and who are alert both to the recurrent problems in our personal lives, and to the crises that periodically come upon society, must be aware that the merely virtuous or good life is not enough, and that unless we can go beyond and discover something of greater significance—a wider vision, more fullness of life—then, however noble our efforts and endeavor, we shall always remain in this state of turmoil and ceaseless strife. The good life is obviously necessary, but surely that by itself is not religion. And is it possible to go beyond all that?

Some of us, I think, have seen the stupidity of dogmas, of beliefs, of organized religions, and have set them aside. We fully realize the importance of the good life, the balanced, sane, unexaggerated life—being content with little, being kindly, generous—yet somehow we do not seem to discover that vital something which brings about the truly religious life. One may be virtuous, very active in doing good, satisfied with little, unconcerned about oneself, but surely the truly religious life must mean something much more. Any respectable person, any good citizen, is all those things in one degree or another, but that is not religion. Belonging to a church, going to Sunday gatherings, reading an occasional book on religious matters, worshiping a symbol, dedicating one's life to a particular idea or ideal—surely, none of that is religion. Those are all man-made things; they are within the limits of time, of culture and civilization. And yet even those of us who have dropped all such things seem unable to go beyond.

What is the difficulty? Is it the gift of the few to go beyond? Can only a few understand or realize or experience reality—which means that the many must depend on the few for help, for guidance? I think such an idea is utterly false. In this whole idea that only a few can realize, and the rest must follow, lie many forms of thoughtlessness, exploitation, and cruelty. If once we accept it, our lives become very shallow, meaningless, trivial.

And most of us accept that idea very easily, do we not? We think that only the few can understand, or that there is only one Son of God, and the rest of us are just—whatever we are. We accept such an idea because in ourselves we are very lazy, or perhaps we do not have the capacity to penetrate. It may be mostly our lack of this capacity to penetrate, to go to the root of things, that is preventing deep understanding, this extraordinary sense of unity—which is not identification with the idea of unity. Most of us identify ourselves with something—with the family, with the country, with an idea, with a belief—hoping thereby to forget our petty, little selves. But I am afraid that is no solution. The greater does contain the lesser, but when the lesser tries to identify itself with the greater, it is merely a pose and has no value.

So, is it possible for each one of us to have this capacity to go beyond routine virtue, goodness, sensitivity, compassion? These are essential in daily life, but can we not awaken the capacity to penetrate beyond them, beyond all the conscious movements of the mind, beyond all inclinations, hopes, aspirations, desires, so that the mind is no longer an instrument which creates and destroys, which is caught in its own projections, in its own ideas?

If we can sanely and diligently find out for ourselves how this capacity comes into being, without trying to cultivate it or wishing for it to happen, then I think we shall know what it is to lead a religious life. But this demands an extraordinary revolution in our thinking—which is the only real revolution. Any merely economic or social revolution only breeds the need of further reform, and that is an endless process. Real revolution is inward, and it comes into being without the mind seeking it. What the mind seeks and finds, however reasonable, however rational and intelligent, is never the final answer. For the mind is put together, and what it creates is also put together; therefore, it can be undone. But the revolution of which I am speaking is the truly religious life, stripped of all the absurdities of organized religions throughout the world. It has nothing to do with priests, with symbols, with churches.

How is this revolution to take place? As we do not know, we say that we must have faith, or that grace must descend upon us. This may be so; grace may come. But the faith that is cultivated is only another creation of the mind, and therefore it can be destroyed. Whether there is grace or not is not our concern; a mind that seeks grace will never find it.

So, if you have thought at all about these matters, if you have meditated upon life, then you must have asked yourself whether this inward revolution can take place, and whether it is dependent upon a capacity that can be cultivated, as one cultivates the capacity for accountancy or engineering or chemistry. Those are cultivable capacities; they can be built up, and will produce certain results. But I am talking of a capacity which is not cultivable, something that you cannot go after, that you cannot pursue or search out in the dark places of the mind. And without that something, virtue becomes mere respectability—which is a terrible thing; without that something, all activity is contradictory, leading to further conflict and misery.

Now, being aware of our own ceaseless struggling within the field of self-conscious activity, our self-concern—taking all this multifarious action and contradiction into account, how are we to come to that other state? How is one to live in that moment which is eternity? All this is not mere sentiment or romanticism. Religion has nothing whatsoever to do with romanticism or sentimentality. It is a very hard thing—hard in the sense that one must work furiously to find out what is truly religious.

Perceiving all the contradiction and confusion that exists in the outward structure of society and the psychological conflict that is perpetually going on within oneself, one realizes that all our endeavor to be loving or brotherly is actually a pose, a mask. However beautiful the mask may be, behind it there is nothing; so we develop a philosophy of cynicism or despair; or we cling to a belief in something mysterious beyond this ceaseless turmoil. Again, this is obviously not religion, and without the perfume of true religion, life has very little meaning. That is why we are everlastingly struggling to find something. We pursue the many gurus and teachers, haunt the various churches, practice this or that system of meditation, rejecting one and accepting another. And yet we never seem to cross the threshold; the mind seems incapable of going beyond itself.

So, what is it, I wonder, that brings the other into being? Or is it that we cannot do anything but go up to the threshold and remain there, not knowing what lies beyond? It may be that we have to come to the very edge of the precipice of everything we have known so that there is the cessation of all endeavor, of all cultivation of virtue, and the mind is no longer seeking anything. I think that is all the conscious mind can do. Whatever else it does only creates another pattern, another habit. Must not the mind strip itself of all the things it has gathered, all its accumulations of experience and knowledge, so that it is in a state of innocency which is not cultivated?

Perhaps that is our difficulty. We hear that we must be innocent in order to find out, so we cultivate innocence. But can innocence ever be cultivated? Is it not like the cultivation of humility? Surely, a man who cultivates humility is never humble, any more than the man who practices nonviolence ceases to be violent. So it may be that one must see the truth of this—that the mind which is put together, which is made up of many things, cannot do anything. To see this truth may be all that it can do. Probably there must be the capacity to see the truth in a flash—and I think that very perception will cleanse the mind of all the past in an instant.

The more serious, the more earnest we are, the greater danger there is of our trying to become or achieve something. Surely, only the man who is spontaneously humble, who has immense unconscious humility—only such a man is capable of understanding from moment to moment and never accumulating what he has learned. So this great humility of not-knowing is essential, is it not?

But you see, we are all seeking success, we want a result. We say, "I have done all these things, and I have got nowhere, I have received nothing; I am still the same." This despairing sense of desiring success, of wanting to arrive, to attain, to understand, emphasizes, does it not, the separativity of the mind; there is always the conscious or unconscious endeavor to achieve a result, and therefore the mind is never empty, never free for a second from the movement of the past, of time.

So I think what is important is not to read more, discuss more, or to attend more talks, but rather to be conscious of the motives, the intentions, the deceptions of one's own mind—to be simply aware of all that and leave it alone, not try to change it, not try to become something else, because the effort to become something else is like putting on another mask. That is why the danger is much greater for those of us who are earnest and deeply serious than it is for the flippant and the casual. Our very seriousness may prevent the understanding of things as they are.

It seems to me that what each one of us has to do is to capture the significance of the totality of our thinking. But much concern over detail, over the many conflicting thoughts and feelings, will not bring about an understanding of the whole. What is required is the sudden perception of the totality of the mind—which is not the outcome of asking how to see it but of constantly looking, inquiring, searching. Then, I think, we shall find out for ourselves what is the truly religious life.

Question: What are your ideas about education?

KRISHNAMURTI: I think mere ideas are no good at all because one idea is as good as another, depending on whether the mind accepts or rejects it. But perhaps it would be worthwhile to find out what we mean by education. Let us see if we can think out together the whole significance of education, and not merely think in terms of my idea or your idea or the idea of some specialist.

Why do we educate our children at all? Is it to help the child to understand the whole significance of life, or merely to prepare him to earn a livelihood in a particular culture or society? Which is it that we want? Not what we should want, or what is desirable, but what is it that we as parents actually insist on? We want the child to conform, to be a respectable citizen in a corrupt society, in a society that is at war both within itself and with other societies, that is brutal, acquisitive, violent, greedy, with occasional spots of affection, tolerance, and kindliness. That is what we actually want, is it not? If the child does not fit into society—whether it be communist, socialist, or capitalist—we are afraid of what will happen to him, so we begin to educate him to conform to the pattern of our own making. That is all we want where the child is concerned, and that is essentially what is taking place. And any revolt of the child against society, against the pattern of conformity, we call delinquency.

We want the children to conform; we want to control their minds, to shape their conduct, their way of living, so that they will fit into the pattern of society. That is what every parent wants, is it not? And that is exactly what is happening, whether it be in America or in Europe, in Russia or in India. The pattern may vary slightly, but they all want the child to conform.

Now, is that education? Or does education mean that the parents and the teachers themselves see the significance of the whole pattern, and are helping the child from the very beginning to be alert to all its influences? Seeing the full significance of the pattern, with its religious, social, and economic influences, its influences of class, of family, of tradition—seeing the significance of all this for oneself and helping the child to understand and not be caught in it—that may be education. To educate the child may be to help him to be outside of society, so that he creates his own society. Since our society is not at all what it should be, why encourage the child to stay within its pattern?

At present we force the child to conform to a social pattern which we have established individually, as a family, and as the collective; and he unfortunately inherits not only our property but some of our psychological characteristics as well. So from the very beginning he is a slave to the environment.

Seeing all this, if we really love our children and are therefore deeply concerned about education, we will contrive from the very beginning to bring about an atmosphere which will encourage them to be free. A few real educators have thought about all this, but unfortunately very few parents ever think about it at all. We leave it to the experts—religion to the priest, psychology to the psychologist, and our children to the so-called teachers. Surely, the parent is also the educator; he is the teacher, and also the one who learns—not only the child.

So this is a very complex problem, and if we really wish to resolve it, we must go into it most profoundly; and then, I think, we shall find out how to bring about the right kind of education.

Question: What is the meaning of existence? What is it all about?

KRISHNAMURTI: This is a question that is constantly arising all over the world: What is the purpose of life? We are now asking it of ourselves, and I wonder why we ask it? Is it because life has very little significance for us, and we ask this question in the hope of being assured that it has a greater significance? Is it that we are so confused in ourselves that we do not know how to find the answer, which way to turn? I think that is most likely. Being confused in ourselves, we look, we ask; and in asking, in looking, we invent theories, we give a purpose or a meaning to life.

So what is important is not to define the purpose, the significance, the meaning of existence, but rather to find out why the mind asks this question. If we see something very clearly, we do not have to ask about it, so probably we are confused. We have been in the habit of accepting the things imposed upon us by authority; we have always followed authority without much thought, except the thoughts which authority encourages. Now, however, we have begun to reject authority because we want to find things out for ourselves, and in trying to find things out for ourselves, we become very confused. That is why we again ask, "What is the purpose of life?" If someone tells you what is the purpose of life, and their answer is satisfactory, you may accept it as your authority and guide your life accordingly, but fundamentally you will still be confused. The question, then, is not what the purpose of life is, but whether the mind can clear itself of its own confusion. If it can and does, then you will never ask that other question.

But the difficulty for most of us is to realize that we are thoroughly confused. We think we are only superficially confused, and that there is a higher part of the mind which is not contaminated by confusion. To realize that the totality of the mind is confused is very difficult because most of us have been educated to believe that there is a higher part of the mind which can direct, shape, and guide us; but surely this again is an invention of the mind.

To free oneself from confusion, one must first know that one is confused. To see that one is really confused is the beginning of clarification, is it not? But it requires deep perception and great honesty to see and to acknowledge to oneself that one is totally confused. When one knows that one is totally confused, one will not seek clarification because any action on the part of a confused mind to find clarification will only add to the confusion. That is fairly obvious, is it not? If I am confused, I may read or look or ask, but my search, my asking, is the outcome of my confusion, and therefore it can only lead to further confusion. Whereas, the mind that is confused and really knows it is confused will have no movement of search, of asking, and in that very moment of being silently aware of its confusion, there is a beginning of clarification.

If you are really following this, you are bound to see the truth of it psychologically. But the difficulty is that we do not really know, we are not actually aware of how extraordinarily confused we are. The moment one fully realizes one's own confusion, one's thought becomes very tentative, hesitant, it is never assertive or dogmatic. Therefore the mind begins to inquire from a totally different point of view, and it is this new kind of inquiry alone that will clear up the confusion.

Question: Do you believe in God?

KRISHNAMURTI: It is easy to ask questions, and it is very important to know how to ask a right question. In this particular question, the words *believe* and *God* seem to me so contradictory. A man who merely believes in God will never know what God is, because his belief is a form of conditioning—which again is very obvious. In Christianity you are taught from childhood to believe in God, so from the very beginning your mind is conditioned. In the communist countries, belief in God is called sheer nonsense—at which you are horrified. You want to convert them, and they want to convert you. They have conditioned their minds not to believe, and you call them godless, while you consider yourself God-fearing, or whatever it is. I do not see much difference between the two. You may go to church, pray, listen to sermons, or perform certain rituals and get some kind of stimulation out of it—but none of that, surely, is the experiencing of the unknown. And can the mind experience the unknown, whatever name one may give it? The name does not matter. That is the question—not whether one believes or does not believe in God.

One can see that any form of conditioning will never set the mind free, and that only the free mind can discover, experience. Experiencing is a very strange thing. The moment you know you are experiencing, there is the cessation of that experience. The moment I know I am happy, I am no longer happy. To experience this immeasurable reality, the experiencer must come to an end. The experiencer is the result of the known, of many centuries of cultivated memory; he is an accumulation of the things he has experienced. So when he says, "I must experience reality," and is cognizant of that experience, then what he experiences is not reality but a projection of his own past, his own conditioning.

That is why it is very important to understand that the thinker and the thought, or the experiencer and the experience, are the same; they are not different. When there is an experiencer separate from the experience, then the experiencer is constantly pursuing further experience, but that experience is always a projection of himself.

So reality, the timeless state, is not to be found through mere verbalization, or acceptance, or through the repetition of what one has heard—which is all folly. To really find out, one must go into this whole question of the experiencer. So long as there is the 'me' who wants to experience, there can be no experiencing of reality. That is why the experiencer—the entity who is seeking God, who believes in God, who prays to God—must totally cease. Only then can that immeasurable reality come into being.

June 25, 1956

Hamburg, Germany, 1956

First Talk in Hamburg

I think it is important to establish a right relationship between yourself and myself because you may be under the erroneous impression that I am going to talk about a complicated philosophy, or that I am bringing a particular system of philosophical thought from India, or that I have peculiar ideas which I want you to accept. So I think we should begin by establishing a relationship between us in which there is mutual understanding of each other.

I am not speaking as an Indian, nor do I believe that any particular philosophy or religion is going to solve our human problems. No human problem can be understood or resolved through a special way of thinking or through any dogma or belief. Though I happen to come from India, we have essentially the same problems there as you have here. We are human beings, not Germans or Hindus, English or Russians; we are human beings, living in a very complex society, with innumerable problems—economic, social, and above all, I think, religious. If we can understand the religious problem, then perhaps we shall be able to solve the contradictory national, economic, and social problems.

To understand the complex problem of religion, I think it is essential not to hold on to any particular idea or belief but to listen with a mind that is not prejudiced so that we are capable of thinking out the problem together. Surely we must approach all our human problems with a very simple, direct clarity and understanding.

Our minds have been conditioned from childhood to think in a certain way; we are educated, brought up in a fixed pattern of thought. We are tradition-bound. We have special values, certain opinions, and unquestioned beliefs, and according to this pattern we live—or at least we try to live. And I think there lies the calamity. Because, life is in constant movement, is it not? It is a living thing, with extraordinary changes; it is never the same. And our problems also are never the same, they are ever changing. But we approach life with a mind that is fixed, opinionated; we have definite ideas and predetermined evaluations. So, for most of us, life becomes a series of complex and apparently insoluble problems, and invariably we turn to someone else to guide us, to help us, to show us the right path.

Here, I think, it would be right for me to point out that I am not doing anything of that kind. What we are going to do, if you are willing, is to think out the problem together. After all, it is your life, and to understand it, surely, you must understand yourself. The understanding of yourself does not depend on the sanctions of another.

So it seems to me that if we are at all serious, and if we would understand the many problems that exist in the world at the present time—the nationalism, the wars, the hatred, the racial divisions, and the divisions which the organized religions bring about—if we would understand all this and eliminate the conflict between man and man, it is imperative that we should first understand ourselves. Because, what we are, we project—which is a very simple fact. If I am nationalistic, I help to create a separative society—which is one of the seeds, the causes of war. So it is obviously essential that we understand ourselves, and this, it seems to me, is the major issue in our lives.

Religion is not to be found in a set of dogmas, beliefs, rituals; I think it is something much greater and far beyond all that. Therefore it is imperative to understand why the mind clings to any particular religion or belief, to any particular dogma. It is only when we understand and free the mind from these beliefs, dogmas, and fears that there is a possibility of finding out if there is a reality, if there is God. But merely to believe, to follow, seems to me an utter folly.

So, if we are to understand each other, I think it is necessary for you to realize that I am not speaking to you as a group, as a number of Germans, but to each one as an individual human being. Because, the individual problem is the world problem. It is what we are as individuals that creates society—society being the relationship between ourselves and others. I am speaking—and please believe it—as one individual to another, so that together we may understand the many problems that confront us. I am not establishing myself as an authority to tell you what to do because I do not believe in authority in spiritual matters. All authority is evil, and all sense of authority must cease, especially if we would find out what is God, what is truth, whether there is something beyond the mere measure of the mind. That is why it is very important for the individual to understand himself.

I know the inevitable question will arise: If we have no authority of any kind, will there not be anarchy? Of course there may be. But does authority create order? Or does it merely create a blind following which has no meaning at all except that it leads to destruction, to misery? But if we begin to understand ourselves—which is a very complex process—then we shall also begin to understand the anatomy of authority. Then I think we shall be able to find out, as individuals, what is true. Without the compulsion of society, without the authority of a religion or of any person, however great, without the influence of another, we shall be able to discover and experience for ourselves something beyond mere intellection, beyond the clever assertions of the mind.

So, I hope this much is very clear between us—that I am not speaking as an Indian, with a particular philosophy, nor am I here to convince you of anything. I am asking, as one individual to another, whether it is possible to find out what is true, what is God—if there is God. It seems to me that one must begin by understanding oneself. And to understand yourself, surely, you must first know what you actually are, not what you think you should be—which is an ideological fallacy. After all, if I want to know myself, I must see myself exactly as I am, not as I think I ought to be. The "ought to be" is a form of illusion, an escape from what I am.

So, what we are concerned with—as individuals, not as a group—is to find out what is beyond the beliefs and theories, beyond the sentimental hopes and intellectual assertions of the various organized religions. We are trying to experience directly for ourselves if there is such a thing as reality, something more than the mere projections of the mind—which is what most religions are, however pleasant, however comforting. Can the mind find out, experience directly? Because, direct experience alone has validity. Can you and I as individuals, by going into this question now, discover or experience something which is immeasurable? Because, such an experience—if it is valid, if it is not just an illusion, a vision, a passing fantasy—has an extraordinary significance in life. Such an experience transforms one's life and brings about a morality which is not mere social respectability.

So, is it possible for you who are listening to me to experience that which is immeasurable? Just to say yes or no would be an absurdity. All that we can do is to find out if the mind is capable of experiencing something which is not a projection of its own demands. Which means, really, can you, the individual, free yourself from all your conditioning? Can you cease completely to be the Christian who believes, who has certain formulas, certain ideals? After all, each one is brought up in a particular tradition, and his God is the God of that tradition. Surely, that is not reality; it is merely a repetition of what he has been told. To find out if there is a reality, one must free oneself from the tradition in which one has been brought up—and that is an extraordinarily difficult thing to do. But only then is it possible to go beyond the mere measure of the mind and experience something which is immeasurable. If we do not experience that, life is very empty, trivial, lonely, without much meaning.

So, how is one, being serious and earnest, to set about it? Because without the fragrance, without the perfume of that reality, life is very shallow, materialistic, miserable; there is constant tension, striving, ceaseless pain and suffering. So a serious person must surely ask himself this question: Is it possible to experience something which is not a mere wish or intellectual concept from which one derives a certain satisfaction but something entirely new, beyond the fabrications of the mind? And if it is possible, then what is one to do? How is one to set about it?

I think there is only one approach to this problem, which is to see that until I know myself, until I know the whole content of the mind, the unconscious as well as the conscious, with all its intricate workings—until I am cognizant of all that, fully aware of it, I cannot possibly go beyond. Can I know myself in this way? Can I know myself as a whole—all the motives, the urges, the compulsions, the fears—and not just a few reactions and responses of the conscious mind? And can anyone help me, or must this be done entirely by myself? Because if I look to another for help, I become dependent, which means that the other becomes my authority; and when I only know myself through the authority of another, I do not know myself at all. And merely reading psychological books is of very little importance because I can only know myself as I am by observing my living from day to day, watching myself in the mirror of my relationship with another. To watch myself in that mirror is not to be merely introspective or objective but to be constantly alert, watchful of what is taking place in the mind, in myself.

You will find that it is extraordinarily difficult to watch yourself in the mirror of relationship without any sense of condemning what you see, and if you condemn what you see, you do not understand it. To understand a thing as it is, condemnation, judgment, evaluation, must go—which is extremely difficult because at present we are trained, educated to condemn, to reject, to approve, to deny.

And that is only the beginning of it, a very shallow beginning. But one must go through that, one must understand the whole process of the mind, not merely intellectually, verbally, but as one lives from day to day, watching oneself in this mirror of relationship. One must actually experience what is taking place in the mind—examine it, be aware of the whole content of it, without denying, suppressing, or putting it away. Then, if you go so far, and if you are at all serious, you will find that the mind is no longer projecting any image, no longer creating any myth, any illusion; it is beginning to understand the totality of itself, and therefore it becomes very clear, simple, quiet.

This is not a momentary process but a continual living, a continual sharpening of the mind. And in the very process of sharpening, the mind spontaneously ceases to be as it is. Then the mind is no longer creating images, visions, fallacies, illusions; and only then, when the mind is completely still, silent, is there a possibility of experiencing something which is not of the mind itself. But this requires not just one day of effort, or a casual observation, or attending one talk, but a slow maturity, a deepening search, a greater, wider, totally integrated outlook, so that the mind—which is now driven by many influences and demands, inhibited by so many fears—is free to inquire, to experience.

Only such a mind is truly religious—not the mind that believes or disbelieves in God, that has innumerable beliefs, that joins, agrees, follows, or denies; such a mind can never find out what is truth. That is why it is very important for those who are serious, for those who are concerned with the welfare of mankind, to put aside all their vain beliefs and theories, all their associations with particular religious organizations, and inquire very deeply within themselves.

For after all, religion is not dogma, it has nothing to do with belief; religion does not mean going to church or performing certain rituals. None of that is religion; it is merely the invention of man to control man. And if one would find out whether there is a reality, something beyond the inventions of the mind, one must put aside all these absurdities, this childish thinking. It is very difficult for most people to put it all aside because in clinging to beliefs, they feel secure, it gives them some hope. But to discover reality, to experience something beyond the mind, the mind must cease to have any form of security. It must be totally denuded of all refuges. It is only such a mind that is purified, and then it is possible for the mind to experience something which is beyond itself.

I have been given some questions, and I shall try to answer some of them—or rather, together we shall try to unravel the problem. There is no one answer to a problem, there is no isolated solution. If we merely look for a solution to a problem, we shall find that our search for the solution creates other problems. Whereas, if we are capable of examining the problem itself, without trying to find an answer, we shall discover that the answer is in the problem. So it is very important to know how to approach the problem. The mind which has a problem, and seeks an answer, cannot possibly inquire into the problem itself because it is concerned only with the solution. To understand any problem, you must give your whole attention to it, and you cannot give your whole attention to it if you are seeking a solution, an answer.

Question: We are full of memories of the last war, with all its terror. Can we ever free our minds of the past and start anew?

KRISHNAMURTI: The problem of memory is very complex, is it not? We have pleasant memories and unpleasant memories. We want to reject the unpleasant, the terrible, the painful memories, and keep the pleasant ones. That is what we are always trying to do, is it not? The pleasant memories of our youth, the interesting things we have read, the stimulating experiences we have had—all this has significance for us, and we want to hold on to it; but the things which are painful, sorrowful, unpleasant, irritating, we reject. So we divide our memories into the pleasant and the unpleasant, and what we are mostly concerned with is how to put away the unpleasant memories and keep alive those that are pleasant. But so long as we divide memory into the pleasant and the unpleasant and try to get rid of the unpleasant, there will always be conflict, both within and without.

I do not know if I am making myself clear. The mind is full of memories, it is made up of memories. You have no mind without memory—the memories of your past, of all the things you have learned, experienced, lived, suffered. Mind is memory, conscious or unconscious. In memory there is the pleasant and the unpleasant, and we want to reject the unpleasant; we want to keep the desirable and get rid of the undesirable, so there is always a conflict going on. What we have to understand is not how to retain the pleasant and be free of the terrible memories, but rather how to eliminate the desire to keep some memories and reject others, which creates conflict. What is important is to be aware of this conflict, and to understand why it is that the mind gathers memories and holds on to them.

Obviously one needs certain memories in order to live in this world. I must remember how to get back to the place where I live, and so on. But such memories are no problem to us. For most of us the problem is how to get rid of the memories which are painful, destructive, while retaining those which are significant, purposeful, enjoyable. But why does the mind cling to the one and seek to reject the other? Please follow this. If you do not hold fast to the pleasant memories, what are you? If you had no memories of the pleasant, of the hopeful, of the enjoyable, of the things that you have lived for, you would feel nonhuman, you would feel lost, a nobody. The mind clings to its pleasant memories because without them it would be lonely, in despair.

So I do not think the problem is how to get rid of the unpleasant memories, the terrors of the past. That is fairly easy. If you deliberately set about to wipe out the past, it can be done comparatively simply. But what is much more complex, what demands much deeper thought and inquiry, is to go into the whole problem of memory—not only the conscious memories, but the deep, underlying memories which guide our lives.

After all, a memory much deeper than the memory of the war and all the bestiality of it is that which makes you call yourself a German or a Christian or a Hindu; that also is part of memory, is it not? And that gives you solidarity, it gives you companionship, it makes you feel equal or superior to others, it gives you a sense of courage, and so many other things. But must you not also be free of that memory? Must one not be free to inquire, to go much further than the mere reaction to memories, which is a process of living in the past?

You see, memory does not yield to the newness of life. Memory is only the past, and anything born of memory is always old, never new. To discover something totally new, the mind must be astonishingly quiet, still, not active, not desiring and reacting to memories.

Question: We have had enough of war. We want peace. How can we prevent a new war?

KRISHNAMURTI: I do not think there is a simple answer because the causes of war are many. So long as there is nationalism, so long as you are a German or a Russian or an American, clinging to sovereignty, to an exclusive nationality, you are sure to have war. So long as you are a Christian and I am a

Hindu, or you are a Muslim and I am a Buddhist, there is bound to be war. So long as you are ambitious, wanting to reach the top of your society, seeking achievement and worshiping success, you will be a cause of war.

But we are brought up on all this. We are trained to compete, to succeed, to be ambitious, to serve a particular government, to belong to a particular country or religion. Our whole education cultivates the competitive spirit and guides the mind towards war. And can we, as individual human beings, change all this? Can you and I individually cease to be ambitious, cease to regard ourselves as Germans or Indians, cease to belong to any particular religion, to any particular group or ideology—communist, socialist, or any other—and be concerned only with human welfare?

So long as we remain attached to a group or to an ideology, so long as we are ambitious, seeking success, we are bound to create war. It may not be a war of outward destruction, but we will have conflict between each other and within ourselves, which is actually a form of war. I do not think we see this, and even if we do, we are not serious about it. We want some miraculous event to take place to stop war, while we continue to live as we are in the present social structure, making money, seeking position, power, prestige, trying to become famous, and all the rest of it. That is our pattern, and so long as that pattern exists in our minds and hearts, we are bound to produce war.

After all, war is merely the catastrophic effect of our daily living, and so long as we do not change our daily living, no amount of legislation, controls, and sanctions will prevent war. Is peace in the mind and heart, in the way of our life, or is it merely a governmental regulation, something to be decided in the United Nations? I am afraid that for most of us, peace is only a matter of legislation, and we are not concerned with peace in our own minds and hearts; therefore, there can be no peace in the world. You cannot have peace, inward or outward, so long as you are ambitious, competitive, so long as you regard yourself as a German, a Hindu, a Russian, or an Englishman, so long as you are striving to become somebody in this mad world. Peace comes only when you understand all this and are no longer pursuing success in a society which is already corrupt. Only the peaceful mind, the mind that understands itself, can bring peace in the world.

September 5, 1956

Second Talk in Hamburg

I think it is important, in listening to each other, to find out for oneself if what is being said is true; that is, to experience it directly and not merely argue about whether what is said is true or false, which would be completely useless. And perhaps this evening we can find out if it is possible to set about the very complex process of forgetting oneself.

Many of us must have experienced, at one time or another, that state when the 'me', the self, with its aggressive demands, has completely ceased, and the mind is extraordinarily quiet, without any direct volition—that state wherein, perhaps, one may experience something that is without measure, something that it is impossible to put into words. There must have been these rare moments when the self, the 'me', with all its memories and travails, with all its anxieties and fears, has completely ceased. One is then a being without any motive, without any compulsion, and in that state one feels or is aware of an astonishing sense of immeasurable distance, of limitless space and being.

This must have happened to many of us. And I think it would be worthwhile if we could go into this question together and see whether it is possible to resolve the enclosing, limiting self, this restricting 'me' that worries, that has anxieties, fears, that is dominating and dominated, that has innumerable memories, that is cultivating virtue and trying in every way to become something, to be important. I do not know if you have noticed the constant effort that one is consciously or unconsciously making to express oneself, to be something, either socially, morally, or economically. This entails, does it not, a great deal of striving; our whole life is based on the everlasting struggle to arrive, to achieve, to become. The more we struggle, the more significant and exaggerated the self becomes, with all its limitations, fears, ambitions, frustrations; and there must have been times when each one has asked himself whether it is not possible to be totally without the self.

After all, we do have rare moments when the sense of the self is not. I am not talking of the transmutation of the self to a higher level but of the simple cessation of the 'me' with its anxieties, worries, fears—the absence of the self. One realizes that such a thing is possible, and then one sets about deliberately, consciously, to eliminate the self. After all, that is what organized religions try to do—to help each worshiper, each believer, to lose himself in something greater, and thereby perhaps to experience some higher state. If you are not a so-called religious person, then you identify yourself with the state, with the country, and try to lose yourself in that identification, which gives you the feeling of greatness, of being something much larger than the petty, little self, and all the rest of it. Or, if we do not do that, we try to lose ourselves in social work of some kind, again with the same intention. We think that if we can forget ourselves, deny ourselves, put ourselves out of the way by dedicating our lives to something much greater and more vital than ourselves, we shall perhaps experience a bliss, a happiness, which is not merely a physical sensation. And if we do none of these things, we hope to stop thinking about ourselves through the cultivation of virtue, through discipline, through control, through constant practice.

Now, I do not know if you have thought about it, but all this implies, surely, a ceaseless effort to be or become something. And perhaps in listening to what is being said, we can together go into the whole process and discover for ourselves whether it is possible to wipe away the sense of the 'me' without this fearful, restricting discipline, without this enormous effort to deny ourselves, this constant struggle to renounce our wants, our ambitions, in order to be something or to achieve some reality. I think in this lies the real issue. Because all effort implies motive, does it not? I make an effort to forget myself in something, in some ritual or ideology, because in thinking about myself, I am unhappy. When I think about something else, I am more relaxed, my mind is quieter, I seem to feel better, I look at things differently. So I make an effort to forget myself. But behind my effort there is a motive, which is to escape from myself because I suffer, and that motive is essentially a part of the self. When I renounce this world and become a monk or a very devout religious person, the motive is that I want to achieve something better, but that is still the process of the self, is it not? I may give up my name and just be a number in a religious order, but the motive is still there.

Now, is it possible to forget oneself without any motive? Because, we can see very well that any motive has within it the seed of the self with its anxiety, ambition, frustration, its fear of not-being, and the immense urge to be secure. And can all that fall away easily, without any effort? Which means, really, can you and I, as individuals, live in this world without being identified with anything? After all, I identify myself with my country, with my religion, with my family, with my name, because without identification I am nothing. Without a position, without power, without prestige of one kind or another, I feel lost; and so I identify myself with my name, with my family, with my religion, I join some organization or become a monk—we all know the various types of identification that the mind clings to. But can we live in this world without any identification at all?

If we can think about this, if we can listen to what is being said, and at the same time be aware of our own intimations regarding the implications of identification, then I think we shall discover, if we are at all serious, that it is possible to live in this world without the nightmare of identification and the ceaseless struggle to achieve a result. Then, I think, knowledge has quite a different significance. At present we identify ourselves with our knowledge and use it as a means of self-expansion, just as we do with the nation, with a religion, or with some activity. Identification with the knowledge we have gained is another way of furthering the self, is it not? Through knowledge the 'me' continues its struggle to be something, and thereby perpetuates misery, pain.

If we can very humbly and simply see the implications of all this, be aware, without assuming anything, of how our minds operate and what our thinking is based on, then I think we shall realize the extraordinary contradiction that exists in this whole process of identification. After all, it is because I feel empty, lonely, miserable, that I identify myself with my country, and this identification gives me a sense of well-being, a feeling of power. Or, for the same reason, I identify myself with a hero, with a saint. But if I can go into this process of identification very deeply, then I will see that the whole movement of my thinking and all my activity, however noble, is essentially based on the continuance of myself in one form or another.

Now, if I once see that, if I realize it, feel it with my whole being, then religion has quite a different meaning. Then religion is no longer a process of identifying myself with God, but rather the coming into being of a state in which there is only that reality, and not the 'me'. But this cannot be a mere verbal assertion, it is not just a phrase to be repeated.

That is why it is very important, it seems to me, to have self-knowledge, which means going very deeply into oneself without assuming anything, so that the mind has no deceptions, no illusions, so that it does not trick itself into visions and false states. Then, perhaps, it is possible for the enclosing process of the self to come to an end—but not through any form of compulsion or discipline because the more you discipline the self, the stronger the self becomes. What is important is to go into all this very deeply and patiently, without taking anything for granted, so that one begins to understand the ways, the purposes, the motives and directions of the mind. Then, I think, the mind comes to a state in which there is no identification at all, and therefore no effort to be something; then there is the cessation of the self, and I think that is the real.

Although we may swiftly, fleetingly experience this state, the difficulty for most of us is that the mind clings to the experience and wants more of it, and the very wanting of more is again the beginning of the self. That is why it is very important, for those of us who are really serious in these matters, to be inwardly aware of the process of our own thinking, to silently observe our motives, our emotional reactions, and not merely say, "I know myself very well"—for actually one does not. You may know your reactions and motives superficially, at the conscious level. But the self, the 'me', is a very complex affair, and to go into the totality of the self needs persistent and continuous inquiry without a motive, without an end in view, and such inquiry is surely a form of meditation.

That immense reality cannot be found through any organization, through any church, through any book, through any person or teacher. One has to find it for oneself—which means that one has to be completely alone, uninfluenced. But we are, all of us, the result of so many influences, so many pressures, known and unknown; and that is why it is very important to understand these many pressures, influences, and be dissociated from them all so that the mind becomes extraordinarily simple, clear. Then, perhaps, it will be possible to experience that which cannot be put into words.

Question: You said yesterday that authority is evil. Why is it evil?

KRISHNAMURTI: Is not all following evil? Why do we follow authority of any kind? Why do we establish authority? Why do human beings accept authority—governmental, religious, every form of authority?

Authority does not come into being by itself; we create it. We create the tyrannical ruler, as well as the tyrannical priest with his gods, rituals, and beliefs. Why? Why do we create authority and become followers? Obviously, because we all want to be secure, we want to be powerful in different ways and in varying degrees. All of us are seeking position, prestige, which the leader, the country, the government, the minister, is offering—so we follow. Or we create the image of authority in our own minds and follow that image. The church is as tyrannical as the political leaders, and while we object to the tyranny of governments, most of us submit to the tyranny of the church or of some religious teacher.

If we begin to examine the whole process of following, we will see, I think, that we follow, first of all, because we are confused, and we want somebody to tell us what to do. And being confused, we are bound to follow those who are also confused, however much they may assert that they are the messengers of God or the saviors of the state. We follow because we are confused, and as we choose leaders, both religious and political, out of our confusion, we inevitably create more confusion, more conflict, more misery.

That is why it is very important for us to understand the confusion in ourselves, and not look to another to help us to clear it up. For how can a man who is confused know what is wrong and choose what is right, what is true? First he must clear up his own confusion. And once he has cleared up his own confusion, there is no choice; he will not follow anybody.

So we follow because we want to be secure, whether economically, socially, or religiously. After all, the mind is always seeking security, it wants to be safe in this world and also in the next world. All we are concerned with is to be secure, both with mammon and with God. That is why we create the authority of the government, the dictator, and the authority of the church, the idol, the image. So long as we follow, we must create authority, and that authority becomes ultimately evil because we have thoughtlessly given ourselves over to domination by another.

I think it is important to go deeply into this whole question and begin to understand why the mind insists on following. You follow, not only political and religious leaders, but also what you read in the newspapers, in magazines, in books; you seek the authority of the specialists, the authority of the written word. All this indicates, does it not, that the mind is uncertain of itself. One is afraid to think apart from what has been said by the leaders because one might lose one's job, be ostracized, excommunicated, or put into a concentration camp. We submit to authority because all of us have this inward demand to be safe, this urge to be secure. So long as we want to be secure—in our possessions, in our power, in our thoughts—we must have authority, we must be followers; and in that lies the seed of evil, for it invariably leads to the exploitation of man by man. He who would really find out what truth is, what God is, can have no authority, whether of the book, of the government, of the image, or of the priest; he must be totally free of all that.

This is very difficult for most of us because it means being insecure, standing completely alone, searching, groping, never being satisfied, never seeking success. But if we seriously experiment with it, then I think we shall find that there is no longer any question of creating or following authority because something else begins to operate—which is not a mere verbal statement but an actual fact. The man who is ceaselessly questioning, who has no authority, who does not follow any tradition, any book or teacher, becomes a light unto himself.

Question: Why do you put so much emphasis on self-knowledge? We know very well what we are.

KRISHNAMURTI: I wonder if we do know what we are? We are, surely, everything that we have been taught; we are the totality of our past; we are a bundle of memories, are we not? When you say, "I belong to God," or "The self is eternal," and all the rest of it—that is all part of your background, your conditioning. Similarly, when the communist says, "There is no God," he also is reflecting his conditioning.

Merely to say, "Yes, I know myself very well," is just a superficial remark. But to realize, to actually experience that your whole being is nothing but a bundle of memories, that all your thinking, your reactions, are mechanical, is not at all easy. It means being aware not only of the workings of the conscious mind but also of the unconscious residue, the racial impressions, memories, the things that we have learned; it means discovering the whole field of the mind, the hidden as well as the visible, and that is extremely arduous. And if my mind is merely the residue of the past, if it is only a bundle of memories, impressions, shaped by so-called education and various other influences, then is there any part of me which is not all that? Because, if I am merely a repeating machine, as most of us are—repeating what we have learned, what we have gathered, passing on what has been told to us—then any thought arising within this conditioned field obviously can only lead to further conditioning, further misery and limitation.

So, can the mind, knowing its limitations, being aware of its conditioning, go beyond itself? That is the problem. Merely to assert that it can or it cannot would be silly. Surely it is fairly obvious that the whole mind is conditioned. We are all conditioned—by tradition, by family, by experience, through the process of time. If you believe in God, that belief is the outcome of a particular conditioning, just as is the disbelief of the man who says he does not believe in God. So belief and disbelief have very little importance. But what is important is to understand the whole field of thought, and to see if the mind can go beyond it all.

To go beyond, you must know yourself. The motives, the urges, the responses, the immense pressure of what people have taught you, the dreams, the inhibitions, the conscious and hidden compulsions—you must know them all. Only then, I think, is it possible to find out if the mind, which is now so mechanical, can discover something totally new, something which has never been corrupted by time.

Question: You say that true religion is neither belief nor dogma nor ceremonies. What then is true religion?

KRISHNAMURTI: How are you going to find out? It is not for me just to answer, surely. How is the individual to find out what is true religion? We know what is generally called religion—dogma, belief, ceremonies, meditation, the practice of yoga, fasting, disciplining oneself, and so on. We all know the whole gamut of the so-called religious approach. But is that religion? And if I want to find out what is true religion, how am I to set about it?

First of all, I must obviously be free from all dogmas, must I not? And that is extraordinarily difficult. I may be free from the dogmas imposed upon me in childhood, but I may have created a dogma or belief of my own—which is equally pernicious. So I must also be free from that. And I can be free only when I have no motive, when there is no desire at all to be secure, either with God or in this world. Again, this is extremely difficult because surreptitiously, deep down, the mind is always wanting a position of certainty. And there are all the images that have been imposed upon the mind, the saviors, the teachers, the doctrines, the superstitions—I must be free of all that. Then, perhaps, I shall find out what it is to be truly religious—which may be the greatest revolution, and I think it is. The only true revolution is not the economic revolution, or the revolution of the communists, but the deep religious revolution which comes about when the mind is no longer seeking shelter in any dogma or belief, in any church or savior, in any teacher or sacred book. And I think such a revolution has immense significance in the world, for then the mind has no ideology, it is neither of the West nor of the East. Surely, this religious revolution is the only salvation.

To find out what is true religion requires, not a mere one-day effort or one-day search and forgetfulness the next day, but constant questioning, a disturbing inquiry, so that you begin to discard everything. After all, this process of discarding is the highest form of thinking. The pursuit of positive thinking is not thinking at all; it is merely copying. But when there is inquiry without a motive, without a desire for a result, which is the negative approach—in that inquiry the mind goes beyond all traditional religions; and then, perhaps, one may find out for oneself what God is, what truth is.

September 6, 1956

Third Talk in Hamburg

I do not think that we realize the significance or the importance of the individual. Because, as I was saying the other day, to bring about a fundamental, religious revolution, one must surely cease to think in terms of the universal, in terms of the collective. Anything that is made universal, collective, belonging to everybody, can never be true—true in the sense of being directly experienced by each individual, uninfluenced, without the impetus of self-centered interest. I think we do not sufficiently realize the seriousness of this. Anything really true must be totally individual—not in the sense of self-centeredness, which is very limiting and which in itself is evil, but individual in the sense that each one of us must experience for himself, uninfluenced, something which is not the outcome of any self-centered interest or drive.

One can see in the modern world how everything is tending towards collective thought—everybody thinking alike. The various governments, though they do not compel it, are quietly and sedulously working at it. Organized religions are obviously controlling and shaping the minds of people according to their respective patterns, hoping thereby to bring about a universal morality, a universal experience. But I think that whatever is made universal, in that sense, is always suspect because it can never be true; it has lost its vitality, its directness, its truth. Yet throughout the world we see this tendency to shape and to control the mind of man. And it is extraordinarily difficult to free the mind from this false universality and to change oneself without any self-interest.

It seems to me that we must have a change—a fundamental, radical change in our thinking, in our feeling. To bring about change, we use various methods; we have ideals, disciplines, sanctions, or we look to social, economic, and scientific influences. These things do bring about a superficial change, but I am not talking of that. I am talking of a change which is uninfluenced, without any self-interest, without self-centeredness. It seems to me that such a change is possible, and that it must come about if we are to have this religious revolution of which I was speaking the other day.

We think that ideals are necessary. But do ideals help to bring about this radical change in us? Or do they merely enable us to postpone, to push change into the future, and thereby avoid the immediate, radical change? Surely, so long as we have ideals, we never really change but hold on to our ideals as a means of postponement, of avoiding the immediate change which is so essential. I know it is taken for granted by the majority of us that ideals are indispensible, for without them we think there would be no impetus to change, and we would rot, stagnate. But I am questioning whether ideals of any kind ever do transform our thinking.

Why do we have ideals? If I am violent, need I have the ideal of nonviolence? I do not know if you have thought about this at all. If I am violent—as most of us are in different degrees—is it necessary for me to have the ideal of nonviolence? Will the pursuit of nonviolence free the mind from violence? Or is the very pursuit of nonviolence actually an impediment to the understanding of violence? After all, I can understand violence only when, with my whole mind, I give complete attention to the problem. And the moment I am wholly concerned with violence and the understanding of violence, what significance has the ideal of nonviolence? It seems to me that the pursuit of the ideal is an evasion, a postponement. If I am to understand violence, I must give my whole mind to it and not allow myself to be distracted by the ideal of nonviolence.

This is really a very important issue. Most of us look upon the ideal as essential in order to make us change. But I think it is possible to bring about a change only when the mind understands the whole problem of violence, and to understand violence, you must give your complete attention to it, and not be distracted by an ideal.

We all see the importance of the cessation of violence. And how am I, as an individual, to be free of violence—not just superficially, but totally, completely, inwardly? If the ideal of nonviolence will not free the mind from violence, then will the analysis of the cause of violence help to dissolve violence?

After all, this is one of our major problems, is it not? The whole world is caught up in violence, in wars; the very structure of our acquisitive society is essentially violent. And if you and I as individuals are to be free from violence—totally, inwardly free, not merely superficially or verbally—then how is one to set about it without becoming self-centered?

You understand the problem, do you not? If my concern is to free the mind from violence, and I practice discipline in order to control violence and change it into nonviolence, surely that brings about self-centered thought and activity because my mind is focused all the time on getting rid of one thing and acquiring something else. And yet I see the importance of the mind being totally free from violence. So what am I to do? Surely, it is not a question of how one is not to be violent. The fact is that we are violent, and to ask, "How am I not to be violent?" merely creates the ideal, which seems to me to be utterly futile. But if one is capable of looking at violence and understanding it, then perhaps there is a possibility of resolving it totally.

So, how are we to resolve violence without becoming self-centered, without the 'me' being completely occupied with itself and its problems? I do not know if you have thought about this matter. Most of us, I think, have accepted the easy path of pursuing the ideal of nonviolence. But if one is really concerned, deeply, inwardly, with how to resolve violence, then it seems to me that one must find out whether ideals are essential, and whether discipline, practice, the constant reminding of oneself not to be violent, can ever resolve violence or will merely exaggerate self-centeredness under the new name of nonviolence. Surely, to discipline the mind towards the ideal of nonviolence is still a self-centered activity and therefore only another form of violence.

If the problem is clear, then perhaps we can proceed to inquire into whether it is possible to free the mind from violence without being self-centered. This is very important, and I think it would be worthwhile if we could go into it hesitantly and tentatively and really find out. I see that any form of discipline, suppression, any effort to substitute an ideal for the fact—even though it be the ideal of love, or peace—is essentially a self-centered process, and that inherent in that process is the seed of violence. The man who practices nonviolence is essentially self-centered and therefore essentially violent because he is concerned about himself. To practice humility is never to be humble because the self-conscious process of acquiring humility, or cultivating any other virtue, is only another form of self-centeredness, which is inherently evil and violent. If I see this very clearly, then what am I to do? How am I to set about to free the mind from violence?

I do not know if you have thought about the problem at all in this manner. Perhaps this is the first time you have considered it, and so you may be inclined to say, "What nonsense!" But I do not think it is nonsense. After all, most idealists are very self-centered people because they are concerned with achievement. So the question is: Is it possible to free the mind from violence without the self-centered influence and activity? I think it is possible. But to really find out, one must inquire into it, not as part of a group, or the collective, but as an individual. As part of the collective, you have already accepted the ideal, and you practice virtue. But surely one must dissociate oneself totally from that whole process and inquire directly for oneself.

To inquire directly, one must ask oneself if the entity, the person who wants to get rid of violence, is different from the violence itself. When one acknowledges, "I am violent," is the 'I' who then wishes to get rid of violence different from the quality which he calls violence? This may all sound a bit complicated, but if one will go into it patiently, I think one will understand without too much difficulty.

When I say, "I am violent," and wish to free myself from violence, is the entity who is violent different from the quality which he calls violence? That is, is the experiencer who feels he is violent different from the experience itself? Surely the experiencer is the same as the experience; he is not different or apart from the experience. I think this is very important to understand because if one really understood it, then in freeing the mind from violence, there would be no self-centered activity at all.

We have separated the thinker from the thought, have we not? We say, "I am violent, and I must make an effort to get rid of violence." In order to get rid of violence, we discipline ourselves, we practice nonviolence, we think about it every day and try to do something about it—which means we take it for granted that the 'I', the maker of effort, is different from the experience, from the quality. But is this so? Are the two states different, or are they really a unit, one and the same?

Obviously, there is no thinker if there is no thought. But the thinker, the 'I', who is the maker of effort, is always exercising his volition in getting rid of violence, so he has separated himself from the quality which he calls violence. But they are not separate, are they? They are a unity. And actually to experience that unitary state—which means not differentiating between the thinker and his thought, between the 'I' who is violent and the violence itself—is essential if the mind is to be free from violence without self-centered action.

If you will think about it a little, I am sure you will see the truth of what I am trying to say. After all, just as the quality of the diamond cannot be separated from the diamond, so the quality of the thinker cannot be separated from thought itself. But we have separated them. In us there is ever the observer, the watcher, the censor, who is condemning, justifying, accepting, denying, and so on; the censor is always exercising influence on his thought. But the thought is the censor; the two are not separate, and it is essential to experience this in order to bring about a revolutionary change in which there is no self-centered activity.

After all, it is urgent that we change. We have had so many wars, such destruction, violence, terror, misery, and if we do not change radically, we shall go on pursuing the same old path. To change radically and not merely accept a new set of slogans, or give ourselves over to the state or to the church, to really understand the fundamental revolution that must take place in order to put an end to all this misery, it seems to me essential to discover whether there can be an action which is not self-centered. Surely, action will ever be self-centered as long as we do not experience directly for ourselves the fact that there is only thought and not the thinker. But if once we do experience this, I think we will find that effort then has quite a different significance.

At present we make an effort, do we not, in order to achieve a result, in order to arrive, to become something. If I am angry, ambitious, brutal, I make an effort not to be. But such effort is self-centered because I am still wanting to be something, perhaps negatively; there is still ambition, which is violence.

So if I am to change radically, without this self-centered motive, I must go very deeply into the problem of change. This means that I must think entirely differently, away from the collective, away from the ideal, away from the usual habit of discipline, practice, and all the rest of it. I must inquire who is the thinker, and what is thought, and find out whether thought is different from the thinker. Although thought has separated itself and set the thinker apart, he is still part of thought. And so long as thought is violent, mere control of thought by the thinker is of no value. So the question is: Can the mind be aware that it is violent, without dividing itself as the thinker who wants to get rid of violence?

This is really not a very complex problem. If you and I who are discussing it could go into it very carefully as individuals, we would see the extraordinary simplicity of it. Perhaps we are missing the significance of it because we think it is very complex. It is not. The simple fact is that there is no experiencer without the experience; the experiencer is the experience, the two are not separate. But so long as the experiencer sets himself apart and demands more experience, so long as he wishes to change this into that, there can be no fundamental transformation.

So the radical change we need is possible only when there are no ideals. Ideals are reform, and a mind that is merely reforming itself can never radically change. There can be no fundamental change if the mind is concerned with discipline, with fitting itself into a pattern, whether the pattern be that of society, of a teacher, or a pattern established by one's own thinking. There can be no radical change so long as the mind is thinking in terms of action according to its self-centered interest, however noble. The mere cultivation of virtue is not virtue.

So we have to inquire into the problem of change from a wholly different point of view. The totality of comprehension comes only when there is no division between the thinker and the thought—and that is an extraordinary experience. But you must come to it tentatively, with care, with inquiry, for mere acceptance or denial of the fact that the thought and the thinker are one will have no value. That is why a man who desires to bring about a fundamental change within himself must go into this problem very seriously and very deeply.

Question: Crime among young people is spreading everywhere. What can we do about it?

KRISHNAMURTI: You see, there is either a revolt within the pattern of society or a complete revolution outside of society. The complete revolution outside of society is what I call religious revolution. Any revolution which is not religious is within society and is therefore no revolution at all, but only a modified continuation of the old pattern. What is happening throughout the world, I believe, is revolt within society, and this revolt often takes the form of what is called crime. There is bound to be this kind of revolt so long as our education is concerned only with training youth to fit into society—that is, to get a job, to earn money, to be acquisitive, to have more, to conform. That is what our so-called education everywhere is doing—teaching the young to conform, religiously, morally, economically; so naturally their revolt has no meaning, except that it must be suppressed, reformed, or controlled. Such revolt is still within the framework of society, and therefore it is not creative at all. But through right education we could perhaps bring about a different understanding by helping to free the mind from all conditioning—that is, by encouraging the young to be aware of the many influences which condition the mind and make it conform.

So, is it possible to educate the mind to be aware of all the influences that now surround us, religious, economic, and social, and not be caught in any of them? I think it is, and when once we realize it, we shall approach this problem entirely differently.

Question: If we transform ourselves and become peaceful, while others do not transform themselves but remain aggressive and brutal, are we not inviting them to attack and violate us as helpless victims?

KRISHNAMURTI: I wonder if this question is put seriously? Have you tried to transform yourself, to be really peaceful, and see what happens? Without actually being peaceful, we say to ourselves, "If I am peaceful, another may attack me," and so we set up the whole mechanism of attack and defense.

But surely, sirs, we are concerned, are we not, with the transformation of the individual, irrespective of what is done to him. We are not thinking in terms of nations, of groups, of races. So long as society exists as it is now, there must be attack and defense because the whole structure of our thinking is based on that. You are a German or a Muslim, and I am a Russian or a Hindu; being afraid of each other, we must be prepared to defend ourselves; therefore, we dare not be peaceful. So we keep that game going, and we live in its pattern. But now we are not talking as members of any particular society, of any particular group, nationality, or religion. We are talking as individual human beings. Any great thing, surely, is done by the individual, not by the mass, the collective.

The mass is composed of many individuals who are caught in words, slogans, in nationalism, in fear. But if you and I as individuals begin to think about the problem of peace, then we are not concerned with whether another is peaceful or not. Surely love is not a matter of your loving me, and therefore I love you. Love is something entirely different, is it not? Where there is love, there is no problem of the other. Similarly, when I know for myself what peace is, I am not concerned with whether others are going to attack me or not. They may. But my interest is in peace and the understanding of it, which means totally eliminating from myself the whole fabric of violence. And that requires tremendously clear thinking, deep meditation.

Question; You say the mind must be quiet, but it is always busy, night and day. How can I change it?

KRISHNAMURTI: I wonder if we are actually aware that our minds are busy night and day? Or is this merely a verbal statement? Are you fully conscious that your mind is ceaselessly active, or are you merely repeating a statement you have heard? And even if you know it directly for yourself, why do you wish to change it? Is it because someone has said you must have a quiet mind? If you want a quiet mind in order to achieve something more or to get somewhere else, then the acquisition of a quiet mind is just another form of self-centered action. So, does one see, without any motivation, that it is essential to have a quiet mind? If so, then the problem is: Can thought come to an end?

We know that when we are awake during the day, the mind is active with superficial things—with the job, the family, catching a train, and all the rest of it. And at night, in sleep, it is also active in dreams. So the process of thinking is going on ceaselessly. Now, can thought come to an end voluntarily, naturally, without being compelled through discipline? For only then can the mind be completely still. A mind that is made still, that is forced, disciplined to be still, is not a still mind; it is a dead mind.

So, can thought, which is incessantly active, come to an end? And if thought does come to an end, will this not be a complete death to the mind? Are we not therefore afraid of thought coming to an end? If thought should come to an end, what would happen? The whole structure which we have built up of 'myself' being important, my family, my country, my position, power, prestige—the whole of that would cease, obviously. So, do we really want to have a quiet mind?

If we do, then we must inquire, must we not, into the whole process of thinking; we must find out what thinking is. Is thinking merely the response of memory, or is thinking something else? If it is merely the response of memory, then can the mind put away all memory? Is it possible to put away all memory? That is, can thought cease to make an effort to retain the pleasant and discard the unpleasant memories?

Perhaps this all seems a bit too complex and difficult, but it is not, if you go into it. The state of a mind that is really silent is something extraordinary. It is not the silence of negation. On the contrary, a silent mind is a very intense mind. But for such a mind to come into being, we must inquire into the whole process of thinking. And thinking, for most of us, is the response of memory. All our education, all our upbringing, encourages the continuance of memory identified as the 'me', and on that basis we set the ball of thought rolling.

So it is impossible to have a really still mind, a mind that is completely quiet, as long as you do not understand what thinking is, and the whole structure of the thinker. Is there a thinker when there is not thought based on memory? To find out, you have to trace your thought, inquire into every thought that you have, not just verbally or casually, but very persistently, slowly, hesitantly, without condemning or justifying any thought. At present there is a division between the thinker and the thought, and it is this division that creates conflict. Most of us are caught in conflict—perhaps not outwardly, but inwardly we are seething. We are in a continuous turmoil of wanting and not-wanting, of ambition, jealousy, anger, violence; and to have a really still, quiet mind, we must understand all that.

September 9, 1956

Fourth Talk in Hamburg

To understand what it is another is trying to convey, one must give a certain attention—not enforced attention or tremendous concentration, but that attention which comes with natural interest. After all, we have many problems in life—problems arising out of our relationship with society, the problems of war, of sex, of death, of whether or not there is God, and the problem of what this everlasting struggle is all about. We all have these problems. And I think we might begin to understand them deeply if we did not cling to one particular problem of our own, which is perhaps so close to us that it absorbs all our attention, all our effort, all our thinking, but tried instead to approach the problem of living as a whole. In understanding the problem of living as a whole, I think we shall be able to understand our personal problems.

That is what I want to deal with, if I can, this evening. Each one of us has a problem, and unfortunately that problem generally consumes most of our thought and energy. We are constantly groping, searching, trying to find an answer to our problem, and we want somebody else to supply that answer. It is probably for this very reason that you are here. But I do not think we will understand the totality of our existence if we merely look for an answer to a single problem. Because all problems are related; there is no isolated problem. So we have to look at life not as something to be broken up into parts, made fractional, but as something to be understood as a whole. If we can realize this, get the feeling of it, then I think we shall have a totally different approach to our individual problems, which are also the world problems.

What is happening now is that we are all so concerned with our own problems, with earning a livelihood, with getting ahead, with our personal virtue, and all the rest of it, that we do not have a general comprehension of the complete picture. And it seems to me that unless we get the feeling of the totality of our life with all its experiences, miseries, and struggles, unless we comprehend it as a whole, merely dealing with a particular problem, however apparently vital, will only create further problems, further misery.

I hope this is clear between us—that we are not considering one isolated problem, but we are trying to understand together the totality of the problem of our existence. So, whatever may be our immediate problem, can we, through that problem, look at our life as a whole? If we can, then I think the immediate problem which we have will undergo quite a change, and perhaps we shall be able to understand it and be free of it entirely.

Now, how does one set about to have this integrated outlook, this comprehensive view of life which reveals the significance of every relationship, every thought, every action? Surely, before we can see the whole picture, we must first be aware that we are always trying to solve our immediate problem in a very limited field. We want a particular answer, a satisfactory answer, an answer which will give us certainty. That is what we are seeking, is it not? And I think we must begin by being conscious of that; otherwise, we shall not be able to grasp the significance of this whole problem.

All this may at first seem very difficult; it may even sound rather absurd to those of you who are hearing it for the first time, and what we hear for the first time, we naturally tend to reject. But if one wants to understand, one must neither reject nor accept what is being said. One must examine it, not with sentimentality or intellectual preconceptions, but with that intelligence and common sense which will reveal the picture clearly.

So, why is it that most of us are incapable of looking at the whole picture of life which, if understood, would resolve all our problems? We look at the picture of Germans or Russians or Hindus or what you will. We look at the picture with our knowledge, with our ideas, with a particular training or technique, with a mind which is conditioned. We are always translating the picture according to our background, according to our education, our tradition. We never look at the picture without this influence of the past, without thinking about the picture. Do you see what I mean? After all, if I want to understand something, I must come to it with a fresh mind, with a mind that is not burdened with accumulated experience, knowledge, with all the conditioning to which it has been subjected.

Life demands this, does it not? Life demands that I look at it afresh. Because life is movement, it is not a dead, static thing, and I must therefore approach it with a mind that is capable of looking at it without translating it in certain terms—as a Hindu, a Christian, or whatever it is I happen to be. So, before I can look at the whole picture, I must be aware of how my mind is burdened with knowledge, tradition, which prevents it from looking afresh at that which is moving, living. Knowledge, however wide, however necessary at one level, does not bring comprehension of life, which is a constant movement. If my mind is burdened with technique, training, so that it can understand only that which is static, dead, then I can have no comprehension of life as a whole. To comprehend the totality of life, I must understand the process of knowledge, and how knowledge interferes with that comprehension. This is fairly obvious, is it not?—that knowledge interferes with the understanding of life.

And yet, what is happening in the world? All our education is a process of accumulating knowledge. We are concerned with developing techniques, with how to meditate, how to be good; the "how," the technique, becomes knowledge, and with that we hope to understand the immeasurable. So when one says, "I understand what you are talking about," is it merely a verbal understanding, or has one really grasped the truth of the matter? If we really grasp the truth of what is being said, that very comprehension will free the mind from the accumulated knowledge which interferes with perception.

So, is it possible for one who has had many experiences, who has read the various philosophies, the learned books, who has accumulated information, knowledge, to put all that aside? I do not think one can put it aside, suppress, or deny it; but one can be aware of it, and not allow it to interfere with perception. After all, we are trying to find out what is truth, if there is reality, if there is God; and to discover this for oneself is true religion—not the acceptance of some silly ritual or dogma, and all the rest of that nonsense.

To find something original and true, something timeless, you cannot come to it with the burden of memory, knowledge. The known, the past, can never help you to discover the moving, the creative. No amount of technique or learning, no amount of attending talks and discussions, can ever reveal to you the unknown. If you really see the truth of this, actually experience if for yourself, then you are free of all Masters and gurus, of all teachers, saints, and saviors. Because, they can only teach you what is known, and the mind which is burdened with the known can never find what is unknowable.

To be free from the known requires a great deal of understanding of the whole process of the accumulative mind. It would be silly to say, "I must forget the past"—that has no meaning. But if one begins to understand why the mind accumulates and treasures the past, why the whole momentum of the mind is based on time—if one begins to understand all that, then one will find that the mind can free itself from the past, from the burden of accumulated knowledge. There is then the discovery of something totally new, unexperienced, unimagined, which is a state of creativity and which may be called reality, God, or what you will.

So, being surrounded by problems, by innumerable conflicts, our difficulty is to know how to look at them, how to understand them, so that they are no longer a burden, and through those very problems we begin to discover the process by which the mind is everlastingly caught in time, in the known. Unless we can do that, our life remains very shallow. You may know a great deal, you may be a great scientist, you may be a great historian or just an ordinary person; but life will always be shallow, empty, dull, until you understand for yourself this whole process, which is really the beginning of self-knowledge.

So it seems to me that our many problems can never be solved until we approach them as an integral part of the totality of existence. We cannot understand the totality of existence as long as we break it up into compartments, as we are doing now. The difficulty is that our problems are so intense, so immediate, that we get caught in them; and not to be caught in them, the mind must begin to be aware of its own process of accumulation, by which it gains a sense of security for itself. After all, why do we accumulate property, money, position, knowledge, and so on? Obviously, because it gives us a sense of security. You may not have much property or money, but if you have knowledge, it gives you a feeling of security. It is only to the man who has no sense of security of any kind that the new is revealed because he is not concerned about himself and his achievements.

So, how is the mind to free itself from time? Time, after all, is knowledge. Time comes into being when there is the sense of achievement, something to be arrived at, something to be gained. "I am not important, but I shall be"—in that idea, time has come into being, and with it the whole struggle of becoming. In the very idea, "I shall be," there is effort to become; and I think it is this effort to become which creates time, and which prevents a comprehension of the totality of things. You see, so long as I am thinking about myself in terms of gain and loss, I must have time. I must have time to cover the distance between now and tomorrow when I hope I shall be something, either in terms of virtue or position or knowledge. This creation of time breaks life up into segments, and that becomes the problem.

To understand the totality of this extraordinary thing called life, one must obviously not be too definite about these things. One cannot be definite with something which is so immense, which is not measurable by words. We cannot understand the immeasurable so long as we approach it through time.

To grasp the significance of all this is not an intellectual feat, nor a sentimental, emotional realization, but it means that you must really listen to what is being said; and in that very process of listening, you will find out for yourself that the mind, though it is the product of time, can go beyond time. But this demands very clear thinking, a great alertness of mind, in which no emotionalism is involved. To understand the immeasurable, the mind must be extraordinarily quiet, still; but if I think I am going to achieve stillness at some future date, I have destroyed the possibility of stillness. It is now or never. That is a very difficult thing to understand because we are all thinking of heaven in terms of time.

Question: Are yogic exercises helpful in any way to human beings?

KRISHNAMURTI: I think one must go into this question fairly deeply. Apparently in Europe as well as in India, there is this idea that by doing yogic exercises, practicing virtue, being good, participating in social work, reading sacred books, following a teacher—that by doing something of this kind, you are going to achieve salvation or enlightenment. I am afraid you are not. On the contrary, you are going to be caught in the things you are practicing, and therefore you will always be held a prisoner and your vision will be everlastingly limited.

Yogic exercises are all right, probably, for the body. Any kind of exercise—walking, jumping, climbing mountains, swimming, or whatever you do—is on the same level. But to suppose that certain exercises will lead you to salvation, to understanding, to God, truth, wisdom—this I think is sheer nonsense, even though all the yogis in India say otherwise. If once you see that anything that you practice, that you accept, that you develop, always has behind it the element of greed—wanting to get something, wanting to reach something, wanting to break a record—then you will leave it alone. A mind that is merely concerned with the "how," with doing yogic exercises, this or that, will only develop a sense of achievement through time, and such a mind can never comprehend that which is timeless.

After all, you practice yogic exercises in the hope of reaching something, gaining something; you hope to achieve happiness, bliss, or whatever is offered. Do you think bliss is so easily realized? Do you think it is something to be gained by doing certain exercises or developing concentration? Must not the mind be altogether free of this self-centered activity? Surely a man who practices yoga in order to reach enlightenment is concerned about himself, about his own growth; he is full of his own importance. So it is a tremendous art—an art which can be approached only through self-knowledge, not through any practice—to understand this whole process of self-centered activity in the name of God, in the name of truth, in the name of peace, or whatever it be—to understand and be free of it.

Now, to be free does not demand time, and I think this is our difficulty. We say, "I am envious, and to get rid of envy I must control, I must suppress, I must sacrifice, I must do penance, I must practice yoga," and all the rest of it—all of which indicates the continuance of self-centered activity, only transferred to a different level. If one sees this, if one really understands it, then one no longer thinks in terms of getting rid of envy in a certain period of time. Then the problem is: Can one get rid of envy immediately? It is like a hungry man—he does not want a promise of food tomorrow, he wants to be fed now, and in that sense he is free of time. But we are indolent, and what we want is a method to lead us to something which will ultimately give us pleasure.

Question: A well-known author has written a great deal about the use of certain drugs which enable man to arrive at some visionary experience of union with the divine ground. Are those experiences helpful in finding that state of which you speak?

KRISHNAMURTI: You can learn tricks or take drugs or get drunk, and you will have intense experiences of one kind or another, depressing or exciting. Obviously the physiological condition does affect the psychological state of the mind, but drugs and practices of various kinds do not in any way bring about that state of which we are talking. All such things lead only to a variety, intensity, and diversity of experience—which we all want and hunger after because we are fed up with this world. We have had two world wars, with appalling misery and everlasting strife on every side, and our own minds are so petty, personal, limited. We want to escape from all this, either through psychology, philosophy, so-called religion, or through some exercise or drug—they are all on the same level.

The mind is seeking a sensation; you want to experience what you call reality, or God, something immense, great, vital. You want to have visions, and if you take some kind of drug or are sufficiently conditioned in a certain religion, you will have visions. The man who is everlastingly thinking about Christ or Buddha or what not will sooner or later have experiences, visions; but that is not truth, it has nothing whatever to do with reality. Those are all self-projections; they are the result of your demand for experience. Your own conditioning is projecting what you want to see.

To find out what is real, the mind must cease to demand any experience. So long as you are craving experience, you will have it, but it will not be real—real in the sense of the timeless, the immeasurable; it will not have the perfume of reality. It will all be an illusion, the product of a mind that is frustrated, that is seeking a thrill, an emotion, a feeling of vitality. That is why you follow leaders. They are always promising something new, a utopia, always sacrificing the present for the future, and you foolishly follow them because it is exciting. You have had that experience in this country, and you ought to know better than anyone else the miseries, the brutality of it all. Most of us demand the same kind of experience, the same kind of sensation, only at another level. That is why we take various drugs, or perform ceremonies, or practice some exercise that acts as a stimulant. These things all have significance in the sense that their use indicates that one is still craving experience; therefore, the mind is everlastingly agitated. And the mind that is agitated, that is craving experience, can never find out what is true.

Truth is always new, totally unknown, and unknowable. The mind must come to it without any demand, without any knowledge, without any wish; it must be empty, completely naked. Then only truth may happen. But you cannot invite it.

Question: Is our life predetermined, or is the way of life to be freely chosen?

KRISHNAMURTI: So long as we have choice, surely there is no freedom. Please follow this; do not merely reject or accept it, but let us think it out together. The mind that is capable of choosing is not free because in choice there is always conflict, conscious or unconscious, and a mind that is in conflict is never free. Our life is full of conflict; we are always choosing between good and bad, between this and that; you know this very well. We are always comparing, judging, evaluating, accepting, rejecting—that is the process of our life, which is a constant struggle, and a mind that is struggling is never free.

And are we individuals—individuals in the sense of being unique? Are we? Or are we merely the result of our conditioning, of innumerable influences, of centuries of tradition? You may like to separate yourself as being of the West, and set yourself still further apart as being German. But are you an individual in the sense of being completely uncorrupted, uninfluenced? Only in that state are you free—not otherwise. Which does not mean anarchy or selfishly individual existence—on the contrary.

But now you are not individuals; you are anything but that. You are German, English, French; you are Catholics, Protestants, communists—something or other. You are stamped, shaped, held within the framework in which you have been brought up, or which you have subsequently chosen. So your life is predetermined. You saw ten years ago how your life was predetermined. And every Catholic, every churchgoer, every person who belongs to any religious organization—his life is predetermined, fixed; therefore, he is never free. He may talk about freedom, he may talk about love and peace, but he cannot have love and peace, nor can he be free because for him those are mere words.

Your life is shaped, controlled by the society which you have created. You have created the wars, the leaders; you have created the organized religions of which you are now slaves. So your life is predetermined. And to be free, you must first be aware that your life is predetermined, that it is conditioned, that all your responses are more or less the same as those of everybody else throughout the world. Superficially your responses may be different; you may respond one way here, another way in India or in China, and so on, but fundamentally you are held in the framework of your particular conditioning, and you are never an individual. Therefore it is absurd to talk about freedom and self-determination. You can choose between blue cloth and red cloth, and that is about all; your freedom is on that level. If you go into it very deeply, you will find that you are not an individual at all.

But in going into it very deeply, you will also find that you can be free from all this conditioning—as a German, as a Catholic, as a Hindu, as a believer or a nonbeliever. You can be free from it all. Then you will know what it is to have an innocent mind, and it is only such a mind that can find out what is truth.

Question: Will awareness free us, as you suggest, from our undesirable qualities?

KRISHNAMURTI: I think it is important to understand what we mean by awareness. I am going to explain what I mean, and please do not add something mysterious, complicated, or mystical. It is very clear and simple if one cares to go right to the end of it.

We are aware, are we not, of many things. You are aware that I am standing here, that I am talking, and that you are listening. And if you are alert, you are also aware of how you are listening. To know how you are listening is also part of awareness, and it is very important because if you are aware of how you are listening, you will know in what way you are conditioned. You are probably interpreting what is being said according to your conditioning, according to your prejudices, according to your knowledge; and when you are interpreting, you are not listening. To be conscious of all this is part of awareness, is it not?

Now if you go still further, you will find that the moment you are really listening, and not interpreting according to your prejudices, you begin to see for yourself what is true and what is false. Because true and false are not a matter of prejudice or opinion; either it is so or it is not. But if you are concerned with interpretation all the time, then your vision is blurred and there is no clear perception. That is why most of us are not really listening to what is being said—because we are interpreting it in terms of our upbringing or preconceptions. If you are a Christian, you listen and compare what is being said with the teaching of the Bible or the Christ; or if you do not do that, you refer to some other information which you have gathered. So you are always listening with a barrier. To see this whole process going on in one's mind is part of awareness, is it not?

The questioner wants to know if through awareness he can be free of any unpleasant qualities. That is, can one be free, let us say, of envy? If you will follow what I am saying, you will see the full implication of what lies in this question.

Most of us, if we are at all aware, cognizant, conscious of ourselves, know when we are envious. Furthermore, we can see that our whole society is based on envy, and that religions are also based on it—wanting something more, not only in this world, but also in the next. We know the feeling of being envious, the superficial as well as the very complex process of envy.

Now, being aware of envy, what happens? We either condemn or rationalize it. We generally condemn it because to condemn is part or our upbringing; we are educated to condemn envy; it is the thing to do, even though we are envious all the time. By condemning envy, we hope to be free of it, but we are not free; it keeps on returning. Envy exists so long as there is a comparative mind. When I am comparing myself with somebody who is greater, more popular, more virtuous, and so on, I am envious. So a comparative mind breeds envy.

And you will see, if you go into this problem still deeper, that so long as you verbalize that feeling by calling it *envy,* the feeling goes on. I hope you are following this. You name the feeling, do you not? You say, "I am envious." But cannot one know that one is envious without naming it? Is it only by naming the feeling that one becomes conscious of it?

How do you know you are envious? Please take it very simply, and you will see. Do you know it only after you have given a name to it, calling it envy? Or do you know it as a feeling, independent of all terms? Is not all this also part of awareness?

Let us go slowly. I am envious, and I condemn it because to condemn envy is part of my social upbringing, but it goes on. So if I really want to be free of envy, what am I to do? That is the problem. I do not want the feeling to continue because that would be too silly; I see the absurdity of it, and I want to be free of it. So, how is the mind to be free of envy? First I have to see that all comparison must cease, and to really see that requires very arduous inquiry because one's whole upbringing is based on comparison—you must be as good as your brother or your uncle or your grandfather or Jesus or whoever it is. So, can the mind cease to compare?

Then the problem is: When one has a certain feeling, can the mind stop naming it, stop calling it envy? If you will experiment with this, you will see how extraordinarily alert the mind must be to differentiate the word from the feeling. All this is part of awareness, in which no effort is involved, because the moment you make an effort, you have a motive or gain, and therefore you are still envious.

So the mind is envious as long as it is comparing itself with somebody else, and it is envious as long as it gives a name to the feeling, calling it envy, because by giving it a name it strengthens that feeling. And when the mind does not compare, when the mind does not give a name to the feeling and thereby strengthen it, you will find, if you proceed very hesitantly, carefully, diligently, that awareness does free the mind from envy.

September 14, 1956

Fifth Talk in Hamburg

I think these meetings will be useless if what we are discussing is regarded merely as a verbal communication without much significance. Most of us, it seems to me, listen rather casually to something very serious, and we have little time or inclination to give our thought to the profound things of life and go deeply into them for ourselves. We are inclined to accept or to deny very easily. But if, during these meetings, instead of just listening superficially, we can actually experience what we are talking about as we go along, then I think it will be worthwhile to discuss a problem which must be confronting most of us. I am referring to the problem of dependence. It is really a very complex problem, but if we can go into it deeply and not merely listen to the verbal description, if each one of us can be aware of it, see the whole implication of dependence and where it leads, then perhaps we shall discover for ourselves whether man, you and I, can be totally free from dependence.

I think dependence, in its deeper psychological aspects, corrupts our thinking and our lives; it breeds exploitation; it cultivates authority, obedience, a sense of acceptance without understanding. And if we are to bring about a totally new kind of religion, entirely different from what religion is now, if there is to be the total revolution of a truly religious person, then I think we must understand the tremendous significance of dependence and be free of it.

Most of us are dependent, not only on society, but on our neighbor, on our immediate relationship with wife, husband, children, or on some authority. We rely on another for our conduct, for our behavior, and in the process of dependence we identify ourselves with a class, with a race, with a country; and this psychological dependence does bring about a sense of frustration. Surely it must have occurred to some of us to ask ourselves whether one can ever be psychologically, inwardly free—free in one's heart and mind of all dependence on another.

Obviously we are all interdependent in our everyday physical existence; our whole structure is based on physical interdependence, and it is natural, is it not, to depend on others in that sense. But I think it is totally unnatural to depend on another for our psychological comfort, for our inward security and well-being.

If we are at all aware of this process of dependence, we can see what it involves. There is in it a great sense of fear, which ultimately leads to frustration. Psychological dependence on another gives a false sense of security. And if it is not a person on whom we depend, it is a belief or an ideal or a country or an ideology or the accumulation of knowledge.

We see, then, that psychologically we do depend. I think this is fairly obvious to any person who is at all aware of himself in his relationship with another and with society.

Now, why do we depend? And is it possible not to depend psychologically, to be free of this inward dependence of one mind on another? I think it is fairly important to find out why we depend. And if we did not depend, what would happen? Is it a feeling of loneliness, a sense of emptiness, insufficiency that drives us to depend on something? Are we dependent because we lack self-confidence? And if we do have confidence in ourselves, does that bring about freedom or merely an aggressive, self-assertive activity?

I do not know if you think, as I do, that this is a significant problem in life. Perhaps we are not aware of our psychological dependence; but if we are, we are bound to see that behind this dependence there is immense fear, and it is to escape from that fear that we depend. Psychologically we do not want to be disturbed or to have taken away from us that on which we depend, whether it be a country, an idea, or a person; therefore, that on which we depend becomes very important in our life, and we are always defending it.

It is in order to escape from the fear which we unconsciously know exists in us that we turn to another to give us comfort, to give us love, to encourage us—and that is the very process of dependence. So, can the mind be free of this dependence, and thus be able to look at the whole problem of fear? Without deeply understanding fear and being free of it, the mere search for reality, for God, for happiness is utterly useless because what you are seeking then becomes that on which you again depend. Only the mind that is inwardly free of fear can know the blessing of reality, and the mind can be free of fear only when there is no dependence.

Now, can we look at fear? What is fear? Fear exists, surely, only in relation to something. Fear does not exist by itself. And what is it that we are afraid of? We may not be consciously aware of our fear, but unconsciously we are afraid, and that unconscious fear has far greater power over our daily thoughts and activities than the effort we make to suppress or deny fear.

So what is it that most of us are afraid of? There are superficial fears, such as the fear of losing a job, and so on, but to those fears we can generally adjust ourselves. If you lose your job, you will find some other way of making a living. The great fear is not for one's social security; it lies much deeper than that. And I do not know if the mind is willing to look at itself so profoundly as to be able to find out for itself what it is intrinsically frightened of. Unless you discover for yourself the deep source of your fear, all efforts to escape from fear, all cultivation of virtue, and so on is of no avail because fear is at the root of most of our anxious urges. So can we find out what it is we are afraid of, each one of us? Is the cause of fear common to us all, like death? Or is it something that each one of us has to discover, look at, go into for himself?

Most of us are frightened of being lonely. We are unconsciously aware that we are empty, that we are nothing. Though we may have titles, jobs, position, power, money, and all the rest of it, underlying all that there is a state of emptiness, an unfulfilled longing, a vacuum which we translate as loneliness—that state in which the self, the 'me', has completely enclosed the mind. Perhaps that is the very root of our fear. And can we look at it in order to understand it? For I think we must understand it if we would go beyond it.

Most of our activity is based on fear, is it not? That is, we never want to face ourselves exactly as we are, to know ourselves completely. And the more deeply and drastically you go into yourself, the greater the sense of emptiness you will find. All that we have learned—the knowledge we have acquired, the virtues we have cultivated—all this is on the surface, and it has very little meaning if one penetrates more and more deeply into oneself, for as one penetrates, one comes upon this enormous sense of emptiness. You may sometimes have caught a fleeting glimpse of it as a feeling of loneliness, of insufficiency, but then you turn on the radio, or talk, or do something else to escape from that feeling. And that feeling, that sense of 'not-being', may be the cause of fear.

I think most of us have, at rare moments, experienced that state. And when we do fleetingly experience it, we generally run away from it through some form of amusement, through knowledge, through the vast mechanism of escape offered by the so-called civilized world. But what happens if we do not escape? Can the mind go into that? I think it must. Because in going deeply into that state of emptiness, we may discover something totally new and be completely free of fear.

To understand something, we must approach it without any sense of condemnation, must we not? If I want to understand you, I must not be full of memories; my mind must not be burdened with knowledge about Germans, Hindus, Russians, or whatever the label may be. To understand, I must be free of all sense of condemnation and evaluation. Similarly, if I am to understand this state which I have called emptiness, loneliness, a feeling of insufficiency, I must look at it without any sense of condemnation. If I want to understand a child, I must not condemn him or compare him with another child. I must observe him in all his moods—when he is playing, crying, eating, talking. In such a manner the mind must watch the feeling of emptiness, without any sense of condemnation or rejection. Because, the moment I condemn or reject that feeling, I have already created the barrier of fear.

So, can one look at oneself, and at this sense of insufficiency, without any condemnation? After all, condemnation is a process of verbalization, is it not? And when one condemns, there is no true communication.

I hope you are following this because I think it is very important to understand it now, to really experiment with it as you are listening, and not merely go away and think about it later. This does not mean experimenting with what I say but experimenting with the discovery of your own loneliness, your own emptiness—the feeling of insufficiency which causes fear. And you cannot be free to discover if you approach that state with any sense of condemnation.

So, can we now look at that thing which we have called emptiness, loneliness, insufficiency, realizing that we have always tried to escape from it rather than comprehend it? I see that what is important is to understand it, and that I cannot understand it if there is any sense of condemnation. So condemnation goes; therefore, I approach it with a totally different mind, a whole, free mind. Then I see that the mind cannot separate itself from emptiness because the mind itself is that emptiness. If you really go into it very deeply for yourself, free of all condemnation, you will find that out of the thing which we have called emptiness, insufficiency, fear, there comes an extraordinary state, a state in which the mind is completely quiet, undemanding, unafraid; and in that silence there is the coming into being of creativity, reality, God, or whatever you may like to call it. This inward sense of having no fear can take place only when you understand the whole process of your own thinking, and then I think it is possible to discover for oneself that which is eternal.

Question: Most of us are caught up in and are bored with the routine of our work, but our livelihood depends on it. Why can we not be happy in our work?

KRISHNAMURTI: Surely, modern civilization is making many of us do work which we as individuals do not like at all. Society as it is now constituted, being based on competition, ruthlessness, war, demands, let us say, engineers and scientists; they are wanted everywhere throughout the world because they can further develop the instruments of war and make the nation more efficient in its ruthlessness. So education is largely dedicated to building the individual into an engineer or a scientist, whether he is fit for it or not. The man who is being educated as an engineer may not really want to be one. He may want to be a painter, a musician, or who knows what else. But circumstances—education, family tradition, the demands of society, and so on—force him to specialize as an engineer. So we have created a routine in which most of us get caught, and then we are frustrated, miserable, unhappy for the rest of our lives. We all know this.

It is fundamentally a matter of education, is it not? And can we bring about a different kind of education in which each person, the teacher as well as the student, loves what he is doing? *Loves*—I mean exactly that word. But you cannot love what you are doing if you are all the time using it as a means to success, power, position, prestige.

Surely, as it is now constituted, society does produce individuals who are utterly bored, who are caught in the routine of what they are doing. So it will take a tremendous revolution, will it not, in education and in everything else, to bring about a totally different environment—an environment which will help the students, the children, to grow in that which they really love to do.

As things are now, we have to put up with routine, with boredom, and so we try to escape in various ways. We try to escape through amusements, through television or the radio, through books, through so-called religion, and so our lives become very shallow, empty, dull. This shallowness in turn breeds the acceptance of authority, which gives us a sense of universality, of power, position. We know all this in our hearts, but it is very difficult to break away from it all because to break away demands, not the usual sentimentality, but thought, energy, hard work.

So if you want to create a new world—and surely you must after these terrible wars, after the misery, the terrors that human beings have gone through—then there will have to be a religious revolution in each one of us, a revolution that will bring about a new culture and a totally new religion, which is not the religion of authority, of priestcraft, of dogma and ritual. To create a wholly different kind of society, there must be this religious revolution—that is, a revolution within the individual, and not the terrible outward bloodshed which only brings more tyranny, more misery and fear. If we are to create a new world—new in a totally different sense—then it must be our world, and not a German world or a Russian world or a Hindu world, for we are all human beings, and the earth is ours.

But unfortunately very few of us feel deeply about all this because it demands love, not sentimentality or emotionalism. Love is hard to find, and the man who is sentimentally emotional is generally cruel. To bring about a totally different culture, it seems to me that there must take place in each one of us this religious revolution, which means that there must be freedom, not only from all creeds and dogmas, but freedom from personal ambition and self-centered activity. Only then, surely, can there be a new world.

Question: You reject discipline and outward order and suggest that we should act only by inner impulse. Will this not add to the great instability of people and encourage the following of irresponsible urges, especially among the youth of our time, who only want to enjoy themselves and are already drifting?

KRISHNAMURTI: I am afraid the questioner has not understood what we are talking about at all. I am not suggesting that you should abandon discipline. Even if you did try to abandon it, your society, your neighbor, your wife or husband, the people around you would force you to discipline yourself again. We are discussing not the abandonment of discipline but the whole problem of discipline. If we could understand the very deep implications of discipline, then there might be order which is not based on coercion, compulsion, fear.

Surely, discipline implies suppression, does it not? Please think it out with me and do not just reject it. I know you are all very fond of discipline, of obeying, following, but do not merely reject what I am suggesting. In disciplining myself, I suppress what I want in order to conform to some greater value, to the edicts of society, or whatever it is. That suppression may be a necessity, or it may be voluntary, even pleasurable, but it is still a form of putting away desire of one kind or another—suppressing it, denying it, and training myself to conform to a pattern laid down by society, by a teacher, or by the sanctions of a particular regime. If we reject that outward form of discipline, then we establish a discipline of our own. We say, "I must not do this, it is wrong; I must do only what is right, what is good, what is noble. When I have an ugly thought, I must suppress it; I must discipline myself, I must practice constant watchfulness."

Now, where there is conformity, discipline, suppression, conscious or unconscious, there is a constant struggle going on, is there not? We are all familiar with this fact. I am not saying anything new, but we are directly examining what is constantly taking place. And a mind that is suppressed, compelled to conform, must ultimately break out into all kinds of chaotic activities—which is what actually happens.

When we discipline ourselves, it is in order to get something we want. After all, the so-called religious people discipline themselves because they are pursuing an idea in the distance which they hope someday to achieve. The idealist, the utopian, is thinking in terms of tomorrow; he has established the ideal for the future and is always trying to conform to what he thinks he should be. He never understands the whole process of what is actually taking place in himself, but is only concerned with the ideal. The 'what should be' is the pattern, and he is trying to fit himself into it because he hopes in that pattern there will be greater happiness, greater bliss, the discovery of truth, God, and all the rest of it.

So, is it not important to find out why the mind disciplines itself, and not merely say that it should not? I think there would be not conformity, not enforcement, but a totally different kind of adjustment if we could really understand what it is the mind is seeking through discipline. After all, you discipline yourself in order to be safe. Is that not essentially true? You want to be secure, not only in this world, but also in the next world—if there is a next world. The mind that is seeking security must conform, and conformity means discipline. You want to find a Master, a teacher, and so you discipline yourself, you meditate, you suppress certain desires, you force your mind to fit into a frame. And so your whole life, your whole consciousness is twisted.

If we understand, not superficially, but really deeply, the inward significance of discipline, we will see that it makes the mind conform, as a soldier is made to conform; and the mind that merely conforms to a pattern, however noble, can obviously never be free, and therefore can never perceive what is true. This does not mean that the mind can do whatever it likes. When it does whatever it likes, it soon finds out there is always pain, sorrow, at the end of it. But if the mind sees the full significance of all this, then you will find that there is immediate understanding without compulsion, without suppression.

One of our difficulties is that we have been so trained, educated to suppress, to conform, that we are really frightened of being free; we are afraid that in freedom we may do something ugly. But if we begin to understand the whole pattern of discipline, which is to see that we conform in order to arrive, to gain, to be secure, then we shall find that there comes into being a totally different process of awareness in which there is no necessity for suppression or conformity.

Question: What happens after death? And do you believe in reincarnation?

KRISHNAMURTI: This is a very complex problem that touches every human being whether he is young or old, and whether he lives in Russia, where there is officially no belief in the hereafter, or in India, or here in the West, where there is every shade of belief. It really requires very careful inquiry and not merely the acceptance or rejection of a particular belief. So let us please think it out together very carefully.

Death is the inevitable end for all of us, and we know it. We may rationalize it or escape from the uncertainty of that vast unknown through belief in reincarnation, resurrection, or what you will, but fear is still there. The body, the physical organism, inevitably wears itself out, just as every machine wears itself out. You and I know that disease, accident, or old age will come and carry us away. We say, "Yes, that is so," and we accept it, so that is really not our problem. Our problem is much deeper. We are frightened of losing everything that we have gained, understood, gathered; we are frightened of not-being; we are frightened of the unknown. We have lived; we have accumulated, learned, experienced, suffered; we have educated the mind and disciplined ourselves, and is death the end of it all? We do not like to think that it is. So we say there must be a hereafter; life must continue, if not by returning to earth, then it must continue elsewhere. And many of us have a comforting belief in the theory of reincarnation.

To me, belief is not important because belief in an idea, in a theory, however comforting, however satisfactory, does not give understanding of the full significance of death. Surely, death is something totally unknown, completely new. However anxiously I may inquire into death, it ever remains something which I do not know. All that you and I know is the past, and the continuity of the past through the present to the future. Memory identified with my house, my family, my name, my acquisitions, virtues, struggles, experiences—all that is the 'me', and we want the 'me' to continue. Or if you are tired of the 'me', you say, "Thank God, death ends it all," but that does not solve the problem either.

So we must find out, surely, the truth of this matter. What you happen to believe or disbelieve about reincarnation has no truth in it. But instead of asking what happens after death, can we not discover the truth of what death is? Because, life itself may be a process of death. Why do we divide life from death? We do so because we think life is a process of continuity, of accumulation, and death is cessation, the annihilation of all that we have accumulated. So we have separated living from death. But life may be entirely different; it may be a process the truth of which we do not know, a process of living and dying each minute. All that we know is a form of continuity—what I was yesterday, what I am today, and what I hope to be tomorrow. That is all we know. And because the mind clings to that continuity, it is afraid of what it calls death.

Now, can the living mind know death? Do you understand the problem? It is not a question of what happens after death, but can a living mind—a mind that is not diseased, that is fully alert, aware—experience that state which it calls death? Which means, really, do we know what living is? Because living may be dying, in the sense of dying to our memories. Please follow this, and perhaps you will see the enormous implication of this idea of death.

We live in the field of the known, do we not? The known is that with which I have identified myself—my family, my country, my experiences, my job, my friends, the virtues, the qualities, the knowledge I have gathered, all the things I have known. So the mind is the result of the past; the mind is the past. The mind is burdened with the known. And can the mind free itself from the known? That is, can I die to all that I have accumulated—not when I am a doddering old man, but now? While I am still full of vitality, clarity, and understanding, can I die to everything that I have been, that I am going to be, or think that I should be? That is, can I die to the known, die to every moment? Can I invite death, enter the house of death while living?

You can enter the house of death only when the mind is free from the known—the known being all that you have gathered, all that you are, all that you think you are and hope to be. All this must completely cease. And is there then a division between living and dying, or only a totally different state of mind?

If you are merely listening to the words, then I am afraid you will not understand the implication of what is being said. But if you will, you can see for yourself that living is a process of dying every minute, and renewing. Otherwise you are not really living, are you? You are merely continuing a state of mind within the field of the known, which is routine, which is boredom. There is living, surely, only when you die—consciously, intelligently, with full awareness—to everything that you have been, to the many yesterdays. Then the problem of death is entirely different. There may be no problem at all. There may be a state of mind in which time does not exist. Time exists only when there is identification with the known. The mind that is burdened with the known is everlastingly afraid of the unknown. Whatever it may do, whatever may be its beliefs, its dogmas, its hopes, they are all based on fear, and it is this fear that corrupts living.

September 15, 1956

Sixth Talk in Hamburg

It seems to me that the whole world is intent on capturing the mind of man. We have created the psychological world of relationship, the world in which we live, and it in turn is controlling us, shaping our thinking, our activities, our psychological being. Every political and religious organization, you will find, is after the mind of man—"after" in the sense of wanting to capture it, shape it to a certain pattern. The powers that be in the communist world are blatantly conditioning the mind of man in every direction, and this is also true of the organized religions throughout the world, who for centuries have tried to mold the way of man's thought. Each specialized group, whether religious, secular, or political is striving to draw and to hold man within the pattern of that which its books, its leaders, the few in power, think is good for him. They think they know the future; they think they know what is the ultimate good for man. The priests, with their so-called religious authority, as well as the worldly powers—whether it be in Rome, in Moscow, in America, or elsewhere—are all trying to control man's thought process, are they not? And most of us eagerly accept some form of authority and subject ourselves to it. There are very few who escape the clutches of this organized control of man and his thinking.

Merely to break away from a particular religious pattern, or from a political pattern of the left or of the right, in order to adopt another pattern, or to establish one of our own, will not, it seems to me, simplify the extraordinary complexity of our lives, or resolve the catastrophic misery in which most of us live. I think the fundamental solution lies elsewhere, and it is this fundamental solution that we are all trying to find. Groping blindly, we join this organization or that. We belong to a particular society, follow this or that leader, try to find a Master in India or somewhere else—always hoping to break away from our narrow, limited existence, but always caught, it seems to me, in this conflict within the pattern. We never seem to get away from the pattern, either self-created or imposed by some leader or religious authority. We blindly accept authority in the hope of breaking through the cloud of our own strife, misery, and struggle, but no leader, no authority is ever going to free man. I think history has shown this very clearly, and you in this country know it very well—perhaps better than others.

So if a new world is to come into being, as it must, it seems to me extremely important to understand this whole process of authority—the authority imposed by society, by the book, by a set of people who think they know the ultimate good for man and who seek to force him through torture, through every form of compulsion, to conform to their pattern. We are quick to follow such people because in our own being we are so uncertain, so confused, and we also follow because of our vanity and arrogance and out of desire for the power offered by another.

Now, is it possible to break away from this whole pattern of authority? Can we break away from all authority of any kind in ourselves? We may reject the authority of another, but unfortunately we still have the authority of our own experience, of our own knowledge, of our own thinking, and that in turn becomes the pattern which guides us, but that is essentially no different from the authority of another. There is this desire to follow, to imitate, to conform in the hope of achieving something greater, and so long as this desire exists, there must be misery and strife, every form of suppression, frustration, and suffering.

I do not think we sufficiently realize the necessity of being free of this compulsion to follow authority, inward or outward. And I think it is very important psychologically to understand this compulsion; otherwise, we shall go on blindly struggling in this world in which we live and have our being, and we shall never find that other thing which is so infinitely greater. We must surely break away from this world of imitation and conformity if we are to find a totally different world. This means a really fundamental change in our lives—in the way of our action, in the way of our thought, in the way of our feeling.

But most of us are not concerned with that; we are not concerned with understanding our thoughts, our feelings, our activities. We are only concerned with what to believe or not to believe, with whom to follow or not to follow, with which is the right society or political party, and all the rest of that nonsense. We are never concerned deeply, inwardly, with a radical change in the way of our daily life, in the way of our speech, the sensitivity of our thought towards another—we are not concerned with any of that. We cultivate the intellect and acquire knowledge of innumerable things, but we remain inwardly the same—ambitious, cruel, violent, envious, burdened with all the pettiness of which the mind is capable. And seeing all this, is it possible to break away from the petty mind? I think that is the only real problem. And I think that in breaking away from the petty mind, we shall find the right answer to our economic, social, and other problems.

Without understanding the pettiness of ourselves, the narrow, shallow thoughts and feelings that we have—without going into that very deeply and fundamentally, merely to join societies and follow leaders who promise better health, better economic conditions, and all the rest of it seems to me so utterly immature. Our fear may perhaps be modified, moved to another level, but inwardly we remain the same; there is still fear and the sense of frustration that goes with self-centered activity. Unless we fundamentally change that, do what we will—create the most extraordinary legislative order, bring about a welfare state which guarantees everyone's social well-being and all the rest of it—inwardly we shall always remain poor.

So how is the mind to break away from its own pettiness? I do not know if you have ever thought about this, or if it is a problem to you. Perhaps you are merely concerned with improving conditions, bringing about certain reforms, establishing a better social order, and are not concerned with a radical change in human thinking. It seems to me that the real problem is whether a fundamental change comes about through outward circumstances, or through any form of compulsion, or whether it comes from a totally different direction. If we rely on any form of compulsion, on outward changes in the social order, on so-called education, which is the mere gathering of information, and so on, surely our lives will still be shallow. We may know a great deal about many things, we may be able to quote the various authorities and be very learned in the expression of our thought, but our minds will be as petty as before, with the same ache of deep anxiety, uncertainty, fear. So there is no fundamental transformation through outward change, or through any form of pressure, influence. Fundamental transformation comes from quite a different direction, and this is what I would like briefly to talk about, even though I have already talked about it a great deal during the last five meetings, because it seems to me that this is the only real issue.

So long as we ourselves are confused, small, petty, whatever our activity may be, and whatever concept we may have of truth, of God, of beauty or love, our thinking and our action are bound to be equally petty, confused, limited. A confused mind can only think in terms of confusion. A petty mind can never imagine what God is, what truth is, and yet that is what we are occupied with. So it seems to me important to discover whether the mind can transform itself without any compulsion, without any motive. The moment there is compulsion, the mind is already conforming to a pattern. If there is a motive for change, that motive is self-projected; therefore, the change, being a product of self-centered activity, is no change at all. It seems to me that this is the real thing which we have fundamentally to tackle, put our teeth into—and not whom to follow, who is the best leader, and all that rubbish.

The question is: Can the mind, without any form of compulsion, without a motive, bring about a transformation within itself? A motive is bound to be the result of self-centered desire, and such a motive is self-enclosing; therefore, there is no freedom, there is no transformation of the mind. So, can the mind break away from all influence and from all motive? And is not this very breaking away from all influence and from all motive in itself a transformation of the mind? Do you follow what I mean?

You see, we must abandon this world in which we are caught—the world of authority, of power, of influence, the world of conditioning, of fear, of ambition and envy—if we are to find the other world. We must let this world go, let it die in us without compulsion, without motive, because any motive will be a mere repetition of the same thing in different terms.

I think just to look at the problem, just to comprehend the problem, brings its own answer. I see that, as a human being, I am the result of innumerable influences, social compulsions, religious impressions, and that if I try to find reality, truth, or God, that very search will be based on the things I have been taught, shaped by what I have known, conditioned by my education and by the influences of the environment in which I live. So, can I be free of all that? To be free, I must first know for myself that my mind is conditioned, that is, I must be fully aware that I am not really a human being, but a Hindu, a Catholic, a German, a Protestant, a communist, a socialist, or whatever it may be. I am born with a label, and this, or some other label of my own choosing, sticks to me for the rest of my life. I am born and die in one religion, or I change from one religion to another, and I think I have understood reality, God, but I have only perpetuated the conditioned mind, the label. Now, can I, as a human being, put all that away from me without any compulsion?

I think it is very important to understand that any effort made to free oneself from one's conditioning is another form of conditioning. If I try to free myself from Hinduism, or any other ism, I am making that effort in order to achieve what I consider to be a more desirable state; therefore, the motive to change conditions the change. So I must realize my own conditioning and do absolutely nothing. This is very difficult. But I must know for myself that my mind is small, petty, confused, conditioned, and see that any effort to change it is still within the field of that confusion; therefore, any such effort only breeds further confusion.

I hope I am making this clear. If your mind is confused, as the minds of most people are, then your thought, your action, and your choice of a leader will also be confused. But if you know that you are confused, and realize that any effort born of that confusion can only bring still further confusion, then what happens? If you are fundamentally, deeply aware of that fact, then you will see quite a different process at work. It is not the process of effort; there is no wanting to break through your confusion. You know that you are totally confused, and therefore there is the cessation of all thinking.

This is a very difficult thing to comprehend because we are so certain that thinking, rationalizing, logical reasoning, can resolve our problems. But we have never really examined the process of thinking. We assume that thinking will solve our problems, but we have never gone into the whole issue of what thinking is. So long as I remain a Hindu, a Christian, or what you will, my thinking must be shaped by that pattern; therefore, my thinking, my whole response to life, is conditioned. So long as I think as an Indian, a German, or whatever it is and act according to that petty, nationalistic background, it inevitably leads to separation, to hatred, to war and misery. So we have to inquire into the whole problem of thinking.

There is no freedom of thought because all thought is conditioned. There is freedom only when I understand that all thought is conditioned and am therefore free of that conditioning—which means, really, that there is no thought at all, no thinking in terms of Catholic, Hindu, Buddhist, German, or what you will, but pure observation, complete attention. In this, I think, lies the real revolution—in the immense understanding that thought does not solve the problem of existence. Which does not mean that you must become thoughtless. On the contrary. To understand the process of thinking requires not acceptance or denial but intense inquiry. When the mind understands the whole process of itself, there is then a fundamental revolution, a radical change, which is not brought about through conscious effort. It is an effortless state, out of which comes a total transformation.

But this transformation is not of time. It is not a thing about which you can say to yourself, "It will come eventually; I must work at it, I must do this and not that." On the contrary, the moment you introduce time as a factor of change, there is no real change at all.

The immeasurable is not of this world; it is not put together by the mind because what the mind has put together, the mind can undo. To understand the immeasurable, which is to enter into a different world altogether, we must understand this world in which we live, this world which we have created and of which we are a part—the world of ambition, greed, envy, hatred, the world of separation, fear, and lust. That means we must understand ourselves, the unconscious as well as the conscious, and this is not very difficult if you set your mind to it. If you really want to know the totality of your own being, you can easily discover it. It reveals itself in every relationship, at every moment—when you are entering the bus, getting a taxi, or talking to someone.

But most of us are not concerned with that because it requires serious endeavor, persistent inquiry. Most of us are very superficial; we are easily satisfied with such words as *God, love, beauty.* We call ourselves Christians, Buddhists, or Hindus and think we have solved the whole problem. We must shed all that, let it drop away completely, and it will drop away only when we begin to know ourselves deeply. It is only through understanding ourselves that we shall find something which is beyond all measure.

These are not mere words for you to learn and repeat. What you repeat will have no meaning unless you directly experience this. If you do not have your own direct understanding of it, the world of effort and sorrow, of misery and chaos, will continue.

Question: You talk so much against the church and organized religion. Have they not done a lot of good in this world?

KRISHNAMURTI: I am not talking against the church and organized religion. It is up to you. Personally I do not belong to any church or organized religion because to me they have no meaning, and I think that if you are earnestly seeking what is real, you will have to put all those things aside—which does not mean that I am attacking. If you attack, you have to defend, but we are neither attacking nor defending. We are trying to understand this whole problem of existence, in which the church and organized religions are included.

I do not think any organized religion helps man to find God, truth. They may condition you to believe in God, as the communist mind is conditioned not to believe in God, but I do not see much difference between the two. The man who says, "I believe in God," and who has been trained from childhood to believe in God, is in the same field as the man who says, "I do not believe in God," and who has also been conditioned to repeat this kind of nonsense. But a man who wants to find out begins to inquire for himself. He does not merely accept some authority, some book or savior. If he is really in earnest, pursuing understanding in his daily thoughts, in his whole way of life, he abandons all belief and disbelief. He is an inquirer, a real seeker, without any motive; he is on a journey of discovery, single, alone. And when he finds, life has quite a different significance. Then perhaps he may be able to help others to be free.

The questioner wants to know if the organized religions have not done good. Have they? I believe there is only one organized religion which has not brought misery to man through war—and it is obviously not Christianity. You have had more wars, perhaps, than any other religion—all in the name of peace, love, goodness, freedom. You have probably suffered more than most people the terrors of war and degradation—with both sides always claiming that God is with them. You know all this so well, without my repetition.

I think it is we who have made this world what it is. The world has not been made by wisdom, by truth, by God; we have made it, you and I. And until you and I fundamentally change, no organized religion is going to do good to man. They may socially do good, bring about superficial reforms. But it has taken centuries to civilize religions, and it will take centuries to civilize communism. A man who is really in earnest must be free from all these things. He must go beyond all the saviors, all the gods and demagogues, to find out what is true.

Question: Will self-knowledge put an end to suffering, which apparently necessitates the soul taking birth over and over again?

KRISHNAMURTI: The idea is that so long as you have to suffer, you must be reborn, until you transcend suffering. That is the old Hindu, Buddhist, or Asiatic idea. They say you must return to the earth, be reborn over and over again and continue to suffer until you understand the whole process of suffering and step out of it.

In one way it is true, is it not? Our life is suffering. Year after year, from the time we are born until we die, our life is a process of struggle, suffering, pain, anxiety, fear. We know this all too well. It is a form of continuity—the continuity of suffering, is it not? Whether you will be reborn, to suffer again until you understand, is irrelevant. You do suffer now, within the present lifetime. And can we put an end to suffering, not at some future date, but immediately, and not think in terms of time?

I think it is possible. Not that you must accept what I say because acceptance has no validity. But can one not begin to inquire for oneself whether suffering can come to an end? I am talking of psychological suffering, not the bodily aches and pains—although if we understand the psychological state of the mind, it may perhaps help to ameliorate our physical suffering also. So, can suffering come to an end? Or is man doomed to suffer everlastingly—not in the Christian sense of hellfire and all that rubbish, but in the ordinary sense? After all, fifty years or so of suffering is good enough. You don't have to speculate about the future.

If we begin to inquire into it, I think we shall find that suffering exists so long as there is ignorance of the whole process of one's own being. So long as I do not know myself, the ways and compulsions of my own mind, unconscious as well as conscious, there must be suffering. After all, we suffer because of ignorance—ignorance in the sense of not knowing oneself. Ignorance is also a lack of understanding of the ordinary daily contacts between man and man, and out of that ignorance comes much suffering also, but I am talking of our utter lack of self-knowledge. Without self-knowledge, suffering will continue.

Question: Is it possible to influence the thinking of mankind in the right direction by suitable thoughts and meditation?

KRISHNAMURTI: I think this is one of the most extraordinary concerns of man—the desire to influence somebody else. That is what you are all doing, is it not? You are trying to influence your son, your daughter, your husband, your wife, everybody around you—thinking that you know and the other does not. It is a form of vanity.

Really, what do you know? Very little, surely. You may be a great scientist and know a lot of facts; you may know many things that have been written in books, you may know about philosophy and psychology—but these are all merely the acquisitions of memory. And beyond that, what do you know? Yet you want to influence people in the right direction. That is what the communists are doing. They think they know; they interpret history in a certain way, as the church does, and they all want to influence people. And they jolly well are influencing people—putting them in concentration camps, trapping them with threats of hell-fire, excommunication, and all the rest of it. You know all this business—which is supposed to be influencing people in the right direction. Those who do the influencing think they know what the right direction is. They all claim to have the vision of what is true. The communists claim it, and in the case of the church, it is supposed to be God-given. And you want to join one or the other of them, through "right thinking," as you call it.

But first of all, do you know what thinking is? Can there ever be right thinking so long as the mind is conditioned, so long as you are thinking of yourself as a Christian, a communist, or what you will? Surely the whole idea of trying to influence people is totally wrong.

Then you may ask, "What are you trying to do?" I assure you I am not trying to influence you. I am pointing out certain obvious things, which perhaps you have not thought about before—and the rest is up to you. There is no "good" influence or "bad" influence when you are seeking what is true. To find out for oneself what is true, all influence must cease. There is no "good" conditioning or "bad" conditioning—there is only freedom from all conditioning. So the idea of trying to influence another for his "good" seems to me utterly immature, completely false.

Then there is this problem of meditation, which the questioner raises. It is a very complex problem, and I do not know if you want to go into it.

Unless we know for ourselves what meditation is and how to meditate, life has very little depth. Without meditation there is no perfume to life, no beauty, no love. Meditation is a tremendous thing, requiring a great deal of insight, perception. One may know that state, one may feel it occasionally. When one is sitting very quietly in one's room or under a tree looking at the blue sky, there comes a feeling of immensity without measure, without comparison, without cognition. But that is entirely different from the things that you have learned about meditation. You have probably read various books from India, telling how to meditate, and so you want to learn a technique in order to meditate.

The very process of learning a technique in which to meditate is a denial of meditation. Meditation is something entirely different. It is not the outcome of any practice, of any discipline, of any compulsion or conformity. But if you begin to understand the process of conformity, of compulsion, the desire to achieve, to gain something, then the understanding of all that is part of meditation. Self-knowledge—which is to know the ways of your own thought and to pursue thought right to the end—is the beginning of meditation.

It is very difficult to pursue a thought to the end because other thoughts come in, and then we say we must learn concentration. But concentration is not important. Any child is capable of concentration—give him a new toy and he is concentrated. Every businessman is concentrated when he wants to make money. Concentration, which we think we should have in order to meditate, is really narrowness, a process of limitation, exclusion.

So when you put the question, "How am I to meditate?" what is important is to understand why you ask "how." If you go into it, you will find this very inquiry is meditation.

But that is only a beginning. In meditation there is no thinker apart from thought; there is neither the pursuer nor the pursued. It is a state of being in which there is no sense of the experiencer. But to come to that state, the mind must really understand the whole process of itself. If it does not understand itself, it will get caught in its own projection, in a vision which it has created, and to be caught in a vision is not meditation.

Meditation is the process of understanding oneself; that is the beginning of it. Self-knowledge brings wisdom. And as the mind begins to understand the whole process of itself, it becomes very quiet, completely still, without any sense of movement or demand. Then, perhaps, that which is not measurable comes into being.

September 16, 1956

Athens, Greece, 1956

First Talk in Athens

I do not think that the social problem can be separated from the individual problem, and to resolve the social as well as the individual problem, surely one must begin with oneself. If one wants to bring about a fundamental change in society, it seems to me that it is first necessary to bring about a fundamental change in oneself. So I am going to talk this evening, and at the next two meetings, about those problems which I feel are fundamental to the individual, and which reflect in our social activities; and I hope you will understand that I am talking to you as an individual, and not as a collective group.

It seems to me that it is very important for the individual to bring about a fundamental, unforced revolution or transformation within himself. Considering the many problems that we have, not only in this country, but all over the world, I think that the right response to them can come about only if there is a totally different kind of religion, a wholly new approach. The world is broken up, as we can see only too well, into conflicting ideologies, competing religions, and various forms of social culture. There is not only the communist ideology but the many religious ideologies, all of which separate man from man. So it seems to me very important that we should try to bring about a different kind of world, a different view of life altogether, so that we can have a totally new comprehension of religion.

I do not mean by religion an organized set of beliefs but something which is totally different from that which exists everywhere at present. Because, after all, religion is a fundamental necessity for man—more so, it seems to me, than bread. And what I mean by religion is the discovery of the fundamental solution, the ultimate answer to all our major problems. I do not mean by religion a mere belief, a dogma, nor following a certain ecclesiastical authority—which is what is called religion today. But is it not possible for something else to take place? Is it not possible for the mind to be totally free from the vast tradition of centuries? Because it is only a free mind that can discover truth, reality, that which is beyond the projections of a conditioned mind. That is why I think that the unconditioned mind is the only truly religious mind, and that only the truly religious mind is capable of a fundamental revolution.

Our life, both in our work and during our free time, leads to a very superficial relationship between man and man, does it not? It is a false life. And I feel that a fundamental change depends upon understanding what is true, and not upon belief in any religious dogma or spiritual authority. If you feel really deeply the need to be aware of what is true, then you will see that every form of belief or dogma is a hindrance. We are, after all, brought up to believe in certain ideas, whether of the communist world, of the Western world, or of the Eastern world; we have accepted established beliefs, and to free ourselves from this conditioning is not easy. But surely it is impossible, under any circumstances, to find out what is true, what is God, so long as one merely believes in certain ideas, certain concepts which man has himself created for his own security.

If I am born in India, for instance, and am educated in a certain sphere of thought, subjected to certain influences and pressures, my mind is obviously conditioned; it is as conditioned to believe as the communist mind is conditioned not to believe. And if I would find out what is true, what is God, what is beyond the mere measure of the mind, surely I must free my mind from this conditioning—which seems so obvious.

And is it possible for the mind to free itself from its conditioning? That, it seems to me, is the only realistic approach. If the Hindu merely continues to repeat certain words and perform certain ceremonies because he has been brought up in that way, and the Christians, the Buddhists, and others do likewise, then surely there is no freedom; and without freeing the mind from all conditioning, we cannot find out what is true. To me, this freedom of the mind from all conditioning is therefore the only real solution.

So, first of all, it is very important to become aware of our conditioning. And I assure you, it is extremely difficult to realize that one is conditioned and be free of all conditioning. What usually happens is that we move away from one set of concepts to follow another. We give up Christianity for communism, or we leave Catholicism for some other equally tyrannical group, thinking that we are progressing towards reality, but we have merely changed our prison.

Surely, what is important is to free the mind from all conditioning, and not just find a so-called better conditioning. Only freedom from all conditioning can bring about this revolution which I call religious. I am talking about an inner revolution, a revolution within the mind itself, whether it be a Christian mind, a Hindu mind, or a Buddhist mind; for without this revolution, this freedom, surely there can be no deep understanding. I think this is fairly clear—that the mind can find out what is true only when it is free of all beliefs, however apparently good and noble.

Economic or social revolutions do not solve our problems because, being superficial, they can only bring about superficial results. When we look to outward reforms to bring about a fundamental change, it is surely a wrong approach to the problem. We obviously need a fundamental change in our way of thinking and feeling, and to rely on any social or economic solution only brings further problems on the same level.

So the solution to all our problems, it seems to me, lies in bringing about a fundamental, religious revolution in ourselves. This really means, does it not, finding out whether the mind can free itself from all the impositions, from the ambitions, the beliefs and dogmas in which at present it feels so secure. Can the mind—your mind and my mind—which has been conditioned from childhood to believe or not to believe, free itself from all its present conditioning without falling into a different kind of conditioning?

The problem is complicated because it is not merely a matter of freeing the conscious mind from its conditioning. Besides the waking consciousness of our daily activities, there are also the deep layers of the unconscious, in which there are the accumulated influences of the past. All these hindrances make up the conditioning of the mind, and unless it is totally free from them, our inquiry is bound to be limited, narrow, without much significance. Merely to drop certain beliefs or daily habits does not solve the problem. There must be a change, not in just a part of our consciousness, but in the totality of our being, must there not?

Now, how is this to be done? That is our problem. Is there a particular technique or method which will bring about a fundamental revolution in one's consciousness? We see that necessity for a radical change, and by following a method, a technique, we hope to bring it about. But is there any method that can bring it about? Or does the very action of seeking a method, the very desire to find the "how," create another conditioning of the mind? I think it is very important, instead of merely desiring a method, to find out for ourselves whether a method is necessary at all; and to find out, we shall have to go very deeply into this question. After all, when we ask for a method, it is because we want a result; but the desired result is a projection of the conditioned mind; and in pursuing it, the mind is merely moving towards another form of conditioning.

First of all we must inquire, must we not, why we are seeking, and what it is we are seeking. We know that we go from one teacher to another. Each teacher offers a different method of discipline or meditation—and all that is so absurd. What is important, surely, is not the teacher and what he offers but to find out what it is you are seeking. By delivering yourself into the hands of another, by following some authority, by practicing a discipline, controlling yourself, sooner or later you will find what you want, but it will not be the truth. The following of any method only perpetuates conditioning, perhaps in a new form, and so the mind is never free to understand what is true.

Now, if one really perceives that the very demand for a method—whether it be the Buddhist method, the Christian method, or any other—is only another form of conditioning which prevents the mind from finding the truth, then what is one to do? One can understand superficially, perhaps, that dependence on authority, however promising, is detrimental to the discovery of what is true; but it is very difficult, is it not, to free ourselves from all dependence on authority, whether it be the authority of the church, of society, or the authority which one has created for oneself through one's own experience. If you are serious in these matters, if you are really trying to find out whether the mind can free itself from authority, you will know how difficult it is. Yet the mind must be free from authority, obviously; otherwise, it can never find out what is true. We depend on authority because, among other things, we are afraid of not attaining salvation, and the mind that is dependent cannot know the immeasurable, that which is beyond all churches, all dogmas and beliefs. There must be total freedom, which means that the mind must be capable of standing completely alone.

So, can the mind completely free itself from fear, from the dictates of society and so-called religious beliefs? Surely, if one really desires to find the truth, one must be totally free from all conditioning, from all dogmas and beliefs, from the authorities that make us conform. One must stand completely alone—and that is very arduous. It is not a matter of going out into the country on a Sunday morning, sitting quietly under a tree, and so on. The aloneness of which I am speaking is pure, incorruptible; it is free of all tradition, of all dogma and opinion, of everything that another has said. When the mind is in this state of aloneness, it is quiet, essentially still, not asking for anything, and such a mind is capable of knowing what is true. Otherwise we are ever burdened with fear, which creates so much conflict and confusion in us and in the world.

So the religious revolution of which I am speaking can come about only when the mind is free from all the so-called religions, with their dogmas and beliefs, and from self-created inward authority. And there can be this freedom, surely, only through self-knowledge. But self-knowledge cannot be found in books; it is not a matter of reading psychology or following the description of another as to what the self is made up of. Self-knowledge comes only in understanding oneself, in watching the movement of one's own mind in relationship with people, with things, and with ideas; it lies in being aware of the whole content of the mind, in observing the total operations of one's consciousness from moment to moment.

I shall now read a question which has been sent to me, but I think we must all understand that I am not answering the question, but rather we are considering the problem together. Most of us have problems and want to solve them. Whatever the problem may be, we want an answer or a solution which will be satisfactory to us. That is, we are concerned with the answer, the solution, and not with the problem. Our attention is divided; with one part of the mind we are seeking a solution, instead of trying with the totality of our being to understand the problem. The solution may or may not come, but to understand the problem, our concern must be with the problem itself, and not with the solution.

Question: What makes up a problem? And is any problem solved by dissecting it and finding its cause?

KRISHNAMURTI: What is a problem? Please do not just wait for an answer from me. You are not merely listening to someone talking, but we are trying to find out together what creates a problem. You each have your own problems. How do they come into being?

We have contradictory desires, do we not? I want to be rich, let us say, and at the same time I know or have heard that wealth is detrimental to the discovery of truth. So there is a contradiction in my desires—the contradiction of wanting and not wanting. It is this conflict of contradictory desires in us that creates a problem, is it not? We have many contradictory desires, many conflicting pursuits, ambitions, urges, and all these contradictions create a problem. Now, can the mind ever resolve the problem of self-contradiction by imposing one desire on another?

Take hatred, for example. What causes hatred? Surely, one of the biggest factors is chauvinism; another is the sense of superiority or inferiority created by economic differences; still another is the division created between man and man by what are called religions. These are the principal causes of hatred, and they give rise to many other major problems in the world today. Knowing all this, can the individual free himself from hatred? This is where our difficulty lies, and if you will listen carefully I think you will see it.

When I say, "I know the cause of hatred," what do I mean by the words "I know"? Do I know it merely through the word, the intellect, or do I know it with the totality of my being? Am I aware of the root of hatred in myself, or do I know its cause only intellectually or emotionally? If the mind is totally aware of the problem, then there is freedom from the problem, but I cannot be aware of it with the totality of my being if I condemn the problem. It is very difficult for the mind not to condemn, but to understand a problem, there must be no condemning of that problem, no comparing of it with another problem.

I do not think we realize that we are all the time either condemning or comparing. Let us not try to excuse ourselves but just watch our daily life, and we shall see that we never think without judging, comparing, evaluating. We are always saying, "This book is not as good as the other one," or "This man is better than that man"; there is a constant process of comparison through which we think we understand. But do we really understand through comparison? Or does understanding come only when one ceases to compare, and just observes? When your mind is integrated, you have no time to compare, have you? But the moment you compare, your attention has already moved elsewhere. When you say, "This sunset is not as beautiful as that of yesterday," you do not really see the sunset, for your mind has wandered off to the memory of yesterday.

When the mind is capable of not condemning, not comparing, but merely examines the problem, then surely the problem has undergone a fundamental change, and then the problem ceases. Simple awareness is enough to put an end to the problem.

What do we mean by awareness? If you observe your own mind, you will see that it is always comparing, judging, condemning. When we condemn or compare, do we understand? If we condemn a child or compare him with his brother, obviously we do not understand him. So, can the mind be simply aware of a problem without condemning or comparing? This is extremely difficult because from childhood we have been brought up to condemn and to compare. And can the mind cease to condemn and compare without being compelled? Surely, when the mind sees for itself that to condemn or to compare does not bring about understanding, then that very perception frees the mind from all condemnation and comparison. This means a complete separation of the mind from all traditions and beliefs.

To free one's mind in this deep sense requires a great deal of insight because the mind is very easily influenced. It is always seeking security, not only in this world, in society, but also in the so-called spiritual world. If you go into the whole process of your own mind, you will see that this is so, and a mind that is seeking security can never be free.

To observe the total process of the mind without condemnation or comparison, to be conscious of it without judgment, to recognize and understand it from moment to moment—this is awareness, is it not?

You have listened to what is being said, and probably you either approve or disapprove of it, which means that you accept or reject it. But we are not just dealing with ideas, which can be accepted or rejected; we are not putting new ideas in the place of old ones. We are concerned with the totality of the mind, the totality of yourself, of your whole being, which cannot be approached through ideas. Please do not accept or reject but try to find out, as you listen, how your own mind is operating. Then you will see that the mere observation of the process of the mind is in itself sufficient to bring about a fundamental transformation within the mind.

We see that there must be in us a radical change, and we think that we have to make an effort to bring it about. But any effort in that direction is merely another form of wanting a result, so we are back again in the same old process. What is necessary, surely, is not more control, more knowledge, but rather awareness of the totality of oneself, without any sense of condemnation or approval. Then you will find that the mind is renewed and absolutely still. For this an exceptional amount of energy is required, but it is not energy spent in the usual way—on comparison, on suppression, on the imposition of discipline, nor is it the energy acquired through prayer. It is the energy that comes with full attention. Every movement of thought in any direction is a waste of energy, and to be completely still, the mind needs the energy of absolute attention. When the mind is alert, aware, wholly attentive, it becomes very quiet, very still, and only then is it possible for that which is immeasurable to come into being.

September 24, 1956

Second Talk in Athens

Communication is always difficult because in communicating we must employ words, and certain words have different meanings for different people, and I think it is very difficult for most of us to go beyond the words and feel out for ourselves the full significance of what lies beyond. There are words which have not only a dictionary meaning but more than that; our minds are heavily conditioned to them. Take words like *love* and *God*. Such words have come to have a particular meaning for each one of us, and they affect us in different ways, physiologically as well as psychologically. We accept such words very easily because we have been brought up to believe in what they represent. But what they represent for most of us is very restricted and superficial, and it will be a waste of time if we merely remain at the threshold of the meaning of words.

To follow what is being communicated and not be misled by words requires a particular kind of attention, and this attention is difficult to come by. Most of us are satisfied with a certain set of words or phrases which we have often heard and which we repeat. But perhaps this evening we could go beyond the words and feel out for ourselves the significance of what is being said. Because after all, in these talks we are not merely trying to express certain ideas—however pleasant or unpleasant—but if possible to go beyond the meaning of words and experience a new state which we all feel must exist.

Understanding depends on the way one listens. As we listen, are we discussing inwardly what is being said, interpreting it according to our individual opinions, knowledge, and idiosyncrasies? Or are we simply listening, without any movement of adjustment or interpretation? There are two ways of listening. One can listen merely to the words, see their usual significance and understand only their outward meaning; or one can listen to the verbal exposition, and follow it inwardly—that is, understand what is being described as one's own experience. So may I suggest, if this experiment is to be useful and worthwhile, that we should not merely listen to the words, but in listening, examine, if we can, the very process of our own thinking.

We are trying to find out what is the real process of life, and what lies behind the superficial activities of our daily existence. If we would really experience what we are talking about, it must be done directly, now; it is of no value to wait and think about it afterwards. That is, if you are taking notes, trying to capture certain phrases in order to think about all this afterwards, it will be of no value because you will merely be remembering words. To discover for yourself the significance of your own thinking, you must directly examine how you think and actually experience the whole process of it. Because it seems to me that thought is not going to solve our many problems; however reasonable, however clever, logical, thinking surely will not put an end to our ceaseless conflict. Not that you must accept this statement, but can we find out for ourselves what thinking is?

Please examine your own thought process as I am talking, and ask yourself what thinking is. Thinking is a process or reaction, is it not? It is a reaction according to our background, according to the environment in which we live and have been brought up; and without understanding this background, we shall never find out whether it is possible for the mind to go beyond the process of its own activities.

What happens when we think? Without realizing it, the mind divides itself, and then one section of the mind investigates the other, giving an answer out of its own accumulated experience or according to the accepted experiences of others. This effort makes up what we call thinking, and the resulting answer is but the projection of a conditioned mind.

Surely our problems demand quite a different approach; they demand a really new psychological outlook, but we must understand the process of our own thinking before we can go beyond thought. That is why it is important to inquire for ourselves into how our thinking begins and where it stops, because if we do not understand the activity of our own thought, we shall only create more problems, and perhaps bring about our own destruction.

When we think, we do so within a framework which society has imposed on us, or which we ourselves have adopted; and it seems to me that so long as we think within a framework, our problems, whether social or individual, will remain unsolved. I feel it is very important that you and I as two individuals, not as a group, should investigate for ourselves the process of our own thinking.

Is there freedom in thinking, or is all thought limited? If you look into yourself, you will see that all thinking is conditioned. The mind, the conscious as well as the unconscious, is the result of time, of memory; it is the residue of various cultures, of centuries of knowledge and experience. The totality of consciousness is made up of thought, and thought, surely, derives from this residue of the past, both individual and collective. So our thinking is obviously conditioned.

If we examine ourselves, we shall see that our consciousness is the outcome of many influences: climate, diet, various forms of authority, the do's and don'ts of society and of the religion in which we have been brought up, the books we have read, the reactions we have felt, and so on. All these influences condition and shape the mind, and from this background comes our thought. Furthermore, our thinking is based on hope, on fear, on the desire to become something, all of which is encouraged and stimulated by the competitive society in which we have been brought up. So all thinking is conditioned; it is merely a process of reaction according to the past, and the question is: Can such thinking solve our many problems?

I hope you are giving close attention to all this; otherwise, you will miss the significance of it. There is no unlimited thinking; thinking is always limited, and to find out what lies beyond thought, thought must first come to an end. After all, being limited, prejudiced, shaped by society, how can thought inquire into something which is measureless? If I want to find out what love is, for example, how shall I proceed? Shall I think about it, read what has been said in the Bible, in the sacred books, or by some priest? Surely, to find out what love is, I must first see whether my mind is conditioned by the idea which society calls "love," or by organized religion—which preaches love, but which has actually destroyed human beings. Because it is only when my mind is free from all conditioning that I shall be able to find out what love is. In the same way, to find out if there is truth, if there is God, my mind must be free from all the beliefs and prejudices in which it has been brought up.

So to discover something true, not conditioned, not contaminated, you must in one sense cease to think. I hope you understand what I mean. After all, if you have beliefs, if you hold on to certain ideas, they are obviously going to interfere with your listening to what is being said. In order to experience something real, something which is not merely an opposite, the mind must free itself from its own beliefs and be completely still. Having been brought up in a certain society, educated according to a particular ideology, with its dogmas and traditions, the mind is conditioned; and any movement of the mind to free itself, being the result of that conditioning, only leads to still further conditioning. The mind can free itself only when it is completely alone. Even though it is burdened with problems, with innumerable tendencies, conflicts, ambitions, through awareness without condemnation or acceptance, the mind can begin to understand its own functioning; and then an extraordinary silence comes about, a stillness in which there is no movement of thought. Then the mind is free because it is no longer desiring anything, no longer asking for anything; it is no longer anchored to an ideology or aiming at a purpose—all of which are merely the projections of a conditioned mind. Unless you undergo this actual experience so that it is not merely a verbal statement which you have heard from another, life remains very superficial and sorrowful.

So for those who are really serious about this matter, it seems to me that what is important is not what you believe or do not believe but to understand the process of your own thinking. In that direct understanding of one's own thinking, a radical change in one's living will take place which is not according to any social plan or religious dogma, and only then will it be possible for the external structure of society to change also.

A number of questions have been sent to me, and I shall try to go into some of them.

Question: Psychoanalysts offer the panacea of analysis, asserting that by just knowing what it is all about, one is cured, but this does not always hold true. What is one to do when in spite of knowing the cause of one's trouble, one is still unable to get rid of it?

KRISHNAMURTI: You see, in this problem there is involved the analyzer and the analyzed. You may not go to a psychoanalyst; you may analyze yourself, but in either case there is always the analyzer and the analyzed. When you try to examine the unconscious or interpret a dream, there is the examiner and the examined; and the examiner, the interpreter, analyzes what he sees in terms of his own background, according to his pleasure. So there is always a division between the analyzer and the analyzed, with the analyzer trying to reshape or control that which he has analyzed. And the question is not only whether the analyzer is capable of analyzing, but more fundamentally whether there is actually any division between the analyzer and the analyzed. We have assumed that there is such a division, but is there in actuality? The analyzer, surely, is also the result of our thinking. So really there is no division at all, but we have artificially created one. If we see the truth of this, if we realize the fact that the thinker is not separate from his thought, that there is only thinking and no thinker—and it is very difficult to come to that realization—then our whole approach to the problem of inner conflict changes.

After all, if you do not think, where is the thinker? The qualities of thinking, the memory of various experiences together with the desire to be secure, to be permanent, have created the thinker apart from thinking. We say that thinking is passing, but that the thinker is permanent. You may call the thinker permanent, enduring, divine, or anything else you like, but in reality there is no thinker, but only the process of thinking. And if there is only thinking, and not a thinker who thinks, then without a thinker, an analyzer, how shall we solve our problem?

Am I explaining the matter clearly or only complicating it? Perhaps it is not very clear because you are merely listening to my words; you are not directly experiencing the thing. There is a great difference between having a toothache and listening to the description of a toothache, is there not? And I am afraid something of that sort is what is happening now. You are merely listening to the description, hoping to find a way to solve your problems.

Briefly, what I am saying is this: If you once fully understand that there is only thinking and no thinker, then there is a tremendous revolution in your whole approach to life, because in experiencing for yourself that there is only thinking, and not a thinker who must control thought, you have at one stroke removed the very source of conflict. It is the division between the thinker and the thought that creates conflict, and if one is capable of removing that division, there is no problem.

Question: What would happen to the world if all men and women were to arrive at a state so far removed from attachment to a definite person that marriage and love affairs became unnecessary?

KRISHNAMURTI: Is not the questioner putting a very hypothetical question? Should we not rather ask ourselves whether there is love when there is attachment? Our attachments are based on mutual satisfaction, mutual support, are they not? Each one needs the companionship of another. So instead of asking this theoretical question, I think it is important to find out if there is love at all when there is attachment.

Is there love when we are attached, when we possess somebody? And why are we attached? To really go into it, to inquire why one is attached, not only to a man or a woman, but to children, to ideas, to property, and find out for oneself if it is possible to be free of all possessing and possessiveness—this, I think, demands a great deal of hard inner work. If you were not attached, what would happen? You would be at a loss, would you not? We are attached because in ourselves we are insufficient, psychologically dependent, and therein lies our misery.

Question: How is one to deal with a very small child if one is to avoid influencing him in any way?

KRISHNAMURTI: Why does one try not to influence a small child? Let us consider. Are we not all influenced? You are influenced by climate, by society, by the food you eat, by the papers you read—you are influenced by everything around you. It is not a matter of good or bad influence—we are considering influence itself. What you call a good influence, another society might call bad or false. What is important, I think, is to understand the whole problem of influence, and then perhaps we shall approach differently the education of the child. We know that we are being influenced in some degree by everything around us, and is it possible to be free from the influences which are strongly or subtly impressing us, dominating us? To be free of such influences, we must be aware, must we not, of the many factors which create them.

Take, for instance, the influence of the flag, of the nation, of the word *patriotism.* We accept that influence all over the world, for every school, every government is sedulously conditioning us to accept it, and that is one of the basic causes of war because it separates man from man. So can we, the grown-up people, free ourselves from this influence? If we can, then perhaps we shall be able to help the child to be free. But to be free from this particular influence demands a great deal of insight, understanding, for there is the possibility that you may be ostracized, you may lose your job, and you will be a nobody in society.

Let us take another example. Whether we live as of the world or try to be religious, most of us are ambitious. We can see that ambition is destructive, but socially and religiously we accept it. The ambitious man can never love because he is concerned with himself and his success—success in the name of God, in the name of family, in the name of country. The worship of success is also an influence throughout the world, is it not? And can one free oneself from this influence? Can you as an individual do it? Do not say, "If I am not ambitious, I shall be crushed by society." If you really see the truth that ambition is destructive and deeply understand the whole process of influence, you will be a different person, and then perhaps you will be able to help the child to understand and be free of all influence.

Question: Is it possible to live without any attachment?

KRISHNAMURTI: Instead of asking this question, why don't you find out? And to ask, "How am I to become detached?" is another false question. Find out to what you are attached, and why. You are attached to your family, to your property, to your name, to your beliefs and ideas, to your business—to a dozen things. To be free from this attachment, you must first be aware that you are attached, and not merely ask if it is possible to live without attachment; you must experience the fact that you are attached, and understand why. You are attached, for instance, to the idea of God, of truth, or to some belief or ideal because without that concept and the feeling it evokes, your life would be empty, miserable; you would have nothing to rely on. So your attachment is a form of drug, and knowing the fundamental reason for attachment, you then try to cultivate detachment, which is still another escape. That is why it is very important to study the process of one's whole being, and not merely try to clarify what to believe and what not to believe, which is all so superficial.

The key to freedom lies within ourselves, but we refuse to use it. We are always asking someone else to open the door and let the light in.

September 26, 1956

Third Talk in Athens

It seems to me that one of the most difficult problems we have to face is how to bring about a fundamental change in our selves, and everyone who is seriously interested in these things must surely face this problem. How is the mind to bring about a change in itself which will be a revolution, and not merely a new division, another alteration, a disciplined reform? If we want to create a world that is without hatred, a world in which there is love, in which man does not turn against man, then I think it is essential that you and I as individuals should contribute to the realization of such a revolution by a fundamental transformation in ourselves. This is the subject on which I am going to talk this evening, and as it is rather complicated, I hope you will be patient enough to listen with attention.

To find out if it is possible to bring about such a revolution, I think one has to begin by experimenting with oneself. In this country, as in every other, you have many troubles. Although everyone is trying to bring peace, unconsciously we go on working towards war. We desperately need peace in the world, but the fact is that we are creating still more confusion and misery. That is what is happening in the world around us and within ourselves. We have many contradictory desires, deep-rooted urges and restraining ideals which bring about conflict. We strive after harmony, but whatever we do only seems to create more confusion and less peace.

Seeing all this confusion taking place around us and within ourselves, one wonders how a radical change is to be brought about. If we look into ourselves, we can see that the mind is capable of improving a part of itself, but it remains only a part, and even if that one part manages to dominate all the rest, the mind will be in a state of continuous conflict. Conflict is inevitable, is it not, so long as one part of ourselves is trying to improve or to control the other part. The conflict arises, surely, from this division in the mind.

Now, is it possible to bring about a total change, and not merely a partial one? I do not know if you understand the problem, but I think it is very important to do so. Is it possible to bring about a fundamental transformation without conflict, without one part of the mind trying to dominate another part? It seems to me that this is possible only if we realize the urgency of a total change, and see the falsity of one part of ourselves, which we call "higher," striving to dominate the "lower"; for surely the "higher" is still within the field of the mind, and is therefore also the outcome of conflict.

To change fundamentally, completely, without one part of the mind seeking to dominate another part and thereby creating further conflict, we must give our total attention to it. But usually we never give our full attention to anything, do we? We give only a partial attention. We look at a problem of this kind through the screen of our religious beliefs and social convictions, or we give attention to it with the desire to achieve a result; therefore, our attention is divided, it is never complete, whole. There can be full attention only when there is not the conflict of wanting a result or pursuing an ideal, and it is only when the mind is capable of giving full attention that this radical change takes place within us.

Most of us think we must have ideals to entice us to change, but to me ideals are a distraction from the fact; they are merely a projection of the opposite of what we really are. We hope that by clinging to an ideal, we shall achieve a radical change; but the continuous effort to discipline, to control ourselves, only brings about endless conflict.

Surely, a radical change can come about only when there is no effort. So long as there is any sense of achieving an ideal, of bringing about a change through compulsion, there cannot be complete attention. A person who is really concerned with transforming himself totally will have no ideals because ideals are a distraction from the fact of *what is*. When you have an ideal, your mind is not looking at the actual, but at 'what should be', and so attention is incomplete. To bring about a fundamental change, a new way of thinking, a revolution within oneself, one must understand the necessity of total attention without any distraction—which is, after all, a state of love. Love is not the product of effort, of distraction, of control according to an ideal; it is total attention in which the contradictory impulses, with all their accumulative memories, completely cease.

To put it differently, what most of us are trying to do is to change through time. We think that time will give to the mind an opportunity to bring about a gradual change within itself. Being envious, we have the ideal of becoming free from envy in the future, and through time we think we shall achieve this ideal—which to me is an escape, a distraction from the actual fact. So, can one give one's total attention to the problem of envy, without any distraction? That is, can one approach the problem of envy completely anew?

It is true, is it not, that we generally move from the known to the known, and this is not a radical change, it is not a revolution. The ideal is still within the field of the known and does not bring about a fundamental transformation. The process of changing through time is based on the principle preached by religious teachers and sacred books, "I am this, I must become that, and the change will come about in time through discipline, control." We can see how the mind works, how it has invented various systems of discipline to control itself; but surely this process is totally false because all forms of discipline, control, compulsion are still within the field of the known and do not contribute to a radical change. In this process of continuity, moving from yesterday through today towards tomorrow, there is no fundamental transformation.

So the problem is—and I hope you are not just listening to words, but are experiencing the thing we are talking about—can the mind come to an end without compulsion, without any form of discipline, which means that it has understood itself completely? Because that very understanding is a process of revolution. Truth or God is something totally unknown; you may imagine, you may speculate about it, you may believe it is this or that, but it is still the unknown. The mind must come to it completely stripped of the past, free of all the things it has known; and the known is, after all, the accumulated memories and problems of everyday existence. So if there is really to be a radical change, a fundamental transformation, the mind must move away from the known. For love is not something which you experienced yesterday and are able to recapture at will tomorrow; it is totally new, unknown.

The mind, being the result of the known, of time, can never bring about a radical change within itself. Any change which it brings about can only be a superficial alteration within the field of the known. There can be a fundamental change in the mind only when the mind dies, when thinking dies—which means, really, when the self ceases to exist. This is not a system of philosophy to be conveyed by teaching. It is an inner experience to be lived, day in and day out, by the person who is seriously inquiring and who does not restrict himself to the mere repetition of phrases without meaning.

Many questions have been sent in, and I cannot go into all of them in the course of a few talks, so if your particular question is not answered, you will know why. Also, I am not "answering" these questions, but we are together trying to investigate the problem. The problem is yours, and you have to find the answer within the problem itself, not away from it.

Question: In what way can self-knowledge help to solve the many pressing problems of the world—for instance, starvation?

KRISHNAMURTI: Is not the world, with all its lies, its corruption, hatred, and starvation, brought about by human beings? Surely the problems which exist in this country and throughout the world are the product of each one of you because you are nationalistic; you want to be somebody, and therefore you identify yourself with the country; you consider yourself a Greek or a Christian, which gives you a sense of importance, and through your envy you have created a society based on acquisition. So to bring about a tremendous change in the world, you and I must change, must we not? We must know ourselves. Unfortunately most of us think that tyranny, politics, or various forms of legislation will solve our problems. But what the individual is, the world is, and to bring about a fundamental change, you, the individual, must understand yourself; and the understanding of yourself must be complete, not just partial.

Self-knowledge is the beginning of wisdom, and to know yourself is not a miracle or something extraordinary to be learned from books. You can see yourself exactly as you are in the mirror of relationship. Nothing can live in isolation; you are related to people, to things, to ideas, to nature, and in the mirror of that relationship you can see the totality of your own being. But if you condemn what you see, then obviously you stop all inquiry and understanding. Most of us have the instinct to condemn, to compare, to judge what we see. But if you once realize that to understand something, you must not condemn it, then condemnation ceases; and through the self-knowledge which comes when there is observation without condemnation, the whole mind, the unconscious as well as the conscious, can be understood. Only then is the mind completely quiet and therefore able to inquire further.

Question: If a man has no ambition, how is he to live in this world of competition?

KRISHNAMURTI: I wonder why we are ambitious? You are ambitious in your job, in your school, in everything that you do, are you not? Why are we envious, ambitious? Is it because there are a hundred motives encouraging us to be ambitious? Or is it that without ambition, without trying to get somewhere or to be something, we are nothing? If we were not ambitious, what would happen? We would be nobody, would we not? We would be unrecognized, have no dreams of success, of being great, and we would merely live, but just to live in that way does not seem very gratifying. So we create a competitive society in which ambition is encouraged, and anyone who wants to get rid of it is ignored by his neighbor. I am not talking of ambition only in the worldly sense. Anyone who wants to become something, whether in this world or the next, is ambitious. The priest who wishes to become a bishop, the clerk who wants to become an executive, the man who strives to have some so-called religious experience—they are all on the same level because they are anxious to be or to have something.

Now, seeing the havoc that ambition is causing in the world today, and realizing that a man who is ambitious can have no love, the question naturally arises: Is it possible to be completely free from ambition? I cannot answer for you; you will have to find out for yourself. But you see, the fact is that most of us want security, we want safety, we want guarantees; therefore, we live with ambition. Such people are not serious, though they may ask serious questions.

Question: What is the real meaning of brotherhood?

KRISHNAMURTI: It is fairly obvious, is it not? A man who is nationalistic is not brotherly. Nor is he brotherly who is a communist, a socialist, a capitalist, or who belongs to a particular religion, because anyone devoted to an ideology, to a system, to a belief, obviously separates himself from other men. After all, this is our world, it is yours and mine—not to live in as Greeks or Americans or Indians or Russians, but as human beings. But unfortunately we have national, economic, and religious barriers, and living behind these barriers, we talk about brotherhood, we talk about love, peace, God. To really know what love is, we must abolish all these barriers, and each one of us must begin with himself.

Question: Should one give any importance to one's dreams or not?

KRISHNAMURTI: To investigate this question directly, we must understand the process of our own consciousness. Consciousness is surely the totality of one's being, but we have divided it as the conscious and unconscious. Most of us are concerned with cultivating the conscious mind, and every school, every society is busy with the same thing. Society, of which we form a part, gives great importance to the so-called education of the conscious mind, and it tries to make us efficient, capable citizens by giving us a job.

Now, if you will observe yourself, you will see that, while the conscious mind is concerned with your daily activities, there is at the same time a hidden activity going on in the mind, of which you are largely unconscious. You will also see that there is a division or conflict between the conscious and the unconscious mind—the unconscious being not only the hidden personal motives, but also the racial influences and the collective experience of centuries. When the conscious mind goes to sleep and is relatively quiet, the unconscious draws near, and its urges then become dreams. This is what actually happens to most of us because during the day, our conscious minds are so taken up with our superficial motives and pursuits that there is no time to receive the promptings of the unconscious. So we dream, and then the problem arises of how to interpret these dreams, so we go to specialists who interpret dreams according to their pleasure, or in terms of their so-called knowledge.

It seems to me that the problem is not how to interpret dreams, but whether it is possible not to dream at all. Please do not reject this; do not drive it away. A mind that is perpetually active during the day and unconsciously active when it is asleep can never be creative. It is only when the mind is completely still, without movement, without action, that there is a possibility for a new state to come into being.

So, can the conscious mind be in such close relationship at all times with the unconscious, during the day as well as during the night, that there is never this state of confusion which necessitates the projection of dreams? Surely, when the conscious mind already knows the movements of the unconscious so that the unconscious has no need to project dreams for the conscious mind to interpret, then it is possible not to dream at all. That is, if you are constantly aware of your motives, of your prejudices, of your conditioning, of your fears, of your likes or dislikes—if you are aware of all this during the day, then when you sleep, the mind is not everlastingly disturbed by dreams. That is why it is important to be aware of one's thinking, of one's ambition, of one's motives, urges, jealousies—not to push them aside, but to understand them completely. Then the mind is very quiet, silent, and in that silence it can be free from all its conditioning. Such a mind is a religious mind, and only such a mind is capable of receiving that which is true. The mind that seeks truth will never find it; but when the mind is completely still, without any movement, without any desire, then it is possible for the immeasurable to come into being.

September 30, 1956

New Delhi, India, 1956

First Talk in New Delhi

Considering the number of problems that each human being has, not only in India, but throughout the world, it seems to me that what is important is to find a new approach to these many problems. But to find a new approach is very difficult for most of us because we think with a conclusion, and to think with a conclusion is obviously not to think at all. And it is not easy, is it, to be free from thought based on a conclusion. Most of us think of any problem, however complex it may be, as Hindus, as Christians, as Buddhists, or as communists, which indicates that we approach the problem with a mind already made up; so the problem, which demands a totally new approach, always evades us and multiplies.

Now, is it possible for human beings like you and me, as individuals, to be free from all conclusions, from any thought which is conditioned, psychologically shaped, and controlled by society, by so-called culture? I don't know if you have thought about it at all, but surely the question is not how to resolve our many problems, rather it is how to understand the problem, whatever it be. We have many problems in life, not only economic and social, but also the problem of death and whether there is immortality, the problem of whether there is reality, God, or what you will; and it seems to me that we can understand and resolve these problems only if we are able to approach them, not with a divided mind, but a mind that is totally integrated. There lies, I think, our whole difficulty. How is it possible to approach these many issues with a mind that is cleansed of all the obstructions, of all the prejudices, of all the religious conclusions and psychological pressures which have been inflicted upon it through the ages? The problem, surely, is never old; it varies and is constantly in movement, but our minds are static; they are already made up, already shaped, conditioned by our past thoughts, fears, and hopes.

So we invariably approach our problems with a mind that has already concluded, and I think the whole issue lies in being able to free the mind from all conclusions because any thinking that starts with a conclusion is no thinking at all. If I think as a Hindu, obviously my thought is not vital; it starts with an assumption, which has no validity, and tries to solve the complex problems of existence through the screen of a particular conclusion, prejudice, or idea.

Is it possible, then, to free the mind from ideation? Because these talks are not going to be an exchange of ideas. I am not going to put forward a new philosophy, a new set of ideas, dogmas, doctrines. To me, all these—beliefs, ideas, dogmas, doctrines—are impediments to the perception of what is true, and if you are expecting a new set of ideas with which to confront the swift movement of life, I am afraid you will not only be disappointed but also confused. Whereas, if we can together think out the problem anew, not as Hindus, Muslims, Buddhists, communists, or Christians, nor as the one who knows and the one who does not know, which is really absurd, but as individual human beings who are trying to solve the problem of existence, then I think these talks will be worthwhile. Because there is fundamentally only one problem, which is the whole process of existence—not a religious as opposed to a mundane existence, nor a spiritual existence as opposed to that of society.

The many human problems which confront us are becoming more and more complex, more and more vitally destructive, bringing great sorrow not only to individuals but to the collective life of peoples; and if we are to approach this whole process of existence with an integrated outlook, there must be a vital change in our thinking. Surely that is obvious, is it not? If I think as a communist, my thinking is based on an already-established conclusion which, however clever, cunning, cannot resolve the problem because the problem is totally new each time I approach it. As a human being who is desirous of understanding this whole process of existence with all its complexities—with its sorrows, divisions, and incessant conflict—I must approach it, surely, with a mind that is not conditioned as a Hindu, a Buddhist, a communist, or a Christian; but unfortunately our minds are conditioned. You know what I mean by a conditioned mind. Through education, through religious sanctions and the psychological compulsions of society, your mind has been shaped to a particular pattern. You think as a Hindu, as a Muslim, or what you will; or if you have rejected the more orthodox patterns, you think as a man who is free of all that, but who is conditioned by his own ideas, his own conclusions based on his personal study and experiences. So, is it possible to approach the problem of human existence with a mind that is entirely free from conditioning?

Our inquiry, then, is not how to resolve the problem, but rather how the mind can free itself from its conditioning so that it is made fresh, new, and can therefore tackle the problem creatively, not in this destructive, fractional way.

Please, as I said, we are discussing not to exchange ideas or to promulgate some new philosophy, which is utter nonsense, but rather to inquire deeply into ourselves as human beings and find out whether it is possible to free the mind—your mind, not somebody else's mind—from the conditioning which has been imposed upon it through centuries. If you say it is impossible to free the mind from its conditioning, or if you assume that it is possible, you have already concluded; therefore, there is no creative thinking. What matters is that through listening to what is being said, you become conscious of yourself, of your own conditioning, your own thinking, so that you are aware of how your mind operates. Then you will be able to free the mind from its conditioning, not by listening to me, but by observing your own mind through the description which I give. I think it is important to understand this right from the beginning because only then is the right relationship established between us. To me the whole idea of guru and disciple is utterly false because it only breeds slavery of thought. That is why it is so important to establish from the very beginning the right relationship between the speaker and yourself.

What we are trying to do is to find out without being told what to find, which means that you and I must have a mind capable of discovery; but we cannot discover if we start from a series of conclusions or experiences, our own or somebody else's, and in that lies our greatest difficulty. If you observe yourself, you will see that your thought is only a series of quotations from the Gita, the Koran, or the Bible, or from what Buddha or the latest saint has said, and such a mind is incapable of discovery. To discover is not only to find the solutions to our problems but also, through the understanding of our problems, to discover for ourselves what is true, whether there is reality, God, and not merely to assert that there is or there is not.

Now, how is the mind, being so conditioned, so bound by authority, by tradition, to free itself from the past? Please, this is not a theory, nor am I telling you what to do. If I told you what to do, and you did it, it would be totally wrong because then you would be following another. You may leave the old and follow the new, but you are still a follower, and he who follows will never find out what is true; he will never discover for himself whether there is truth, God, peace.

So I am not pointing out the way to truth because truth has no way, no system; it is not to be found through the cultivation of virtue, for the cultivation of virtue is only a form of self-centered activity. You must have a free mind to discover what is true, and it is extraordinarily difficult to have a free mind, a mind not bound by tradition, a mind that is no longer accepting or rejecting conclusions, a mind that is not burdened with experience, however noble or transient. What is important is not just to follow what I say but to find out for yourself how your mind is conditioned, and to see if it is possible to free the mind from that conditioning. Your mind is obviously conditioned; that is a fact whether you like it or not, and as long as you call yourself an Indian, a Hindu, a communist, or what you will, you are maintaining that conditioning.

Now, how is one to be aware of one's conditioning? Do you understand the problem? You may verbally assert that you are conditioned, but merely to assert it and to discover that you are conditioned—in your speech, in your thought, in dozens of ways—are two entirely different states. To know that you suffer is one thing, and merely to speculate about suffering is another. Most of us, unfortunately, superficially speculate about being conditioned, and so we create a division between ourselves as we actually are and the idea of our being conditioned. That is clear, is it not?

Throughout the world man has broken up his existence as spiritual and worldly, and that division exists in your life. You seek God, you meditate and do all that kind of stuff, while in daily life you are ambitious, you are seeking power, position, prestige, and you try to mix the two and create something out of it. So you live a schizophrenic existence, an existence that is broken up, split, and to realize for yourself that this cleavage exists is quite different from the mere acceptance of the idea, is it not? To know that I am hungry, to feel the misery of it, is one thing, and to think about the idea of hunger is a totally different state. Most of us are merely thinking about these problems, we are not feeling them. If we were capable of feeling any problem totally, then our approach to it would be entirely different; there would be no split approach, and I think it is very important to understand how the mind is caught in words and is therefore incapable of looking at the fact without the word.

If you listen to all this as mere talk, then what is being said becomes another lecture with very little meaning. It will be worthwhile only if you listen to find out how your own mind operates, observing as you are sitting there how it is broken up into fragments, each fragment in conflict with another like so many opposing desires, with yourself caught in the middle trying to bring peace amidst all this confusion.

So there is a vast difference between the fact and an opinion or idea about the fact. Which is it that is actually happening to you? Is it the fact that you are confronting, whatever the fact may be, or your opinion about the fact? And can we free the mind from the opinion, the conclusion, and look directly at the fact? If we can look at the fact in that way, then there is an integrated action, a complete comprehension of the fact, and therefore the resolution of that fact.

You see, the difficulty is that if a problem exists in our life, as it does—the problem of sorrow, of loneliness, of division—we want a solution, but the solution does not lie beyond the problem. Please do follow this a little bit. The answer to the problem lies in the problem itself, not away from it. Now, our very existence has become a problem, and to understand our existence, we have to look at it, surely, not in terms of what has been said, but as it actually is. It is important to know oneself, is it not? Because without knowing oneself, whatever one may think, whatever one may believe, will have no basis, no validity. So you have to know yourself first, and that is the foundation on which you can build; but without self-knowledge, your building has no significance. You see, the difficulty is that most of us do not want to know ourselves. We are bored with ourselves, and we want to escape from our boredom through some form of amusement: going to a guru, attending church, performing rituals, seeking power, position—the whole business of modern society.

What is important, then, is to know oneself. Self-knowledge is the beginning of wisdom, and to have self-knowledge is not a complex problem. You can know yourself as you actually are by observing yourself every minute of the day, or whenever it is possible to do so. If I want to know myself, the conscious as well as the unconscious, if I want to understand the whole buildup of the 'me', I must watch myself as I get into the bus, when I am conversing with a friend; I must observe the way I talk to my wife, to my boss, to my servant. Surely, I can see myself as I am only in the mirror of relationship. Do you follow? If you really go into it, you will find that it is extraordinarily simple.

Without knowledge of yourself there can be no solution of either the world problem or your own problem. You know very well what is happening in the world. There is more and more confusion, more and more tyranny. Everywhere the one-party system is spreading, with one so-called great leader. Man is being shaped, conditioned to think according to a certain pattern, within a certain field, and thereby he avoids a religious revolution. And one sees that such a revolution is necessary, a revolution not based on economic or social upheaval but a total revolution, a revolution which is truly religious. I am not talking of the religion of the Hindu, of the Buddhist, or the Christian. That is not religion at all; it is merely a dogma, a set of beliefs born of fear, of the desire to be secure, to sit on the right hand of God, or what you will. Religion is something entirely different from all that, and to find the religious life, there must be a total revolution in our thinking. To bring about a different kind of world, an altogether new culture, each one of us must begin with the right foundation, and that foundation is laid through self-knowledge. You must begin to know yourself, the whole of your being, and not just the superficial part of your upper consciousness.

I have been given some questions, and I shall try to go into them, but first of all, I wonder why you ask questions. Either you want another to point the way out of your confusion, or you are hoping someone is going to answer in a way that will resolve your problems. It is good to question, to criticize, to inquire, and never accept; but when we do inquire, we always have an end in view, and therefore it is no longer an inquiry. If you have a problem, you want a satisfactory answer to that problem, do you not? Otherwise you would not put the question. You are not trying to understand the problem but to find a gratifying solution, a safe haven in which you will never be disturbed; therefore, you are no longer inquiring into the problem, and I think it is very important to realize this.

So, in considering these questions I am not giving an answer, because life has no answer; life must be lived, understood, and not run away from into some secure haven. To understand this extraordinarily complex existence and to find out if there is reality, God, one must approach it very hesitantly, tentatively, for only then can one begin to understand oneself, the whole structure of one's being.

Question: I read in the newspaper today your statement that to solve man's problems, what is needed is not an economic or social revolution but a religious revolution. What do you mean by religious revolution?

KRISHNAMURTI: First of all, let us find out what we mean by religion. What is religion for most of us—not the theory of what religion should be, but the actual fact? For most of us, religion is obviously a series of dogmas, traditions, what the Upanishads or the Gita or the Bible has said; or it is made up of the experiences, visions, hopes, ideas which have sprung from our conditioned minds, from our minds which have been shaped according to the Hindu, the Christian, or the communist pattern. We start with a particular conditioning and have experiences based on it. What we call religion is prayer, ritual, dogma, wishing to find God, the acceptance of authority, and a vast number of superstitions, is it not? But is that religion? A man who is really trying to find out what is true must surely abandon all that, must he not? He must totally discard the authority of the guru, of the Upanishads, and the authority of his own experiences so that, being purged of all authority, his mind is capable of discovery. That means you must cease to be a Hindu, a Christian, a Buddhist; you must see the absurdity of that whole business and break away from it. And will you? Because if you do, you are against the present society and may lose your job. So fear dominates the mind, and you go on accepting authority.

What we call religion, then, is not religion at all. Whether we believe in God or do not believe in God depends upon our conditioning. You believe in God, and the communist believes in no-God. What is the difference? There is no difference whatsoever because you are trained to believe, and he is trained not to believe. Therefore a man who is seriously inquiring must totally reject that process, must he not?—reject it because he understands the whole significance of it.

Being insecure, frightened, inwardly insufficient, we identify ourselves with a country, with an ideology, or with a belief in God, and we can see what is happening throughout the world. Every religion, though they all profess love, brotherhood, and all the rest of it, is actually separating man from man. You are a Sikh and I am a Hindu, he is a Muslim and somebody else is a Buddhist. Seeing all this confusion and separation, one realizes there must be a different kind of thinking; but the different kind of thinking obviously cannot come into being as long as one remains a Hindu, a Christian, or what you will. To be free of all that, you have to know yourself, the whole structure of your being; you have to see why you accept, why you follow authority, which is fairly obvious. You want success; you want to be assured that there is a God on whom you can rely in moments of trouble. A man who is really joyous, happy, never thinks about God. We think about God when we are in misery, conflict, but we have created the misery, the conflict, and without understanding the whole process of it, merely to inquire after God leads to utter illusion.

So the religious revolution of which I am talking is not the revival or reformation of any particular religion but the total freedom from all religions and ideologies—which means, really, freedom from the society which has created them. Surely, a man who is ambitious cannot be a religious man. A man who is ambitious does not know love, though he may talk about it. A man may not be ambitious in the worldly sense, but if he wants to be a saint, a spiritual somebody, if he wants to achieve a result in the next world, he is still ambitious. So the mind must not only be stripped of all ceremonies, beliefs, and dogmas, but it must also be free of envy. The total freedom of man is the religious revolution, for only then will he be able to approach life entirely differently and cease to create problem after problem.

You have probably listened to all this only verbally or intellectually because you say to yourself, "What would I do in life if I had no ambition? I should be destroyed by society." I wonder if you would be destroyed by society. The moment you understand society and reject the whole structure on which it is based—ambition, envy, the pursuit of success, the religious dogmas, beliefs and superstitions—you are outside of society and can therefore think of the whole problem anew, and perhaps then there will be no problem. But you have probably listened only on the verbal level and will continue with the same old thing tomorrow; you will read the Gita or the Bible, go to your guru or a priest, and all the rest of it. You may listen to all this and accept it intellectually, verbally, but your life continues in the opposite direction, so you have merely created another conflict; therefore, it is much better not to listen at all because you have enough conflicts, enough problems, without introducing a new one. It is very nice to sit and listen to what is being said here, but if it has no relationship to your actual life, it is much better to shut your ears, because if you hear the truth and do not live it, your life becomes a hideous confusion, the sorrowful mess which it is.

Question: You seem to be against the very essence of authority. Is not the acceptance of authority inevitable in our individual lives? Without it would not society be reduced to chaos?

KRISHNAMURTI: Let us find out what we mean by authority, and why we accept it, rather than speculate as to whether, without authority, society would disintegrate. Society is disintegrating, whether you like it or not; it is going to pieces because we have followed authority, so let us inquire into that.

Why do we follow another? This is a very complex problem, and we must therefore approach it carefully, wisely, patiently. It involves the problem of knowledge, that is, the problem of accepting the authority of one who has knowledge, assuming that you don't know and the other does. We accept the authority of a doctor, and the civil authority which says we must drive on the left side of the road. If you haven't the common sense to follow the general rule of driving on the left side of the road, you will end up in a police station. So we follow normal activity in certain things which are common to us all. If I want to build a bridge, I cannot reject the knowledge that has been accumulated through the centuries; that would be absurd. We are not talking of such authority. We are talking of authority at quite a different level—the authority of the teacher, the guru who says he knows, and who is followed by the person who does not know and who wishes to be led to reality. Let us be very clear that it is such authority we are talking about, not the authority of factual knowledge which has been accumulated through centuries in medicine, engineering, or any other branch of science. To reject all that would be too stupid. We are talking of the authority that you create in the person who says he knows God, truth, and can lead you to that reality. So the problem is clear, is it not? We are talking of spiritual authority—if I may use that word *spiritual* without being misunderstood—the authority of the guru who knows, in his relationship with the disciple who does not know.

When the guru says he knows, what does it mean? It means that he has experienced God, truth, perfect peace, and all the rest of it; he knows and you do not, so you follow him, hoping to be led to that reality. That is how we create so-called spiritual authority.

Now, please follow this. What do we mean by knowing? When I say, "I know," what does that signify? I can only know something which is already over. Do you understand? I can only know what has been, and when a guru says he knows, he only knows the past, what he has experienced, and what he has experienced is always static; it is a dead thing, it is not living. Truth, God, cannot be known; you cannot know or experience it because the moment you say, "I know, I have experienced," you don't know. You can only know what has been, and what has been has no validity; it is no longer truth. When the teacher says he will help you to reach truth, reality, he can only help you to reach something which is fixed, within the field of time, and therefore not true.

Sirs, do listen to this. Don't accept what I am saying; see the truth of it, and seeing the truth of it will free you.

We think truth, God, is a fixed point in time; it is over there, and to gain it, to travel the intervening distance and reach it, we say we must have time. What we call reality is fixed; therefore, we can make a path to it—or rather, many paths, the paths of the various religions, sects, beliefs. But reality can never be fixed; it is immeasurable, alive, beyond time; it has no being in the terms we know. It can only be approached when the mind has ceased to be caught within the field of time, and so no guru, no book, no system of meditation can lead you to it. The mind must be totally free from all the past compulsions, past influences; it must be without movement, completely silent, no longer inquiring in order to be safe, in order to be happy, in order to achieve. That is why the truly religious man has no authority, no dogma, no tradition, no belief. Tradition, belief, dogma, authority, are all within the field of time, and a mind that is caught within that field can never find that which is timeless. To free the mind from time is an immense problem because the mind is the result of time; it is the result of innumerable influences, memories, and can such a mind be free from the past? Until the mind is free from the past, it cannot discover what is true.

Because they are suffering, lost in their confusion, human beings go to another, hoping to find an answer, a sense of comfort, a haven of security; and they do find a haven of security because that is their desire, but their haven of security is not God; it is not truth. It is a thing made by the mind, put together by man, and what has been put together can be torn asunder. That is why it is very important to understand yourself. Self-knowledge is the beginning of wisdom. But the self, the 'me,' is a very complex thing, and knowing yourself is not just a matter of reading a book or practicing some stupid form of introspection and then saying, "I have learned all about myself." That does not bring self-knowledge. The ways of the self are to be discovered from moment to moment, not through accumulation. Observe how your mind operates, what you think, your impulses, your compulsions, your hidden motives—be aware of all that from moment to moment, and then free the mind from this curse of authority, from all the books, from all the leaders, political or otherwise, because they are just as ambitious as you are. The ambitious, the successful will never create the new world. The new world can be created only by the man who is free from ambition, from the desire to be successful, free from all dogmas, beliefs—which means, really, free from himself, free from his ego, his 'me'. It is only through this religious revolution, and not through the economic revolution of the communists or the socialists, that the new world can come into being.

October 10, 1956

Second Talk in New Delhi

It seems to me that it is very important to understand the totality of all problems and not merely resolve one problem after another; but most of us are inclined, I think, to solve each problem on its own particular level and not to have a total, comprehensive view of the whole problem of existence. What matters, surely, is to see the whole and not be caught up in the particular, for in understanding the whole, the particular will be resolved and understood. Most of us are concerned with a particular problem, economic, social, or religious, and we do not seem to be aware of the whole. Though the particular is important, if we could see the whole and not get lost in the particular, then I think we should be able to resolve the many disturbing issues that confront us.

We all have many problems, have we not? Our existence is fraught with innumerable contradictory issues, and how are ordinary human beings like you and me to resolve this enormous complex of problems? We have the economic problem, the problem of our relationship with each other, the problem of war and peace, the problem of death, the problem of whether there is God, truth, the problem of social reformation, the problem of what system to follow—the communist, the socialist, or the capitalist, and so on.

Now, how do you and I approach these many problems? Do we look at the problems of life as separate from the totality of existence, or do we consider the totality of existence and then deal with the particular? Do you understand what I mean?

Our life consists of political activity, religious activity, the activity of a job, and the personal activity of self-centered action; we are concerned with what leader we should follow, what authority we should obey, which teacher we should imitate, and so on. That is our life, and without understanding the totality of it, most of us try to deal with each issue separately, hoping thereby to solve the whole problem. The political leader is concerned with one issue, the religious leader with another, while the social reformer is concerned with the amelioration of society—he wants to abolish the caste system, and all the rest of it. There are innumerable problems, but I don't think any problem can be solved by itself because all problems are interrelated. Most of us regard education, political reformation, and the religious life, for example, as separate problems, unrelated to each other, and therefore our confusion grows. The politician is only concerned with legislation; the so-called religious person is only concerned with the pursuit of reality, God, and the social worker is only concerned with the reformation of society. To me this fragmentary outlook, with its isolated activity, is most dangerous because it merely creates further misery—which is exactly what is happening throughout the world.

Now, seeing this whole process and being aware of its significance, how is each one of us to understand the totality of existence and then apply our understanding to the particular? What makes a great painter? Surely, a great painter is one who first sees the whole and then paints the details. Similarly, can each one of us see the totality of existence and not merely be concerned with the particular? The totality of existence includes all our particular idiosyncracies, our particular vanities, our social relationships, our conditioning by a particular religion, culture, or political system, and if we do not understand the totality, merely dealing with a particular issue will not solve any of our problems. I think it should be very clear to anyone who is at all serious that no problem can be solved on its own level, but must be approached through the understanding of the totality.

What does it mean to understand the totality? It means, surely, that I must understand the totality of my own being because I am not different from society. I am the product of society, as society is the projection of myself; and to bring about a fundamental transformation in society, I must totally transform myself. It is only through being concerned with the total transformation of myself that I am capable of dealing with society. It is now the fashion to be concerned with the reformation of society, as though society were something different from ourselves. But you and I have created society by our ambition, by our cruelty, by our stupidity, by our pursuit of something which we think is God, so the individual problem is the problem of the world. Each one of us is intimately related to the world, to society, and to solve the problem of society, we must understand the creator of the problem, which is you, which is me.

To understand the totality of action, then, I must understand the whole structure of my own being, the conscious as well as the unconscious; I must understand the ways of my thought and feeling. Without bringing about a basic revolution in myself, there is no possibility of creating a new society, and this should be fairly obvious, at least to anyone who thinks about these problems fundamentally. And how are you and I as individuals to understand and bring about this transformation in ourselves? Do you understand the problem? The problem is not which party to join, what legislation to support, which leader to follow, which guru to imitate, but how am I—who am composed of all these fragmentary views and contradictions—to bring about a complete revolution in myself? To know what I am matters infinitely because my action reflects the contradiction in myself and therefore creates a contradiction in society. This does not mean emphasis on individual salvation, on the individual and his attainment; on the contrary, to find out what we are is to inquire whether we are individuals at all. Do you understand?

Most of us think we are individuals, that we are capable of thinking independently and therefore acting freely, but is that so? Are you an individual? You have a particular name, a private bank account, certain features and qualities which distinguish you from someone else, but are you an individual in the sense that your mind is completely uncontaminated by society? Or is your mind merely the product of society, of a particular culture?—in which case you are not an individual at all, though your many activities, reflections, and memories make you think that you are an individual. Do you understand all this?

We think we are individuals, but are we? When you say you are a Hindu, a Muslim, a Buddhist, or a Christian, you are repeating what you have been told from childhood, and the repetition of what you have been told does not constitute individuality. To be truly individual is not to be the result of the collective, but you are the result of the collective because you merely repeat the things which society has taught you. You may think you have an individual soul, but that belief is merely the imprint of a particular culture.

I think it is very important to understand this one thing. You see, truth, reality, God, or what name you will, can only be experienced by a mind that is completely alone; and the mind is not alone as long as it is contaminated by society, put together by so-called knowledge, by a particular culture. Only the individual who has really understood the full significance of truth is truly religious, and such an individual, being in a state of total revolution, will have a revolutionary effect on society. That is why it is very important to find out if the mind can ever be free to think independently.

Can thinking ever be independent? As long as the mind is conditioned, surely, there can be no freedom in thinking. And your mind is conditioned, is it not? As a Hindu you are shaped by many centuries of tradition—the Brahmin, the untouchable, or what you will—which means that you are the product of the society in which you have been brought up; your mind is conditioned by certain beliefs, information, ideals which have been given to you, and with that background you proceed to think. But unless one is free of the background completely, there is no possibility of thinking independently. Until I totally cease to be a Hindu, it is not possible for me to discover what is true, and I think it is very important to realize this. A conditioned mind, a mind that is put together by society, by time, is incapable of finding the timeless.

So there must be this sense of individuality which comes only when the mind is uncontaminated by society, that is, when it is no longer thinking in terms of the Hindu, the Christian, the Buddhist, and so on. A mind that is constantly freeing itself from the memories, the traditions, the values which society has imposed upon it is an individual mind, and only such a mind is capable of inquiring into what is true. As long as the mind is conditioned, shaped by society, by economic and religious influences, it is never free, and it is only the free mind that can discover what is new. And truth is something totally new; God must be something which has never been experienced before. That is why a mind that is conditioned, that is shaped by authority, by tradition, by religious books, can never find out if there is a reality or not.

The totality of this revolution lies in the mind's discovery of how it is conditioned, and freeing itself from that conditioning. After all, a mind that is ambitious, envious, at whatever level—political, religious, or social—is incapable of understanding what is true. For most of us it is very difficult to be free of ambition because ambition is the very essence of the self, the 'me'; and the mind that seeks to attain a so-called spiritual state, to reach the other shore, is as ambitious as the mind that wants a good position in society. A total revolution is necessary if we are to bring about a completely different kind of world, and a total revolution is possible only when the mind of each one of us is not bound by society, that is, when it is no longer the result of the collective and is therefore capable of stepping out of the whole structure of society.

Sirs, I have been handed some questions. Please bear in mind that we are going to investigate the problem and find the answer together. Don't wait for me to give an answer to the question, but let us together explore the problem. Though I may describe and explain, you are watching the problem operating in yourself; and that observation, that very awareness and understanding of the problem in yourself, will resolve the problem.

Question: People well versed in the Hindu scriptures say that sadhana *is essential for* mukti. *Vinoba Bhaveji has said that what you speak of as freedom cannot be the same as* mukti *because you do not seem to believe in* sadhana. *Kindly explain.*

KRISHNAMURTI: Now, sir, what is important in this question? Not what Vinoba Bhaveji says, or what I say, or what is written in the scriptures, but to find out for yourself what is true. *Sadhana,* I am told, means the method, the system, the practice towards an end; and the question is: Is *sadhana* necessary or not? So please understand that we are discussing, not what X or Y has said, but whether in fact a practice with an end in view leads to freedom, to reality.

Most of us think that by doing certain things—practicing yoga, meditating, disciplining, suppressing, denying, torturing oneself—the mind will be led to reality, to God. That is what you have been brought up on, but I say that no method, no system can lead you to reality because you will become a prisoner of that system, and it is only the free mind that can discover what is true. Besides, truth has no fixed abode, it is not static, it is a living thing which is in constant movement, and a path can only lead to that which is fixed, which is static. The practicing of any method or system merely produces the result which that system offers. Do you understand?

Sirs, I am not trying to convince you of the truth of what I am saying, but if you see the truth of this for yourself, you will be free of the system which you hope will lead you to truth. The moment you see that no system can lead you to truth, you are free of systems.

First of all, you think that truth, reality, God, or what you will, is a fixed point, and that to get there, all you have to do is diligently to practice a certain discipline every day, make your mind conform to a certain pattern. That is what your books, your leaders, your swamis and yogis all say; but they may be totally wrong, including the Gita. So you håve to find out, and how will you find out? You must begin, surely, by abandoning all authority. That means you cannot have any fear. And then what happens? You begin to inquire into what is implied by a practice, a method. Surely, a practice, method, or discipline implies the suppression of your own thoughts to conform to a particular pattern which you think will lead you to reality.

Does all this interest you, or are you going to sleep? You see, what I am saying goes entirely opposite to everything that you believe, and obviously most of you want to continue to think along the old lines because what I am saying means real revolution, not the economic or social kind, but the fundamental revolution that comes into being when the whole structure of authority is questioned—the authority not only of the guru but also of tradition and of your own experience.

So what are we discussing? We are trying to find out the truth or falseness of the common belief, which includes the ideas of your various gurus, that certain practices are necessary to reach *mukti,* to reach freedom. If you examine the whole process very carefully, you will see that by practicing a method, your mind is not made free but merely conforms itself to the method, and so becomes a slave to that method and to what it will produce. I think that much is very clear if you once see it. To be creative, the mind must be free, and not conform to a pattern or a framework which you think will lead you to the real.

Sirs, another factor involved in all this is the question of discipline. Can discipline free the mind? Or to be free, must the mind, through intense alertness, understand the implications of discipline and thereby be free of discipline? Discipline implies suppression in order to achieve a result of which you know nothing. What you "know" of *moksha*, and all the rest of it, is only what you have been told, and in order to gain what you think is truth, you practice disciplines, but can truth ever be known to a mind that is ambitious, envious, cruel? Why do you not concern yourself with freeing the mind from envy, to take that as a simple example? And can you free the mind from envy by discipline?

Do you understand, sirs? Have you ever tried freeing the mind from envy by compelling it to be nonenvious? When you do that, what happens? The mind that is forced not to be envious is a dead mind, is it not? It has built a wall around itself; therefore, it is an insensitive mind. You may be unworldly and possess only a loincloth, but you are still envious inwardly because you want to get somewhere in the so-called spiritual sense. If you go into it very deeply, you will find that the mind can never be free of envy through any form of discipline, but only when it understands the whole process of envy—which means studying envy, not condemning it or comparing it with something else. Envy comes into being when there is comparison, when you want to be better than X, more this or more that. As long as the mind is thinking in terms of the 'more', there must be envy; and when you discipline yourself not to be envious, you are still demanding the 'more'; therefore, you are still envious. If you understand this very clearly, you will see that truth is not somewhere in the distance; it is not over there, separated from you by a gap, an interval of time. When you create such a gap, you must have time to bridge it, you must perform various disciplines to achieve what you call truth.

So *sadhana* of any kind is unnecessary, and the very perception that *sadhana* is unnecessary brings a profound understanding of the ways of the mind. The mind has a continual craving to be certain. It wants a result, it wants to be reassured, it wants to reach an end which will be permanent, secure; and so we do these things in order to find comfort, in order to be gratified, in order to feel that we have arrived, all of which is the process of the self, the 'me'. If you understand this, not merely verbally or intellectually, but really see the truth of it, then there is no distance between *what is* and the truth. But to see the truth of it, you must begin by putting away all authority—the authority of the book, however good, however religious, the authority of the gurus, of all those who think they have arrived. The man who says he knows, does not know because all that he can know is the past, not truth.

To be free of authority, you must understand fear, and fear will exist as long as the mind is pursuing security, comfort, gratification, power, position, whether here or in the so-called spiritual world. If you really see this, then what is the necessity for any discipline? If you understand something to be poisonous, surely you leave it alone; there is no temptation, there is no conflict, you don't have to discipline yourself not to touch it. You just leave it alone. In the same way, if you understand the poison of ambition, envy, you just drop it; you don't have to practice a discipline to be free of it. But to understand that ambition is poison, you must give your whole attention to it, and you cannot give your whole attention to it if you are afraid or if you are seeking a comforting result.

The question, then, is not which is the right *sadhana*, or whether there should be any *sadhana* at all, but can the mind free itself from fear? Fear comes into being as long as the mind is trying to become something. If you see the truth of this, then no discipline is necessary. But to see the truth, you need a mind that is unafraid, that is not anxious, not covetous, that is not seeking position, power, prestige, either in this world or in the next. Actually you are seeking these things, and you also want to reach truth or happiness, so there is a conflict; and you want to know how to get rid of the conflict without giving up either this or that.

So, to understand what is true or what is false, there must be freedom from fear, and you cannot discipline your mind to be free from fear. You must see for yourself that ambition, covetousness, violence, greed, and all the rest of it is poison, and then you will leave it alone. That means going totally against society, against many things that you have maintained as being essential to life.

Question: What is habit? There are certain needs which are fundamental, and others which are based on the psychological memory of pleasure. Does this mean that one should indulge, or not indulge, depending on whether the need is fundamental or based on memory?

KRISHNAMURTI: Sirs, this is a very interesting and complex question because a great deal is involved in it. If you will, kindly follow the description which I am going to give, but also watch your own minds through the explanation. Do you understand what I mean? I am describing or explaining something, but the explanation will remain merely verbal and therefore useless if you don't observe your own habits and become aware of how they function.

Now, what do we mean by habit? Let us go slowly, step by step. It is a very complex problem, demanding a great deal of attention, and if you don't follow the sequence, you will miss the whole significance of it. What do we mean by *habit?* We are not seeking a definition but the content of that word. A person takes a cup of coffee every morning, for example, because without it he feels he will have a headache. That action has become a habit, based on what he considers a necessity; that is, the stimulation of coffee has become a necessity. That much is fairly simple and clear. It is like smoking. Though the first cigarette may have nauseated you, smoking gradually becomes pleasurable and you keep on repeating the act. That is one form of habit.

Then there is the process of eating. It is essential for my body to have food, and does eating become a habit? It becomes a habit only when I demand that food shall have such and such a taste based on pleasure. I must have pickles, I must have rice, I must have this or that, which means that my tongue is dictating the habit of eating based on pleasure.

Similarly, there is the habit of sex and all that is implied in it. Glandular secretion takes place, which is a function of the body, and it must have an outlet. Then what happens? The mind stores up as memory the pleasure of the sexual act. Now, is glandular secretion a habit, or does habit arise only when the mind derives pleasure from resuscitating the memory of the sexual act and thereby becomes a slave to that memory? Are you following all this?

Surely, habit is the repetition of a pleasure based on the memory of yesterday. Please follow this, sirs, because if you follow alertly, watchfully, not just my words, but your own mind, you will see how the mind creates habit through the demand for pleasure. Habit is not the natural demand of hunger, for example, but the demand for pleasure and the repetition of that pleasure based on memory. A body that is hungry needs food, but habit arises only when it demands that the food shall have a particular taste which is the repetition of a pleasure it has had before. So habit is the recollection of a pleasure which the mind has had and wants the constant repetition of. All right? Or is this too complex? It does not matter, sirs. You come with me, let us look at it together.

The mind is the result of habit, it only knows the memories of a thousand yesterdays, and every act based on that background becomes a habit. Now, follow this. The mind establishes a habit based on the memory and repetition of a particular pleasure. Then society, your guru, or sacred book says that the habit is very wrong, so you have the opposite: you must be celibate, you must be this or that. Hence there is a conflict between the fact, which is the habit, and what you think you should be; so you go to somebody to tell you how to get rid of that conflict, thereby creating another problem. You had one conflict, now you have two conflicts—and that is our life, a series of never-ending conflicts. The mind is always being frustrated, it is miserable, fearful, and such a mind wants something beyond itself. It is impossible.

The mind seeks the repetition of a particular pleasure, sexual or whatever it is, and as long as it demands that pleasure, it functions in the groove of habit. That is a fact. Then the mind says, "I must be free from this habit," so it is always resisting, fighting, and it seeks to cultivate another habit which will not be like this one. So what has happened? The mind is in conflict; it wants a certain pleasure and at the same time it is pushing away that which it wants. I am not saying it must or must not yield to pleasure; that is not the problem. We will see it presently.

I see a lovely sunset, with billowing clouds lighted by the sun and Mars riding on top. There is great delight, for it is a beautiful thing to behold. That is pleasure, is it not? Now, why do we say that watching a cloud is all right, and that certain other forms of pleasure are wrong? When we deny pleasure in one field and maintain it in another, we are becoming insensitive. Do you understand? It is like the mind that says, "I must have only beautiful things around me; therefore, I am going to close the window and not see the dirty village." Life is both the ugly and the beautiful, but we only want one and not the other, and the denial of the ugly makes us insensitive.

So, when you are caught in one habit and resist that habit in order to have some other habit which you think is better, you are cultivating insensitivity. Habit is based on pleasure and the repetition of that pleasure, but if you want to destroy pleasure, which is what the swamis, the yogis, and the whole lot of them do, then you must not live at all because pleasure is part of life. When you see a cloud, a smile, a tear, when you watch a child, a woman, or a man, all that is life, and if you deny any part of life, you become insensitive. A man who is sensitive has no habit. Please follow this. If you say, "I must have no pleasure," then you must also deny love. No? That is what you have done. When the mind is caught in habit and is therefore insensitive, how can there be love?—just love, not the godly love and the physical love. Do you understand what I mean? I am talking of love, which is to love a human being, a flower, an animal, and not to think of yourself and your pleasures, your vanities, your ambitions. The mind must be completely sensitive to love; it must be vulnerable to love. But how can the mind be vulnerable to love if it has habits, good or bad?

Follow this, sirs; just see the truth of it for yourselves. Surely, a mind that is insensitive cannot know what beauty is. How can it? And if it is insensitive to beauty, there is no austerity. A yogi, swami, or mahatma who has only one loincloth and practices all kinds of austerities is not austere. Austerity is to be sensitive to beauty, to love. You cannot be austere if you are not simple. And simplicity is not a matter of the clothes you wear or don't wear—that is merely immature thinking. To be simple is to be inwardly without ambition, without resistance, which means being completely vulnerable, totally sensitive. You cannot be sensitive if there is conflict; therefore, a man who is denying, resisting, struggling to cultivate good habit as opposed to bad habit is not sensitive. Such a mind will never know what love is because it is only concerned with its own advancement, with its own ideas, however noble. A man who does not love does not know what it is to be austere; therefore, he does not know what it is to be simple.

So, if you understand the totality of all this, you will see that a mind that is in conflict, that is making an effort to become something, can never be sensitive; and such a mind, whatever it may do, however much it may try to bring reformation to the world, can only create more harm, more mischief. It is only the mind that is sensitive, that knows what it is to love and is therefore free of ambition, of envy, of the desire for power, position, prestige—it is only such a mind that can do good in the world.

October 17, 1956

Third Talk in New Delhi

For most of us, if we have thought about these things at all, the idea of change must be rather confusing because we see that the so-called revolutions, though they have produced certain outward and perhaps beneficial effects, have ultimately been deeply detrimental to man. After all, a fundamental change must be more than just a shift from one limited field of thinking to another. As things are in the world, one can see that there must be some kind of radical change, not only at the economic and social levels, but deep within each one of us; and for those who are at all serious about these matters, the problem must be how to bring about that change. A change that is brought about through any form of compulsion is obviously no change at all. If I am compelled or influenced to change, it is not really a change because I am merely conforming to a pattern, either externally imposed upon me or established by myself. Nor does change consist in adapting oneself to an environment, which is merely to adjust oneself to a pattern which one thinks will be beneficial or a better way of life.

Now, if one sees that adjustment, conformity, or any form of change brought about by compulsion or influence is no change at all, then how is a change to be brought about? A fundamental change is obviously essential, not only in this country, but throughout the world; and how can such a change, which is not the result of compulsion, conformity, or adjustment, be set going?

Most of us think that adjustment, conformity, or being compelled to act in a certain direction is a process of change, and we have never questioned whether it is really a revolutionary change. I don't think it is because if you observe yourself when you are conforming, adjusting, being influenced or compelled, you will see that you are merely fitting into a pattern of thinking, whether ancient or modern, and that the core of your being has not changed at all.

So the problem is: How can one radically change at the core of one's being? I don't know if you have given much thought to it because most of us are willing to be forced to conform to a pattern; we think it is sufficient to bring about a modified change in the world, and with that we are satisfied. But if you go into the matter sufficiently deeply, then you must ask yourself how it is possible for the totality of one's being, the whole of one's consciousness to be changed, how a complete revolution in thinking and in valuation is to be brought about. Because it is obviously only such a revolutionary change—

deep, inward, at the heart of oneself—that can ultimately release the creativeness of reality and bring about a totally different kind of world. Without this fundamental inward change, mere outward adjustment, acquiring a little more knowledge, establishing a few more reforms, and all that, is really very superficial. It is like putting on a new coat, but underneath, the old condition continues to exist. So, if you are at all interested in the matter, how is one to change completely?

May I suggest that you should listen to what I am explaining without judging, without saying it is impossible. Please do not translate what is being said in terms of your own information or listen to it with a defensive attitude, comparing it with what you have been told or with what you have read in the sacred books—which are no more sacred than any other books. To listen is quite an arduous task, and most of us never listen to anything but the voice of our own thinking, so there is really no communication at all. To listen with judgment, comparing what we hear with what we already know or have read, is a form of distraction. But if we can listen without comparison, with effortless attention, then I think that that very listening is an act of meditation which does bring about a deep transformation. Try observing yourself sometimes to see if you ever really listen to anything—to what your friends say, to what your wife or husband says, to what your boss says—and you will find that your mind is not there at all. You pretend to listen, but you are only half-listening; either you are frightened, or bored, or you just don't want to listen, so there is no direct communication. As I said, listening in itself does bring about an extraordinary miracle. The very act of listening produces an immense understanding without any effort on your part, and since you are here and I am talking, I would suggest, if I may, that you listen to find out what it is I am trying to convey.

I think that a fundamental change, not a revival, but a religious revolution, must come into being because without it our problems will multiply, though we may have more refrigerators and all the rest of it, we shall become increasingly superficial and have yet greater miseries. And to bring about this deep transformation at the core, surely we have to inquire into the whole problem of what is consciousness and understand the anatomy of change. Most of us try to change through effort, do we not? That is, we see ourselves as being cruel, for example, and we say, "I must change," so we make an effort to change; we try to force ourselves through discipline not to be cruel. Now, let us examine the urge which makes us want to change, for without understanding that, without understanding the total process of consciousness which says, "I must change," there can be no fundamental change, though there may be superficial adjustments.

Please do not listen to all this against a background of what you have read about consciousness in the Gita or any other book because what we are trying to do is not to communicate ideas but to directly experience what we are listening to. Unless we experience what we hear, these talks will have no value at all; they will merely be another set of ideas, a process of mentation which, however exciting, will have very little significance. Whereas, if you and I are actually experiencing what is being said as you are sitting there and I am talking, if through the verbal description each one of us is watching the operation of his own mind, then I think these talks will be really worthwhile.

So we are trying to find out how to change, not just superficially, but at the very center of our being, which means that we have to inquire into the question of what is consciousness. When I ask myself, "What is consciousness?" there is the questioner apart from the question, is there not? There is the entity who has asked the question and is waiting for an answer, and that process is the beginning of consciousness, is it not? The questioner says, "I must know how consciousness works," and then begins to inquire, and both the inquiry and the answer depend on how he asks the question.

To put it differently, I want to know what consciousness is, and it is not a vain or merely curious question. I ask myself what is consciousness because I see that I must fundamentally change, the totality of my being must undergo a complete transformation. Now, does this revolutionary change come about through a series of efforts on the part of the one who says, "I must change"? Must he develop the quality of will and change according to that will? Do you understand?

I am asking myself, and I hope you are asking yourself, too, what is this consciousness, the 'me', that says, "I must change"? And what is the momentum, the action, the force of the inquirer who is trying to change? That whole process is within the field of consciousness, within the field of thinking, is it not? Are you following this? It is not complex, it is very simple.

When I wish to change, I already have the pattern or the idea towards which I must change. That is true, is it not? Now, is that really change, or is it merely a movement from the known to another known? Do you understand? Because I am cruel, I say I must be kind. The process of trying to be kind is a movement towards something which is already known, and is that change at all? Is there a change if I move towards something which I know? Surely, there is a change only when the mind moves towards the unknown. When it pursues that which it has already experienced, its movement is merely a continuation of the known in a modified form; therefore, it is no change at all.

Suppose, being violent, I have the ideal of nonviolence. The ideal is already known. I have imagined what it is not to be violent, so the ideal is born out of my actual state of violence, and when I change towards that ideal, I am moving within the field of the known; therefore, it is not a change at all. That is the whole process of consciousness, is it not? Sirs, don't agree with me, because you have to think it out, feel it out.

I make an effort to change in conformity with what I call the ideal, which is the opposite of what I have experienced as violence; therefore, I have created a conflict between *what is* and 'what should be', and I think this conflict is necessary to bring about a change. All this is the process of consciousness, is it not? Whether it is conscious or unconscious, it is still consciousness. If you see this very clearly for yourself, you will discover something extraordinary.

So I am asking myself, is there a change when there is an effort to change? When I try to change, is there a change, or merely conformity to a pattern which has been established by me or by some external agent? That is, any form of change based on tradition or authority is no change at all because one is merely conforming to an idea, and all ideas are of the known, they are the result of the background which projects them. So any change through effort towards that which you call the ideal, which is the known, is no change at all. When you are pursuing the ideal of nonviolence, for example, you are still violent because you want to achieve a state through compulsion, conformity to a pattern, which is another form of violence.

Consciousness is this movement from the known to the known, a movement of compulsion, of effort. When the communist says, "I have the right pattern for existence," that pattern is the result of what he has known. He creates a utopia according to his knowledge and interpretation of history, and if he is a big man, he pushes it through, while we little people conform. That is what has happened in one form or another throughout the world. The Shankaras, the leaders, the teachers have ideas, we read and conform, and we think we are changing. There may be a superficial adjustment, but there is no change at all in the sense in which I am speaking, which is the total transformation of our being so that our way of thinking is entirely new.

What is new cannot be brought about through effort, through moving from the known to the known, which is the pursuit of the ideal. And yet that is what you are doing in your daily life, is it not? You realize you are ambitious or cruel or envious, and you say, "I must change," so you proceed to conform to the pattern of an ideal which you or others have established, and you think that is an enormous change. But if you really go into it, penetrate into the whole psychological process of thinking, you will see that as long as the mind is thinking in terms of a duality, such as violence and nonviolence, as long as it is making an effort to conform to the opposite of what it is—which is merely the projection of the known and therefore a continuation of the same thing in a modified form—there can be no fundamental change.

What is important, then, is to realize, to actually see or experience the falseness of your effort to change. The gurus, the mahatmas, the Masters, and all the religious books tell you to make an effort, to control, to discipline yourself; and to realize that this effort is really false means that you must be capable of looking at it without the authority of any leader, political or religious, including myself. To experience the truth or the falseness of what you see, you cannot interpret it according to somebody else; it does not matter who it is. If you go into this matter and see very clearly for yourself that there can be no change as long as there is conformity—that is, as long as you are forcing yourself to fit into a pattern established by you or by somebody else—if you really see the truth or the falseness of that, then you will find that your mind has stripped itself of all authority, and is not that the very beginning of a fundamental revolution?

It seems to me that there must be, especially at this time, people who are really serious about these things—by which I do not mean the people who are seriously dedicated to the Gita, to communism, or to some other pattern, because such people are merely conformists. I am talking of people who seriously and earnestly want to find out how to bring about in themselves a revolution which is total. So we come to the question: Can the mind free itself from the known?—for only then is there a fundamental change.

Please, sirs, this requires a great deal of insight, inquiry. Don't agree with me but go into it, meditate, tear your mind apart to find out the truth or the falseness of all this. Does knowledge, which is the known, bring about change? I must have knowledge to build a bridge, but must my mind know towards what it is changing? Surely, if I know what the state of the mind will be when it is changed, it is no longer change. Such knowledge is a detriment to change because it becomes a means of satisfaction, and as long as there is a center seeking satisfaction, reward, or security, there is no change at all. And all our efforts are based on that center of reward, punishment, success, gain, are they not? That is all most of us are concerned with, and if it will help us get what we want, we will change, but such change is no change at all. So the mind that wishes to be fundamentally, deeply in a state of change, in a state of revolution, must be free from the known. Then the mind becomes astonishingly still, and only such a mind will experience the radical transformation which is so necessary.

Question: You often use the term understanding *in connection with the dissolution of problems. What exactly do you mean by understanding?*

KRISHNAMURTI: If I want to understand a child, what must I do? I must watch him, must I not? I must watch him when he sleeps, when he plays, when he cries, when he is mischievous, and not condemn him or compare him with his elder brother. I must not have a pattern of what he should be. Is that not so? In the same way, if I have a problem, I must watch it, and I cannot watch it if I want a particular solution of that problem, or if I condemn or fear it. Fear, comparison, judgment, condemnation, prevent me from understanding the problem. That is, if I condemn, judge, compare, or identify myself with the problem, I don't understand the problem. But if I don't do any of these things, then does the problem exist? Do you understand? The problem exists as long as I am separate from the problem, does it not? I wonder if you are getting this?

Look, take the problem of violence, envy, greed, or what you will. If I am violent and say, "I must not be violent," I have already condemned my violence. That very word *violence* contains condemnation. Is that not so? If I want to understand the whole process of violence, I must not judge it, I must not compare it with what I should be, and there must be no fear. When I remove fear, when there is no condemnation, no comparison, then is there violence and all the problems connected with it?

Do you understand, sirs? You are waiting for me to answer. Please don't. Experiment with yourself; don't wait for me to answer because I have nothing to answer. You see, what we consider to be positive thinking is a process of being told what to do, and is that thinking? Or is there only one form of thinking, the highest, which is to push, to probe, to inquire, and never to accept? And you cannot inquire if you are caught in a so-called positive form of thinking. I wonder if you are following this, sirs?

We are trying to find out what it means to understand a problem, and we are examining the word *understanding*. I see that I cannot understand the problem of envy, for example, if I condemn, judge, identify, compare, and all the rest of it; and I am asking myself, when the mind ceases to do these things, does the problem exist? The problem exists as long as I am comparing, judging, evaluating, accepting, or denying it, struggling against it. But the moment there is no comparison in the profound sense of the word, the moment I cease comparing myself with my guru, my ideal, or with the man above me in my job, does not the problem of envy disappear? So, to understand a problem and dissolve it totally, there must be no form of condemnation, judgment, comparison, which only increase and do not resolve the problem.

Question: You said the other day that one has to see the totality of a problem to comprehend it. What is it that enables one to see the problem in its entirety?

KRISHNAMURTI: I shall go into this question, but let us approach it differently. What do we mean by attention? Is there attention when I am forcing my mind to attend? When I say to myself, "I must pay attention, I must control my mind and push aside all other thoughts," would you call that attention? Surely that is not attention. What happens when the mind forces itself to pay attention? It creates a resistance to prevent other thoughts from seeping in; it is concerned with resistance, with pushing away; therefore, it is incapable of attention. That is true, is it not? When you struggle to pay attention to something, other thoughts come in, and you have to keep pushing them away; your whole energy goes into that battle. So there is no attention as long as effort is made to pay attention. Similarly, there is no attention when you are examining a problem with the hope of resolving it, or with the hope of getting a reward out of it. Is that not so? Are you getting tired?

Comment: No, sir.

KRISHNAMURTI: But I see people yawning. Sirs, all this may be somewhat new to you, and listening is bound to be a very tiring process for you if your mind is struggling to follow. Don't struggle to follow, just listen, play with it, and you will understand much more than when you struggle.

So there is obviously no attention when the mind forces itself to attend. Nor is there attention when the mind is seeking a reward, when it is avoiding, escaping, wanting, because in that state your mind is distracted. To understand something totally you must give your complete attention to it. But you will soon find out how extraordinarily difficult that is because your mind is used to being distracted, so you say, "By jove, it is good to pay attention, but how am I to do it?" That is, you are back again with the desire to get something, so you will never pay complete attention. You must see for yourself the importance of being completely attentive, not just to what I am saying, but to everything in life. When you see a tree or a bird, for example, to pay complete attention is not to say, "That is an oak," or "That is a parrot," and walk by. In giving it a name, you have already ceased to pay attention. To look at the moon with complete attention is to look at it without saying, "That is the moon, it will be full moon the day after tomorrow," and so on, chattering all the time to yourself or to somebody else. But we never look at anything in that way. Whereas, if you are wholly aware, totally attentive when you look at something, then you will find that a complete transformation takes place, and that total attention is the good. There is no other, and you cannot get total attention by practice. By practice you get concentration, that is, you build up walls of resistance, and within those walls of resistance is the concentrator—but that is not attention, it is exclusion.

To understand the totality of a thing, there must be the absence of the 'me', the 'me' being preoccupation with "my wife," "my children," "my property," "my job," with who is ahead of me and whether I can get ahead of him. The 'me' includes the atma. Don't divide the atma from the 'me' because the 'me', which is the process of thinking, has invented the atma, and if there is no thinking, there is no atma. Try it and you will find that when all thought completely ceases—when it is not induced to cease, but really ceases—there is a state of being which is not the atma invented by the mind.

So the questioner wants to know what it is that enables one to see the problem in its entirety? Can one see the problem in its entirety? Most of us have never even asked ourselves that question, have we, sirs? All that we are concerned with is how to solve the problem, and the quicker it is solved, at whatever level, the more satisfied we are. We have never put to ourselves the question: Can I look at the problem entirely, totally? The moment you seriously ask yourself that question, you will find that you are doing it; you are looking at the problem in its totality because then you are not concerned with interpretation, evaluation, and all the rest of the nonsense. You are completely watching the problem without naming it. To watch a thing in its entirety, you cannot name it because the very naming process is a distraction. And what has happened to a mind that is free from naming, evaluating, comparing? Such a mind is capable of total awareness—not a continued total awareness, which is silly, because the moment anything continues, it has no life in it, it is already dead. Only the mind that is capable of seeing a problem in its totality understands the problem and is therefore free of the problem. Such a mind is in a state of extraordinary movement, but I cannot tell you of that movement; you have to find it for yourself. And a lazy mind, a mind that is ridden by authority, by tradition, by fear, can never find it.

October 21, 1956

Fourth Talk in New Delhi

I think it would be a waste of time, and this a useless gathering, if we were to treat what has been said, and what is going to be said, as mere intellectual amusement. To rely on any form of stimulation invariably makes the mind heavy, dull, incapable of swift thought, and if we are merely using the talks as a different kind of stimulant, then I think it would be better if these meetings had not taken place at all. On the other hand, if we can examine profoundly the ways of our thinking in daily life and begin to understand the process of our own minds, then perhaps these meetings will be worthwhile.

Though we may repeat certain words which have deep significance, most of us live very superficially; we live in a verbal world, a world of superficial actions and emotions. Our minds are shallow, petty, narrow, and one of the vital problems of life is how to make such a mind deep, rich, and full. The mind that is burdened with knowledge is not a rich mind, but only the mind that has delved deeply into itself and discovered its own innumerable recesses, its secret ideas, motives, is capable of penetrating, going beyond thought.

I am using the word *mind* to mean not only the superficial mind of everyday activity but also the unconscious mind—the mind which has many hidden compulsions and motives, the mind that is pursuing its secret fulfillments, that is aware of its frustrations, its capacities, its limitations, the mind that is ever seeking, ever probing. I am talking about the totality of the mind, the conscious as well as the unconscious. We know very little of that totality because most of us only function in the upper layers of our consciousness; we are wholly occupied with our job, with the routine of life, with beliefs, dogmas, and the easy repetition of prayers, all of which the superficial mind clings to because it is convenient, profitable, and with that we are satisfied.

Now, if we can go much more profoundly into the whole process of the mind, delve deeply into the unconscious, then perhaps we shall be able to find out for ourselves the full extent and limitation of the power of thinking. The unconscious is surely not a mystery, it is not a thing that we must learn about from psychologists, or from people who have studied philosophy. It is part of our daily existence and is constantly indicating something, giving hints; only our conscious mind is so occupied, so busy with its own trivial problems that it has no time or attention to receive these intimations—but the hidden mind is there. It is no more sacred or holy than the conscious mind because both are part of the total process of our consciousness, and to really go beyond the limitations of this consciousness, it seems to me that we must understand its ways.

Most of us think that struggle, conflict, various sorrows and frustrations have to be gone through, that the mind must be disciplined, that certain things have to be conquered or put aside in order to arrive at a stage which is beyond the mind, but I do not think it is possible to go beyond the mind in that way. To find out what is beyond the mind, one must go into it very deeply and understand the ways of the mind, because the mind that has not completely understood itself projects ideas, illusions which assume a false reality. Until I understand the ways of my mind, the ways of the self, any urge to seek is based on the desires, the motives of the mind. So, without really understanding the ways of the mind, it is impossible to find out what is true. I may say that there is an atma, an oversoul, a timeless reality, but it will be a mere repetition based on my conditioning, my belief, which has no validity. Until I understand the whole field of my thought, the total content of my mind, it is not possible to go beyond, and one *must* go beyond because without discovering something totally new, life becomes very repetitive, very shallow, uncreative.

So, how is the mind to understand itself? Is there within the field of the mind an entity who is superior to the mind? Do you understand, sirs? Is there within the process of thought an entity who is above and beyond thought, and who can therefore control thought? Or is the thing that we have called the atma, the sublime, the soul, merely an invention of thought and therefore still within the field of thought? I think it is very important to understand this because if there is a super entity, an outside agent who is beyond our whole process of thinking, then it is no good our thinking about it because it is not within the field of thought. We can think about something which we already know and are able to recognize, but to find that which is beyond the mind, thought must come to an end.

Most of us believe, do we not, that there is something beyond the mind, an observer who is watching not only the mind but the things of the mind, who is controlling, shaping, disciplining thought. Until we question whether there is such an entity beyond the mind, beyond the field of thought, we will look to that entity as a means of guiding our life and shaping our conduct.

Now, is there such an entity as the atma, the soul, or what you will, which is shaping, guiding, helping us to live a sane, balanced life? Or is that entity within the field of our own thinking, an invention of our own thought, and therefore not real? The mind is the product of time, of innumerable experiences, it is the result of many conditionings. The communist does not believe in an atma, a soul, because he has been conditioned to believe otherwise, as you have been conditioned to believe that there is a soul, an atma. You start with a postulate, an assertion, as he also does, both resulting from a mind which is conditioned. Until one really sees this fact and deeply realizes its significance, the mind is incapable of going beyond itself—or, to put it differently, thought can never be still, the mind can never be completely quiet, because there is always the observer and the observed; there is always the experiencer who is wishing for greater experience, so our life becomes the endless series of struggles which it actually is.

When you have an experience which is pleasurable, you want to repeat it; and when the experience is painful, you as the experiencer want to put away the pain. The thinker is inviting pleasure and discarding pain, so there is a constant battle going on within, which is obvious when you look into yourself. But you have the idea that the thinker, the observer, the watcher, exists above and beyond thinking. You believe, because you have read in your religious books, that the atma, or soul, exists and is watching thought. But if you look very closely, you will see that where there is no thinking, there is no thinker; where there is no demand for more and more experience, and no gathering of experience, there is no experiencer. We have stipulated that there is an entity who is beyond all this. But that entity is still the result of thinking and so still within the field of time; therefore, it is not timeless, nor something divine.

After all, what is the mind? Please, sirs, do not merely listen to my words, to my explanations or descriptions, but watch your own mind in operation. I am not giving positive directions because, as I explained, any positive thinking is really thoughtlessness. Whereas, if you think negatively, which is to observe your own mind without directing, without telling it what to do—because the director, the entity who says, "This is right, that is wrong," is still part of the mind—if you can merely watch your mind as you would observe a flower, without demanding anything, without translating what you see, then you will discover that this very observation brings clarification because the mind is not then seeking a result, it is not concerned with reward or punishment; it just wants to observe, to know what is true. And you cannot know what is true if there is a director who is already shaped by the past, by a particular conditioning. So please listen to find out for yourself, and you can find out for yourself only when you watch your own mind, that is, when the mind watches itself.

Now, what is the mind? It is not only a series of responses to the various challenges which are always impinging upon us but also a series of memories, conscious or unconscious, which are constantly shaping the present according to the conditioning of the past to conform to a future pattern. Watch yourselves, sirs; don't merely listen to my words and repeat them. Watch yourself and you will see that your mind is a series of desires, and the urge to fulfill those desires, in which are involved fear and frustration—I want something, I can't get it, so I am frustrated, unhappy. You love me, I don't love you; therefore, you feel frustrated, and so on and on.

The mind is also a series of ideas related to the past and to our desires; that is, the mind thinks in terms of progress. I am this, I want to be that, and I need time to arrive. Being envious, I say I must have time to arrive at the state of nonenvy, which is what we call progress, evolution. But is it? Please watch your own mind in operation. Can thought progress towards truth, reality, God, or can it only move from the known to the known? And is thinking independent of memory, or is it merely the repetition of the background, which is memory?

All this is the content of the mind, the mind being both the conscious and the unconscious. In the unconscious are stored up the racial memories as well as the individual experiences which I have not understood, and all these memories, the collective and the individual, impinge on the mind in that process which we call thinking, do they not? Desire, fear, frustration, wanting to act, wanting to improve, trying to fulfill oneself through some ambition, thinking that there is an atma, a supersoul, or that there is none—all that is the mind.

Now, if you do not understand the totality of the 'me', that is, if the mind does not understand the totality of itself, its activity will always be within the field of its own making. Unless the mind breaks away from its conditioning, the conscious as well as the unconscious, there is no real inquiry because your search will be according to your conditioning, and your experiences according to your background. The experiences of a man who has visions of Christ, Krishna, this or that, are obviously based on his background, his tradition. So a mind that is really seeking what is true, that wants to find out if there is truth, if there is reality, if there is God, must be free of its background; and without discovering what is true, our life becomes a repetitive pattern, modified by circumstances perhaps, but still a repetitive pattern, which we call progress, evolution.

Now, let us go a little further. Being aware of this totality of itself, the mind realizes that any effort it makes to alter itself is still part of that same pattern, however modified. Do you understand? The mind that seeks freedom, for example, is a mind which has created the idea of freedom and is pursuing it. Knowing only bondage, it says, "I must be free," and then struggles to be free. So we have always thought that effort is necessary to be free, but if we realize that effort exists only when the mind has separated itself as the maker of effort, as the watcher, as the thinker apart from the bondage, then effort is seen to be futile. All right, sirs?

Let me put it much more simply. My mind is in bondage to a tradition, and I want to be free of it because I see how absurd it is for the mind to be enslaved by something. But the moment I have said, "The mind must be free," what has happened? I have created effort, have I not? And the effort is according to the new pattern of what I want to be.

Let us look at it differently. If there is no watcher apart from the watched, if there is no observer apart from the observed, how can there be effort? There is effort only as long as there is a watcher who is trying to alter the thing watched. But if you understand that the watcher is the watched—which is not an intellectual formula, it is a tremendous experience to know that there is no thinker apart from thought—then you will find that there is no effort at all. Then quite a different process comes into being, quite a different way of looking at what you call envy, or whatever it is that is watched. As long as there is an observer who is making an effort to reach a certain state, there must be conflict, and it is not through conflict that there is understanding.

Now, this total process is the mind, and when the mind understands its total process, it becomes quiet, utterly still, because there is no desire to be or not to be. Such a mind is not made still, or induced to be still, but it becomes still because it has totally understood the content of itself. Then only is it possible to find out for yourself whether there is reality or not. Until your mind has come to that state, your assertions that there is or is not reality, God, or the atma, have no meaning whatsoever. They are merely the repetitions of a mind that is conditioned like a gramophone record to repeat a phrase over and over again.

So, self-knowledge is essential, but it is not to be found in books; self-knowledge arises from watching ourselves in the mirror of relationship, which reveals the whole operation of the mind. It is only when we have understood the totality of the mind that there is stillness.

Question: In the process of thinking, one has to draw on one's knowledge and experience. Are you not doing the same? Then why do you condemn knowledge and experience?

KRISHNAMURTI: Well, sirs, this is a very interesting question because if you can go into it really carefully, it will be very revealing.

Words are necessary for communication. If I talked in the Chinese language, for example, you would not understand. So words which have a common meaning for you and me are a means of communication. These words are stored up in the mind as memory. That is one fact.

Another fact is that most of us have experiences of innumerable kinds stored up as memory, and from this background of memory, there is a response. If you did not know where you lived, there would obviously be something very wrong with you. Knowledge is a series of experiences, not only of the individual, but also of the collective. Scientific knowledge, the knowledge based on your own experiences, the experiences arising from your particular conditioning—all this has been stored up in the mind as memory. That is the background, is it not? And most of us function from that background. That is, if I have been brought up as a Hindu, if that is my tradition, my background, and I meet a Muslim, my reaction is immediate; I don't like him, though I may be tolerant because I am civilized. So when I meet someone new, I respond according to my conditioning, my prejudices, as he responds according to his. That is our state, is it not?

Now, the questioner asks, "Why do you condemn knowledge and experience?" I am not condemning. I must have knowledge to go where I live, or to build a bridge, or to communicate certain things to you. I must have knowledge not to burn myself. To keep on burning myself would be stupid, neurotic. What I am saying is that experience based on knowledge, on one's background, is merely the continuation of that background, and therefore, there is no new experience. Surely that is simple. If I am translating every challenge in terms of my conditioning, there is no new experience. I can respond to the challenge anew only when my mind has understood and freed itself from the background. If the mind is to discover anything new, it cannot depend on knowledge, which is based on conditioning, memory, experience, and so on. So what has happened? The questioner wants to know if I am not doing that very thing when I am speaking. I am depending on words to communicate, obviously. But there is something more implied in the question, which is: Are you not speaking from the knowledge of some past experience which you have had? I will explain what I mean.

Let us say I was happy yesterday. There was a lovely sunset, the dark hills outlined against the setting sun with a single tree and many birds; it was an extraordinarily beautiful thing to behold, to feel. Now, in speaking to you of that sunset, am I living in the memory of it, or am I free of that memory and am merely describing the experience without the emotional content? Do you understand what I am talking about? No?

Sirs, this is very interesting, and you will find out something if you watch your own mind and not just listen to my words. Your life is based on past experience, and your past experiences are shaping your present thinking. Now, is it possible to be in a state of experiencing, and not in a state of having had experience? Do you understand the difference? They are two entirely different states: the state of experiencing and the state of having had experience. Experiencing is a living process whereas the other is not—it is the memory of an experience which is over. From which state do you talk?—that is what the questioner wants to know. I am doing all the thinking, am I not?

Now, what is the actual fact with most of us? Don't bother with me for the time being. What is the fact with you? You are thinking, and your thought is based on past experience, which is what you call knowledge. So your mind is living in the past; it is living on experience that you have had, or on experience that you hope to have, based on your conditioning, on your knowledge. Are you ever aware of the other state, the state of experiencing? Or are you only aware of the experience when it is over? Do you follow?

Look, sirs, when you are happy, are you aware that you are happy? When something delights you, are you aware that you are delighted? The moment you know that you are happy, happiness is gone. The moment you are aware that you are virtuous, virtue has obviously ceased to be; therefore, the cultivation of virtue is a self-centered activity, and not virtue at all.

So the questioner wants to know whether I speak from a past experience which is remembered and communicated through words, or whether experiencing and communicating are going on simultaneously. Is that clear?

To put it differently, the word *love* can be communicated. You and I both know that word. Now, if you have had the taste of love, you can speak of that experience from the past; but if you are living, experiencing love, you can communicate it; and that is a state entirely different from the other, which is to experience and then communicate. If you understand this, if you really see the falseness of the one and the truth of the other, then your mind is in a state of continual experiencing, which is not to experience a thing and then communicate it. Reality is something which is living; it cannot be recognized through experience and then communicated through words. When you are feeling something intensely, living it, communication has meaning, but it has no meaning when you have had an experience and repeat that experience from memory.

Sirs, when you repeat the word *atma*, when you quote the Gita, the Upanishads, and other sacred books, the mind is merely a repetitive machine; but if the mind sees the futility of all that and is free—not free from something, but free—then it is in a state of experiencing which never ceases. Do you understand, sirs? There is always the state of experiencing; therefore, the mind is always fresh, young, innocent, and only such a mind can understand that which is immeasurable.

Question: We find the need for discipline even in our daily living. Is not discipline necessary for the proper education of the young?

KRISHNAMURTI: Sir, what do we mean by discipline? Don't be on the defensive, I am not attacking you; don't put me in the position of the prosecutor, with you as the defendant. We are trying to understand. What do we mean by discipline? Does it not mean conforming to a pattern which society has laid down or which you have established for yourself? That is one form of discipline. Discipline also means suppression. I have a certain feeling, but the guru, the authority says, "No, you must suppress it." Discipline also means creating a pattern for my action in order to achieve my ambition, does it not? I want to be the biggest something, so I discipline myself according to my ambition.

Now, what happens when you suppress, conform, adjust yourself to a pattern? What has happened to a mind that has forced itself to fit into a mold? Obviously it is a dead mind, it is not a living mind. As we build barriers to keep the river from overflowing its banks and inundating the land, so the mind is held in a particular pattern. To hold the mind in a pattern, we need discipline, and so we say discipline is essential even in our daily life.

Do you follow, sirs? I am just investigating the implications of discipline. What you suppress remains in the unconscious and keeps on acting in various ways. Through discipline you merely push it further down, thereby giving it greater vitality to repeat in different directions. All this is implied in the discipline which you think is necessary. You say, "If I do not discipline myself, I shall lead a chaotic, miserable, and stupid life"; but you are leading a chaotic, miserable, and stupid life as it is. Similarly the educator says, "We must discipline the child because look what has happened to students in universities all over India." But is discipline what is needed in our life, or is it the understanding of the whole process of discipline?—which will bring its own order, an order not imposed by society or by ambition. Order is obviously essential in life, but not order according to a tradition.

Now, the questioner asks, "Is not discipline necessary for the proper education of the young?" What do you mean by education? When you say that you must educate the child, what do you mean by that? Essentially you mean that he must be taught to conform to society, he must learn a technique so that he can get a job and be capable of earning a livelihood. Is not that what you are all concerned with? And you also teach him about so-called religion—or, if you are a communist, you want him to accept communism, and so on and on. The governments throughout the world want the educated to be efficient, to be trained to kill in the name of the country, to be capable of building dams, or to possess other engineering and technical capacities, and you also are concerned with that. You want the student to fit himself into the pattern of society, to conform to tradition and be able to earn a livelihood, so you are really not concerned with the child at all, are you? You are only concerned with what he should be, and the government is also concerned with that, and to make him what he should be is what we call education, is it not?

Seeing this whole process, you say, "How are we to educate the child differently, creatively, without inventing new patterns, new ways of conditioning?" Before going into that, we have first to find out if you are an educator, if you are a parent who really loves his child—and I doubt that you do love your child. If you loved your child, you would not want him to fit into this rotten society; on the contrary, you would help him to be free so that he could create a new society with totally different values. If you really loved your child, you would stop all wars, and you would not think in terms of hierarchical authority.

If you deeply understood all this and really meant it, what would you do as an educator, as a parent? Life is a series of influences; you cannot avoid them. Every book, every newspaper, everything that you read, hear, or see is being imprinted on your mind, which is shaped by these influences, and you choose one influence as opposed to another depending on your tradition, your environment, your society.

So the child is conditioned from the very beginning by the many influences about him, and the wise educator will obviously point all this out, helping the child to be aware of these influences and to be free of them without creating a new conditioning which he thinks is nobler. No system, no method, will help the child to be free from influence. The parent as well as the teacher has to be very watchful not to be caught in any influence, which means that he must have a very alert mind, but neither the parent nor the teacher has an alert mind. Most of us think that we shall have an alert mind by creating a new method, a new system, and we look to the system, the method, the technique to help us to be free—which is an impossibility. Only when the mind of the educator, of the parent, understands the whole process of discipline, with all its implications, is it possible to help the child to be free. Freedom is not at the end but at the beginning.

I have spoken for an hour and five minutes. There is one more question. Can you bear it if I go into it?

Comment: Yes, sir.

KRISHNAMURTI: Which means that you are merely listening to my words and not watching your own mind. If you were watching your own mind and had observed all the things implied in what you have heard, you would be exhausted, obviously, because your mind is not accustomed to being acutely watchful, alert. I am not criticizing you, sirs; I would not be so impudent, and I mean it. But when you say, "Please go on," it indicates a great deal because if you took one question, like discipline, or what is experience, and went completely into it, followed it to the very end, you would not need to ask any other question, for you would have found the totality of all questions and all answers. But unfortunately, most of us ask many questions, hoping that by putting many parts together, we shall come to the whole. The whole is not understood through the part. The whole must be seen immediately.

And I think that is enough for this evening.

October 24, 1956

Fifth Talk in New Delhi

I think one of our greatest difficulties is the incapacity to resolve our human problems. We have many human problems, one after another, and most of us seem to be utterly incapable of resolving them. And is it possible to gather this capacity through the process of time, or does it come into being not so much through the process of time but with the immediate comprehension of the problem? It seems to me that it is not a matter of cultivating capacity, but rather of applying an attention which is not distracted. I will explain what I mean.

We all have many conflicting human problems, social, economic, religious, and so on; and we are aware of these problems, not only individually, in our private lives, but also collectively. We see that the present society is everlastingly in conflict with itself, and that within it there is always the factor of deterioration; and we also see that in our own minds, however eager, alert, there is this same process of deterioration going on.

Now, is it possible for the mind to tackle all these problems as a whole, and not partially, one by one? Do you understand? We are confronted with this complex of problems, and we think we can resolve it by tackling the problems one by one, trying to do something about the part unrelated to the whole. The politician, for example, always deals with a part and not with the whole, so he can never bring about peace, though he may talk about it. It is like pruning a branch when the whole root system of the tree is without proper nourishment, insufficiently watered, and so on.

So what is important is to see that the complex problem of human existence is not to be solved little by little, one part at a time, but must be attacked totally, as a whole, and I think that is where our difficulty lies. Through education, through tradition, we have created the division of a religious life and a worldly life, a spiritual formula and a material technique, and with this fragmentary outlook we are trying to resolve our many conflicts. It is this fragmentary outlook, I think, which is the real cause of the multiplication of our conflicts, and not the lack of capacity to deal with the problem. We think we lack that capacity, and so we look to some authority to help us; we practice discipline in various forms, and so on, but I don't think that is the issue. The issue is not the cultivation of a particular technique, or the following of a particular path, but to see that we are not approaching life as a totality.

There is no such thing as an isolated existence. Nothing can exist in isolation, for everything is related to something else. If we can actually feel the truth of this and not just grasp it intellectually—that is, if the mind can look at the whole complex of existence and see it as an interrelated totality, which is not to create a series of divisions and partial understandings—then I think we shall deal with our problems from a completely different point of view.

So, can the mind empty itself of its Hindu, Christian, or Buddhist way of thinking? Can it cease to think as a politician, an ambitious man, a virtuous man, and so on, and not function in part all the time? Can it stop looking at life fragmentarily? Can you free yourself, for example, from the idea that you are an Indian, an American, a Russian, or a communist—free yourself, not just from the word, but from the whole content of the word, from the whole tradition and outlook—and think as a human being who has got to deal with the complex problem of existence? Surely life must be dealt with, not according to any particular pattern, system, or ideology, but as an integrated whole; and the question invariably arises, "How am I to do it, what is the method?"

Now, there is no "how." There is a "how" in the cultivation of the fragmentary outlook, but the outlook which is complete, which sees the whole problem of existence at once, cannot be cultivated through any method. So what is one to do? Surely, what is necessary is that you who were born in this or that country, who have been educated or conditioned according to certain traditions and beliefs, should see that your education, your conditioning, does interfere with the perception of the whole—the whole being man with his many problems. That is, you must be capable of dealing with the problems of life, not as the communist, the socialist, the Hindu, or the so-called religious person would deal with them, but as a human being who is constantly responding to the challenge anew. A mind that does not respond fully and adequately to the challenge of life soon finds itself in a state of deterioration. Only the mind that is capable of meeting the challenge totally, adequately, that responds fully to what is demanded of it—only such a mind is not deteriorating.

As long as the mind thinks in terms of the part and does not respond to the whole complex of existence, it can never resolve our many problems, however clever it may be in the political, economic, or so-called religious field. A mind whose thinking is fragmentary, partial, cannot respond to the challenge of life with freshness, with clarity; its response is incomplete, inadequate, and it is such a mind that has within it the deteriorating factor. If you and I realize this fact, really see the truth of it, then is a technique necessary? Do you understand the issue?

What is important, surely, is to see the necessity of approaching life anew, not with the bias of Hinduism, communism, and all the rest of the stupid stuff—which means that one's mind must not think in terms of the old, nor create a future pattern based on the old. One must be capable of approaching the problem, whatever it be, with a mind that is entirely devoid of any fragmentary, separative, or partial outlook, and I think this is the basic issue confronting the world. We are neither Indians nor Americans nor Hungarians, but human beings. This is our earth, to be lived on totally, and we cannot live a total life if we are thinking as Christians, Buddhists, communists, or what you will.

Now, if you have really listened to this, if you really see it, feel completely the necessity of it, then your mind is already free from the conditioning of the past; and when that conditioning does arise, you will know how to deal with it because your mind is thinking in terms of the whole and not of the part. To respond anew to any challenge—and challenge is always new—the mind must totally empty itself of the past. The past cannot be revived. The idea of reviving an old religion, however fascinating, is really detrimental. A thing that is dead cannot be revived, and religion is not a matter of revival. Religion is something entirely different from the social conditioning of the mind. A man who is a Hindu, a Buddhist, or a Christian, and who seeks reality along that path, will never find it. There is no path to God. Paths have been invented by man for his convenience, and however assiduously he may follow the path to which his mind has been conditioned, he will never find reality because he is thinking in part, and that is why he does not know the quality of love. Love is not a thing of the mind, and one can understand the totality of love only when the mind can look at life as a whole and not as a part.

There are several questions which we are going to consider, and in doing so we are not trying to find an answer to the problem but rather to think out the problem together. We seek an answer when we don't understand the problem. If you and I understand the problem, no answer is necessary; but a mind that is seeking a solution, expecting an answer, will only increase the problem because it is moving away from the problem and is not concerned with the problem itself.

This is something which I think it is very important to understand and to feel the truth of—that the answer, the solution to a problem lies in the problem itself and not away from it. A mind which looks for an answer is not concerned with the problem, it is concerned with the answer; therefore, it is incapable of looking at the problem and understanding it. Nor is the mind capable of understanding the problem if it starts with a conclusion. Surely, the mind that thinks from a conclusion is not thinking at all. If I have a conclusion about what love should be and what it should not be, and start my thinking process from there, my mind is obviously not thinking; it is only moving from one conclusion to another, which is what most minds do. Having never understood what it is to love, they function only in the intellectual realm of conclusions, and therefore their world is barren.

So, in considering these questions, we are not looking for an answer, and please bear this in mind. An answer is very cheap to come by; you can find it in any book, or buy it from any authority—give him a garland or a few rupees, and there is your answer. The man who really wishes to understand the problem has to put aside all temptation to find an answer, but that is not the only difficulty. He has also to start without any conclusion. The mind that is burdened with a conclusion is incapable of looking at the problem; therefore, it can only increase and multiply the problem.

Question: Sleep is a period of rest for both the mind and the body. What is it that actuates dreams?

KRISHNAMURTI: What is a dream, and why do we dream? And is it possible not to dream at all? We know that we dream and that there are various kinds of dreams. Some dreams are very superficial, while others have a deep significance, the implications of which we are incapable of understanding, so we turn to a psychologist for an interpretation; but the interpreter of dreams obviously interprets according to his conditioning, which means that we become slaves to the interpreter. I hope you see all this. First there is a dream, and then the effort to find out the meaning or significance of the dream, and finally there is the question of whether the mind need dream at all—which may be the really important issue, and not the other.

Please, we are trying to think out this problem together. Watch your own mind at work; do not merely listen to my words. I am describing the process of dreaming, but if you are content with the description, at the end of it you will not understand, and you will be left with the mere ashes of words.

We dream. What does that mean? When the physical organism goes to sleep, the mind is still working, and this working of the mind in sleep is indicated by dreams—which does not mean that the mind is not functioning when we don't dream. The mind is not merely the upper levels of consciousness; it is also the unconscious, and in sleep it begins to dream. Why?

Now, what is happening during the day when the mind is not dreaming—at least when it thinks it is not dreaming? What is actually taking place? On the superficial levels the mind is very occupied with a job, with learning a particular technique, or what you will; it is busy, active, constantly occupied with many things. Being occupied during the day, the superficial mind is not open to the intimations of the unconscious, obviously, because as long as it is occupied, how can it listen to anything but its own occupation? It is closed not only to the unconscious but also to the extraordinary beauty of the skies, to the marvels of the earth, to the appalling poverty and squalor that exist about us. A mind that is occupied is incapable of being sensitive. But when the physical organism goes to sleep and the superficial mind, being tired out with the many occupations of the day, is relatively quiet, then in that quietness it is capable of receiving the intimations of the unconscious. These intimations take the form of symbols, visions, ideas, dreams. This is actually what happens; there is nothing mysterious about it. We may think we are having extraordinary experiences, meeting the Master and all that nonsense, but it is nothing of the kind. The unconscious is as conditioned as the conscious, and it projects certain ideas in the form of dreams. That is actually what is going on. The conscious mind, which is occupied during the day, is quiet during sleep, so the intimations of the unconscious are projected into it, and when you wake up you say, "I have had a dream." Then you want to find out the meaning of the dream, so you turn to some authority, or you try to interpret it yourself.

That is one process. There is also another process, though I don't know if it has ever happened to you: one dreams, and as one dreams, the interpretation is going on at the same time so that when one wakes up, there is no necessity for any further interpretation.

Are you following all this just verbally, or are you actually feeling your way into it? If you don't really feel it, then you are merely listening to words, and you will say at the end of it, "I have listened to you, but I have not got anything." Perfectly right, because you will not have listened with the intention to find out for yourself, watching your own mind in operation.

So the unconscious—which is a storehouse of racial memories, of cultural patterns, of innumerable experiences, individual as well as collective—wants to tell the conscious mind something; but the conscious mind, being active, occupied during the day, is incapable of receiving intimations from the unconscious except in the form of dreams when the physical organism sleeps.

Now, the next question is: Need the mind dream at all? If your mind is aware during the day—do you understand, sirs? It is not a matter of how to be aware—just aware, actively alert and not merely occupied, watching the movement of a tree, or a bird, seeing the smile of a child, the attitude of a beggar, observing your own occupation, your routine, your reaction to what the boss says, how you treat your servants and curry the favor of the rich—if you watch all that, if you are really sensitive to all that, then you are receiving intimations from the unconscious all the time. It is not a very complicated process. You are awake on the superficial level, and at the same time the unconscious, which is the residue of the past, is telling you things like an encyclopedia. The conscious is no longer a thing separate from the unconscious, into which the unconscious has to project certain ideas during sleep. So, to the extent that you are alert, watchful, what is the necessity of dreaming at all? Is that clear? The mind is then astonishingly sensitive during the day, receiving and understanding from moment to moment, not withholding, not accumulating. Please listen to this. The moment you accumulate, you have a residue which becomes a dream that must be interpreted. A sensitive mind is not an accumulative mind, but the mind which has accumulated is insensitive, and this accumulation is the unconscious which must unburden, cleanse itself, and so it begins to project symbols and all the rest of it.

If you are alert, sensitive, not only to what is happening in your own process of thinking, but to everything about you; if when you read the newspapers or your sacred books, you are aware of all the stupidities contained in them; if when you listen to your particular authority, you see his assumptions, his desire for power, position, knowing at the same time your own desire for power, position, authority—if you are awake to all that, then you will find that there is no longer a division between the conscious and the unconscious. Then experience leaves no residue, which means that there is no necessity for dreaming and the interpretation of dreams.

What happens to a mind that is so astonishingly sensitive during the day that it is not withholding, not accumulating? What happens to such a mind when it goes to sleep? *Is* it asleep? Do you understand? The physical organism sleeps, naturally, because it must rest. But need the mind rest that has been so intensely alert all during the day? Or does such a mind continue in that state of sensitivity, but without the many impressions from outside, so that it is able to penetrate to great depths without any motivation, and is therefore capable, when the physical organism wakes up, of seeing something totally new?

These are just words to you, naturally, because you have never experimented with all this. You have never been sensitive during the day, really active—which is not to be active in the sense of chattering, gossiping, being caught up in a routine, and all the rest of it. A mind that is really active is acutely sensitive to both the beautiful and the ugly, and for such a mind, there is no longer the division of waking and sleeping, the conscious and the unconscious. Then the mind functions totally, as an integrated whole.

Question: We all have moments of inward clarity, but we seem unable to relate these glimpses of light to our personal, national, and international problems. Unless we can establish a relationship between clarity and action, of what value is this clarity?

KRISHNAMURTI: We all have moments of clarity, but that clarity is a rare thing, and most of our life is spent in a state of contradiction, confusion, and struggle. And the questioner asks, "How can I who know moments of clarity, apply this clarity to the confusion in which I live? Of what value is clarity if I don't relate it to my daily action?"

Now, that is a wrong question, is it not? And if you put a wrong question, you will have a wrong answer. The question is: Can our moments of clarity help us to bring order into our activities and live a better life? I say that is a wrong question because you have clarity only when confusion is not. You cannot relate clarity to confusion. When you do, you are still more confused. Do you understand? Clarity comes only when the mind is not occupied with itself, with its virtues, with its gods, with its little quarrels, ambitions, and the whole petty business of its existence. When the mind is not occupied, there is clarity. Having felt that clarity, you say, "How can I relate it to my ambition?" Obviously you cannot. That clarity is of no value in terms of your ambition, yet that is what all the religio-political leaders say—that God must intervene in your life, must guide you, show you how to be free or spiritual. But God is not interested in your petty, little mind, obviously, because it is only when the mind ceases to function in its own frame that there is clarity.

So our function is not to pursue clarity. A petty mind cannot see the immeasurable. All that it can do is to free itself from pettiness—which is to cease to be ambitious. An ambitious man may talk of God, but that is merely a political trick of the exploiter. It is only when we cease to be envious, greedy, when we have real love and not ideas about love—it is only then that there is a clarity unrelated to that which is petty. Do you understand, sirs? How can a petty mind, a mind which is confused, contradictory, ambitious, vain, stupid, mediocre, understand that which is sweeping, limitless? We have occasional glimpses of something wide, full, rich, and we say, "How can I relate that state to the petty mind?" When we put a wrong question, we shall have a wrong answer, and our life is full of wrong answers because we are always putting wrong questions.

Question: Our most constant fear throughout life is the fear of death. Are we afraid of dying because we do not want to part with life, or because we do not know what lies beyond?

KRISHNAMURTI: Sir, this is a very complex question involving many problems: the problem of karma or cause-effect, the problem of complete loneliness, and the whole problem of séances, materialization, of trying to meet again an individual whom you have known and who you think lives on the other side. Then there is also involved the belief in reincarnation or in some form of resurrection. So this question has many side issues, and we cannot go into all of them now. Perhaps we can discuss them another time. Let us tackle the main issue, for if we can understand that, we shall be able to deal with the secondary issues.

Again, please listen, not just to my words, but to the whole feeling of what is being said, because it is your life you are concerned with, not my life. I shall be going away from here in a few days, which is probably a good thing, and your concern is not with me but with your own daily existence, with the misery, the fear, the turmoil, the anxiety, and the innumerable other things that make up your life. So this is your problem, and you have to deal with it; therefore, you are not merely listening to my words.

Now, what is living and what is dying, and why do we divide living from dying? Is living apart from the process of dying? That is the primary issue involved in this question, is it not? If I really understand the primary issue, then I can go after the side issues with a full heart and resolve them; but unless I understand the primary issue, I cannot deal with the secondary. The primary issue is: Do I know what living is? And if I know what living is, then will I be frightened of dying? Surely, if I know what living is, then in that very living, my mind will understand the full significance of dying. So we are now going to find out what is living.

What do we mean by living? And are we living? Living for most of us is a routine, a series of repetitious happenings—going to the office, sex, repeating some mantra, following an authority, accumulating and translating in our own terms other people's experience and knowledge, thinking it is something original, and so on. That whole process is what you call living, and if you are aware of it, watch it critically, you will see there is nothing in it that is original, pristine, unpremeditated. You are full of the Gita, of the Bible, you merely repeat what Christ or Krishna has said; you are driven by sex, or by the desire to fulfill some ambition with all its frustration and ugly horror. You beget a child, and through the child, through property, you try to find immortality; your child is important because he is carrying on your name. Do you understand, sirs? All that is what you call living.

Now, is that living? Is living a process of satisfaction and sorrow, a mere series of events, or is living something entirely different? And what do we mean by dying? Seeing that the physical organism dies through long use, disease, or accident, the mind says, "I have accumulated, I have suffered, I have acquired virtue, I have worked for my country, for God, and what will happen to me when the physical organism dies? Is there a continuity in the hereafter?" There is a continuity in our living which is mere repetition. Do you understand, sirs? If you look into your own mind, into your own heart, do you see anything living, or merely a process of repetition? There is a repetition, a continuity in so-called living, and you say, "When I die, that repetition, that center of continuity must go on." Is it not so?

To put it differently, the 'me' that has learned, suffered, accumulated, has not fulfilled, and you say, "Must it not have another chance?" So the 'me' is a complex entity made up of accumulated memory, and that is what you want to continue. You may think there is an atma, an entity beyond time, but that is still within the field of thinking and therefore part of the whole process of continuance. What you are concerned with, then, is a continuance, and therefore you are frightened of an ending. You say, "I have lived, worked so much, and if I shall come to an end at death, what is the good of it all?" So either you become a rationalist, brushing death away intellectually, or you invent a comforting theory called reincarnation and continue in that. I am not against reincarnation. I am showing you the whole process of how the mind operates.

I want to know what death is, as I know what living is. I see that repetition, in which there is the burden of tradition, memory, is not living; and because I see the falseness or the truth of not living, I know what living is. Are you getting what I am talking about? Is this clear? A mind that is caught in the net of repetition is not living. I see the truth of that; therefore, seeing the truth of that, I am free of repetition. Please listen.

I know that living is not a repetition; it is something incredibly new every minute, something which has never been experienced before. And as I know what living is in the real sense of the word, I must also know what dying is. Now, can I experience dying, as I know what living is? Through living, can I also experience dying? If I don't, I am not living. Do you understand? Dying is part of living, and if I understand only one part, I am insensitive to the whole. Therefore I must understand, know what death means, experience it, not in moments of accident or disease, when the physical mechanism wears out, but while I am living, healthy, active.

Sirs, this is not a theory, this is not oratory, nor is this a meeting for you to be intellectually stimulated by; if you are, you will be dull human beings afterwards.

So I want to know what it means to die. Dying is a coming to an end, is it not?—not only of the physical organism, but of the mind which thinks in terms of continuity. To die is to cease to be; it is the cessation of being as we know it, which is a continuity. Do you understand, sirs? "My house," "my property," "my job," "my wife," "my virtues," and all the rest of it is a continuity, and death may be the ending of that continuity. Can I end consciously, with the full feeling of what I am doing, this whole process of continuity?

Sirs, don't agree or disagree with me; don't say, "I can" or "I cannot," because you don't know what it means. You don't know what it means to live; if you did, you would never put this question about what it means to die because then there would be no continuity. Death is this living without continuity. Surely, a mind that is living invites or enters the house of death because it must also know the meaning, the whole significance of that word. Such a mind is not concerned with reincarnation, whether it is true or false, because it is thinking in a different field altogether.

Surely, that which has continuance is not capable of being creative. Only in that which ends is there a possibility of renewal. Do you understand, sirs? A mind that lives, that has continuance in memory—what can such a mind know of anything new? It can only know its own vanity, its own projections. There is renewal only for the mind that dies to all its yesterdays, literally dies, so that it has no sense of property. You may then live in a house, but it has no value as yours; you keep it tidy, but you have no identification with it. Similarly with your son, your daughter, your wife. This nonidentification is love. Therefore a mind that has no identification through continuance is a mind that is really creative—which is not the creativeness of writing books, inventing new schemes, and all the rest of that nonsense. A mind that is creative is limitless, and only such a mind is not afraid of living and therefore not afraid of dying.

October 28, 1956

Sixth Talk in New Delhi

It seems to me that what is important is not the problem but the mind that approaches the problem. We have many problems of every kind: the growth of tyranny, the multiplication of conflicts in the individual as well as in the collective life, and the utter lack of any directive purpose in life except that which is artificially created by society or by the individual himself. Our many problems seem to be increasing; they are not diminishing. The more civilization has progressed, the greater has become the complexity of the problems of living, and I think most of us are aware that the various ways of life which most people follow—the communist way of life, the so-called religious way of life, and the purely materialistic or progressive way of life, the life of many possessions—have not solved these problems. Seeing all this, those of us who are at all serious must have considered the question of how to bring about a change, not only in ourselves and in our relationship with particular individuals, but also in our relationship with the collective, with society. Our problems multiply, but as I said, I don't think the problem, whatever it be, is the real issue. The real issue, surely, is the mind that approaches the problem.

If my mind is incapable of dealing with a problem, and I act, the problem multiplies, does it not? That is a fairly obvious fact. And seeing that whatever it does with regard to the problem only multiplies the problem, what is the mind to do? Do you understand the issue? The problem—whether it be the problem of God, the problem of starvation, the problem of collective tyranny in the name of government, and so on—exists at different levels of our being, and we approach it hoping to solve it, which I think is a wrong approach altogether because we are laying emphasis on the problem. It seems to me that the real problem is the mind itself and not the problem which the mind has created and tries to solve. If the mind is petty, small, narrow, limited, however great and complex the problem may be, the mind approaches that problem in terms of its own pettiness. If I have a little mind and I think of God, the God of my thinking will be a little God, though I may clothe him with grandeur, beauty, wisdom, and all the rest of it.

It is the same with the problem of existence, the problem of bread, the problem of love, the problem of sex, the problem of relationship, the problem of death. These are all enormous problems, and we approach them with a small mind; we try to resolve them with a mind that is very limited. Though it has extraordinary capacities and is capable of invention, of subtle, cunning thought, the mind is still petty. It may be able to quote Marx, or the Gita, or some other religious book, but it is still a small mind, and a small mind confronted with a complex problem can only translate that problem in terms of itself, and therefore the problem, the misery increases. So the question is: Can the mind that is small, petty, be transformed into something which is not bound by its own limitations?

Are you following what I am talking about, or am I not making myself clear? Take, for example, the problem of love, which is very complex. Though I may be married, have children, unless there is that sense of beauty, the depth and clarity of love, life is very shallow, without much meaning, and I approach love with a very small mind. I want to know what it is, but I have all kinds of assumptions about it, I have already clothed it with my petty mind. So the problem is not how to understand what love is but to free from its own pettiness the mind that approaches the problem, and the minds of most people are petty.

By a petty mind I mean a mind that is occupied. Do you understand? A mind that is occupied with God, with plans, with virtue, with how to carry out what certain authorities say about economics or religion; a mind that is occupied with itself, with its own development, with culture, with following a certain way of existence; a mind that is occupied with an identity, with a country, belief, or ideology—such a mind is a petty mind.

When you are occupied with something, what happens psychologically, inwardly? There is no space in your mind, is there? Have you ever watched your own mind in operation? If you have, you will know that it is everlastingly busy with itself. An ambitious man is concerned from morning till night, and during his sleep, with his successes and failures, with his frustrations, with his innumerable demands, and the fulfillment of his ambition. He is like the so-called religious man who endlessly repeats a certain phrase, or is occupied with an ideal and with trying to conform to that ideal. So the mind that is occupied is a petty mind. If one really understands this, then quite a different process is at work.

After all, a mind that is vain, arrogant, full of the desire for power, and that tries to cultivate humility is occupied with itself; therefore, it is a petty mind. The mind that is trying to improve itself through the acquisition of knowledge, that is trying to become very clever, to be more powerful, to have a better job—such a mind is petty. It may occupy itself with God, with truth, with the atma, or with sitting in the seats of the mighty, but it is still a petty mind.

So what happens? Your mind is petty, occupied, it starts with certain conclusions, assumptions, it posits certain ideas, and with this occupied mind you try to solve the problem. When a small mind meets an enormous problem, there is action, obviously, and that action does produces a result—the result being an increase of the problem; and if you observe, that is exactly what is happening in the world. The people in the big seats are occupied with themselves in the name of the country; like you and me, they want position, power, prestige. We are all in the same boat, and with petty, little minds we are trying to solve the extraordinary problems of living, problems which demand an unoccupied mind. Life is a vital, moving thing, is it not? Therefore one must come to it afresh, with a mind that is not wholly occupied, that is capable of some space, some emptiness.

Now, what is the state of the mind that knows it is occupied and sees that occupation is petty? That is, when I realize that my mind is occupied, and that an occupied mind is a petty mind, what happens?

I don't think we see sufficiently clearly the truth that an occupied mind is a petty mind. Whether the mind is occupied with self-improvement, with God, with drink, with sexual passion, or the desire for power, it is all essentially the same, though sociologically these various occupations may have a difference. Occupation is occupation, and the mind that is occupied is petty because it is concerned with itself. If you see, if you actually experience the truth of that fact, surely your mind is no longer concerned with itself, with its own improvement, so there is a possibility for the mind that has been enclosed to remove its enclosure.

Just as an experiment, observe for yourself how your whole life is based on an assumption—that there is God or there is no God, that a certain pattern of living is better than other patterns, and so on. A mind which is occupied starts with an assumption, it approaches life with an idea, a conclusion. And can the mind approach a problem totally, removing all its conclusions, its previous experiences, which are also a form of conclusion? After all, a challenge is always new, is it not? If the mind is incapable of responding adequately to challenge, there is a deterioration, a going back; and the mind cannot respond adequately if it is consciously or unconsciously occupied, occupation being based on some ideology or conclusion. If you realize the truth of this, you will find that the mind is no longer petty because it is in a state of inquiry, in a state of healthy doubt—which is not to have doubts *about* something because that again becomes an occupation. A mind that is truly inquiring is not accumulating. It is the accumulating mind that is petty, whether it is accumulating knowledge or money, power, position. When you see the truth of that totally, there is real transformation of the mind, and it is such a mind that is capable of dealing with the many problems.

I am going to answer some questions, and as I have pointed out, the answer is not important. What is important is the problem, and the mind cannot give undivided attention to the problem if it is distracted by trying to find a solution to the problem. All solutions are based on desire, and the problem exists because of desire—desire for a hundred things. Without understanding the whole process of desire, merely to respond to the problem through one particular activity of desire, hoping it will produce the right answer, will not bring about the dissolution of the problem. So we are concerned not with an answer but with the problem itself.

Question: I entirely agree with you that it is necessary to uncondition one's mind. But how can a conditioned mind uncondition itself?

KRISHNAMURTI: The questioner states that he agrees with what I have said. Before we go into the question of unconditioning the mind, let us find out what we mean by agreement. You can agree with an opinion, with an idea; you cannot agree with a fact. You and I may agree in the sense that we share an opinion about a fact, but an opinion held by many does not make truth. To understand, there must be a living, vital skepticism, not acceptance or agreement. If you merely agree with me, you are agreeing with an opinion which you think I have. I have no opinions, so we are not in agreement. If you and I both see a poisonous snake, there is no question of agreement—we both stay away from it. When we say we agree, we are intellectually agreeing about an idea; but this inquiry into how to free the mind from conditioning does not demand an intellectual agreement. As long as the mind is conditioned as a Hindu, a communist, or what you will, it is incapable of thinking anew. That is not a matter of opinion. It is a fact. You don't have to agree.

So the question is: How can a mind which is conditioned, uncondition itself? You realize that your mind is conditioned as a Hindu, with all the various beliefs of Hinduism, or as a communist, a Christian, a Muslim, and so on. Your mind is conditioned, that is obvious. You believe in something, in the supernatural, in God, whereas another who has been brought up in a different social and psychological environment says there is no such thing, it is all rubbish. You are both conditioned, and your God is no more real than the no-God in which the other fellow believes.

So, whether you like it or not, your mind is conditioned, not partially, but all the way through. Don't say the atma is unconditioned. You have been told that the atma exists; otherwise, you don't know anything about it, and when you think of the atma, your thought is conditioning the atma. This again is so obvious. It is like the man who believes in Masters. He has been told there are Masters, and through his own desire for security he longs to find them, so he has visions, which are psychologically very simple and immature.

Now, the question is this. I know that my mind is conditioned, and how am I to free my mind from conditioning when the entity that tries to free it is also conditioned? Do you understand the issue? When a conditioned mind realizes that it is conditioned and wishes to uncondition itself, that very wish is also conditioned, so what is the mind to do?

Are you following this? Please, sirs, don't merely listen to my words, but watch your own minds in operation. This is a very difficult issue to discuss with such a large group, and unless you pay real attention, you will not find the answer. I am not going to give you the answer, so you have to observe your own minds very intently.

I know that my mind is conditioned as a Hindu, as a Buddhist, or whatever it is, and I see that any movement of the mind to uncondition itself is still conditioned. When the mind tries to uncondition itself, the maker of that effort is also conditioned, is he not? I hope I am explaining this.

Sirs, can you not take a pill and stop coughing? I can go on, but coughing and taking notes disturbs the others who are listening. So I will begin again.

Your mind is conditioned right through; there is no part of you which is unconditioned. That is a fact, whether you like it or not. You may say there is a part of you—the watcher, the supersoul, the atma—which is not conditioned; but because you think about it, it is within the field of thought; therefore, it is conditioned. You can invent lots of theories about it, but the fact is that your mind is conditioned right through, the conscious as well as the unconscious, and any effort it makes to free itself is also conditioned. So what is the mind to do? Or rather, what is the state of the mind when it knows that it is conditioned and realizes that any effort it makes to uncondition itself is still conditioned? Am I making myself clear?

Now, when you say, "I know I am conditioned," do you really know it, or is that merely a verbal statement? Do you know it with the same potency with which you see a cobra? When you see a snake and know it to be a cobra, there is immediate, unpremeditated action; and when you say, "I know I am conditioned," has it the same vital significance as your perception of the cobra? Or is it merely a superficial acknowledgement of the fact, and not the realization of the fact? When I realize the fact that I am conditioned, there is immediate action. I don't have to make an effort to uncondition myself. The very fact that I am conditioned, and the realization of that fact, brings an immediate clarification. The difficulty lies in not realizing that you are conditioned—not realizing it in the sense of understanding all its implications, seeing that all thought, however subtle, however cunning, however sophisticated or philosophical, is conditioned.

All thinking is obviously based on memory, conscious or unconscious, and when the thinker says, "I must free myself from conditioning," that very thinker, being the result of thought, is conditioned; and when you realize this, there is the cessation of all effort to change the conditioning. As long as you make an effort to change, you are still conditioned because the maker of the effort is himself conditioned; therefore, his effort will result in further conditioning, only in a different pattern. The mind that fully realizes this is in an unconditioned state because it has seen the totality of conditioning, the truth or the falseness of it. Sirs, it is like seeing something true. The very perception of what is true is the liberating factor. But to see what is true demands total attention—not a forced attention, not the calculated, profitable attention of fear or gain. When you see the truth that whatever the conditioned mind does to free itself, it is still conditioned, there is the cessation of all such effort, and it is this perception of what is true that is the liberating factor.

Question: How can I experience God, which will give a meaning to my weary life? Without that experience, what is the purpose of living?

KRISHNAMURTI: Can I understand life directly, or must I experience something which will give a meaning to life? Do you understand, sirs? To appreciate beauty, must I know what its purpose is? Must love have a cause? And if there is a cause to love, is it love? The questioner says he must have a certain experience that will give a meaning to life—which implies that for him life in itself is not important. So in seeking God, he is really escaping from life, escaping from sorrow, from beauty, from ugliness, from anger, pettiness, jealousy, and the desire for power, from the extraordinary complexity of living. All that is life, and as he does not understand it, he says, "I will find some greater thing which will give a meaning to life."

Please listen to what I am saying, but not just at the verbal, intellectual level because then it will have very little meaning. You can spin a lot of words about all this, read all the sacred books in the land, but it will be worthless because it is not related to your life, to your daily existence.

So, what is our living? What is this thing that we call our existence? Very simply, not philosophically, it is a series of experiences of pleasure and pain, and we want to avoid the pains while holding on to the pleasures. The pleasure of power, of being a big man in the big world, the pleasure of dominating one's little wife or husband, the pain, the frustration, fear, and anxiety which come with ambition, the ugliness of playing up to the man of importance, and so on—all that goes to make up our daily living. That is, what we call living is a series of memories within the field of the known, and the known becomes a problem when the mind is not free of the known. Functioning within the field of the known—the known being knowledge, experience, and the memory of that experience—the mind says, "I must know God." So, according to its tradition, according to its ideas, its conditioning, it projects an entity which it calls God, but that entity is the result of the known; it is still within the field of time.

So you can find out with clarity, with truth, with real experience whether there is God or not only when the mind is totally free from the known. Surely, that something which may be called God or truth must be totally new, unrecognizable, and a mind that approaches it through knowledge, through experience, through ideas and accumulated virtues, is trying to capture the unknown while living in the field of the known, which is an impossibility. All that the mind can do is to inquire whether it is possible to free itself from the known. To be free from the known is to be completely free from all the impressions of the past, from the whole weight of tradition. The mind itself is the product of the known; it is put together by time as the 'me' and the 'not-me', which is the conflict of duality. If the known totally ceases, consciously as well as unconsciously—and I say, not theoretically, that there is a possibility of its ceasing—then you will never ask if there is God because such a mind is immeasurable in itself; like love, it is its own eternity.

Question: I have practiced meditation most earnestly for twenty-five years, and I am still unable to go beyond a certain point. How am I to proceed further?

KRISHNAMURTI: Before we inquire into how to proceed further, must we not find out what meditation is? When I ask, "How am I to meditate?" am I not putting a wrong question? Such a question implies that I want to get somewhere, and I am willing to practice a method in order to get what I want. It is like taking an examination in order to get a job. Surely, the right question is to ask what meditation is, because right meditation gives perfume, depth, significance to life, and without it life has very little meaning. Do you understand, sirs? To know what is right meditation is much more important than earning a livelihood, getting married, having money, property, because without understanding, these things are all destroyed. So the understanding of the heart is the beginning of meditation.

I want to know what is meditation. I hope you will follow this, not just verbally, but in your own hearts, because without meditation you can know nothing of beauty, of love, of sorrow, of death and the whole expanse of life. The mind that says, "I must learn a method in order to meditate," is a silly mind because it has not understood what meditation is.

So, what is meditation? Is not that very inquiry the beginning of meditation? Do you understand, sirs? No? I will go on and you will see. Is meditation a process of concentration, forcing the mind to conform to a particular pattern? That is what most of you do who "meditate." You try to force your mind to focus on a certain idea, but other ideas creep in; you brush them away, but they creep in again. You go on playing this game for the next twenty years, and if at last you can manage to concentrate your mind on a chosen idea, you think you have learned how to meditate. But is that meditation? Let us see what is involved in concentration.

When a child is concentrating on a toy, what is happening? The attention of the child is being absorbed by the toy. He is not giving his attention to the toy, but the toy is very interesting and it absorbs his attention. That is exactly what is happening to you when you concentrate on the idea of the Master, on a picture, or when you repeat mantras, and all the rest of it. The toy is absorbing you, and you are merely a plaything of the toy. You thought you were the master of the toy, but the toy is the master.

Concentration also implies exclusiveness. You exclude in order to arrive at a particular result, like a boy trying to pass an examination. The boy wants a profitable result, so he forces himself to concentrate, he makes tremendous effort to get what he wants, which is based on his desire, on his conditioning. And does not this process of forcing the mind to concentrate, which involves suppression, exclusiveness, make the mind narrow? A mind that is made narrow, one-pointed, has extraordinary possibilities in the sense that it may achieve a great deal, but life is not one-pointed; it is an enormous thing to be comprehended, to be loved. It is not petty. Sirs, this is not rhetoric, this is not mere verbiage. When one feels something real, the expression of it may sound rhetorical, but it is not.

So, to concentrate is not to meditate, even though that is what most of you do, calling it meditation. And if concentration is not meditation, then what is? Surely, meditation is to understand every thought that comes into being, and not to dwell upon one particular thought; it is to invite all thoughts so that you understand the whole process of thinking. But what do you do now? You try to think of just one good thought, one good image; you repeat one good sentence which you have learned from the Gita, the Bible, or what you will; therefore, your mind becomes very narrow, limited, petty. Whereas, to be aware of every thought as it arises, and to understand the whole process of thinking, does not demand concentration. On the contrary, to understand the total process of thinking, the mind must be astonishingly alert, and then you will see that what you call thinking is based on a mind that is conditioned. So your inquiry is not how to control thought but how to free the mind from conditioning. The effort to control thought is part of the process of concentration in which the concentrator tries to make his mind silent, peaceful, is it not? "To have peace of mind"—that is a phrase which all of us use.

Now, what is peace of mind? How can the mind be quiet, have peace? Surely, not through discipline. The mind cannot be *made* still. A mind that is made still is a dead mind. To discover what it is to be still, one must inquire into the whole content of the mind—which means, really, finding out why the mind is seeking. Is the motive of search the desire for comfort, for permanency, for reward? If so, then such a mind may be still, but it will not find peace because its stillness is forced; it is based on compulsion, fear, and such a mind is not a peaceful mind. We are still inquiring into the whole process of meditation.

People who "meditate" and have visions of Christ, Krishna, Buddha, the Virgin, or whoever it be think they are advancing, making marvelous progress, but after all, the vision is the projection of their own background. What they want to see, they see, and that is obviously not meditation. On the contrary, meditation is to free the mind from all conditioning, and this is not a process that comes into being at a particular moment of the day when you are sitting cross-legged in a room by yourself. It must go on when you are walking, when you are frightened, when you are getting into the bus; it means watching the manner of your speech when you are talking to your wife, to your boss, to your servant. All that is meditation.

So meditation is the understanding of the meditator. Without understanding the one who meditates, which is yourself, inquiry into how to meditate has very little value. The beginning of meditation is self-knowledge, and self-knowledge cannot be gathered from a book, nor is it to be had by listening to some professor of psychology, or to someone who interprets the Gita, or any of that rubbish. All interpreters are traitors because they are not original experiencers; they are merely secondhand repeaters of something which they believe someone else has experienced and which they think is true. So beware of interpreters.

The mind which understands itself is a meditative mind. Self-knowledge is the beginning of meditation, and as you proceed deeply into it, you will find that the mind becomes astonishingly quiet, unforced, completely still, without motion—which means there is no experiencer demanding experience. When there is only that state of stillness without any movement of the mind, then you will find that in that state something else takes place. But you cannot possibly find out intellectually what that state is; you cannot come to it through the description of another, including myself. All that you can do is to free the mind from its conditioning, from the traditions, the greed, and all the petty things with which it is now burdened. Then you will see that, without your seeking it, the mind is astonishingly quiet; and for such a mind, that which is immeasurable comes into being. You cannot go to the immeasurable, you cannot search it out, you cannot delve into the depths of it. You can delve only into the recesses of your own heart and mind. You cannot invite truth, it must come to you; therefore, don't seek it. Understand your own life and then truth will come darkly, without any invitation; and then you will discover that there is immense beauty, a sensitivity to both the ugly and the beautiful.

October 31, 1956

Madras, India, 1956

First Talk in Madras

I think we must all be very gravely concerned with the affairs of the world because one can see that there is a great deal of tyranny and appalling butchery going on in the name of some ideology, and that even in the so-called democracies there is slowly arising the tendency to mold the mind of man according to a particular pattern of thought. Everywhere, in religious circles as well as in the political world—and regardless of whether man lives in a village or in the most modern of towns—there is this tendency to shape his mind in a particular way; and we think that by controlling the mind of man, we are going to achieve a social order that will not have within it the seed of deterioration and destruction. We have done this throughout the centuries, have we not? Through education, through religious dogmas and beliefs, through the worship of some God, through every form of coercion, punishment, and reward, we hope that man can be conditioned to act gently, without too much exploitation, with a sense of social relationship, and that society will then continue in an orderly fashion. This is not only the modern idea, for it has existed down the centuries. Since ancient times, religions throughout the world have successfully shaped the mind of man to think in a certain way, and now the politicians are using modern psychological methods to control his thought. They want collective action on a planned basis, so they seek to shape the mind of man according to a certain ideology, whether communist, socialist, or capitalist, hoping that you and I can thereby be made to live amicably in our relationship with each other, which is society.

This is what is actually happening all over the world. In the so-called democracies there is more leniency; you can read what you like and say what you like within limits, but the newspapers to a large extent control your thought and determine what your prejudices shall be. The literature you read influences your thinking, and the politician, with his promises of a future utopia, shapes your action. So the political or religious authorities are gradually shaping the mind of man. This is a fact, whether you accept it or not.

The central government, for example, issues certain legislative orders, and the newspapers never disagree too violently because their action is dictated by vested interests, as it is vested interests that create the politician. Every politician, from the highest to the lowest, is involved in vested interests, not only in terms of money, but also in terms of idea. The politician and his party have certain ideas as to what the country should be. Their ideas are obviously based on their limited knowledge, their inclinations, their prejudices, their personal experiences, and the whole country is subtly made to comply through propaganda, and it is the same with religious organizations throughout the world. The more cunning the organizer, the greater the possibility of controlling man's mind. You can see this process going on in the so-called Christian religion, particularly in Catholicism, as well as in the communist countries; and it is also going on in this country—only we are inefficient at it, thank God. But the politician here as elsewhere wants to be efficient, and he is going to succeed because, though you may profess all kinds of religious ideals and try mildly to follow them, for most of you the thing of first importance is security in the form of bread and butter, so the politician has got you.

This is the actual state of affairs in the world. Your mind is shaped as a Hindu, a Buddhist, or a socialist; you are conditioned to believe or not to believe, and merely to change the form of belief, dropping Hinduism and becoming a Christian, a communist, or something else, seems to me so utterly futile—not only futile, it is really a form of criminality because it does not solve the fundamental problem. We merely move from one set of words to another set of words, and this change of words in itself has an extraordinary effect on the mind. I don't know if you have ever observed what slaves we are to words. We shall discuss this presently in the course of these talks.

Now, what is a man to do who sees exactly what is taking place in the world, and who really wants to find out if God, truth, is an actuality, or merely a clever invention of the priest? After all, you and I are the result of the collective, are we not? And there must be individual human beings who have completely broken away from the collective, from society, who are free from conditioning, not in layers or in spots, but totally, for it is only such individuals who can find out what truth or God is—not the man of tradition, not the man who does *japa*, rings the bell, quotes the Gita, and goes to the temple every day. It is the irreligious people who do that. But the man who really wants to find out what this extraordinary movement of living is must not only understand the process of his own conditioning but be able to go beyond it, because the mind can find out what is true only when it is free from all conditioning, not when it merely repeats certain words or quotes the sacred books. Such a mind is not free.

So it is extraordinarily difficult in this world for the mind to be free. The politician and the so-called religious person talk about freedom—that is one of their catchwords—but they jolly well take care that you are not free because the moment you are free, you obviously become a danger to society, to organized religion, to all the rotten things that exist about you. It is only the free mind that will find out what is true, it is only the free mind that can be creative; and it is essential, in a culture of this kind, that importance be given, not to the following of a pattern, a doctrine, or a tradition, but to allowing the mind to be creative. But the mind can be creative only when it is free from conditioning, and such freedom is not easily come by; you have to work extraordinarily hard for it. You work hard for your daily living; you spend years at the whole business of being bossed around in order to earn a livelihood, swallowing the insults, the discomforts, the indignity, the sycophancy—but to work so that the mind is free is much more arduous. It requires great insight, great comprehension, an extensive awareness in which the mind knows all its impediments, its blockages, its movements of self-deception, its fantasies, its illusions, its myths. Once the mind is free, it can begin to investigate, to search out, but for a mind to seek when it is not free has no meaning. Do you understand? The mind which would find truth, God, this extraordinary beauty and depth of life, the fullness of love, must first be free. It has no meaning for a mind that is shaped, conditioned, held within the boundaries of tradition, to say, "I am seeking truth, God." Such a mind is like a donkey tethered to a post, it cannot wander further than the length of its rope.

So, if we want to find out what is this extraordinary state that lies beyond the vagaries of the mind—really experience it, live with it and know its full meaning—surely there must be freedom, and freedom implies harder work than most of us are willing to undertake. We would rather be led than discover, but one cannot be led to truth. Do please understand this very simple fact. No swami, no system of yoga, no religious organization, no doctrine or belief can lead you to the discovery of truth. Only the free mind can discover. That is obvious, is it not? You cannot discover the truth of anything by merely being told what it is because then the discovery is not yours. If you are merely told what happiness is, is that happiness?

To find out what this life is all about, to know the whole content of it and not just the superficial layers which we call living, to be aware of its joy, its extraordinary depths, its width and beauty, which includes the squalor, the misery, the strife, the degradation—to understand the significance of all that, your mind must obviously be free. If that is clearly understood, then your relationship with me, and my relationship with you, is not based on authority. I cannot lead you to truth, nor can anyone else; you have to discover it every moment of the day as you are living. It is to be found when you are walking in the street or riding in a tramcar, when you are quarreling with your wife or husband, when you are sitting alone or looking at the stars. When you know what is right meditation, then you will find out what is true; but a mind that is prepared, so-called educated, that is conditioned to believe or not to believe, that calls itself a Hindu, a Christian, a communist, a Buddhist—such a mind will never discover what is true, though it may search for a thousand years. So the important thing is for the mind to be free, and can the mind ever be free?

Do you understand the problem, sirs? Only the mind that is free can discover what is true—discover, not be told what is true. The description is not the fact. You may describe something in the most lovely language, put it in the most spiritual or lyrical words, but the word is not the fact. When you are hungry, the description of food does not feed you. But most of us are satisfied with the description of truth, and the description, the symbol, has taken the place of the factual. To discover whether there is a reality or not, we must be capable of seeing the true as the true, the false as the false, and not wait to be told like a lot of immature children.

So, to find out what is true, the mind must first be free, and to be free is extraordinarily hard work, harder than all the practices of yoga. Such practices merely condition your mind, and it is only the free mind that can be creative. A conditioned mind may be inventive; it may think up new ideas, new phrases, new gadgets; it may build a dam, plan a new society, and all the rest of it, but that is not creativity. Creativity is something much more than the mere capacity to acquire a technique. It is because this extraordinary thing called creativity is not in most of us that we are so shallow, empty, insufficient, and only the mind that is free can be creative.

So our problem is: How is the mind to be set free? And is it possible to set the mind free—not in layers or patches, not in little bits here and there, but totally, right through, the unconscious as well as the conscious? Or is the mind ever to be conditioned, ever to be shaped? You have to find out for yourself, and not wait for me to tell you whether the mind can ever be free. Can the mind only think about freedom, as a prisoner does, and so be doomed never to be free but always to be held within the bondage of its conditioning?

Do you understand the problem? Can the mind ever be totally free, or is it the very nature of the mind to be conditioned? If it is the fundamental quality of the mind to be limited, then there is no question of ever finding out what is reality; then you can go on repeating that there is God or there is no God, that this is good and something else is bad, all of which is within the pattern of a given culture. But to find out the truth of the matter, you have to inquire for yourself into whether the mind can really be free. I say it can be—which is not for you to accept or reject. It may be true, or it may be my opinion, my fancy, my illusion, and you cannot base your life on somebody else's discovery, or on his illusion, his fancy, or on a mere idea. You have to find out.

So, our inquiry throughout all these talks will be concerned not with how to further condition the mind according to a nobler pattern, a better system or ideology—which is what most people want—but with whether it is possible to free the mind totally. Because you see, sirs, there must be a creative explosion to bring about a new society. Mere reformation within the pattern is no change at all. There is change only when you break through the pattern and find something new. Whether or not what you discover will have an influence on society is irrelevant. To be capable of having this extraordinary, explosive creativity outside the pattern is what is vital. This explosive creativity has its own action which may or may not influence society, but it will create a totally new culture, a new way of thinking which is not within the pattern. So we are not concerned with the reformation of society; on the contrary, our inquiry is to find out if it is possible to break away from society, that is, from our own conditioning.

Now, how do we set about to inquire into the truth of anything? Do you understand, sirs? If we are at all serious, in earnest, not merely given to words and phrases, to a slipshod way of thinking, you and I want to know how to inquire into the question of whether or not the mind can be free. How are we to set about it? Surely, one of the most essential factors in all inquiry, in all questioning, is not to assume or postulate anything, not to start thinking from a conclusion, because if you start thinking from a conclusion, there is no thinking at all. Thought starting from an established idea is not thinking, it is merely repetition. To be free from conclusions, from assumptions, is extraordinarily difficult; but that is the first essential, it seems to me, in all real inquiry. You cannot inquire if you start with a ready-made foundation, which may be utterly false, and therefore your so-called inquiry is bound to lead to something equally false.

So, can you and I as individuals—not as Hindus, not as people living in India or in Europe—start to inquire without any assumption? I do not mean the assumptions implicit in facts like tomorrow, yesterday, time, food, and all the rest of it, but the assumptions arising from the state of mind which demands psychological security—the assumption that there is God or there is no God, that this is good, that is bad, and so on. Sirs, to find out if there is God or if there is no God, surely I cannot assume anything, can I? If I am really in earnest, if I really want to find out the truth of the matter and not just indulge in cheap talk, if I am eager to discover what reality means, to comprehend the significance, the beauty of it, or its uncertainty, its utter emptiness—if I want to know reality, whatever it may be, then my mind must not assume anything, must it?

Verbally you may agree that you must not assume anything, but will you actually drop your assumptions? Because if you do not assume anything, what will happen? You will be against your family, your society, against every form of tradition; you will have to stand alone, completely dissociated from the values, the ideas which have been imposed upon your mind. And your mind is a bit horrified at that prospect because ideas, traditions, values give it a sense of security, of permanency; your job is based on all that, and you have a psychological investment in it. So consciously or unconsciously your mind rebels against the idea of standing completely alone to find out. To stand completely alone is to be uncontaminated by society—society being envy, greed, vanity, the desire for power, prestige, the pursuit of all the worldly as well as the so-called unworldly things—and it is only such a mind that is free to inquire and to find out the truth or the falseness of that which is beyond the mind. So self-knowledge is the beginning of wisdom. Wisdom is not to be found in books; it arises in the mind that is seeking to understand its own workings, and only such a mind can discover the reality that is beyond the measure of itself.

At all these talks there will be questions and answers—or rather, I am not going to give answers to the questions, but together we shall go into the problem.

Now, why do you put a question? Obviously, you put a question in order to find an answer. And which is more important, the question or the answer? Do please think it out with me. If the answer is more important, then you are really not concerned with the question because you are looking for an answer. Do you understand, sirs? You will see it in a moment as we go along.

There is a problem, whatever it be, and you want an answer to that problem. Now, what is actually taking place when you want an answer to a problem? Your mind is not giving its full attention to the problem. It is divided, it is distracted by the demand for an answer. A problem exists only when there is divided attention, but when you give your complete attention to a so-called problem, then the problem gives its own answer; you don't have to search for the answer outside the problem. But you cannot give your full attention to the problem if you are seeking an answer.

So I am not going to give an answer. Life has no categorical answer to anything; what it tells you is to go into the problem, look at the problem with all the intensity, attention, vitality that you can give to it. Then the problem resolves itself; it is not resolved because you have found an answer. That is the way we are going to look at this question, and you will miss its significance if you are waiting for an answer from me. I am telling you right at the beginning, so that you will have no misconception, that I am not giving an answer, but you and I together are going to inquire into the problem.

Question: Though political leaders, social reformers, and the various holy men are everlastingly denouncing it, exploitation continues to exist in human affairs, from the topmost government official to the illiterate drudge of the village. You too have preached against it for thirty years. How do you envisage action in which there is no exploitation?

KRISHNAMURTI: Sirs, you may be unconscious of this problem of exploitation, or you may not want to think about it, but it is there right in front of your nose, and it exists at every social level. The man who is politically, religiously, or scientifically talented exploits me because he has capacities which I have not. If I have a little learning and live in a petty village, I exploit the illiterate people there, and the village drudge exploits his wife. Now, what do we mean by exploitation?

There is the exploitation of the earth: we use it, we cultivate it, we mine it in order to gather the things of the earth for the benefit of man. That is one kind of exploitation. Then there is the exploitation of the stupid by the clever, of the weak by the strong. The cunning politician, the cunning priest, the cunning leader, the cunning saint—they all have an idea of what society should be, or of morality, righteousness, and they exploit it by their way of life, by their way of talking, and so on. They become examples, and the stupid, the illiterate, the thoughtless follow. So at what level are we talking when we speak of exploitation? Do you understand, sirs? When a man says, "I have found God, I know what it means," and you are eager to get it also, obviously he exploits you. The so-called spiritual leader is supposed to know the Master, and you don't, so you follow him because you want what you think he has, or what he promises. In other words, you are exploited for your own so-called good.

So, when one man knows, or says he knows, and another says, "I don't know, please tell me," is there not exploitation in their relationship? Do you understand, sirs? When there is the teacher and the taught, is there not exploitation? If I say, "I know, I have experienced," and you say you don't know, but you want to have that same experience, whatever it is, have you not put yourself in the position of being exploited by me?

Surely, whether you accumulate property or knowledge, it is essentially the same thing, only at a different level; and as long as the accumulative process is going on, there must be exploitation. The problem is then: Can we ever be in a state of learning, and therefore not in a state of accumulating? If for me life is a process of learning, then there is no exploitation, there is not the division of the teacher and the taught. Then both of us are important, and we learn from each other. Then there is not the high and the low, the more spiritual and the less spiritual, because then both of us are learning and not accumulating.

So, as long as there is accumulation in any form, which is self-centered action, there must be exploitation. That self-centered action may be in the name of society, or in the name of God, it may be in the name of a country or an ideology, but there is still exploitation. The politician at the top thinks he knows what is good for the whole of India. He has power, prestige, capacity, popularity, so he uses you, who don't know, to carry out his ideas; and as you have not the capacity to study, to inquire, and all the rest of it, you just follow. Sirs, this is what we are actually doing. You know, I don't know, so we have established in the world a hierarchical way of thinking based on authority. And the questioner wants to know what I envisage as the action of a man who is not exploiting, that is, who is not accumulating—who may have a few clothes, a little property, but who is without the sense of acquiring, either in terms of property, ideas or belief, and who is free of self-aggrandizement, of all self-centered interest in life.

Now, why do you want to know? Why do you ask how I envisage the state of action in which there is no exploitation? It is because you are lazy, is it not? You want to be told what that state is, you want to discuss it, to accept or reject it; you don't want to be in that state. If you were in that state, you would not ask such a question.

Sirs, please listen. This is really important because if you understand it, it leads to something enormous. Being lazy we say, "Tell me what it means to be free of exploitation, and I will agree or disagree with you." We don't want to be in that state because it demands hard work; it demands inquiry, the breaking up of our present condition of exploitation, whether it be at the topmost level or at the most common level. We don't want to break up our present condition of exploitation, we want that to go on, and yet we ask what is the state of the man who acts without exploitation. I say find out, get into that state, and then you will see that it has its own action, an action which is much more significant, much more vital, more rigorous than the other.

To know what it means not to acquire, to have the feeling of it and not just the mental image conjured up by words, is to feel no sense of self-importance, no sense of accumulation; it is to be really nothing inwardly. Though outwardly you may have a few clothes, a little property, those things are all meaningless. To feel deeply that you are not acquiring means that you are not looking for success, you are not looking for recognition by a rotten society; psychologically you have no vested interest in becoming something. Do you understand? As long as you are becoming something, which is the process of acquiring, there must be exploitation. You may talk a great deal about nonexploitation, but as long as there is this inward urge to become something, to become a saint, a famous politician, a rich man, or what you will—which is the very root of self-centered action—there must be exploitation. And this movement of becoming something is one of the most difficult things to be free of because to be free, one has to understand the whole problem of time as a means of climbing the ladder of success through the acquisition of property, power, position, or knowledge. Any activity or social reform as a means of self-importance or self-forgetfulness leads to exploitation.

If you are really serious about this question, if you earnestly desire to find out whether the mind can ever cease to exploit, then you will discover that it is possible to live in this world without accumulating anything, which means dying every minute to everything that you acquire, to the knowledge, to the virtue, to the things that you have gathered in this world as well as in the psychological realm. But to die totally to everything—to experience, to knowledge, to every process of acquisition—is an arduous task. It means that you must be completely aware, wholly attentive to the movements of the mind, and that is possible only when you watch the process of your mind in operation, that is, in the action of relationship. Observe how you treat your servants, how you play up to the boss, to the big politician, to the governor, to the saint, and to the man who is supposed to know. Only the mind that is really humble is not exploiting, and humility is not a thing to be cultivated. The mind is in a state of nonexploitation when it is silent, alone, when it is not acquiring, not seeking success, not climbing the ladder of recognition; and it is only such a mind that can bring sanity to a world that is full of cruelty and exploitation.

December 12, 1956

Second Talk in Madras

Communication is always difficult, especially when we are dealing with problems which are very complex, because each one is listening not to the problem itself but to his reaction to the problem. As we were saying last week, to discover that which is new, there must be freedom of the mind; and to find out the full significance of that word *freedom,* not the mere dictionary meaning, is very difficult because each one interprets it according to his fancy, prejudice, according to his own limited understanding, and so does not really probe into the depth of it. To understand the meaning of freedom, we cannot start from any supposition, assumption, or conclusion because then, the mind itself is not free. As you are listening to me now, for example, you already have certain ideas, prejudices, conclusions, which means that you are reacting according to the background in which you have been brought up; you are not listening to what is being said, but to these conclusions and interpretations, so actually there is no communication between us. To communicate fully and significantly, you and I must obviously be free from any kind of conclusion, opinion, or dogmatic belief.

The mind must be free to listen, and that is one of our greatest difficulties, is it not? If I want to understand something, my mind must put aside all its prejudices, conclusions, dogmas, and beliefs—which is an extraordinarily difficult thing to do. Yet that is obviously the first essential in all search—to set the mind free from the conclusions or assumptions it has acquired. There is no search if I start with a conclusion, with any form of judgment or evaluation, because my thinking is then merely a movement from one conclusion to another, which is not thinking at all. Is that not so?

Surely we must be clear on this point because, after all, what is it we are trying to do? You and I are trying to find out together the truth about this extraordinary thing called life—not a particular part or segment of life, with its superficial response, but the whole of life; and to find out the significance, the truth of life in its totality, we must surely start without assuming anything, that is, with a mind that is free from conclusions. If you assume that you are a Hindu with certain dogmas, opinions, or a Christian with definite ideas about salvation and how to attain it, obviously that very conditioning prevents real search and discovery. Therefore it is only the free mind that can find out whether there is God, truth, that can know the meaning of love, of death, and of the many problems which confront each one of us.

All this is obvious, is it not? The mind that wishes to find out the truth of anything, especially when it is a psychological matter involving the processes of the mind, must start without any assumption; it cannot assume that there is a soul, an atma, or cling to a particular belief. You must start freely, for you cannot seek if you are bound by a belief. Our concern, then, is not with what truth is, what reality is, or what God is, but with how to free the mind from belief, from influence, from pressure, from conditioning so that it is capable of discovering what is true. We have many problems in life, not only economic, but the many other problems which arise in man's relationship with man, with ideas, and with nature; and we can never find out the truth of all this if our minds are conditioned as communists, socialists, Christians, Hindus, Buddhists, or what you will. There must be a true answer to this enormous and urgent crisis which is confronting us all, but the true answer does not depend upon time because time as we understand it has in itself undergone a tremendous revolution on account of the atom, on account of rapid technological progress, the pressures of war, of economic conflict, and so on—which means that the whole process of our thinking with regard to time has also to undergo a fundamental change. And to bring about such a change, obviously we must free the mind from its conditioning.

Now, can the mind free itself from its conditioning? That is really the issue because, whether you are a communist, a Christian, or a Hindu, you have not solved your problems. On the contrary, your problems are multiplying, with great rapidity. The issue, therefore, is not how to solve the innumerable problems but whether the mind can approach these problems with freshness, with freedom, for it is only when the mind is free that it is capable of finding an answer which must obviously be totally different from the so-called answers to which we are accustomed. The answers that we now have to the problems of life have not resolved these problems, and a man who seriously wishes to understand the deeper significance of life must be concerned with freeing himself from the patterns which society and religion have imposed upon him. I think this is obvious, but the difficulty is that most of us do not accept or realize the necessity of it. We are still Hindus bound to our tradition, or Christians burdened with a particular set of dogmas, beliefs, through which we are trying to understand the very complex problem of living.

So, can the mind free itself from its pressures, from the influences of society, so that it is able to think straight and not be pushed in any direction? Can it free itself from its traditions, from its conclusions, from the experiences based upon its own conditioning, which it calls knowledge? Surely, that is the real issue. Because what is needed in the world is not more planning, more leaders or spiritual guides, but individuals who are explosively creative—not creative merely in the sense of inventiveness, but who have that strange quality of creation which comes when the mind is free from the traditions, the evaluations, the impositions of a particular society or culture. Only when each one of us is such an individual is it possible to bring about a new world, a new culture, a totally new way of looking at life.

Surely, to find out whether the mind can be free is like taking a journey by oneself into the unknown. For obviously, truth, reality, God, or what name you will, is the unknown; it is not the possession of any teacher, it is not to be found in any book, it is not caught in the net of tradition. You must come to it totally alone, you must take the journey without any companion, either Shankara, Buddha, or Christ. Only then will you discover what is true. But most of us walk with companions, which are our memories of all the things we have been told. You have been told about one set of ideas, the communist about another, and the Christian about still another. You have certain leaders, teachers, gurus, priests; you constantly read certain books, which have imposed fixed ideas on your mind. These fixed ideas are your companions in whose company you are always searching for the answer; but you can find the answer, surely, not according to a particular set of ideas, which are merely your prejudices, your conditioning, but only when you walk totally alone, without any companions whatsoever. Truth is something to be discovered, not to be invited or pursued, and to discover it, the mind must be completely free of its conditioning.

I don't know if you have ever thought about this problem of whether the mind, which is a result of time, of association, which is a process of recognition, of accumulated memories, traditions—whether such a mind can free itself from this accumulated residue of memory, from its conditioning as a Hindu, a Christian, a Buddhist, or a communist, and look at life completely anew. Surely, that is the problem—not to find a new teacher, a new doctrine, but to discover for oneself whether the individual mind can separate itself from society and stand completely alone so as to find out what is true.

After all, what is society? Society, surely, is the relationship between man and man. We have created this society; we are part of it, and this society has in turn influenced us, nurtured us, educated us; and without understanding this society, which is our relationship with each other, we shall not be able to understand ourselves. This society is obviously based on acquisitiveness, on greed, envy, ambition, on the search for power, position, prestige; it gives importance to the self, to the 'I'.

Now, can we be free of greed, envy, ambition, fear, not partially, in little bits, but totally? Can the mind be wholly free of the qualities which it calls greed, envy, violence? If it can, then the moment it is free, one's relationship to society has undergone a fundamental change because one is no longer dependent psychologically on the evaluations imposed by society. That is, sirs, to be totally free of envy or jealousy is to be free from the whole complex problem of the 'more': more knowledge, more power, more capacity. The process of imitation, the desire for fame, for success, implies comparison: I am small and you are great, you know and I do not. The mind is caught in this extraordinary process of acquisition, this comparative pursuit of success, in which is involved ambition, with all the frustrations and fears that go with it.

So, can your mind be totally free from this whole process? As long as it is not, you will never find out what is truth or God. You may talk about it, but then it is merely a political word to be bandied about. If the mind is not totally free from envy, for example, there is no possibility of finding out what is true; therefore, a man who seriously and earnestly wants to find out what is true must be concerned with the problem of envy. If you begin to probe into it, you will soon discover that no guru can help you to be free of envy. Please see this fact simply and clearly. When you go to a teacher, a guru, to be taught how to free the mind from envy, you are obviously giving further encouragement to envy; you want to achieve, you want to succeed; therefore, you are still within the net of envy. A mind that is learning about the whole complex problem of envy is not being taught; it has no guide, no philosophy, no system, no teacher. When you have a teacher, a system, you are being taught, and a man who is being taught is fundamentally greedy; therefore, he ceases to learn. Learning is an extraordinary process. The moment you accumulate learning, you cease to learn because that which you have accumulated interprets and therefore impedes any further learning. Is that not so? Knowledge as accumulated learning is an impediment to further learning. Please see this. It is really very simple and essentially real.

After all, what are you and I doing here? If you put yourself in the position of one who is being taught by me, your mind is envious because it wants to achieve success in a particular direction which it calls spiritual. You are concerned with achievement, with gain, with arriving somewhere, which is essentially greed, envy. Whereas, if you and I are both learning without accumulating, then our relationship is entirely different. Do you understand, sirs? Then we are really inquiring together, searching into the totality of envy, and not just remaining on the surface. And what then has actually happened to your mind? You are no longer concerned with ideas about truth, God, with tradition and the compulsions of society, for you are an independent human being who is inquiring, learning, searching. I think it is very important to see this because tyranny is spreading in the world; governments are planning to exercise greater control over the minds of men in order to make them more efficient, and all the rest of it. So in becoming efficient, in becoming powerful, you are losing the capacity for integrated, completely individual thinking, which is really explosive thinking.

To learn about envy is the beginning of freedom from envy. To learn about envy is not to accumulate knowledge about it but to observe all the movements of the mind as they arise from moment to moment, which is to be aware of the mind's response when it sees a man who is rich, or a man who is inferior, or a man who is very happy or erudite. The mind that is thus consciously and unconsciously watching its own movements is in a state of learning, and a mind that is learning has no past; therefore, this whole idea of karma as a binding element is completely wiped away. But the moment you accumulate knowledge as a means to further success, to further security, or as a means of becoming important, you are caught in time. A man who is really experiencing, learning, is completely alone, but not in the sense of being isolated, for the mind of such a man is pure. Do you understand, sirs? Purity of mind is essential to the state of learning, which means that you cannot learn if there is no humility, and you have no humility if you are accumulating knowledge.

If we really see the truth of this, that there can be the state of learning only when there is no accumulation of knowledge, then we shall find that our relationship, not only with each other, but also with the rest of the world, has completely changed. Then a totally new element comes into being, and this whole problem of the superior and the inferior, in the psychological sense, ceases to exist. There are obviously people who have greater capacity than others, and I am not referring to that kind of superficial inequality. But a man who is learning knows neither equality nor inequality; therefore, learning is a process of meditation which frees the mind from the past, from accumulated knowledge. If you are learning about your conditioning, you are already free from that conditioning. It is only the mind that can take the journey alone, without any companion, without any teacher, without any tradition, dogma, or belief—it is only such a mind that is pure and can therefore discover what is true.

There are several questions to be answered, but what is important is one's understanding of the problem, and not the answer. If I understand the problem, I don't ask for an answer. The understanding of the problem itself resolves the problem. Please, sirs, do see this simple fact for yourselves, that the answer is in the problem, not away from the problem. The answer is not at the end of the book, it is not to be given by a teacher or a leader—that is all sheer nonsense. But if you and I can look at the problem totally and see the inward nature of it, all its inward workings, then that very awareness of the problem resolves the problem, and it is in this manner that we are going to consider these questions. If you are waiting for an answer from me, you will be disappointed because I am not concerned with the answer. If I gave you an answer, you would be in a position to refute it, to accept it, to argue about it, and so on, which is utterly futile. That is a political game fit for the newspapers. But if you want to find out the truth of the problem, you must inquire seriously into it, and therefore your mind must not be concerned with the answer. Only the mind that is not concerned with the answer can give full attention to the problem. If you see that simple fact, let us proceed with the question.

Question: There is action as legislation at the governmental level; there is action as reform at the level of Gandhiji and Vinobaji, and there is action according to the various types of religious teachers. It seems to me that all these forms of action are pulling in different directions, and that the individual, being enticed by the promises which each one offers, is caught in conflict within himself. What do you consider to be right action, which will not produce this contradiction?

KRISHNAMURTI: Obviously the government is planning for the next five or ten years because they want to produce a result economically, they must feed the millions, and so on. That is one kind of action. Then there are the various religio-social reformers, each advocating a certain system of thought and action, and promising certain results; and the questioner says we are caught in conflict, being pulled in different directions by the promises of these various leaders.

Now, is that so? Are you as an individual pulled in different directions by the promises and activities of the politicians and the religio-social reformers, or are you yourself creating these contradictory pressures? The government has to control your ambition, your greed, your envy, your ruthlessness, and therefore it must plan, it must impose enormous taxes, and all the rest of it. So it is you, and not the government, that have created the contradiction. You have also created the religio-social reformer, with his promises, because you cannot live totally as an individual. In yourself you are torn in ten different directions. You want a planned economy, and yet you want to be free; you are extraordinarily greedy, vicious, brutal, corrupt, and yet you talk about God, love, truth, peace, and all the rest of that verbal nonsense.

So the contradiction exists within yourself, which is fairly obvious when you consider it. Within yourself there is a pulling in different directions. You want to have a well-ordered society, and you are going to get it. The welfare state, which inevitably means bureaucracy, is going to control your thinking, your feeling, your action, just as the present society controls you in a different way by encouraging you to be greedy, to be envious.

It is a fact, then, that there are conflicting activities going on within each one of us, and within society, which is ourselves in projection. Activity is divided as religious, political, reformatory, educational, scientific, sexual, and so on. We identify ourselves with the particular form of activity which happens for the moment to be convenient, profitable, and the leader of each separate activity thinks he has the answer. Do you understand, sirs? The politician thinks he has the answer, irrespective of the rest of man's problems, and so does the religio-social reformer. Each has certain ideas, prejudices, based on his particular conditioning, each has a plan or a way of life, each says, "This is right, that is wrong"; and you as an individual, with your own passions, lust, greed, ambition, choose from among them a leader and follow him. That is your actual state, is it not? That is what is happening, outwardly and inwardly. And the questioner asks me to tell him what is right action.

Now, that is a false question, surely. If I tell him what is right action and he accepts it, we will merely be creating another leader, another authority, another pernicious pattern of thinking. I really mean this. Please don't laugh it off, sirs; it is much too serious. You have enough patterns, gurus, political leaders; why add one more to the list? Whereas, if you really see that in yourself you are contradictory, torn apart, each part having its own activity and leader in that projection of ourselves which is society; if you think about this fact seriously for even five minutes and ask yourself what is the right thing to do, you will know the answer and will not be caught by economic or religio-social promises.

So, what is right action? I am not going to tell you, but you and I can go into it together and find out. Surely, the question is not what is right action, but whether there can be an action which is total and therefore true under all circumstances, not just at odd moments. Sirs, do we know a total action at any time, or do we know only a series of separate actions which we try to put together, hoping thereby to find the total? Are you getting tired, sirs?

We are trying to find out what is the total action that will respond rightly to all problems, political, religious, social, and moral. Surely, it is only total action that is true under all circumstances, not a separate activity with its limited ideas, leaders, and all the rest of it, which inevitably creates another contradiction. Now, how are we going to find out what is total action? Let us go slowly into it. When do you act as a whole, as a total human being, if you ever do? Don't answer me, please. This is not a discussion. Let me unroll it—but not for you to remember what I say so that you can go home and speculate about it, which is nonsense. We are learning together.

Do you know a total action at any time in your life? And what do we mean by a total action? Surely, there is a total action only when your whole being, your mind, your heart, your body, is in it completely, without division or separation. And when does that happen? Please, sirs, go with me slowly. When does such a thing take place? Total action takes place only when there is complete attention, does it not? And what do we mean by complete attention?

Please, I am thinking this out as I go along, I am not repeating it from memory. I am watching, learning. Similarly, you must watch your own mind, and not just listen to my verbal explanations. What do we mean by attention? When the mind concentrates on an object, is that attention? When the mind says, "I must look at this one thing and eliminate all other thoughts," is that attention? Or is it a process of exclusion, and therefore not attention? In attention, surely, there is no effort, there is no object to be concentrated upon. The moment you have an object upon which you concentrate, that object becomes more important than attention. The object is then merely a means of absorbing your mind; your mind is absorbed by an idea, as a child is absorbed by a toy, and in that process there is no attention because there is exclusion.

Nor is there attention when there is a motive, obviously. It is only when there is no motive, when there is no object, when there is no compulsion in any form, that there is attention. And do you know such attention? Not that you must experience it or learn about it from me, but do you know for yourself the quality of this attention, the feeling of a mind which is not compelled to concentrate, which has no object to gain and is therefore capable of attention without motive? Do you understand, sirs? What is important is not how to get it, but actually to feel the quality of complete attention as you are listening to me.

Now, when does complete attention take place? Surely, only when there is love. When there is love, there is complete attention. There is no need of a motive, there is no need of an object, there is no need of compulsion—you just love. It is only when there is love that there is complete attention, and therefore total action in response to political, religious, and social problems. But we have no love, nor are the political leaders, the social and religious reformers, concerned with love. If they were, they would not talk of mere reform, nor create new patterns of thought. Love is not sentimentality, it is not emotionalism, it is not devotion. It is a state of being—clear, sane, rational, uncorrupted—out of which comes the total action which alone can give the true reply to all our problems. It is because you have no love that you pretend to change; on the circumference you reform, but the core is empty. You will know how to act totally only when you know what it means to love.

Sirs, we have developed our minds, we are so-called intellectuals, which means that we are full of words, explanations, techniques. We are disputatious, clever at arguing, at opposing one opinion with another. We have filled our hearts with the things of the mind, and that is why we are in a state of contradiction. But love is not easily come by. You have to work hard for it. Love is difficult to understand—difficult in the sense that to understand it, you have to know where reason is necessary and go with reason as far as possible, and also know its limitations. This means that to understand what it is to love, there must be self-knowledge—not the knowledge of Shankara, Buddha, or Christ, which you gather from books. Such books are just books, they are not divine revelations. The divine revelation comes into being only through self-knowledge, and you can know yourself, not according to the pattern of some psychologist, but only by observing how your thought is functioning—that is, by watching yourself from moment to moment as you get into the bus, as you talk to your children, to your wife, to your servant.

So if you know yourself, you will know what it means to love, and out of that there is total action, which is the only good action. No other action is good, however clever, however profitable, however reformatory. But to love, you need immense humility—which is just to be humble, not to cultivate humility. To be humble is to be sensitive to everything about you, not only to the beautiful, but also to the ugly; it is to be sensitive to the stars, to the stillness of an evening, to the trees, to the children, to the dirty village, to the servant, to the politician, to the tramcar driver. Then you will see that your sensitivity, which is love, has an answer to the many problems of life because love is the answer to all the problems which the mind creates.

Love is to be found directly by each one of us, and not at the feet of a guru, or through any book. Love must be found alone because it is uncontaminated, pure, and you must come to it completely stripped of greed, of envy, and all the stupidities of society which have made the mind limited, small, petty. Then there is a total action, and that total action is the answer to man's problems, not the separate activities of the reformer, the planner, and the politician.

December 16, 1956

Third Talk in Madras

It seems to me that one of the most difficult things to do is to separate individual thinking and action from the collective thought and activity, yet to free the mind, the whole process of thinking, from the collective is absolutely essential, especially now when the collective is playing such a compulsive part in our daily existence. Throughout the world every means is being used to get hold of the mind of the individual. Not only the communists, but also every type of religious person, is anxious to shape the mind of man; and as governmental efficiency grows, as so-called education becomes universal and technological improvements spread in every direction, thought will be increasingly shaped according to the collective pattern of a given culture.

Most of us are the result of the collective. There is no individual thinking. I am not using the word *individual* in opposition to the collective. I think individuality is entirely different from and is not a reaction to the collective, but as we are now constituted, individuality as something wholly apart from the collective does not exist. What we call individuality is merely a reaction, and reaction is not total action. A reaction produces its own further limitation; it only further conditions the mind.

So I am not using the word *individuality* in the sense of opposition to the collective; I am referring to a state of mind that is totally disengaged, dissociated from the collective process of thinking. Thinking, as we know it now, is almost entirely a response of the collective; and it seems to me that in the face of the present crisis, of this immense challenge with its innumerable problems of starvation, misery, war, and appalling brutality, the collective response has no value. The collective can only respond according to the old conditioning, the old pattern of thought; and what is important, surely, is that there should be the emergence of individuality which is outside the present social structure, not part of the collective pattern of thinking with its dogmas and beliefs, whether communistic or of so-called religion.

I do not know if you are aware of this extraordinary challenge which confronts each one of us and which demands a new approach, a new way of acting towards it. We can see that the old collective response has not been adequate, and this inadequacy of response inevitably creates further problems—which is what is actually happening in the world at the present time. So our problem is: Can the mind, which is a result of the collective, free itself and become individual?—but not in the sense of a reaction, a revolt against the collective, for such a revolt is obviously a process of further conditioning according to a different pattern. Can the mind, by understanding the collective, by investigating, inquiring into the whole process of it, dissociate itself from the collective, and out of the depth of this understanding, not intellectually, but actually, bring about immediate action? Can the mind, which is a result of the collective, free itself and act as a total individuality? I am not using the word *individuality* in the sense that we ordinarily accept, which means an individual who is opposed to the collective, who is self-centered, who is only concerned with his own activity, his own enjoyment, his own success.

This is your problem, is it not? I am not foisting it on you. If you are at all aware of world events, aware of your own social compulsions and pressures, this question must inevitably arise. Can the mind free itself from the collective, which is its own conditioning? To be free of the collective is not just a matter of throwing away your passport or of verbally renouncing a certain state of mind; it means being free of the whole emotional content of such words as *Hindu, Buddhist, Christian, communist, Indian, Russian, American,* and so on. You may strip the mind of the verbal label, but there remains an inward content, the deep feeling of being something in a particular culture or society. You know what I mean. One reacts as a Christian, as a communist, as a Hindu, because one has been brought up in a particular environment, with a superficial, limited outlook, and this reaction of the collective is what we call our thinking.

Since you are listening to me, may I suggest that you listen without any idea of refuting, defending, agreeing, or disagreeing. We are trying to uncover the problem together. The problem being immense, to understand it we have to think clearly and with great depth of feeling. So please do not merely listen to my description, but if you can, through my description, watch the operation of your own mind. You will then see how extraordinarily difficult it is to think totally anew, that is, not to think in terms of Hinduism, Buddhism, Christianity, or what you will. And if you revolt against the pattern of Hinduism only to fall into another cage which you call Buddhism, this or that, then the mind is still held within the field of conditioning.

So your mind is obviously the result of the collective. It responds, not as an individual in the sense in which I am using that word, but as an expression of the collective, which means that it is bound by tradition, by the whole process of conditioning. Your mind is burdened with certain dogmas, beliefs, rituals, which you call religion, and with that background it tries to respond to something which is unprecedently new and vital. But only the mind that is free of its background can respond totally to the challenge, and it is only such a mind that is capable of creating a new world, a new civilization, a wholly new manner of living.

So, can one free the mind from its background, which is the collective, not as a reaction, not in opposition, but through seeing the imperative necessity of a mind that is not merely a repetitive machine? I hope I am making the problem clear. At present we are the result of what we have been told, are we not? That is so obvious. From childhood we have been told to believe or not to believe in certain things, and we repeat it; and if it is not the repetition of the old in which we are caught, then it is a repetition of essentially the same thing in a new form. Whether it lives in the communist world, the socialist world, or the Hindu world, that center which we call the 'I', the self, is the repetitive, accumulative process of the collective.

The problem is then: Can that center be exploded so that no new center is formed and an action takes place which is total and not an activity of the self? After all, the mind is at present a process of self-centered activity, of tradition, is it not? You are a Hindu, a Muslim, a Christian, or a Buddhist, or you may belong to the very latest sect; but the center of your thinking is an accumulative process, either in terms of tradition, or in reaction to the collective, or it is further shaped by experiences based upon its own conditioning. Sirs, all this sounds very difficult, but it is not. If you watch your own mind, you will see how simple it actually is.

What is this center of thinking, the 'I'? Or rather, I won't call it the 'I', the ego, the higher self, or the lower self. There is only the center. This center is a mechanism of thinking based on tradition, and it obviously reacts to any challenge in terms of its own conditioning, which is based on security, fear, greed, envy, and all the rest of it. If you are a politician, you think in terms of nationality; you act for various profitable reasons, and this is your response to a world situation that demands not action in terms of a particular segment of the world but a total action, a completely human outlook of love, of deep thought. All this is denied when you think as a nationalist, when your mind is bound by tradition.

So, can the mind free itself from tradition? And if it can, how is it to set about it? I don't know if you have thought about this problem at all. If you have, you have probably thought about it in the traditional terms of struggling to get rid of the ego by sublimation, by discipline, by control, by various forms of fulfillment, and so on. But perhaps there is another way of looking at it, which is: Can the mind know directly the nature of that center which has subdivided itself into the higher and the lower, the atma and the personal self? That center places itself at different levels and calls itself by different names, thinking there is a permanent entity above and beyond the impermanent; but for the impermanent center to think of a permanent entity is false, because that which is impermanent obviously cannot create a permanent state. You may conceive of a permanent state and build all your theories, your whole way of thinking around it, but that idea of permanency is also impermanent; it is a mere reaction to the impermanency of life.

You may be gone tomorrow. Your thinking, your house, your bank account, your virtues—they are all impermanent. Your relationship with nature, with your family, with ideas, is in a state of flux, of constant movement; everything is transient, and the mind, being aware of that, creates something which it calls permanent. But the very thought which creates the "permanent" is itself impermanent; therefore, what it creates is also impermanent. This is not just logical, sequential; it is an indisputable fact, as clear as that microphone. But a mind which has been brought up, which has been trained to escape from life into the so-called permanent, is incapable of thinking afresh, and therefore it is always in battle with anything new.

I am talking of that center which thinks of a state which is permanent, of God or truth, and which also knows the daily activity of pain and pleasure, of ambition, greed, envy, and the desire for power, prestige. All that is the center, whether you extend it widely or limit it to a little family in Mylapore. And is it possible for that center to come to an end? Please see that unless it does come to an end, you will always know impermanency and sorrow, however much you may pretend to know there is a permanency because some book says so. The books may be mistaken and probably are, including the Gita, the Bible, and the whole lot of them. So you as an individual have to think out this problem as though you were investigating it for the first time, and nobody had ever told you a thing about it. Because what is the actual fact, what is the reality as far as you know it? There is this center which is greedy, envious, vain, which is seeking power, position, prestige, and which constitutes the whole of human existence. That is all you know. Occasionally there is a flash of joy, a movement of something which is not of your making, but the functioning of that center is the primary activity of most human beings.

Now, you and I are going to take a journey into that center, not knowing where it is going to lead. If you already know where it is going to lead, you have preconceived it, and therefore it will not be real. A petty mind, however learned and capable of erudite discussion it may be, is incapable of seeking something totally new. All it can do is to project its own ideas, or induce a devotional or ecstatic state. So we are entering upon an uncharted sea, and each one has to be his own captain, pilot, and sailor. He has to be everything himself. There is no guide, and that is the beauty of existence. If you have companions and guides, you never take the journey alone; therefore, you are not taking the journey at all. The journey is a process of self-discovery, and as you begin to understand it, you will see what an immense relationship it has to your present existence.

So you can only take that journey when you begin to understand yourself, when you begin to understand the nature of your own mind, going into it step by step. And you cannot go far if you condemn, if you evaluate what you discover. The moment you condemn anything, you have put an end to thinking, have you not? If I say you are a wise man or a fool, I have obviously stopped thinking. To inquire, to go into the depths of a thought or an emotion, to unroll it, there must be no sense of judgment, evaluation. One has to move with it, and this inquiry into the self, into the center, is meditation. The practice of going into a corner and looking at a picture, which you call meditation, is phony, it is not meditation at all. That is self-hypnosis. Real meditation is this inquiry into the extraordinary process of thinking to find out how far thinking goes, and whether there is an ending to thought.

If I were to tell you that thought can be ended, you would say, "How am I to arrive at that ending of thought?" which is an immature question. What matters is to find out the nature of the center, to go into it and uncover the whole process of thinking for yourself, not according to somebody else, and you can have no companion on this journey. Neither wife nor husband nor child nor guru nor any book can help you. This journey must be undertaken entirely alone, and there is no religious organization of any kind that can help you. Though such organizations call themselves spiritual, they are exploiters. I am not on my favorite subject. Don't brush it off so easily. Religious organizations merely condition man further; therefore, they are essentially exploiters, though they operate in the name of God, truth, and all the rest of it.

So, to undertake this journey, you must free yourself at the very beginning from all religious organizations, from all tradition. And I assure you, it is very hard work because it demands not mere revolt but a great deal of attention, thought, and inquiry. In the process of inquiry you will find that every form of difficulty comes into being—fear, insecurity, uncertainty—and because we are not capable of facing it, we run away and talk about God and truth. But for a man who is really in earnest, the very undertaking of this journey brings solitude—which is not isolation—because he will know a far greater relationship than the relationship which exists now, which is no relationship at all. Because it has understood the center and is not transposing that center to a different level of consciousness, the mind in that state of aloneness is capable of total individual action—individual in the sense that it is not related to a particular society or culture. Such a mind becomes silent, completely still, and in that very stillness there is an extraordinary movement, a movement which is not put together by the mind. That movement without any center, without any direction or objective, is creation; that movement is the real, beyond the measure of time and man.

Now, sirs, as I explained the other day, there are only questions in life, and no answers, and it is really important to understand this. A mind that seeks an answer is not concerned with the question. It is only when your mind is wholly concerned with the problem—which means it is not distracted by the desire for an answer, or by reacting to the problem in its own way—that you give complete attention to it; and when you give your complete attention to the problem, you will find that the problem undergoes a fundamental change. It is no longer a problem, it has quite another quality. But this demands a mind that can pursue the problem to its end, and you cannot pursue a problem to its end if you are seeking an answer, or if the mind is in any way translating the problem in terms of its own desire.

Question: Is not a certain amount of disciplinary training necessary to understand what you are teaching?

KRISHNAMURTI: Is it? What do we mean by discipline? You know the ordinary meaning of that word: to control, to subjugate, to force thought by the exercise of will to conform to a nobler pattern. Discipline implies resistance, a shaping of the mind, holding thought to a certain line, and so on. All that and more is implied in discipline. In discipline there is the division of the one who disciplines and that which is disciplined, so conflict is everlastingly going on, and we accept this conflict as normal, as a sane way of life. To me it is utter nonsense, and I mean it.

The questioner asks, "Is not a certain amount of disciplinary training necessary to understand what you are teaching?" If you love to do something, is it necessary to discipline yourself to do it? If you are really interested in what I am saying, do you need discipline? Must you train your mind to pay complete attention, to listen with deep feeling? That very listening is the act of understanding—but you are not interested. That is the real problem—you are not interested. Not that you should be. But fundamentally you are superficial; you want an easy way of existence, you want to get on. It is too much of a bother to think very deeply, and besides, you might have to act deeply, you might find yourself in total revolt against this rotten society. So you play with it, you keep one foot here and one foot there, tottering and asking, "Should I discipline myself in order to understand?'' Whereas, if you really inquired into what I am teaching, you would find it very simple; and you can do it yourself, you need no assistance from anybody, including myself. All that you have to do is to understand the operation of your own mind—and a marvelous thing it is, the mind; the most beautiful thing on earth.

But we are not interested in that. We are interested in what the mind can get for us in the way of security, passion, power, position, knowledge, which are the various centers of self-interest. And I say, look at the operation of your own mind, go into it, understand it, all of which you can do by yourself; watch your everyday relationship with people, the way you talk, the way you gesticulate, your pursuit of power, how you behave in front of the important man and in front of the servant. If you observe this whole process of yourself in the mirror of relationship, that is the one necessary action. You don't have to do anything about it, but merely observe it. If you observe, go into the whole process of yourself without condemnation, you will find that the mind becomes extraordinarily sharp, clear, and fearless; therefore, the mind is capable of understanding such human problems as death, meditation, dreams, and the many other things that confront it.

So you don't need any special training. What you need is to pay attention, not to what I say, but to your own mind; you must see for yourself how it is caught in words, in explanations without any basis, without any reality. Perhaps it is the reality of someone else, but if you make that the basis of your life, then it is not reality; it is merely a supposition, a speculation, an imagination, and therefore it is without validity, it has no reality behind it. To find reality you have to work as hard as you work for your daily living, and much harder, because all this is much more subtle, requiring greater attention; for every movement of thought indicates a state of the mind, of the conscious as well as the unconscious. As you cannot observe the operation of your mind all the time, you pick it up, observe it, and let it go. If you watch yourself in this manner, you will find that attention has quite a different significance, and that you can free the mind from the collective. As long as the mind is merely a record of the collective, it is of no more value than a machine. The new computers are extraordinarily capable along certain lines, but human beings are something more than that. They have the possibility of that extraordinary creativity which is not just the writing of poems or books, but the creativity of a mind that has no center.

Question: Most of us seem to be after so many things—sex, position, power, and so on—which promise a sense of happiness and fulfillment, but which bring with them all kinds of frustration and suffering. Is this inevitable?

KRISHNAMURTI: What is it that we are all after? Not what we should be after, which is just idealistic nonsense, but what is it we are all pursuing in fact? And what is it that is making us go after certain things? As the questioner says, we are all after something: sex, position, money, power, prestige, or we want to be near the biggest man, and so on. We all want something—if not in this world, then in the other world, whatever the other world is—and in the pursuit of what we want we meet with frustration, misery.

Now, what is it we are after, and what is driving us to go after it? Do you understand, sirs? What are we seeking, and what is it that is making us seek? I am not answering you, so don't wait for an answer from me. I am exploring it. Together we are going to find out. We all know we are after something: happiness, beauty, comfort, the flowering of goodness, the continuity of satisfaction, and so on and on. We are after something, call it X. And what is making us go after X? Is it discontent—not divine discontent, but plain, everyday discontent? That is, we get something, we are dissatisfied with it, and we want something more. As a boy I want amusement; when I am a little more mature, I want sex, then a house and family, and in a few more years I want position, prestige. So discontent drives me until I find something which will give me contentment: love, knowledge, a person to idolize, a country or an ideology to serve, a Master to whom I can give everything, all in return for my contentment. This may sound cynical, but it is not. I am merely stating an obvious fact, and if you dismiss it as cynicism, that is your affair.

So discontent is driving most of us. We want a little more money, a little more knowledge, more happiness. Perhaps we have momentarily felt the goodness, the beauty, the extraordinary depth and width of life, or someone has described it, and we are after that, but the basis of our search is still this discontent. We are being urged by discontent to find a means of overcoming it. Surely that is a fact—it is the mind's actual response. My wife has died, my son is gone, or my husband has run away with some woman, and I am unhappy; so I go to a guru or turn to some book, hoping to find something which will assuage my agony, my suffering; and when I have found it, I dare not question its reality because it has given me comfort. So, whatever it is, I hold on to it until the next push comes, until again there is the drive of discontent. If a particular guru satisfies me, there I am permanently stuck; if he does not, I move on to the next. It is the same with ideas, with houses, with everything. From the clerk to the highest governmental official, in so-called spiritual as well as in worldly affairs, we are all driven by this burning discontent, which is an actuality in our lives.

So there is this movement of discontent, and the moment you find contentment, which is the opposite of discontent, you go to sleep. This is so, is it not? Have you not noticed people who have found what they call God, or who are encased in a belief? They may be afire with devotion, but they are held in a prison of ideas, their own or those of another, which is their own projection.

That is the way of life as we know it. Driven by discontent, we move from one satisfaction to another; life for most of us is a continuous burning, wanting, pursuing, and that process seems inevitable. But is it inevitable? If you begin to question and to understand the whole process of discontent, out of that understanding there may come a movement which has no fulfillment. Do you understand, sirs?

What is it we are seeking? We are seeking an object that will give us a feeling of fulfillment, are we not? I am forever fulfilling myself in my wife, in my child, in my property, in ideas, in a country, in following somebody, and so on and on; and in the wake of fulfillment, there is always frustration, obviously.

There can never be self-fulfillment because the self is partial, fragmentary, it is never total. It is always broken up. Self-fulfillment must inevitably be incomplete and is therefore frustrating. If my mind sees the truth of that, then my question is not whether there is an ultimate fulfillment, but whether there is a movement totally different from that which we know.

To put it differently, is there a search without a motive? Do you understand, sirs? We are now seeking because we are discontented. We know that very well. We are thoroughly familiar with that process. I am unhappy and I want happiness. The motive is very simple and very clear. But I see that as long as there is a motive in search, there must be frustration. That is very clear, too, not verbally but actually. So the mind says, "Is there a movement which is not the turning of this wheel of content and discontent?" In other words, is there a search, an inquiry which has no causation at all? Because the moment your search has a cause, a motive, you are obviously no longer seeking. Do you understand, sirs? No?

I seek because I have a motive. The motive is: I want to be happy. I already know what happiness is because I know what unhappiness is. So my search for happiness is not a search at all. It is merely an effort to find some means of being what I call happy, which is the opposite of what I am. We know that process very well.

Now, please put yourself the next question, which is: Is there a movement, a search, without any causation, without any pressure, without any motive? Don't say there is or there is not, because it would be mere speculation. The fact is that you don't know. And to find out if there is a movement which has no causation, you cannot translate it in terms of what you have read in books. But what you can do is to say, "I know the way of life which moves from discontentment through fulfillment to discontentment, and I see there is no end to that process." Then you can ask yourself the question: Is there a movement of life which is not a reaction to the ordinary movement and which has no center as causation, as motive? But do not ask me, do not say, "Please tell us about it." It is for you to find out. I say there is such a movement, a movement in which there is no causation, no stimulation, and which is not a mere remembrance of things past. If you can find it, you will see that that movement is completely dissociated from the movement of contentment and discontentment, from this drive towards fulfillment with its shadow of frustration.

But to find that other movement, you must go into this whole question of discontentment; you must think it out, feel it out, grapple with it, and then come to the other, which is to discover it for yourself. To discover it, you must be free from contentment and discontent; you must be free, and not ask how to be free. You will be free only when you understand this whole process of contentment, in which there is frustration, fear, and all the rest of it; and then you will come naturally and easily upon that movement which has no time or causation. It is not metaphysical, mystical, or anything of that kind, but it is an actual fact which the mind can directly experience when it is free of this movement of contentment and discontentment.

So you cannot possibly find out if there is a movement of life in which there is no motive until you have understood the whole problem of causation and the movement arising from that causation. It requires hard work, sirs, and no book, no temple, no god, no guru can reveal it to you. You can just as well throw them all overboard and begin to inquire for yourself. Wisdom lies in the understanding of discontentment, and then you will find that there is an experiencing which is not based upon previous experience. That experiencing has no motive, no ending; therefore, it is timelessly creative.

December 19, 1956

Fourth Talk in Madras

I think it is obvious that our problems are increasing throughout the world. There is every kind of conflict, and the various opinions and answers which are offered for the resolution of our problems only seem to lead to further confusion. If you observe, you will see in this country an extraordinarily rapid deterioration taking place, which is not imaginary but an actual fact; and seeing this whole process of deterioration, this enormous decay of man's endeavor through the centuries, there are those who say you must return to the past, you must go back to the temple, to the sacred books, you must follow the traditional routine, the religious sanctions, and thereby reestablish yourself in righteousness.

But is righteousness in the past? Does righteousness lie in any book? Does righteousness come about through following any leader, any authority? And is not the present decay, this moral corruption and disintegration, the result of a "righteousness" that is based on the authority of another, on the authority of a book, on the authority of several leaders whom you have followed through centuries? Regardless of who it is, whether it is a political leader, a comforting saint, or a religious reformer, is not the very following of another unrighteous?

Is righteousness something that can be stored up, that can be gathered and laid by for actions that demand a right response? Or is righteousness something entirely different? It is not that we have lost righteousness, for probably we have never had it, and that is why there is the present decline. I don't know if you have considered this matter at all seriously, or have merely skimmed along on the surface of life, gratified with the little things—a little work, a little food, a little thought, a little family—not being too disturbed and letting the decline go on as it will. I think there must be some who have given serious thought to the matter—but not in terms of reformation because you can see, if you look around, that reformation has not brought a new release of man's creativity. On the contrary, religious reformation, like political revolution, has merely brought a different group which insists on a different pattern.

Seeing all this, we must have wondered how to bring about that righteousness which is not merely the action of the learned, the action of a mind that has accumulated knowledge, morality, and functions within the groove of a certain virtue. I do not call such a mind righteous. Righteousness is not merely the remembrance of things that are gone; it does not lie in the past of ten thousand years ago, or of yesterday; it is the capacity to meet each challenge with a freshness of mind, with love, with gentleness, with insight into the totality of a happening, whatever it be. The mind that is capable of responding totally to a demand is the only righteous mind, not the mind that calculates, that is shaped by an ideology or is pursuing an ideal, all of which is based on self-interest, on vested interest in morality, in tradition, in values that are profitable. Righteousness is something entirely different from all that, which we shall see as we go along this evening.

A mind that is trained to a pattern of thinking, that demands the "how," the method, that wants to know the path that leads to righteousness, will never be righteous because it is only concerned with success, with getting somewhere. Instead of pursuing money, it invests in so-called righteousness. The ends are fundamentally the same because the desire in each case is fundamentally the same.

So, is it possible to bring about, not a piecemeal change, but a total change, so that your mind, your heart, your whole being is alive and sensitive to everything about you—to the beauty of a cloud, to the breeze among the leaves, to the villager, to the woman who is tortured by bearing many children? What matters, surely, is to be aware of all that and to respond to it fully, not in terms of some social morality, which is not moral at all; it is merely a matter of convenience, of self-interest. Morality is the capacity to respond with the totality of one's being—and I mean that, it is not a rhetorical statement. Words in themselves have very little significance.

What is important is to go beyond the words and to have feeling, because it is feeling that brings the totality of action. Do you understand, sirs? To have feeling is not the process of intellection which breeds all kinds of cunning reasons as to why you should or should not have feeling.

Please, since you have taken the trouble to come here, may I suggest that in listening to what I am saying, you listen to the end, and not just take little bits here and there which happen to suit you; listen to the totality of it, and you will see that the whole thing hangs together. If you take a little part of it, you will have only the ashes which will create more misery, more sorrow, more confusion.

Also, listening itself is quite an art. Most of us never really listen; therefore, we hear only partially. We hear the words that are spoken, but our minds are elsewhere, or our minds respond only to the meaning of the words, and this immediate response prevents us from hearing that which lies beyond the words. So listening is an art, but if you can listen totally to what is being said, then in that very listening, you will find there is a liberation, because such listening is unpremeditated, uncalculated; it is an action of truth because your whole mind is there, your total attention is being given. If you listen without interpreting, without remembering a quotation from some old book, or comparing all this with what you have read, then you will find that your own mind has undergone a really radical change.

Feeling without the paraphernalia of thought is really an extraordinary thing. I don't know if you have ever tried to feel and to ride on that feeling without controlling it, shaping it, without calling it bad or good, without giving a verbal significance to it. You will find that it is very difficult, astonishingly arduous. It is not a thing that comes easily because we have cultivated the mind. To us the intellect is enormously important; we like to argue, to be able to counter one opinion with another which is erudite, very learned, or to quote some ancient book. We have trained our minds to a high degree of efficiency in self-interest, and so we have lost or have never had that feeling.

The immediate objection to this is: If we have a feeling, don't we want to express it? Do we? Or does the mind, clothing it in words, create the sensation which demands an expression? The mind looks beyond the feeling and wants to express it, fulfill it, or to curtail, suppress, hold it back. So the feeling is the real flame, and if you really free the mind from words, if you do not let the verbal significances, all the paraphernalia of our religious and moral instincts shape it, you will find that the feeling does not necessarily demand what you call fulfillment. It is the mind that demands fulfillment, the mind that has an idea about the feeling. Do you understand?

Let us say you pick up a leaf and look at it. The feeling it evokes is one thing, and your opinion about it—"How beautiful," "How green," "How withered"—is another. But the word becomes more important, and the feeling goes away. Observe it, make an experiment with yourself and you will soon find out. Such a feeling does not demand a fulfillment. On the contrary, it has its own movement, unrelated to the verbal movement of thought which demands action.

So it is feeling that really brings a fundamental change in our thinking. And a fundamental change in our thinking is necessary because it is not the outward pressure of economic environment that brings the change. Compulsion in any form does have an effect, but it never brings about a radical change; it only brings a modified perpetuation of things as they have been. What is needed is a radical change, not the superficial quoting of new words, the shouting of new political slogans, or the following of new Masters, new leaders. We have tried all that, and it has not produced a different world.

So, if you are really concerned—as any intelligent and thoughtful person must be when he sees so much poverty, so much degradation and decay—with how to bring about, not a reform, but a fundamental revolution, then I think you will quickly realize that such a revolution is possible only when the mind is truly religious. But religion, the feeling of religion, is not a matter of going to a temple, attending a ceremony, repeating a lot of stupid words, ringing a bell, or putting flowers at the feet of an idol made by the hand or by the mind. Nor is it religion when you can repeat the Gita from beginning to end, or quote any other scripture. Religion is the feeling of sacredness, you understand? It is not your feeling for your guru, for the Masters, which is merely envy, profit, your concern with what you will get in return; and it is not the pursuit of a dogma or a belief, which is merely another form of security, self-interest. Religion is the feeling of that immensity which may be called sacred, and which has nothing to do with the Upanishads, the Gita, the Bible, with symbols, churches, Buddhas, Krishnas, or with me. It has nothing whatever to do with all that. It is because you have given your hearts and minds to things of that kind that you have not this feeling of sacredness which cunning reason cannot pervert, which no mind, however subtle, can destroy. Such feeling is like love, it has its own action. But the mind that thinks it must learn to love creates an action which is a perversion, and such action only brings more complexity, more misery, more confusion.

So religion is not to be found in any temple, in any book; it has nothing to do with putting ashes on your forehead, wearing the sacred thread, or belonging to any particular organization. Religion is something entirely different. There is definitely a state, not a fixed state, but a movement which is beyond the measure of the mind, and the experiencing of that state is religion. Don't translate it as *samadhi*, or some other mystical nonsense, and go off on that; but the actual experiencing of that state, which is creation, brings a new world into being because then our own mind is washed clean of all the rubbish of the centuries. Then your mind is innocent, fresh, sensitive, alive to every problem, and is therefore capable of meeting it. But such a state of mind is not easily come by. You have to understand yourself, the operation of your own thinking.

Religious revolution is the beginning of a new religion—which cannot be organized, which cannot have a priesthood, or a president and a secretary, with property. That is not religion. The religion of which I am speaking is this feeling of sacredness, which is not sentimentality. It is a thing that comes through hard work, through piercing all the illusions, the shadows which the mind has created. That is why it is very important not to have an authority of any kind—either the Masters or a guru or the sacred books or ideals and opinions, whether your own or those of another—because only then are you an individual, free to find out. As long as you depend on another to instruct you, you are lost because you are caught in that instruction.

When the mind is completely denuded of the past, which is knowledge, you will find that a totally different kind of feeling arises, and the people who have that feeling don't belong to any religious organization; they have no country, they don't go near the politicians because they are not seeking power, position, nor are they trying to reform the world. A mind that is concerned with reformation is not a religious mind, it is not kind, compassionate. Such a mind may talk about compassion, goodness, but in the very act of reformation there is destruction, misery, because every reform needs further reform, for all reforms are inadequate. A total action is necessary, but the total action is not brought about by putting the little parts together. It comes when you discover for yourself as an individual human being, that is, when you respond, not as the collective, but as a real individual who has freed himself from society with its greed, envy, possessiveness, and all the rest of it. Only such an individual will know that extraordinary experience of something which is not measurable by the mind. It is not a static experience. It is not an experience to be remembered. What is remembered is not true; it has already joined the dead of yesterday. And without that experience of reality, do what you will, you can never have a sane, ordered, balanced, happy world. But you cannot seek that experience; it must come to you, and it will come to you only when you are not concerned about yourself.

In asking a question, what is important is not the answer but the question because if I know how to look at the question, how to feel my way through it, I shall find, not the answer, but that the problem has ceased to exist. After all, a problem exists in my daily life only when I have not the capacity to meet it adequately. A good mechanic knows what is wrong with a motor immediately; it is not a problem to him, but to another man, who is not a good mechanic, it is a problem. Learning how to deal with a psychological problem is, however, entirely different because the problem varies from moment to moment. It is never the same. You cannot learn a technique of how to deal with the problem because the problem is constantly changing. I don't know if you have noticed it. To say, "I will find an answer and apply it to the problem," or "Having established an end, I will make the problem fit the end," is such a nonsensical way of dealing with a problem. To deal with a problem, one has to have the capacity to look at it. That is all. And you cannot look at a problem if you are interested in the answer. You can look at a problem only if you give your total attention to it, and if you give your total attention to it, the problem is not.

These are not just words. You try it. It is really quite extraordinary how the mind can meet each problem afresh every time. The meeting of every challenge afresh is the renewal of life, but a mind that functions mechanically in the groove of tradition, of memory, cannot adequately meet the challenge, and such a mind only creates further problems. When the mind asks a question looking for an answer, it generally finds an answer, and the answer is invariably gratifying, comforting, so the mind is caught in its own pettiness.

Bearing all this in mind, let us consider these questions.

Question: Is friendship prevented by spreading justice, which is to organize society on an equitable basis? Can the organization of a society with equal opportunities for all lead to that sense of compassion which will ultimately put an end to governmental intermeddling in our personal lives?

KRISHNAMURTI: The first part of the question is, "Is friendship prevented by spreading justice, which is to organize society on an equitable basis?" Obviously, friendship is destroyed if you depend for justice on the organization of an equitable society. Do you understand? If I rely on the so-called order that is enforced by an outside agency, by government, by law, I shall lose the sensitivity of being really friendly. That is fairly obvious, is it not? And that is exactly what is taking place. You carry on as a Brahmin, or whatever it is you are, secluding yourself from others, and the government comes and establishes justice. We are not discussing justice; for the moment that is not the issue.

When man depends on law to hold his greed within limits, invariably his heart withers. Sirs, that is what is happening throughout the world. Society is becoming more and more complex, and as we have to live together and have not got that sense of friendship, of love, compassion, which will find its own action, we are being forced to behave by governments, through legislation—which is called social justice. It is like a man and his wife being forced by law to live together. That you will understand easily because it is part of your daily existence. But the other is not within your experience, it does not pinch your toe every day. You are not conscious of it because your heart is withered.

So where there is no friendliness, the law has to come in. Do you understand, sirs? What is important is the sense of compassion, the feeling of it, not what it will do. You see, again you are thinking of action; and it is because you are thinking of action, and have not the feeling, that your action has to be controlled, shaped, bullied into line. But if you have that feeling of ordinary kindliness, ordinary gentleness, generosity, then you will find that, while legislation continues to exist for those who must be compelled, it does not exist for you because you are acting from a different level, a different depth.

The second part of the question is, "Will the organization of a society with equal opportunities for all lead to compassion?" Do you understand? Will organization, whether it is governmental organization from the center down through the state and the city, or the organization of churches, with their authority, their sanctions, their priests, their sacred books, and excommunications, their shaping of the mind around a belief in the name of love, and all the rest of it—will that organization lead to love, or will it destroy love, compassion? Please do follow this, sirs. It is your life, not mine. You are the person to answer.

When you have to join some society to be brotherly, or belong to some religion which maintains that you must love, and you depend on a priest for the interpretation of that extraordinary beauty—then will you love, will you know what compassion is? Will you be sensitive to the bird, to the tree, to the flower, to the child? Do think about it, sirs. Give your hearts to this question, do not just listen to the words and give your assent or dissent. The fading away of the power of the state is not possible—it is just an idea and therefore valueless, as long as our hearts are empty. On the contrary, governments are going to become more and more powerful because they are run by men like you, men who want power, position, prestige. Like you, they are politicians, they are moved by expediency, they are after immediate results. The more there is the mechanical action of repression, inwardly and outwardly, the more the state will flourish, and organizations like those to which you now belong will continue to shape your mind, so your heart withers and there is no friendliness, no compassion between you and me.

When there is compassion, the feeling of it, it is not just for the poor villager or for a hungry animal; the warmth of it exists wherever you are, whether in a slum or in a palace, and that feeling cannot be organized, nor can you come to it through any organization. No Masters can give it to you; if they say they can, it is a lie. Sirs, it is because you have followed for centuries the authority of the book, of the guru, of the state, the authority of the boss immediately above you, that you have lost all sensitivity to the beauty of life. To look with feeling at the morning sky, at a star over a cloud, to see the villager and give him something out of your heart, not out of your pocket—you have not lost all that, for you have never had it, and that is why you have organizations; and because of these organizations, you will continue not to have it. It is only when you totally break away from every organization and stand completely alone that you will find out. Dependency is self-interest, and as long as you are dependent, there is no compassion. And I assure you, when compassion exists, you don't have to organize society.

Question: Tradition, ideals, and a certain sense of social morality used to keep mediocre people like me occupied in a righteous manner, but such things no longer have any meaning to most of us. How are we to break through our mediocrity?

KRISHNAMURTI: Sir, what is a mediocre mind? Don't define it—you can go and look up that word in the dictionary—but watch your own mind and find out why it is just ordinary, mediocre. The questioner says that tradition, ideals, and a certain sense of social morality used to keep mediocre people like him occupied in a righteous manner. It was not a righteous manner, it was a traditional manner. To do what society tells you is not righteous, it is merely acting like a gramophone, which has nothing to do with righteousness. Righteousness implies breaking away from greed, envy, ambition, power, and standing by yourself. Only then can you talk about righteousness. To act mechanically because you have been educated for centuries to think in a certain manner and to conform to a particular pattern is not righteousness.

So, what is mediocrity? Don't you know? Don't you know what a mediocre mind is? Surely, it is very simple. A mind which is occupied is a mediocre mind. Whatever it is occupied with, whether it be with God, with drink, with sex, with power, it is a mediocre mind. Do you understand, sirs? A mind that practices virtue from morning till night is an occupied mind and is therefore mediocre because it is concerned with itself. You may say, "I am not concerned with myself, I am concerned about India," but that is merely transferring the identification from oneself to something else and being occupied with that. Any occupation—with a book, with a thought, with any one of a dozen things—indicates mediocrity because a mind that is occupied is not a free mind. It is only the free mind that can give attention to something and let it go, which is entirely different from being occupied with it. An occupied mind can never be free. Examine your own mind and you will see how occupied it is with your interests, with your family, with your job; from morning till night there is never a moment when it is empty—which is not a blankness, nor a state of vegetation, of daydreaming. That is not emptiness. When the mind is occupied, it gets tired and vaguely thinks of something else, which is merely another form of occupation. I am not talking of that. The mind that is not occupied is extraordinarily alert, but not about something. It is in a state of complete attention, and the moment such a state exists, there is creation. Such a mind is no longer mediocre; whether it is living in a village or in the capital, it is no longer dominated by the dictates of society. But that requires an astonishingly arduous inquiry into oneself, not the complacency of little successes; it is the outcome of really hard work to find out why the mind is occupied.

Don't you see, sirs, you are occupied with other people's affairs because you are other people, you are not yourself. You don't know yourself. You are occupied with things that you have been told are important. But if you have a real feeling about something, you will see it is no longer occupation. A man who has deep feeling is not a mediocre person, but when he wants to put that feeling into words and makes a lot of fuss about it, when through those words he seeks fame, notoriety, money, or whatever it is, then he has become mediocre. So the inquiry into mediocrity is an inquiry into your own mind, and you will find that a mind that is occupied ever remains mediocre.

Question: You were born in a village of very poor environment, and you say that you have never studied the scriptures. What good karma has brought you to this liberation?

KRISHNAMURTI: This is really a very interesting question, if you care to go into it, not because it is personal, but apart from the person altogether. What makes one see more, what makes one love, what makes one sensitive to the earth and the things of the earth? What makes one understand without words, without gesture? What makes one have a vision or an experience of something beyond the measure of the mind? That is the problem—not why one was born in a little village and not somewhere else, which is without significance. Do think it out with me. Why is it that one mind gets conditioned, shaped, bullied into some kind of action, and another does not? Is it a matter of karma, cause-effect? That is, you have done something good in the past, and the effect is that you are now a kind man, or a rich man, or a talented man—something or other. But is that so? Is cause-effect so clear-cut and defined as all that? Or does the cause, in producing the effect, become again the cause? Therefore there is no isolated cause-effect, but an unbroken series of causes and effects, which become further causes. Do you understand? Karma to most people is a process whereby you benefit from having done something good in the past, and pay for whatever evil you have done. But it is not so simple as that, is it? I know that is what the thoughtless say, those who are always climbing the ladder of success, never thinking of the bootblack, the villager. They are always thinking of karma in terms of achievement—because they are doing good now, in their next life they will have a bigger house, a better position, more money, they will be nearer nirvana, and all the rest of it. Though it may be relevant, that surely is not the essential problem.

So what is the essential problem? If we can put the question rightly, we shall know by investigating it the true content of that question. Why is it that one individual has such an extraordinary sensitivity about him, and another has not? If you put that question through envy, you will never find the answer. Don't laugh it off, sirs. Think it out. Most of us ask through envy because we want the same thing; therefore, our question is not the right one. So, how does it happen that one mind is conditioned and another is not? You can easily say it is karma, or ascribe the whole thing to fancy, imagination, but that is not the answer, surely. Why does one particular mind that is put under pressure, that goes through all the stresses and strains of life, see so much and come out differently? What makes it happen? Is it like some rare thing in botany, or in the field of sport? Or is it something which is possible for everybody? If it is a rare thing, it has no value. You can just as well put it in a museum, label, and forget it—which is what we generally do, only we make the person into a saint or some silly thing like that. But if you really want to know, then you will have to find out for yourself whether there is a reality which can be understood immediately and not through the process of time.

There is a reality—please listen, sirs—there is a reality which, coming upon the mind, transforms it. You don't have to do a thing. It operates, it functions, it has a being of its own; but the mind must feel it, must know it and not speculate, not have all kinds of ideas about it. A mind that is seeking it will never find it, but there is that state, unquestionably. In saying this I am not speculating, nor am I stating it as an experience of yesterday. It is so. There is that state, and if you have it, you will find everything is possible because that is creation, that is love, that is compassion. But you cannot come to it through any means, through any book, through any guru or organization. Do please realize that you cannot come to it through any means. No meditation will lead you to it. When you realize that no sanctions, no pattern of behavior, no guru, no book, no organization, no authority can lead you to that state, you have already got it. Then you will find that the mind is merely an instrument of that creation. And it is that creation operating through the mind that will bring about a totally different world—not the planned world of the politician or the religio-social reformer—because that creation is its own reality, its own eternity.

December 23, 1956

Fifth Talk in Madras

I think it must be a matter of grave concern for most people to see how little they fundamentally change. What is needed is not a modified continuity of things as they are because the immediate problems of war, the pressures and tremendous challenges that confront us every day, demand that we change in a totally different manner than before. The moralists, the politicians, and reformers all urge some kind of change, and change is obviously essential, yet we don't seem to change. By change I do not mean throwing out one particular ideology or pattern of thought and taking up another, or leaving one religious group and joining another. To be caught in the movement of change, if you know what I mean, is not to have a residual point from which change takes place. That is, if I as a Hindu change to Buddhism or Christianity, I am merely changing from one residual thought to another, from one tradition to another, and that is obviously no change at all. So it seems to me very important to be caught in the movement of change, which I shall go into presently.

Most of us are aware that technologically the world is advancing with extraordinary rapidity, but the human problems which technological progress brings cannot be adequately met by a mind that is merely functioning in a routine or according to a pattern. You can see that technology will presently feed man—perhaps not tomorrow, but sooner or later it is going to happen. Through every form of force and compulsion, through legislation, propaganda, ideology, and so on, man is going to be clothed, fed, and sheltered; but even though that is ultimately done, inwardly there will be very little change. You may all be well-fed, clothed, and sheltered, but the mind will remain about the same; it will be more capable of dealing with technological matters, with the machine, but inwardly there will be no compassion, no sense of goodness or the flowering of it. So it seems to me that the problem is not merely how to meet the challenge technologically but to find out how the individual is to change—not just you and I, but how the majority of people are to change and be compassionate, or to change so that compassion is.

Can compassion, that sense of goodness, that feeling of the sacredness of life about which we were talking last time we met—can that feeling be brought into being through compulsion? Surely, when there is compulsion in any form, when there is propaganda or moralizing, there is no compassion, nor is there compassion when change is brought about merely through seeing the necessity of meeting the technological challenge in such a way that human beings will remain human beings and not become machines. So there must be a change without any causation. A change that is brought about through causation is not compassion; it is merely a thing of the marketplace. So that is one problem.

Another problem is: If I change, how will it affect society? Or am I not concerned with that at all? Because the vast majority of people are not interested in what we are talking about—nor are you if you listen out of curiosity or some kind of impulse, and pass by. The machines are progressing so rapidly that most human beings are merely pushed along and are not capable of meeting life with the enrichment of love, with compassion, with deep thought. And if I change, how will it affect society, which is my relationship with you? Society is not some extraordinary mythical entity; it is our relationship with each other, and if two or three of us change, how will it affect the rest of the world? Or is there a way of affecting the total mind of man?

That is, is there a process by which the individual who is changed can touch the unconscious of man? Do you understand the problem, sirs? It is not my problem, I am not foisting it on you. It is your problem, so you have to deal with it. Man is going to be fed, clothed, and sheltered by technology, and that is going to influence his thinking because he will be safe; he will have everything he needs, and if he is not astonishingly alert, inwardly rich, he will become not a mature human being but a repeating machine, and his change will be under pressure, under compulsion of the whole technological process, which includes the use of propaganda to convince a man of certain ideas and condition his mind to think in a certain direction—which is already being done. Seeing all this, you must obviously think, "How am I to change? And if I do change, if I do become an integrated human being—which I must; otherwise, I am merely part of the propaganda machine with its various forms of coercion and so on—will it bring about a change in the collective? Or is that an impossibility?"

Now, must the collective be transformed gradually? Do you understand? When we talk about gradualness, obviously it implies compulsion, slow conviction through propaganda, which is educating the individual to think in a certain direction—to be good, kind, gentle—but under pressure. Therefore the mind is like a machine that is being driven by steam, and such a mind is not good, it is not compassionate, it has no appreciation of something sacred. Its action is all the result of being told what to do.

I don't know if you have thought about all this, but if you have, it must be a tremendous problem to you. More and more people are becoming mere repeaters of tradition, whether communist, Hindu, or whatever tradition it is, and there is no human being who is thinking totally anew of his relationship to society. And if I am concerned with this issue, not verbally or intellectually—not saying that life is one, that we are all brothers, that we must go and preach brotherhood, because all that is mere wordplay—but if I am concerned with compassion, with love, with the real feeling of something sacred, then how is that feeling to be transmitted? Please follow this. If I transmit it through the microphone, through the machinery of propaganda, and thereby convince another, his heart will still be empty. The flame of ideology will operate, and he will merely repeat, as you are all repeating, that we must be kind, good, free—all the nonsense that the politicians, the socialists, and the rest of them talk. So, seeing that any form of compulsion, however subtle, does not bring this beauty, this flowering of goodness, of compassion, what is the individual to do?

If the man of compassion is a freak, then obviously he has no value. You may just as well shut him up in a museum. But the action of a freak is not the action of a man who has really thought it all out deeply, who actually feels compassion, the sense of loving, and does not merely enunciate a lot of intellectual ideas; and has such a man no effect on society? If he has not, then the problem will go on as it is. There will be a few freaks, and they will be valueless except as a pattern for the collective, who will repeat what they have said and moralize everlastingly about it.

So what is the relationship between the man who has this sense of compassion, and the man whose mind is entrenched in the collective, in the traditional? How are we to find the relationship between these two, not theoretically, but actually? Do you understand, sirs? It is like a man who is hungry—he does not talk about the theory of economics, nor is he satisfied with books that describe the good qualities of food. He must eat. So, what is the relationship between the man who is enlightened, not in some mysterious, mystical way, but who is not greedy, not envious, who knows what it is to love, to be kind, to be gentle—what is the relationship between such a man and you who are caught in the collective? Can he influence you? Influence is not the word, surely, because if he influences you, then you are under his propagandistic compulsion, and therefore you have not the real flame; you have only the imitation of it. So what is one to do?

Is there an action which will affect the collective nonthinker so that he thinks totally anew? Will education do that? That is, can the student be helped to understand the whole variety of influences that exist about him so that he does not conform to any influence, thereby bringing into being a new generation with a totally different approach to life? Because the old generation is on the way out; they are obviously not going to change. Most of you will sit here listening for the next twenty years and change only when it suits you. Instead of a dhoti you will put on trousers, or you will drink, or eat meat, and think you have changed marvelously. But I am not talking about such trivialities at all.

Is this change to be brought about by beginning with the young, with the child? But that means there must be a new kind of teacher. Don't just agree with me, sirs. See the whole significance of it. There must be a new kind of mind operating in the teacher so that he helps the child to grow, not in tradition, not as a communist, a socialist, or whatever it be, but in freedom. The student must be helped to be free at the very beginning and not ultimately—free to understand the pressures of his home, of his parents, the pressures of propaganda through newspapers, books, ideas, through the whole paraphernalia of compulsion—and he himself must be encouraged to see the importance of not influencing others. And where are such teachers? You nod your heads in agreement and say that it should be done, but where are the teachers? Which means that you are the teachers. The teachers are at home, not in the school, because nobody else is interested in all this. Governments are certainly not interested. On the contrary, they want you to remain within the pattern because the moment you step out, you become a danger to the present society. Therefore they push you back. So the problem actually devolves upon you and me, not upon the supposed teacher.

Now, can you change immediately, without any compulsion? Sirs, do please listen to this. If you don't change now, you will never change. There is no change within the field of time. Change is outside the field of time because any change within that field is merely a modification of the pattern, or a revolt against a particular pattern in order to establish a new one. So I think the problem is not how the enlightened individual will affect society. I am using that word *enlightened* in the simplest, most ordinary sense—to describe one who thinks clearly and sees the absurdity of all the nonsense that is going on, who has compassion, who loves, but not because it is profitable or good for the state. To ask what effect such a man has on the collective, or of what use he is to society, may be a wrong question altogether. I think it is because if we put the question in that way, we are still thinking in terms of the collective, so let us put the question differently.

Has the man of enlightenment, the man who is inwardly free of religions, of beliefs, of dogmas, who belongs to no organization that brings in the past—has such a man any reality in this world which is bound to the wheel of tradition? Do you understand, sirs? How would you answer that question?

To put it again differently, there is sorrow in the world, sorrow arising from various causes. There is not only physical pain, but this complex psychological process of engendering and sustaining sorrow, which is fairly obvious.

Now, is there freedom from sorrow? I say there is—but not because someone else has said it, which is merely the traditional way of thinking. I say there is an ending to sorrow. And what relation has the man for whom sorrow has ended to the man of sorrow? Has he any relation at all? We may be trying to establish an impossible relationship between the man who is free of sorrow and the man who is caught in sorrow, and creating thereby a whole series of complex issues. Must not the man of sorrow step out of his world, and not look to the man who is free from sorrow? Which means that every human being must cease to depend psychologically, and is that possible?

Dependence in any form creates sorrow, does it not? In depending on fulfillment there is frustration. Whether a man seeks fulfillment as a governor, as a poet, as a writer, as a speaker, or tries to fulfill himself in God, it is all essentially the same because in the shadow of fulfillment there is pain, frustration. And how are you and I to meet this problem? Do you understand, sirs? I may be free, but has that any value to you? If it has no value, what right have I to exist? And if it has value, then how will you meet such a man—not how he will meet you, but how will you meet him? He may want to meet you and go with you, not just one mile, but a hundred miles; but how will you meet him? And is it possible to change so fundamentally, so radically and deeply, that your whole thinking-feeling process is exploded, made innocent, fresh, new?

Sirs, there is no answer to this question. I am only pointing it out. It is for you to expose it, to bite into it, to be tortured by it. It is for you to work hard on it because if you don't, your life is over, finished, gone; and your children, the coming generation, will also be finished. You always say that the coming generation will create the new world, which is nonsense because you are conditioning that generation right off through your books and newspapers, through your leaders, politicians, and organized religions—everything is forcing the child in a particular direction, while you eternally verbalize about nothing.

So this is your problem, and I don't think you are taking it seriously. It is not a thing as vital to you as making money or going to the office and being caught in the routine of that astonishing boredom which you call your life. Whether you are a lawyer, a judge, a governor, or the highest politician, your life for the most part is a dreadful routine that is boring and destructive in the extreme, and you are caught in it; and your children are also going to be caught in it unless you change fundamentally. This is not rhetorical, sirs, it is something that you have to think out, work out, sit together and solve. Because the world does demand human beings who are thinking anew, not in the same old groove, and who do not revolt against the old pattern only to create a new one.

I think you will find the answer in right relationship when you know what love is. Strangely, love has its own action, probably not at the recognizable level; but the man who is really compassionate has an action, a something which other men have not. It is those who are serious, who listen, who think, who work at this thing—it is such people who will bring about a different action in the world, not eventually, but now. And I think the problem is: How is a human being to change so fundamentally in his way of thinking that his mind is totally unconditioned? If you give your thought to it as much as you do to your office, to your puja, and all the rest of the nonsense, you will find out.

Sirs, I am going to answer this one question—or rather, I am not going to answer it, but together we will take the journey into the problem. Because the problem holds the answer, the answer is not outside of the problem. If I am open to the problem, I can see the beauty of it, all its intricacies, its extraordinary nuances and implications, and then the problem dissolves; but if I look at the problem with the intention of finding an answer, obviously I am not open to the problem.

Question: My son and others who have been abroad seem to have had the moral fiber knocked out of them. How does this happen, and what can we do to develop their character?

KRISHNAMURTI: Why do we think only of those people who have been abroad? Has not the moral fiber of most people who are listening been knocked out of them? Seriously, sirs, do not laugh. It is a very complex problem. Let us explore it together. We want to develop character, at least that is what we say. The newspapers, the government, the moralists, the religious people—are they doing it? You think so? How does character develop? How does goodness flower? Does it flower within the frame of social compulsion, which is called moral? Or does goodness flower, does character come into being, only when there is freedom? Freedom does not mean freedom to do what you like. But that is what happens when they go abroad. All the usual pressures are taken off—the pressure of the family, of tradition, of the country, the fear of the father and the mother—and they let loose. But did they have character before they left, or were they merely under the thumb of their parents, of tradition, or society? And as long as a human being is under the thumb of the family, of society, of tradition, of propaganda, and all the rest of it, has he character? Or is he merely a machine functioning repetitiously according to a moral code and therefore inwardly dead, empty? Do you understand, sirs? That is what is happening in India, though the vast majority of people have not gone abroad. Moral fiber is rapidly disintegrating. You ought to know that better than I do. So your problem is, is it not, how to develop character and yet remain within the social pattern so as not to disrupt society. Because, though it may talk about character or morality, society does not want character. It wants people who will conform, who will toe the line of tradition.

So we see that character is not developed in a pattern. Character exists only where there is freedom—and freedom is not freedom to do what you like. But society does not allow freedom. I don't have to tell you. Watch yourself in dealing with your own children. You don't want them to have character, you want them to conform to tradition, to a pattern. To have character there must be freedom, for only in freedom is the flowering of goodness possible, and that is character, that is morality, not the so-called morality that merely conforms to a pattern.

Is it possible, then, to develop character and yet remain within society? Surely, society does not want character, it is not concerned with the flowering of goodness; society is concerned with the word *goodness,* but not with the flowering of it, which can take place only in freedom. So the two are incompatible, and the man who would develop character must free himself from society. After all, society is based on greed, envy, ambition; and cannot human beings free themselves from these things and then help society to break its own pattern?

Sirs, if you look at India, you will see what is happening. Everything is breaking down because essentially there is no character, essentially you have not flowered in goodness. You have merely followed the pattern of a certain culture, trying to be moral within that framework, and when the pressure comes, your moral fiber breaks because it has no substance, no inward reality; and then all the elders tell you to go back to the old ways, to the temple, to the Upanishads, to this and that, which means conformity. But that which conforms can never flower in goodness. There must be freedom, and freedom comes only when you understand the whole problem of envy, greed, ambition, and the desire for power. It is freedom from those things that allows the extraordinary thing called character to flower. Such a man has compassion, he knows what it is to love—not the man who merely repeats a lot of words about morality.

So the flowering of goodness does not lie within society, because society in itself is always corrupt. Only the man who understands the whole structure and process of society, and is freeing himself from it, has character, and he alone can flower in goodness.

December 26, 1956

Colombo, Ceylon, 1957

First Talk in Colombo

It seems to me that the many problems which we have, not only in this country, but throughout the world, are increasing and becoming more and more complex. When we try to solve a particular problem, other problems spring into being, so there arises a wide network of problems endlessly multiplying itself, and there seems to be no way out of it. I think anyone who is at all thoughtful is aware of this dilemma.

Now, if you and I as individual human beings are to understand this complex process of existence, I think it is essential that we approach it in all humility. It is only when the mind is actually in a state of humility that it can learn. We cannot approach our problems with old ideas, with stereotyped answers, with a particular ideology or pattern of thought. We have to approach these problems anew—and there lies our difficulty. As we are now, most of us are incapable of learning from the problem because we approach the problem with a mind that has already learned. I think there is a vast difference between the mind that is open to the problem and a mind that approaches the problem with an ideology. A mind that approaches the problem with an ideology, a preconceived answer, is incapable of learning from the problem.

We have to learn from the problem because the problem is a challenge, and a challenge is always new. But unfortunately most of us approach any problem with conclusions, with a mind already made up, with a mind that is conditioned as a Hindu, a Buddhist, a Christian, a communist, a socialist, or what you will—which means that we are incapable of learning. So it is essential, is it not, that each one of us individually should be open to the problem. I think this is the central issue and that we should see it very clearly.

During the talks that are going to be held here, if you are at all serious in your intent, you have to understand the relationship between yourself and the speaker. It is not a question of someone teaching you; on the contrary, you and I as individuals are going to learn, and there is no division as the teacher and the taught. Such a division is unethical, unspiritual, irreligious. Please understand this very clearly. I am not dogmatic or assertive. As long as we do not understand the relationship between you and the speaker, we will remain in a false position. To me there is only learning, not the person who knows and the person who does not know. The moment anyone says he knows, he does not know. Truth is not to be known. What is known is a thing of the past, it is already dead. Truth is living, not static; therefore, you cannot know truth. Truth is in constant movement; it has no abode, and a mind that is tethered to a belief, to knowledge, to a particular conditioning, is incapable of understanding what is truth.

As you and I are going to explore this whole problem, inquire into it together, we are in a position of learning, are we not? Therefore there is no division of the teacher and the taught. To me the follower is essentially stupid, as is the teacher who admits the following. When you are following, there is no enlightenment; you are not a light unto yourself; you have no love in your heart, but merely the description from the teacher who tells you what love is. So is it not very important, if you are at all serious, that we should establish from the very beginning the right relationship between us? If you are here merely out of curiosity, for amusement, that has its own worth. But the occasion and the immense crisis demand that you be serious—serious, not in the sense of following your prejudices, interests, or bent in a particular direction, but serious to understand.

What we are trying to do, then, is to take a journey of understanding together—together, which means that I am not leading and you are not following. To me, the leader, the teacher, the guru, is essentially unmoral, unethical, unspiritual. We are human beings, free to inquire, to find out if there is God, if there is truth, if there is something beyond the measure of the mind. But you cannot find what is beyond the measure of the mind if you are merely following a pattern of dogma or belief. The problems of life are so immense, so catastrophic, so urgent, and important that the mind must be capable of understanding, of really going into the problem profoundly, and not merely scratching the surface. To do that, the mind has to uncondition itself, for after all, our minds are conditioned, are they not? You are conditioned as a Buddhist, you are conditioned by the climate you live in, by the food you eat, by the books you read, by newspapers, and propaganda. Your mind is obviously the result of influences and pressures, and you are nothing but that. You may think that you are something more, but if you investigate, go into it very seriously, you will see that your mind is actually the result of the collective. When you say you are a Sinhalese, that statement is the result of the collective. You are not an individual, you are the result of the propaganda which says you are a Sinhalese with a particular religion, a particular culture. As a Buddhist you are conditioned by the beliefs, by the dogmas, by the superstitions, by the fears of that particular religion, while a Christian is conditioned from childhood to believe in a Savior, to follow certain rituals, and so on. In the Russian world the communist is conditioned not to believe, and he will tell you that all this belief in God is sheer nonsense. He is conditioned, just as you are conditioned. It is an unpalatable thing to swallow, but it is so.

Now, this conditioning influences our thinking and limits our perception; and it is only when the mind frees itself from its conditioning that it is able to understand the many problems which confront us. So, is the mind capable of freeing itself from its conditioning? Do you understand, sirs? What is important is not to find a better conditioning, a nobler spiritual pattern, but for the mind to free itself from all patterns. And is the mind capable of freeing itself? Surely, it is only a free mind that can respond adequately to the challenge of our ever-mounting problems and misery. Outwardly you may have what you need; sufficient clothing, food, and shelter may be provided by the state. Outwardly, through terror, wars may be stopped, but inwardly there will still be contradiction, strife; there will still be misery, chaos, disturbance, uncertainty within ourselves. We are individually the sum total of all that, and we have to understand it, for it is only the mind that has self-knowledge that understands the whole working process of itself—it is only such a mind that is capable of being free from its conditioning and responding to the challenge anew.

What conditions our minds? It is really very simple if you observe it. Our ambitions, our greed, our envy, our pursuit of personal expansion, of power, position, prestige, our desire to be secure both in the world of relationship and in the world of ideas—all that is what conditions the mind.

Religion as organized belief and dogma is not religion at all. Religion is something entirely different from the mere acceptance of belief or the practice of a ritual. Religion, surely, is the process of freeing the mind from envy, from greed, from ambition, so that the self-centered activity of the 'I' no longer exists, and only such a mind is capable of pursuing in utter silence the movement of reality. That is why it is important to have a religious revolution—which is the only revolution—because mere economic revolution will inevitably fail.

The religious revolution of which I speak has nothing whatever to do with any established religion. On the contrary, to have this religious revolution, one must be free from all organized dogma and belief, for only then is the mind capable of experiencing that which is real. But unfortunately, most of us do not give time to this; we are too busy with our daily lives, with earning a livelihood, with the things of the world. Being too busy, we multiply mischief in the world, and then we say, "What can I as an individual do?"

If you observe, you will see it is only the enlightened individual that is capable of doing anything, not the mass, not the collective; and the enlightened individual is one who has an inward knowledge of himself, of the activities of his own mind, the operations of his own thought. To be truly aware, not only of the workings of the superficial mind, but also of the unconscious, is the beginning of self-knowledge; and without self-knowledge there is self-deception, illusion; therefore, you can never find out what is truth.

Self-knowledge is the beginning of wisdom. This self-knowledge is not to be gathered from books, but you can find it for yourself through observing your daily relationship with your wife or husband, with your children, with your boss, with the conductor of the bus. It is through awareness of yourself in your relationship with another that you discover the workings of your own mind, and this understanding of yourself is the beginning of the freedom from conditioning. If you go into it deeply, you will find that the mind becomes very quiet, really still. This stillness is not the stillness of a mind that is disciplined, held, controlled, but the stillness which comes when, through the understanding of relationship, the mind has ceased to be a center of self-interest. Such a mind is capable of following that which is beyond the measure of the mind.

I have some questions here, but before we consider them, I think we should understand the intention of the questions and the replies.

Why do you ask a question? Obviously, to find an answer—which means that you are interested not in the problem but in the answer. Now, you can understand a problem only when you give your total attention to it, and you cannot give your total attention to it as long as the mind is seeking an answer. Is it not so? I think we ought to see that very clearly.

For example, there is enmity, hate; and what we are concerned with is how to get rid of it. So we go about seeking ways and means of getting rid of hate; we try to get rid of it through disciplines, practices, and so on. But surely that is not the problem. What makes the mind hate? Why is there animosity? Why is there unfriendliness? That is the problem, not how to be free. To understand the whole problem of enmity, jealousy, envy, to go to the very end of it and understand it totally, I must give it my full attention. Then there is no answer; the problem itself is resolved.

I don't know if you have ever tried to give your total attention to something. Have you ever tried to look at a flower completely, without evaluating, without judging? You will find it is an extraordinarily difficult thing to do because your mind immediately says that the flower is beautiful, or that it is of such and such a species, and you either like or dislike it. In the very process of verbalizing, judging, evaluating, your mind has gone away from the object of attention. But if you can give complete attention to something, you will find that that complete attention is the good; you do not have to pursue the good. Such attention is the process of meditation—not the battle to exclude the various thoughts that keep creeping into the mind.

So in considering these questions, we are not trying to answer them, because to the immense problems of life, there is no answer. It is a very superficial and silly mind that seeks an answer. But a mind that gives its whole attention to the problem will find that, in the process of understanding the problem, the problem has ceased.

Question: Like many of my valued friends, I am an ardently religious Sinhalese Buddhist, and I feel intensely for our religion and our culture. But unfortunately, in furthering our religion and our culture, I see that we are unconsciously getting divided into opposing parties. What would you advise me to do?

KRISHNAMURTI: It is not a matter of advice, but together we are going to find out what the problem involves.

The questioner says that he is an ardently religious Sinhalese Buddhist. But is it possible to be a Sinhalese or a Buddhist and still be religious? (Laughter) Don't laugh, sirs, this is not a political meeting. Can you be religious as long as you are a Christian or an Englishman? Can you be religious and belong to India? Are they not contradictory? Is nationalism compatible with love? Please, it is your problem. I am not a Christian, a Buddhist, or a Hindu, nor do I belong to any other religious or nationalistic group. It is your problem because you say you are an ardently religious Sinhalese Buddhist, and you want to maintain a particular culture. You don't see immediately the absurdity of such a statement.

What do you mean by culture? What do you mean when you say you are a Buddhist, a Sinhalese? Since you happen to live on this island, you are made conscious—through propaganda, through the machinations of politicians, through so-called education and other forms of influence—of belonging to a particular group, and you think in terms of that group.

But what does it mean to be religious? Surely, to be religious is not to belong to any organized religion. To be religious is to be kind, to be generous, to love, not to harm, not to kill. That is all. To love, to be kind, you don't have to belong to any religion; not to have enmity, not to be ambitious, not to be self-centered, you don't have to profess any creed or belief. Religion as organized belief does not contain truth. No temple, no church, no mosque has truth in it; they are all man-built, and what man has put together, man can undo. So why call yourself a Sinhalese or a Buddhist? We are human beings, sirs, not labels. We all suffer, we are inwardly tortured by misery, loneliness, sorrow. These are human problems, not the problems of a Buddhist, a Christian, or a Hindu, and we have to solve them together as human beings.

Do please understand this, it is so simple. Religions, organized beliefs, divide and destroy people. See what is happening in the world. There are Catholics and Protestants, Northern Buddhists and Southern Buddhists, Hindus, Muslims, and so on. As the earth is broken up into little patches of nationalistic ownership, so religion has been divided by man; it has become a form of vested interest. So why call yourself a Sinhalese or a Buddhist? If we strip ourselves of all these idiotic labels and remain as simple human beings, then perhaps we shall create a different world, a world in which people are not divided as Sinhalese and Hindus, Christians and Buddhists, Englishmen and Russians. That division is a major cause of your miseries.

Please, sirs, understand this. You have divided man for economic reasons, basically, and also to be secure in a particular pattern of belief, so you are destroying yourselves. You will have no peace in the world until you cease to be labeled as Christians, Buddhists, Hindus. The important thing in all this is to have friendliness, to have compassion, to have love; and we do not have friendliness, compassion, love, so justice comes into being—justice being legislation. Governments make you conform to a pattern, and when justice is a matter of legislation forcing the people to conform, there is no love. A mind-heart that is full of love needs no such justice; a mind-heart that is free from all labels, whether Christian, Buddhist, communist, or what you will, is capable of bringing about a different world.

Now, sirs, you have listened to the problem. What will you do about it? You will probably agree intellectually, that is, verbally, and say, "It sounds reasonable and true," but when you go outside you will again fall into the trap, into the old habit of following the social pattern. Only the man who renounces the social pattern completely—only such a man is a religious person. But unfortunately, though you hear what is being said, you will forget about it and go back to your old way of thinking. What a strange thing!

These meetings are not propagandistic in any sense. I am not trying to propagate an idea. On the contrary, there are no ideas, but only understanding. To understand, we must investigate together, there must be friendliness, a feeling of companionship, a sense of affection. But we cannot have affection, friendliness, if you are a Buddhist and I a Hindu. So those of you who have listened to this, because it is the truth, have an immense responsibility. If you are at all serious, you cannot possibly go back to the old; you may call yourself a Buddhist, a Sinhalese, in applying for a passport, but that is a mere formality. If you are emotionally, inwardly free from all labels, then the authority of the church, of the past, drops away so that the mind is capable of seeing and understanding *what is;* and such a mind, being in a state of real compassion, will solve the many problems that confront each one of us.

Question: In Ceylon we have various religions, but some priests incite their followers to hate those belonging to other religions, which creates serious trouble among the people in general. What is the true function of a priest?

KRISHNAMURTI: Sir, why do we have these various religions at all? Why is there the Christian religion, the Buddhist religion, the Muslim religion, and so on? Have you thought about it at all? Each religion maintains that it is a path, if not the only path to truth, to God, to the highest. Now, is there a path to truth? Or is it that truth is a living thing, and a path can lead only to that which is fixed, static? So, having conceived of truth, of God, as a fixed thing, we have divided ourselves into various religious groups, and each group maintains that its particular system or its particular savior is the path to the highest. Why do they do so? First of all, because of property and vested interests. Religions that have property, vested interests, are no longer religions; they are like any other commercial affair.

Please, sirs, listen diligently. I am not attacking; I am only showing what is actually happening. The Christian says that there is only one savior, and that everyone who does not hold that particular belief is eternally damned. What absurd nonsense, and what cruelty is involved in it! Each religion maintains its own tradition, its guru, its priesthood, and says that it is the path to truth. And why should there be these different religions at all, with their conflicting dogmas and beliefs? If you observe you will see that they exist because you are conditioned from childhood to believe in something, and you are caught for the rest of your life in that belief; and having been conditioned, you are exploited through fear, through vanity, through flattery, through every available means. This is what is actually happening throughout the world. Religions are not interested in reality; they are not interested that men should be free from ambition, from greed, from envy, from hate, from killing each other. No religion has stopped war. That is why religions have failed.

There is no path to reality. Reality is a pathless land, and you must venture out and discover it for yourself. It is because you are frightened inwardly that you depend on something, on the priest or on a belief, and so you get caught in the net of an organized religion. Wherever organized religions may lead you, they will certainly not lead you to truth. You must go beyond organized religions to find truth.

The second part of the question is, "What is the true function of a priest?"

What do you mean by a priest? The man in a yellow robe, the sannyasi, or the man who wears a clerical collar, and so on? The priest is supposed to be a mediator between you and reality, between you and God, between you and the immeasurable, is he not? But can there be a mediator between you and the real? How can there be? Haven't you to be a light unto yourself? Then what need is there for a priest? To love, to be compassionate, to be kind, to be generous, do you need a priest? And if the priest is an interpreter, a mediator between you and reality, does he know reality? Or is he merely conditioned in a particular ideology which he calls reality? Can there be a mediator between you and that which is beyond all measure? If you need a mediator, an interpreter, then you are not seeking truth; what you want is comfort, gratification, and you might just as well take a pill. Please, sirs, I am talking very seriously. Religions with their priests are unnecessary to a man who is seeking truth. A man who is seeking to understand what is compassion, what is love, does not want a priest, he does not want an organized belief; to him, love is more important than belief.

Surely, sirs, to love, to be compassionate, is the only door to reality; there is no other door. But how can you be compassionate, kind, generous, friendly, as long as you are ambitious? You want to be somebody in the world, do you not? You want to be famous, you want to succeed, and your whole social structure is based on acquisitiveness, competition. When your only concern is to get on in the world, to have more property, to achieve success, how can you love, how can there be compassion?

So most of us are not concerned with compassion, with love; we are only concerned with getting ahead, making a success of it, with having labels such as Buddhist, Hindu, Christian—and then we quarrel over the labels. Each one is trying to convert the other, and in converting others, you have more votes, more property, more power. You can see this game going on throughout the world, and this game is called religion.

Surely, religion is something extraordinary; it has nothing to do with any organization, with any belief or dogma. Religion is not to be found in any temple, in any church or mosque. It is to be found only when the mind understands itself and is free from fear, free from the demand to be inwardly secure. Then there is a possibility of being compassionate, kindly, and such a mind-heart will know that which is immeasurable, for then the immeasurable is. It is not a thing to be speculated about, it has to be experienced directly. There is something beyond the measure of the mind, but it is not to be found in the Upanishads, in the Gita, in the Bible, nor in the Buddhist literature. It comes through the understanding of yourself in your relationship with people, with nature, and with ideas. When you understand yourself completely, you will discover without any aid from another, without any organized religion, without any priest, that beyond the mind there is something which is timeless. It is a state that can be experienced only when the mind is completely still.

January 13, 1957

Second Talk in Colombo

We are confronted with a world that is rapidly changing, whose challenges have to be met; and as it is impossible for a mind that is bound by tradition, by the past, to meet these challenges rightly, fully, and adequately, I think it is very important that we understand the fundamental issues. We know from what we read in the papers that extraordinary material progress is being made in America, and we also know what is taking place in Europe, and we can see very clearly that some fundamental change is necessary, that we cannot go on in the way that we have been accustomed to. We cannot possibly continue to think in terms of Asia, Europe, or America. We have to think anew because the challenge is totally new. After all, every challenge is new and has to be met with a fresh mind, a mind that is not conditioned, not influenced by a background or possessed by tradition. Such a total transformation is necessary in each one of us, for we can see that our minds are tethered to the past. Because of our education, because of our religious training, because of our social influences and moral pressures, our minds are at present incapable of meeting the challenge anew.

So our problem is, is it not, how is the mind to undergo a radical transformation? I do not know if you have ever thought about the problem in this manner. We generally think about changing gradually. That is, by the pursuit of an ideal we say that we shall eventually bring about a transformation within ourselves, and thereby change society. Gradualism is a very convenient and satisfying theory, but actually you will see, if you observe, that you do not change through a gradual process. Ideals are not the means of transforming the mind. A man who pursues an ideal, however noble, is really caught in the process of postponement, in the ways of indolence. We shall understand this as we go along.

Before I proceed with what I want to talk about this evening, may I say that I think it is very important to know how to listen. Most of us do not really listen because we always listen with an objection, with interpretations; we translate what is being said in terms of our own ideas, or compare it with what we already know, so actually we never listen. If you have ever attempted really to listen to somebody, you will know how extraordinarily difficult it is because you have innumerable prejudices which come like a screen between yourself and the person to whom you are trying to listen. But if one can listen without judging, without comparing, without translating, then I think such listening has an extraordinary effect. Such listening brings about a total revolution in the mind because it demands complete attention, and complete attention is the complete good.

So I would like to suggest that you try to listen in that way to the talk this evening, and then you will see how very difficult it is. I may say something totally new, and because you happen to be a Buddhist, a Christian, or a Hindu, steeped in a particular ideology, you will naturally have objections, reactions; you will compare what is being said with what you already know, which means that you are actually not listening at all. Your mind is so astonishingly active in comparing, judging, evaluating, that it is really distracted. What matters is to listen with that peculiar attention which is not an effort, which is not absorption—and you do listen in that manner when you really want to find out, when there is urgency. Such an urgency exists at the present period in the world crisis. It cannot wait for you to transform yourself gradually. It demands direct action on the part of each individual immediately.

The difficulty for most of us is that we are mesmerized by the word *collective* and think that individual action is of very little value. We say, "What can I as an individual do against the mass, against this mountain of the collective?" Whereas, if you look more closely, you will find that the total action of the individual—if that total action is very clear, not befuddled by the influences of the collective, of the mass, nor by the influences of the past—is deeply effective. Because the collective is confused, the individual is generally confused. We want guidance and so we look to the past; we try to revive the religion of the past; or we turn to the guru immediately round the corner. But will any guidance clarify a confused mind?

Please follow this a little bit, if you will. Our minds are confused. Each one of us is confused, there are no two ways about it. Religions have failed totally. You may mutter a lot of prayers, go to the temple, attend church, follow a particular routine or practice in accordance with what they say in the books, but that is not religion. Religion is something totally different. A confused mind may seek guidance in the things that have been said by various teachers, or repeat ten thousand prayers, but it will still remain confused because it is confused at the center. Such a mind may clarify itself at the periphery, but at the core of its being there is uncertainty, tremendous confusion, a lack of real clarity of thinking.

The moment an individual realizes that he is confused and cannot possibly look to the past or turn to another to be taught how to clear up his confusion, then his problem will be to find out for himself what has produced this confusion. But most of us are unwilling, I think, to admit that we are confused—and this attitude is obviously a fallacy, a self-deception, because everything around us and in ourselves points to confusion. We are in a state of self-contradiction. We try to lead a religious life, and yet we are worldly; in us there is sorrow, misery, frustration, many desires pulling in different directions. All this indicates, does it not, a sense of confusion. And you have to realize that when you are confused, you cannot possibly rely on anything, because the moment you rely on something when you are confused, that reliance merely breeds further confusion. One of the major causes of confusion is the following of authority. That is what we have done for many thousands of years—we have followed spiritual authority.

Please, as I am talking, look at your own life; observe your own daily activities, observe your thoughts. I am only describing what is actually taking place. If you merely listen to the words and do not relate what is being said to the activities of your own mind, it will have no meaning at all. But if you can relate what is being said to your everyday life, to the actual state of your own mind, then the talk will have an immense significance because then you will find that I am not telling you what to do; on the contrary, through the description, through the explanation, you are going to discover for yourself the process of your own thinking. And when you understand yourself, clarity comes. It is self-knowledge that brings clarity, not dependence on a book, a teacher, or a guide. To observe how you think, the manner of your response to challenge in your various relationships—to be aware of all that, not theoretically but actually, will reveal the process of yourself, and in that understanding there is clarity. So please, if I may most earnestly request it, listen and relate what you hear to the actual state of your own mind. Then these talks will be worthwhile; otherwise, they will be mere words to be soon forgotten.

You may not be aware that you are confused, but if you inquire deeply, you will find that it is so. One of the major causes of this confusion is your reliance on authority for guidance: reliance on the church, on the priest, on the book, on the authority of a teacher. All living based on authority, as has been shown recently both politically and militarily, is the most destructive form of existence. Tyranny, whether of the state or of the priest, is detrimental to thought, to a really spiritual life; and as most of us live in the cage of authority, we have lost the capacity to think clearly and directly for ourselves.

The fundamental change of which I am speaking comes when you no longer depend on any authority for the clarity of your own thinking. Authority is a very complex affair because there is not only the authority of society, of the government, but there is also the authority of tradition, of the book, of the priest, the church, the temple. And even if you reject all that, there is still the authority of your own experience, and that experience is based on the past. After all, life is a process of challenge and response, and your response to challenge is experience. But that experience, which is a response to challenge, is dictated by your conditioning, by your past, so your experience is never original; therefore, you cannot possibly rely on experience for clarity of thought. I think this is very important to understand. Knowledge is the residue of past experience, and if you rely on that knowledge to translate all your experiences, they will only strengthen the past and therefore condition your mind further.

To make it simple: you are a Hindu, a Buddhist, a Muslim, or a Christian, or you are a communist, which means that you have been taught to think in a certain direction, and according to that background you have experience—the experience being your response to challenge. This is taking place every day. You respond to challenge in terms of your past conditioning, and therefore your experience further strengthens your conditioning, which is obvious. So there is the authority not only of the priest, of the church, of the temple, of the book, but also the authority of the knowledge which you have accumulated through personal experience.

As I was saying, there must be a complete inward revolution, a total transformation in your thought, in your whole being; and that is not possible as long as you rely on authority, whether it be the authority of the Buddha, or of one of the Indian teachers, including myself. To rely on authority at any time destroys the capacity to find out what is truth. Freedom from authority is the beginning of the fundamental revolution, of this individual transformation which is essential to the discovery of what is truth, what is God, and it is only this discovery on the part of each one of us that can bring about a different world.

Mind is not made free through a deliberate act, or through any practice. Mind is made free from moment to moment, and then there is the understanding of truth at each moment. You cannot understand what is truth if you merely repeat that which you have been told, so a complete purgation of the mind and heart is necessary. We have to set out on the journey anew, which means that we cannot start with any assumption, any conclusion, however noble or profound it may be. When the mind starts thinking with a conclusion, it is not thinking at all. A mind that is capable of thought in the real sense of the word has no conclusion; therefore, it always starts anew, and it is only for such a mind that there is a possibility of discovering what is truth.

Sirs, if you observe your own minds, you will see how extraordinarily difficult it is to think without a conclusion, whether it be the conclusion of ten thousand years ago or of yesterday. These conclusions, either given to you or self-created, prevent clarity of thought and bring about confusion. So a mind that would clear up its own confusion must be aware of how it is caught in authority. I do not mean the authority which requires you to drive on the right or the left side of the road. I am talking of authority in a much deeper and more profound sense—the authority to which the mind clings.

After all, the mind is everlastingly seeking security for itself. It wants to be safe, it wants to be comfortable; and a mind that is concerned with its own security, or with the security of the particular group with which it has identified itself, is bound to create confusion, which is exactly what is happening in the world. Most of us are identified with a group, with a class, with a country, with a religion, which means that we think fragmentarily, in departments; therefore, we are incapable of thinking out the many problems which are so pressing and urgent. Whereas, an individual who thinks clearly, who is unafraid to go into himself totally, not only at the conscious, but also at the unconscious level—such an individual, I assure you, has an extraordinary vitality, the energy to create. And it is such individuals alone who can bring about a different world—not the scientist, and certainly not the priest or the politician.

Sirs, please, you are all politicians at heart because you are concerned with immediate results, with the past or the future, and not with the totality of the human mind. And this inward revolution, this fundamental change, can take place only when you as an individual free your mind from the authority of society, of the church, of the state, and discover for yourself that which is eternal. It is this individual revolution, with the discovery of truth which it brings, that has a transforming effect on the world—not the economic revolution.

It is imperative, then, that those who are really in earnest should be aware of their own state, of their own idiosyncrasies, of their own conditioning, so that there can be no self-deception. For the beginning of wisdom is in self-knowledge, not in what you learn from the books. It is through observing how you talk, how you behave in your daily relationship with your wife, with your child, with your boss, that you discover yourself, and that discovery is the beginning of wisdom. Out of self-knowledge comes clarity, and then you do not rely on anybody; then you are a guide to yourself, a light in the midst of darkness.

Question: What is the religious life? Is it compatible with the struggle for existence which most of us have to face? Is the religious life necessary at all?

KRISHNAMURTI: For the moment let us not consider what is the religious life; we will come to that presently. But why do we divide the religious life from our daily life? Do we know what our daily life is? Are we aware of it, do we throb with it, suffer with it? Or do we merely say, "I live a routine life and it is terribly boring, unsatisfactory; therefore, I want to take up the religious life"?—as if the religious life were entirely apart from our everyday living. It is because we do not understand our everyday living with all its sufferings, with all its ambitions, cruelties, contradictions, envies, deceptions, that we think we must turn to religion and find God somewhere else. But it is fatal to think in this fragmentary way, in these watertight compartments, is it not? First let us find out what our daily existence is and understand it; then perhaps we shall find out what reality is.

Whether we have to eschew the religious life in order to live in this world and what the religious life is, we shall find out only when we understand our relationship with each other. That much is clear, is it not? If we do not understand our everyday life of going to the office, educating our children; if we do not understand lust, ambition, envy, greed, cruelty, and all the appalling things that are going on within ourselves, with an occasional flash of joy—if we don't understand all that, how can we understand something which is beyond all that? Without understanding the mind, anything that we try to understand beyond the mind will be equally confused, equally stupid. Surely, that is clear, is it not? A petty mind may think of God, but its God will be petty also. It may conceive of nirvana, moksha, heaven, or whatever it be, but its conception will be according to its own state.

So, is the religious life necessary? You will find the answer for yourself when you begin to understand the ways of your own living. The question is very simple, but the understanding of it is extremely complex because it requires a great deal of penetration.

Take, for instance, the very simple fact that our life is based on envy. That is so, is it not? Someone is more intelligent than I am, and I want to be equally intelligent; someone is more handsome, or has more money and can travel, and I want to be like him. The mind is constantly comparing itself with others, and such a mind is envious. An ambitious mind is obviously an envious mind, and that is our life; it is how we live from day to day. You know that very well without my telling you. At least, I am describing a fact, and if you are unwilling to look at the fact, it is your affair. It is a fact that our society is based on envy, and the morality of such a society is mere respectability, the perpetuation of a custom. Our daily life is based on this envious, acquisitive struggle, and we carry the same struggle into the so-called religious life; we want to achieve reality, we want to get nearer to God, closer to heaven, and all the rest of it. The same urge exists there as in this world—we want to be somebody.

Now, is it possible for the mind to be totally free of envy, not just partially or in patches? It is not possible for you because you think you must live as you are living now, and you block yourself by saying, "It is impossible, I have to live in this world." But the man who really sees what is happening in the world, who sees the misery, the struggle, the utter futility of it all, can inquire and find out that it is possible to be free of envy, not only in the superficial layers of the conscious mind, but also in the unconscious, which is much more conservative than the conscious mind. Only the mind that is totally free from envy is capable of understanding what is the religious life and why it is necessary to have a religious life, and such a mind knows the state of being sacred; therefore, it need not go to any temple, church, or priest. It has no need of any book because in itself it is understanding; it has an incorruptible treasure. Such a life is possible. But the mind that wants to be envious and says that it is necessary to live in this world will escape into a religion which has no value at all; it will go to the church or the temple and do whatever it is told. To such a mind religion is just a toy. But a mind that really inquires—and the mind is not free to inquire as long as it is envious—will know what it is to have a profoundly religious life, which has nothing whatever to do with any belief, with any ritual or dogma, with any prayer, because then the mind in itself is the religious life.

Question: To me the greatest fear is the fear of death. How am I to get over this fear?

KRISHNAMURTI: This is a very complex question and needs very careful understanding. Most of us are afraid of death, so we believe in a life hereafter, in reincarnation, and cling to various comforting ideologies.

Now, what is it we are afraid of, sirs? I am just thinking aloud for you. I am not telling you what to believe or not to believe—that would be stupid, it would be childish, immature. But if you and I go into the problem together, as we are doing now, then what you discover will be yours, not mine. It will be your truth, your understanding, and it will free you from the fear of death.

Death is a fact, obviously. Through use, the physical organism wears out, and its end is inevitable. We see death every day in so many forms, but that is not what we are afraid of. We are afraid of something else. What is it we are afraid of? Have you ever thought about it, sirs? Watch your own mind, your reactions, not just my explanations. Surely, we are afraid of not continuing; isn't that it? I have lived in this world twenty, thirty, fifty, or even eighty years; I have accumulated so much knowledge, so many memories; I have suffered and learned so much, and I still want to do so much more. Though there has been frustration, I still long to fulfill, and my life is much too short, so I want to lengthen it. But I know that through disease, old age, or accident, death is inevitable. Even if, through some medical process, I were to live three hundred years, death would still be awaiting me at the end.

So my mind is concerned with continuity, the continuity of my name, my family, my property, my friendships, of the virtues I have gathered, and so on. These are the things which I know, and there is death, which I do not know. So what I am fundamentally afraid of is the known meeting the unknown. Meeting the unknown is death, and continuity is all that I know. From the moment I am born to the moment I die, I know only this continuity of memory, and the responses according to that memory. My friends, my family, my job, my social position, my virtues, my belief in God—these are a series of memories and associations with regard to which the mind says, "This is I." It is these memories and associations that make up the 'me', the self, the ego—and this is what one wants to continue. Sirs, if someone could guarantee that by some miraculous process you would continue indefinitely, then you would have no fear.

But life is not so simple as all that, is it? You have your beliefs, your conclusions. All the religions say there is resurrection, reincarnation, or some other form of continuity, yet the sting of fear goes on. The problem, therefore, is how to die, not eventually but now; to know death while living, and not when death is upon us through old age, disease, or accident. To know death now is to experience a sense of not continuing; it is to enter the house of death willingly, knowingly, with full consciousness. When your mind no longer thinks in terms of continuing, when it dies every day to everything that it has gathered, then you will know what it means to meet the unknown, which is death. I hope I am making myself clear.

What is it that we want to continue? Our memories, our struggles, our pains, our joys, our recognition of friends. We see that memories, knowledge, the things of yesterday move through the present as a passage to the future, and that is all we want, yet we know there is death, an ending. We are afraid of that ending only when we think in terms of continuing, when we say, "I must fulfill my ambition, I must become somebody, I must be famous, I must be the greatest this or that." As long as there is the desire for continuity, there will be fear; and if you observe, you will see that that which continues is never creative. Only that which knows an ending has a beginning which is new.

Is it possible to die every day and not wait for the ultimate death, to die to everything that you have known? Try it and you will see how extraordinarily subtle and vital it becomes, how your mind is made new, fresh. That which has an ending alone has a renewal, not the mind which continues, which knows a thousand yesterdays. To the mind which continues, the present is only a passage to the future, and such a mind is caught in the bondage of time. That sense of continuity is the ego, the 'me', with which the mind identifies itself. The link of identification with property, with people, with ideas is merely memory, and that memory is what we want to continue.

I say there will always be fear unless you know what death is now, even though you are not now suffering, diseased, or involved in an accident. What matters is to experience directly for yourself the ending of everything you have known so that your mind meets the unknown. It is not so very difficult; only the explanation is difficult. If you really observe and are aware of how your mind operates, you will know that in wanting to continue, the mind is like a gramophone record which is everlastingly repeating. Only the mind that is silent, that is free from the past, can know the new, the eternal, the timeless; and such a mind is not concerned with the hereafter.

There is another point which is very interesting if you go into it. Is there a continuity of the mind which does not want to know death now? You are afraid of death; you are nervous, anxious, or you have never thought about it, and you die. Is there the continuity of such a mind? Obviously there is a continuity of the thoughts you are thinking. You have identified yourself with your property, with your wife, and so on, and this identification through recognition sets going a process of thinking, like a vibration or a wave which has its own continuity and which can be got into touch with through mediums and all the rest of it. But that has no vitality; it is all silly and superficial.

What we are concerned with is something totally different: Is it possible to be free from the fear of death? There is freedom from the fear of death only when you know death in the now. It does not mean that you go and commit suicide, but you find out whether the mind, which is the result of time, of many thousands of years, of all the joys, sorrows, pains, and endeavors of man—whether such a mind can end, that is, see the unimportance of continuity. You may have a wife and children and some property, but if you are not identified with any of that, if you die to it all in full vigor, with full comprehension, with a vitality which has its own reward, then you will find that there is no longer fear; then the mind is already in that state in which the unknown is. It is not the virtuous, respectable mind that will know the eternal—for the virtue that is cultivated is no virtue—

but only the mind made innocent because it is free, no longer tethered to the past—and for such a mind there is no fear.

January 16, 1957

Third Talk in Colombo

Considering the critical world situation and seeing the extraordinary conflict that is going on both outwardly and within ourselves, and being aware also of all the pressures—economic, social, and religious—to which we are subject, it seems to me essential to bring about a fundamental change in the life of each one of us. I do not think that most of us appreciate the importance of such a revolution—a revolution that is uninfluenced and not dependent on any circumstances. This fundamental, radical change is not dependent on time, and therefore it has something of the quality of the eternal. But most of us are inclined to wait for change through social reforms, through governmental legislation and outward scientific progress, and so we are always dependent. The changes which are so obviously essential will somehow be brought about, we hope, through the pressure of society, through some kind of vague new educational system, or through social upheaval; but any such change is merely an adaptation to circumstances, and I don't think that adaptation, though it has a certain value, is really a change at all because it does not free the mind to inquire deeply into the reality and the creativity of this thing called life.

Revolution, this inward change which is not brought about by outward invitation or compulsion, is possible only when there is self-knowledge. That is, if I don't know the ways of my own mind, the pressures, motives, compulsions, traditions that guide my thought and feeling, both consciously and unconsciously—if I don't know the totality of myself, then any form of change is really a modified continuity of what has been. Without knowing the whole content of myself, change is no change at all; it is merely an adaptation, a convenience, a conformity, a following of custom, tradition.

So, to bring about a radical change—and a radical change is essential when the crisis is totally new and imminent—there must be self-knowledge; and self-knowledge is not the knowledge that is gathered from books, from a system of philosophy, or from some religious teacher. Self-knowledge comes through observing myself from day to day, from moment to moment, through knowing the urges, the compulsions that spring from the unconscious, and through being aware of my gestures, the way I talk, the manner of my thinking, the anatomy of my feeling. If I don't know all that, then obviously any change is merely a modified continuity of what has been, and it therefore conditions my future action. I think it is important for each one of us to understand this.

Religion should essentially teach man to be a light unto himself and not depend on another, on any church, savior, or system of thought. I think that is clear. Yet the whole social and religious structure which we have built around us makes us dependent; it has become an instrument of compulsion to ourselves and to others. Religions have emphasized, have they not, the importance of rituals, of systems, of beliefs and dogmas; so you have been led away from the one essential fact—which is that you must know yourself. When you know yourself completely, you will find that you don't need a guide because you yourself are the guide, and then there is a total action which operates because the mind is free from every form of fear, whether conscious or unconscious. The mind is then the instrument of this total action, and not the creator of total action. I don't know if I am making myself clear.

In thinking of complete action, most of us want to act in a manner which will be free of contradictions, free of regrets and the fear of future punishment. We want every action to be a total response of our whole being. Because we see the confusion, the misery, the contradiction, the innumerable difficulties that arise from conditioned action, we try to find an action which will be total and in which this misery, this contradiction, can never exist. So the mind, in seeking a total action, inquires, studies, suffers, and possesses an idea which it thinks is total action. That is why you study philosophy, seek out gurus, and all the rest of it—you feel that if you can find a total way of acting, all these contradictions and miseries will not arise. But I say the mind cannot find total action except through self-knowledge. And when through self-knowledge the mind is free, then total action will operate through the mind; the mind will not have to seek it. I think it is important to understand this.

You don't really know yourself. To know yourself is to know the extraordinary capacity of your own mind, to uncover the recesses of your own heart; it is to know how your mind operates, and whether your thinking is action or mere reaction; it is to be aware of the intricacies of the unconscious and see all the intimations and hints that the unconscious is projecting into the conscious. But you are not aware of all that; you are just operating on the surface and going through the routine of daily existence. You go to the office, do your work, and return, carrying on day after day in the same old pattern; and you do not want any disturbance of that pattern, which means that you are superficially satisfied. When you are disturbed superficially, you seek further satisfaction, so your life remains on the superficial level. Though you may meditate, read the scriptures, think of God, it is all on the surface. Your mind is like a gramophone record repeating a song you have heard. It is not even your song; it is the song of another, and there may be no "your song," but only "the song."

So it is very important to understand not only the conscious but also the unconscious mind. The unconscious mind is much more powerful, much more insistent, much more directive and conservative than the conscious mind because the conscious is merely the educated mind which adjusts itself to the environment. I do not know if you have noticed a priest riding on the bus or on a motorbike. This situation is quite contradictory, if you come to think of it. He is adjusting himself, as you do, to the environment, to the pressure from outside, but inwardly he is the same—that is, the unconscious is still the residue of the past.

Sirs, if I may suggest it, watch your own minds; do not merely listen to my words, but through my words observe the operation of your own thinking and discover yourself. I am describing the picture, but it is your picture, not mine. If you really watch yourself as you listen, you will find a radical change taking place in spite of your conscious mind. It is like a seed that, being sown in fertile soil, pushes through the earth and puts out a blossom. So may I respectfully and persistently ask you to listen so that through the activity of listening, you find out the real facts, the truth about yourself. The discovery of that truth will liberate the mind, and then you will not have to pursue the truth which liberates.

The unconscious mind is the residue of all that has been for centuries past; it is the storehouse of tradition, the inheritance of the race, and to bring about a radical change there is much more difficult than to change on the surface. Look at yourselves, sirs, and you will observe a very simple fact—that though you have motorcars, modern buses, gramophones, recording machines, and all the rest of it, inwardly you are steeped in a thousand or ten thousand years of tradition. The unconscious is much more conservative than the conscious mind, much more traditional, and therefore far less capable of real transformation.

So it is very important to understand the unconscious, not merely to scratch on the surface of the mind and think you have understood yourself. To understand the unconscious as well as the conscious mind, there must be a sense of watchfulness which is spontaneous and not enforced. If you watch a child with condemnation, with criticism, with a sense of comparison, what happens? The child feels it and becomes paralyzed, he freezes in his action. You must have noticed it. Whereas, if you begin to play with the child and let him do what he likes, then, even though you are there, he feels free to carry on in his own way, and then you can study him.

Similarly, if the mind watches itself with condemnation, with justification, with a sense of comparison, and so on, then the thinking process freezes and your thoughts become still, but that is not stillness—the mind is simply afraid to move. On the other hand, if you watch with the ease of spontaneity, with the ease of familiarity, without any sense of comparing or justifying, then you will see that the totality of your mind begins to uncover itself. You do not have to uncover it, nor does the conscious mind have to uncover the unconscious. The mind will uncover itself, just as the child begins to play in your presence because he has confidence in you. So the unconscious as well as the conscious mind begins to uncover itself if you approach it without any sense of direction, opposition, or identification, and in this state of awareness you will find that the mind is learning the content of itself.

Learning is not possible if there is accumulation of what has been learned. Please follow this. The mind is capable of learning only when there is no accumulation. The moment there is accumulation, which is knowledge, learning ceases because knowledge interprets what is being learned. Perhaps this is something new and therefore rather difficult, so please pay a little attention. At present you know only one state, the state of being taught, of being told, and a mind that has been taught is incapable of learning because it can move only along the line of what it has been taught. The teaching may give it an opportunity to inquire, but only in a positive or negative direction. A mind that has been taught cannot learn because learning is a new process. You cannot learn if you already know. What is there to learn? Only the mind that does not know, that has not accumulated, is capable of learning.

Most of us are incapable of learning because our minds are filled with things known. When the mind moves in the field of the known, it is not learning; we think it is learning, but in actuality it is merely accumulating or furthering what has been, which is knowledge. To be capable of learning, the mind must be free of this knowledge—the knowledge of what it has been told, of what it has learned. That is why it is tremendously important to know the content of your own mind.

Truth, reality, God, or whatever name you may like to give it, is not something to be learned; you cannot come to it with knowledge. The mind must be free of the known if it is to know the unknowable, and the difficulty for most of us is that we think we can arrive at the unknown by moving from the known to the known. There must be self-knowledge, which means learning about yourself as you live from moment to moment, and you cannot learn about yourself if you begin with what you learned yesterday and carry on with that in order to understand more. There is a possibility of learning about yourself only when there is the death of what you have already learned.

Sirs, please pay a little attention to this because when there is the understanding of yourself, out of that comes an extraordinary sense of release, of complete freedom from fear. This freedom from fear gives an astonishingly vital energy to the mind, and you need this energy if your mind is to be in a state of complete silence so that it is capable of receiving that which is true. You need great energy for the mind to be still—not dull, but still. A petty mind may think about stillness, but it is not still; it may meditate on silence, but silence is not. This silence, this tranquillity, this peace comes only through learning about and understanding yourself so that the mind is in that state of energy which brings stillness. Then only is it possible for the eternal to be.

In considering these questions together, please bear in mind that we are not looking for an answer because the solution lies in the problem itself, and not away from the problem.

Question: You say that the mind will be free when the thinking process ceases. Hinduism and Buddhism advocate various practices towards this end. What method do you advocate?

KRISHNAMURTI: Let us first examine this whole question of pursuing a method in order to achieve a result—a psychological, not a factual result. We are not now considering how to end the process of thinking. We shall come to that later.

What do you mean when you say that the practicing of a method, a system, will give you what you want, very subtly or very obviously? I want peace of mind, and the various religions, including Buddhism and Hinduism, say, "Do these things and you will get it." So day after day I practice a particular method, I sit in meditation, controlling my mind, suppressing unwanted thoughts, and so on. I go through all this, hoping to arrive at a state of mind which I call peace.

Now, what does a method or a system do when you practice it? What is the effect on your mind of practicing a method, whether it be a first-class super-method or a very stupid one? Surely, the effect is to make the mind conform to a pattern of thinking, which is to force it to function in the groove of a particular habit. That is all the method is concerned with. And a mind that is functioning in the groove of habit is not a mind at all, it is merely a mechanism that repeats the same operation day after day.

Do please understand this, sirs. Though a method may promise you bliss, heaven, nirvana, or God, that method does not free the mind; it only enslaves the mind to itself. A mind that practices a method obviously conforms to it. So the method becomes the means of holding the mind within a pattern of thinking, and a mind that thinks in terms of a pattern, a habit, is never capable of being free. If you really understand this, not because I say it, but because you see the truth of it for yourself, then you will find that you are free of all methods. No method, however "good" it may be, can free you; on the contrary, all methods are essentially the same in that they enslave you to themselves. The mind that conforms to any method, to any authority, ceases to function as a free mind, and is therefore incapable of inquiring into what is truth.

I am just pointing out the fact, and I hope it is clear. You can either look at or disregard the fact; it is up to you. If you look at the fact and go into it sanely, reasonably, without any prejudice, you are bound to see that all methods, whether Hindu, Buddhist, Christian, Islamic, or what you will, condition the mind, and that through a method the mind can never be free. Then comes the problem: How is one to free the mind from the thinking process? I am using that word *how* as an inquirer, I am not asking for a method through which to free the mind.

Now, why do you want thought to come to an end? Is it because you have been told or have read that in ending the thought process you will come to something much greater—which means that you are seeking a reward? Or do you want to end thought because you understand the significance of thinking?

What is the significance of thinking? Is thinking the means to a real discovery of what is truth, what is God, what is beyond the measure of the mind? If it is, then we must think completely, fully. But if thinking is not the key that opens the door, then obviously we must put it away.

What do you mean by thinking? When I ask you that question, the whole mechanism of thinking is set going, is it not? My question awakens in your mind a series of associations, memories. Memory responds, and then you give your reply. So what you call thinking is always—and not just when a question is asked—the response of memory, and the response of memory is conditioned thinking. You think as a Sinhalese, as a Buddhist, or a Christian, as a man or a woman, as a businessman or a lawyer. The whole mechanism of your mind is conditioned by the knowledge which you have gathered as a professional or a so-called religious person, by the things you have been trained in, and from that background you think. The background, which is memory, tradition, responds to challenge, and that response, through words, is what you call thinking. This is comparatively simple. Since thinking is the response of memory, and memory is always conditioned, thinking can never be free. There is no such thing as free thinking because thinking is always associated with the past.

So, thinking can never be free. That is a discovery, sirs, not a statement that you have learned from me. If you have really listened, you will find it a tremendous shock and discovery to realize that all thinking about a problem, whether personal or scientific, immediate or in the future, is conditioned by the past, which is memory, and that a human being who would discover something new must put memory aside. He may use memory afterwards, but to use memory to discover is to be conditioned, and a conditioned mind can never find out what is true. The function of thinking is not discovery, but to put into action what has been discovered. Seeing the truth of that, the mind says, "Thought must end"—which is not to confine, suppress, or sublimate thought, but to realize that thought as a process must come to an end. Thought comes to an end only through self-knowledge, that is, when you understand the whole process of thinking and don't just say, "I must end thought," which is an immature statement without any validity or significance.

A petty mind thinks, "I must end thinking in order to find truth." Such a mind is still petty, and it will never find truth. But when the mind says, "I am petty and I must understand this whole process of thinking," which is true self-knowledge, then it is no longer petty. Such a mind understands the significance of thinking, and therefore it is free from the thought process. Being totally still, the mind is made new, fresh, innocent. Only the mind that has put away and is free of the known is capable of receiving the unknown. Such a mind is not the observer of the unknown, it is not a receptacle of the unknown; it is the unknown itself.

Question: You say that the conditioning of the mind, with which we approach all our problems, breeds conflict and prevents the understanding of truth. How can the mind be unconditioned?

KRISHNAMURTI: It is a fact that the mind is conditioned which thinks in terms of Buddhism, Christianity, communism, Hinduism, or any other organized belief, whether it be socio-political or a belief in God. Do you understand, sirs? You can be conditioned to believe in God, and another group of people can be conditioned not to believe in God, which is obvious. The communist does not believe in God; he says it is all tommyrot, it is just the way you have been educated, it is a form of escape, you have merely accepted what you have been told. But the communist himself accepts what he has been told; he too has his books, his leaders, his authorities. He has been conditioned to believe in no-God, just as you have been conditioned to believe in God or in something else. Both are conditioned, obviously. Your conditioning is not superior, nor is his inferior. There is no nobler or less noble conditioning; there is only the fact that the mind is conditioned. You can observe this fact in daily life if you are aware of the functioning of your own mind. You think along a certain line. As a Buddhist or a Christian, you will do or not do certain things, just as a communist will do or not do certain other things, so both minds are conditioned.

Now, the questioner wants to know how to free the mind from its conditioning. First of all, sirs, you must know that your mind is conditioned. The mind cannot free itself until it knows it is conditioned. If I am blind, I must know that I am blind before I can do something about my blindness; otherwise, my talking about blindness has very little value.

Similarly, you must know for yourself that your mind is conditioned, and you must also find out in what manner it is conditioned. You think as a Sinhalese or a Hindu; you have certain customs, a certain social morality, certain ways of approaching problems, a certain disregard for women; you feel contempt for the servant and respect for the big man, which is reflected in the manner of your speech. All this is your conditioning, which is the result of the tradition in which you have been brought up, whether that tradition is comparatively new or ten thousand years old. You cannot be aware of your conditioning if you oppose it, if you think it is right or wrong, good or bad, noble or ignoble, if you say, "This I will keep, that I will throw away." Whereas, if the mind approaches the totality of its conditioning without condemnation or justification, then that very approach will free the mind from conditioning. When you know that you are functioning in the groove of tradition and realize how stupid it is, it drops away; you don't have to struggle against it.

But the difficulty is that you find profit, pleasure in tradition, in being conditioned; you find it is a safe thing, so the unconscious, which is very conservative, hesitant, holds you. Conditioning involves the totality of your thinking-feeling, whether pleasurable or painful; and when you realize that you cannot seek pleasure and discard pain, then you will find that because you understand the whole import of conditioning, the mind is free of conditioning; you do not have to do a thing about it. No effort on the part of the mind to uncondition itself can bring about freedom from conditioning because all such effort is born of conditioning; you have been told from childhood that you must make an effort in order to be free. But if you understand the whole process of conditioning, there is freedom, you don't have to make an effort to be free.

Question: Is it not desirable to revive the great religions and the glorious cultures associated with them, since in their pure form they have helped many people towards the spiritual life?

KRISHNAMURTI: When there is confusion, there is always the urge to revive the past because it is the safe thing to do. All over the Christian world they are shouting that Christianity must be revived, and apparently you are doing the same thing here, saying that the ancient religions must be revived.

Now, can the ancient religions be revived? What do you mean by religion? Surely, religion has nothing whatever to do with dogmas, beliefs, rituals, nor with the authority-bound mentality of the priest. Organized belief has been built up for the profit of the few in the name of the many, and that is obviously not religion. Religion is something entirely different. Religion is love, and can love be "revived"? To be religious is just to love people, to be kind, to be generous, not to hate, not to be ambitious, not to be envious, to have sympathy, to have compassion, and can these things be "revived"? Can you go back and bring the dead books, the dead traditions, to life? Or is it that love cannot be revived because love is only in the present, not in the past or the future? Love is not something that you can get through practice. You can love, be compassionate, only in the present, in the immediate. It is because you do not love, because you are confused, that you seek to revive something which is dead. If you had love, you would never talk about revival. A living man does not talk about revival; he is living. It is the dead man who wants to put life into himself—the so-called life that has made him die.

So religion is not organization, religion is not authority, religion is not dogma, ritual, or belief, nor is it the knowledge accumulated through the past. Religion is a state of living in the present; it is to understand the whole process, the totality of time. This understanding frees the mind from fear, and only then does the mind know what it is to love. A mind that loves does not seek God or truth because love itself is truth. To be completely attentive is the good. The mind that cultivates virtue is not a virtuous mind. Love cannot be revived. Only dead things can be revived—in the sense that you can pump life into them hoping they will live. They never will. Let the dead lie dead. Be concerned with the living. That is much more difficult because it demands great clarity, sympathy, generosity, love.

January 20, 1957

Fourth Talk in Colombo

One of our greatest difficulties is that we do not like to be disturbed, especially when we are a people steeped in tradition, in the easy ways of life, and with a culture that has merely become repetitive. Perhaps you have noticed that we put up a great deal of resistance to anything that is new. We do not want to be disturbed, and if we are disturbed, we soon adjust ourselves to a new pattern and again settle down, only to be again shaken, disturbed, and troubled. So we go on through life, always being driven from a pattern into which we have settled down. The mind objects most violently and defensively to any suggestion of a change from within. It is willing to be compelled by economic, scientific, or political forces to adjust itself to a new environment, but inwardly it remains the same. One can observe this process going on if one is at all aware of things about one and within oneself.

And religion, it seems to me, is the most disturbing state of mind. It is not something from which to get comfort, solace, an easy explanation of the sorrows, travails, and tribulations of life; on the contrary, religion demands a mind that is extraordinarily alert, questioning, doubting, inquiring, that does not accept at all. The truth of religion is to be discovered individually; it can never be made universal. And yet, if you observe, you will see that religions throughout the world have become universal—universal in the sense that a large number of people follow them and adhere to their ideas, beliefs, dogmas, rituals; therefore, they cease to be religion at all.

Religion, surely, is the search for truth on the part of each one of us, and not merely the acceptance of what has been said by another—it does not matter who it is, whether the Buddha, the Christ, or any other. They may point out certain things, but merely to repeat what has been said by them is so immature; it is merely verbal and without much significance. To discover the truth, that reality which is beyond the measure of thought, the mind must be disturbed, shaken out of its habits, its easy acceptance of a philosophy, a system of thought. As the mind is made up of all our thoughts, feelings, and activities, conscious as well as unconscious, it is our only instrument of inquiry, of search, of discovery, and to allow it to settle down and function in a groove seems to me a heinous crime. It is of the utmost importance that we should be disturbed—and we are being disturbed externally. The impact of the West on the East is a shock, a disturbing element. Outwardly, superficially, we are adjusting ourselves to it, and we think we are making progress inwardly; but if you observe, you will see inwardly we are not seeking at all.

Seeking has an extraordinary significance in the life of the individual. Most of us seek with a motive. When we seek with a motive, the motive dictates the end of the search; and when a motive dictates the end, is there a search at all? It seems to me that to seek the realization of what you already know or have formulated is not search. There is search only when you do not know, when there is no motive, no compulsion, no escape, and only then is there a possibility of discovering that which is truth, reality, God.

But most of us are seeking with a motive, are we not? If you observe your own way of life, your own manner of thinking and feeling, you will see that most of us are discontented with ourselves and our environment, and we want to direct this discontent along easy channels until we find contentment. A mind that is pursuing satisfaction easily finds a way of overcoming discontent, and such a mind is obviously incapable of discovering what is truth. Discontent is the only force that makes you move, inquire, search. But the moment you canalize it and try to find contentment or fulfillment through any means, obviously you go to sleep.

That is exactly what is happening in religious matters. We are no longer on a journey, individually seeking what is truth. We are merely being driven by the collective, which means going to the temple, repeating certain phrases, explanations, and thinking that is religion. Surely religion is something entirely different. It is a state of mind in which the inquirer is not urged by any motive and has no center from which to start his inquiry. Truth is not to be found through the motive of wanting contentment, peace, something superior in order to be satisfied. I think it is very important to understand this. We have made religion, have we not, into something which gives us satisfaction, an explanation for our troubles, a solace for our sorrows, for the things that we are, and we easily fit into a satisfying groove of thought, thinking we have solved the problem. There is no individual inquiry on our part, but merely a repetition, a theoretical and not an actual understanding of *what is.*

To find out what is truth, we must be free of the collective, which means we must be truly individual—which we are not. I do not know if you have observed how little individual you are. Being an individual is not a matter of character or habit. After all, character is the meeting of the past with the present, is it not? Your character is the result of the past in response to the present, and that response of the past is still the collective.

To put it differently, are you an individual at all? You have a name, a form, a family; you may have a separate house and a personal bank account, but are you inwardly an individual? Or are you merely the collective acting in a certain approved, respectable manner? Observe yourself and you will see that you are not at all an individual. You are a Sinhalese, a Buddhist, a Christian, an Englishman, an Indian, or a communist, which means that you are the collective; and surely one must be free of the collective, consciously as well as unconsciously, in order to find out what is truth.

To free the mind from the repetitious urge of the collective requires very hard work, and only a mind thus free is capable of discovering what is truth. This actually does happen when you are vitally interested in something. You put aside all the imaginations, ideas, and struggles of the past, and you push forward to inquire. But in religious matters you do not. There you are conservative, you are the collective, you think in terms of the mass, of what you have been told about nirvana, *samadhi*, *moksha*, heaven, or what you will. There is no individual endeavor to discover wholly for yourself. I think such individual endeavor is very important, especially in the present world crisis, because it is only this individual search that will release the creative and open the door to reality. As long as we are not real individuals, as long as we are merely the reaction of the past, as most of us are, life remains a series of repetitive responses without much significance. But if in our search we endeavor as individuals to find out what is truth, then a totally new energy, a totally different kind of creation comes into being.

I do not know if you have ever experimented with yourself by watching your own mind and seeing how it accumulates memory. From memory you act, from knowledge there is action. Knowledge is, after all, experience, and this experience dictates future experience. So you will find that experience does not liberate at all; on the contrary, experience strengthens the past. A mind that would liberate itself from the past must understand this whole process of accumulating knowledge through experience which conditions the mind. The center from which you think, the 'me', the self, the ego, is a bundle of memories, and you are nothing else but that. You may think you are the atma, the soul, but you are still cultivating memory, and that memory projects the coming experience, which further conditions the mind. So experience strengthens the 'me', the self, which is in essence memory—"my house," "my qualities," "my character," "my race," "my knowledge," and the whole structure which is built around that center. In seeking reality through experience, the mind only further conditions itself and does not liberate itself from that center.

Now, is it possible for the mind not to accumulate knowledge around the center, and so be capable of discovering truth from moment to moment? Because it is only the truth discovered from moment to moment that is really important, not the truth which you have already experienced and which, having become a memory, creates the urge to further experience.

There are two kinds of knowledge—there is the factual knowledge of how to build a bridge, all the scientific information that has accumulated through the centuries, and there is knowledge as psychological memory. These two forms of knowledge are not clearly defined. One operates through the other. But it is psychological memory of which the 'me', the self, is made up, and is it possible for the mind to be free of that memory? Is it possible for the mind not to think in terms of accumulation, in terms of gathering experience, but to move without that center? Can we live in this world without the operation of the self, which is a bundle of psychological memories? You will find, if you really inquire into it deeply, that such a thing is possible, and then you can use factual knowledge without creating the havoc which is being created now. Then factual knowledge does not breed antagonism between man and man.

At present there is antagonism, there is hate, separation, anxiety, war, and all the rest of it because psychologically you are using factual knowledge for self-aggrandizement, for a separative existence. One can see very well in the world that religions divide people—religions being idea, belief, dogma, ritual, not the feeling of love, of compassion. Such religions separate people just as nationalism does. What is separating us, then, is not factual knowledge but the knowledge upon which we depend psychologically for our emotional comfort, for our inward security.

So a mind that would find reality, God, or what name you will, must be free of this bundle of memories which is identified as the 'me'. And it is really not so very difficult. This bundle is made up of ambition, greed, envy, the desire to be secure, and if one puts one's mind to the task and works hard, surely one can liberate the mind from this bundle. One can live in this world without ambition, without envy, without hate. We think it is impossible because we have never tried it. It is only the mind that is free from hate, from envy, from separative conclusions, beliefs—it is only such a mind that is capable of discovering that reality which is love, compassion.

Question: What is understanding? Is it awareness? Is it right thinking? If understanding does not come about through the functioning of the mind, then what is the function of the mind?

KRISHNAMURTI: Sir, there are several things involved in this question. First of all, what is thinking?—not right thinking or wrong thinking. Surely, what we call thinking is the response of memory to any challenge. That is, when I ask you a question, you respond quickly if you are familiar with the answer, or hesitantly, with an interval of time, if you are not. The mind looks into the records of memory within itself, and having found the answer, replies to the question; or, not finding the answer in the records of memory, it says, "I don't know."

So thinking is the response of memory, obviously; it is not a very complex thing. You think as a Buddhist, a Sinhalese, a Christian, or a Hindu because your background is that of a particular culture, race, or religion. If you do not belong to any of these groups, and you are a communist, for example, again you respond according to that particular pattern. This process of response according to a certain background is what you call thinking.

You have discovered, then, that there is no freedom in thinking because your thinking is dictated by your background. Thinking as you know it now originates from knowledge, which is memory; it is mechanical because it is the response to challenge of a conditioned mind. There is creativeness, a perception of the new, only when there is no response of memory. In mathematics you may proceed step by step from the known to the known, but if you would go much further and discover something new, the known must for the time being be put in abeyance.

So the functioning of the mind is at present a mechanical response of memory, conscious as well as unconscious. The unconscious is a vast storehouse of accumulated tradition, of racial inheritance, and it is that background which responds to challenge. I think that is fairly obvious.

Now, is there right thinking and wrong thinking? Or is there only freedom from what we call thinking—from which follows right action? Do you understand, sirs? Being brought up in India, Europe, or America, I think in terms of my particular conditioning, according to the way I have been educated. My background tells me what to think, and it also tells me what is right thinking and what is wrong thinking. If I were brought up as a communist, then for me right thinking would be that which is antireligious and anticlerical, according to my communistic background; any other manner of thinking would be a deviation, and therefore to be liquidated. And is a mind that responds according to its background, which it calls thinking, capable of right action? Or is there right action only when the mind is free from the conditioning whose response it calls thinking? Do you understand, sirs? I hope I am making myself clear.

Most of us do not even ask what is right thinking. We want to know what is right thought because right thinking might be very disturbing, it might demand inquiry, and we do not want to inquire. We want to be told what is right thought, and we are told what is right thought by organized religions, by social morality, by philosophies, and by our own experience. We proceed along that line until we are no longer satisfied with the pattern of right thought, and then we ask, "What is right thinking?"—which means that the mind is a little more active, a little more willing to inquire, to be disturbed. Thinking is fluid, whereas right thought implies a static state, and most of us function in static states.

Now, if we really want to inquire into what is right thinking, we must first find out, not what is right thinking, but what is thinking; and we have seen that what we call thinking is a process of response from the background, from that center of accumulated memory which is identified as the 'me'. And I say, is there right thinking in that field at all? Or is there right thinking, right response, right action, only when the mind is free from the background?

The questioner wants to know what is understanding. Surely, understanding is this whole process of uncovering the ways of the mind, which is what we have been doing just now. Understanding implies, does it not, a state of mind that is really inquiring, and you cannot inquire if you start with a conclusion, an assumption, a wish.

Then what is the function of the mind? The mind now functions fragmentarily, in departments, in parts; it does not function as a totality because it is now the instrument of desire, and desire can never be total, whole. Desire is always fragmentary, contradictory. You can easily find out the truth of all this if you observe these things in yourself.

As we know it now, the mind is an instrument of sensation, of gratification, of desire, and desire is always fragmentary; there can never be total desire. Such a mind, with all its self-contradictory desires, can never be integrated. You cannot put hate and love together, you cannot integrate envy and goodness, you cannot harmonize the opposites. That is what most of us are trying to do, but it is an impossibility. So what is the true function of the mind? Is it not to free itself from the contradictions of desire and be the instrument of an action which is not the mere response of memory?

I am afraid all this sounds rather difficult, but if you really observe yourself, you will find that it is not. I am only describing what actually takes place if you do not suppress, sublimate, or find a substitute for desire, but really understand it. You can understand desire only when there is no condemnation, no comparison. If I want to understand you, for example, I must not condemn, I must not justify, I must not compare you with somebody else—I must simply observe you. Similarly, if it would understand desire, the mind must watch itself without condemnation, without any sense of comparison, which only creates the conflict of duality.

So we see what understanding is. We see that there can be no right thinking, which is right action, as long as the mind is conditioned. There is right action only when the mind is free from conditioning. It is not a matter of right thinking, and then right action. Thinking and action are separate only as long as desire functions as memory, as the pursuit of success; but when there is freedom from that bundle of memories which is identified as the 'me', then there is action which is outside the social pattern. But that is much more complicated, and we shall leave it for the moment.

We see, then, that the function of the mind is to understand, and it cannot understand if it condemns, if it thinks segmentally, in parts. The mind will think in fragments, in compartments, as long as there is desire, whether it be the desire for God or for a car, because desire in itself is contradictory, and any one desire is always in opposition to other desires.

So there can be understanding only when the mind, through self-knowledge, discovers the ways of its own operation. And to discover the ways of the mind's operation, there must be awareness; you must watch it as you would watch a child whom you love. You do not condemn or judge the child, you do not compare him with somebody else; you watch in order to understand him. Similarly, you must be aware of the operation of your own mind, see its subtleties, its recesses, its extraordinary depth. Then you will find, if you pursue it further, that the mind becomes astonishingly quiet, very still, and a still mind is capable of receiving that which is truth.

Question: According to the theory of karma, in which many of us believe, our actions and circumstances in this life are largely governed by what we did in our past lives. Do you deny that we are governed by our karma? What about our duties and responsibilities?

KRISHNAMURTI: Sir, again, this is a very complex question, and it needs thinking out to the very end.

It is not a matter of what you believe. You believe that you are the result of the past, that previous lives have conditioned your present circumstances, and there are others who do not believe in all that. They have been brought up to believe that we live only one life and are conditioned only by our present environment. So let us for the moment put aside what you believe or do not believe, and let us find out what we mean by karma, which is much more important, because if you really understand what karma is, then you will find it is not a thing which dictates your present action. We shall go into it and you will see.

Now, what do we mean by karma? The word itself, as you know, means to act, to do. You never act without a cause, or without a motive, or without being compelled by circumstances. You act either under the influence of the past, of a thousand yesterdays, or because you are pushed in a particular direction by the pressure of immediate circumstances. That is, there is a cause and an effect. Please follow this a little bit. For example, you have come here to listen to me. The cause is that you want to listen, and the effect of listening you will find out, if you are really interested. But the point is: there is a cause and there is an effect.

Now, is the cause ever fixed, and the effect already determined? Do you understand, sirs? In the case of an acorn, a seed, there is a fixed cause and a fixed effect. An acorn can never become a palm tree, it will always produce an oak. We think in the same way about karma, do we not? Having done something yesterday, which is the cause, I think the effect of that action today is predetermined, fixed. But is it? Is the cause fixed? And is the effect fixed? Does not the effect of a cause become in its turn the cause of still another effect? Do you understand? I do not want to take more examples because examples do not really clarify the issue, but tend to confuse it. So we must think this out clearly without using examples.

We know that action has a cause. I am ambitious; therefore, I do something. There is a cause and there is an effect. Now, does not the effect become the cause of a future action? Surely, there is never a fixed cause, nor a fixed effect. Each effect, undergoing innumerable influences and being transformed by them, becomes the cause of still another effect. So there is never a fixed cause and a fixed effect, but a chain of cause-effect-cause.

Sirs, this is so obvious. You did something yesterday which had its origin in a previous cause, and which will lead to certain consequences tomorrow; but in the meantime the consequences, being subject to innumerable pressures, influences, have undergone a change. You think that a given cause will produce a fixed effect, but the effect is never exactly the same because something has happened between the two.

So there is a continuous chain of cause becoming effect, and effect becoming cause. If you think in terms of, "I was that in the past, I am this today, and I shall be such-and-such in the next life," it is too immature, utterly silly because that way of thinking is not fluid, it has no living, vital quality. That is decay, deterioration, death. But if you think about the matter deeply, it is really marvelous because then you will see that this chain of cause-effect becoming another cause can be broken at any time, and that the mind can be free of karma. Through understanding the whole process of the mind which is conditioned by the past, you will see for yourself that the effect of the past in the present or in the future is never fixed, never absolute, final. To think that it is final is degradation, ignorance, darkness. Whereas, if you see the significance of cause-effect becoming again the cause, then because that whole process is for you a living, moving thing, you can break it at any time; therefore, you can be free of the past. You no longer need be a Christian, a Buddhist, a Hindu, with all the conditioning that goes with it; you can immediately transform yourself.

Sirs, don't you know that with one stroke you can cut away envy? Haven't you ever tried to break antagonism on the spot? I know it is very comforting to sit back and say, "Well, it is karma that has made me antagonistic to you." It gives a great sense of satisfaction to say that, the pleasure of continuing hate. But if you perceive the whole significance of karma, then you will see that the chain of cause-becoming-effect-becoming-cause can be snapped. Therefore the mind can be astonishingly and vitally free from the past in the immediate.

But that requires hard work; it requires a great deal of attention, a great deal of inquiry, penetration, self-knowledge. And most of us are indolent; we are so easily satisfied by a belief in karma. Good God! What does it matter whether you believe or do not believe? It is what you are now that matters, not what you did in the past and the effects of that in the present. And what are you now? You should know that better than I do. What you are now is obviously the result of the past, the result of innumerable influences, compulsions, the result of food, climate, contact with the West, and so on. Under the pressure of all that, the mind becomes lazy, indolent, easily satisfied by words. Such a mind may talk about truth, God, it may believe in nirvana, and all the rest of it; but that belief has no value at all, any more than has the communist, the Catholic, or any other belief.

The mind can be transformed only when it understands the whole process of itself and the motives, the causations of that process. In that understanding there are immense possibilities for the mind because it opens the door to an astonishing creativity, which is not the writing of a few poems, or the putting of some colors on a canvas, but that state which is reality, God, truth. And for that you need have no ideals. On the contrary, ideals prevent immediate understanding. We are fed on illusions, on things that have no value, and we easily succumb to authority, to religious as well as political tyranny; and how can such a mind discover that which is eternal, that which is beyond the projections of itself? I say it is possible to break this continuity of karma, but only when you understand the operations of karma, which is not static, predetermined, but a living, moving thing; and in breaking itself away from the past, the mind will know what truth or God is.

January 23, 1957

Fifth Talk in Colombo

As I have been pointing out during these talks here, it is surely very important, especially when the world is in such a grave crisis, that we should understand the true significance of religion because religion, it seems to me, is the only basic solution to all the problems of our existence. I do not mean the religions of dogma, of organized belief, which only condition the mind. To me, they are not religion at all. They are like any other propagandistic organization which merely shapes the mind according to a particular pattern of thinking.

To inquire into the whole question of what is true religion, one must first understand what behavior is. To me, behavior is righteousness. But most of us spend our energy and our thought in arguing over what kind of belief we should hold concerning reincarnation and the various other problems involved in religion; we do not start with the fundamental issue. The foundation of right inquiry is surely behavior, which is righteousness, and righteousness is not merely the cultivation of virtue. A man who cultivates virtue ceases to be virtuous; a man who practices humility is no longer humble. The cultivation of humility is arrogance. Similarly, cultivated virtue only leads to respectability. We must have virtue because virtue is essential to all real inquiry, but not the cultivated virtue which is self-centered activity. What is important is to meet the whole movement of that virtue which is not self-centered and which, if we pursue it deeply, not only at the conscious, but also at the unconscious level, does lead to that which is beyond the measure of the mind. This is true religious inquiry, and I think it is very important to understand it.

Most of us are involved in some form of organized belief, such as Buddhism, Hinduism, Christianity, communism, and so on; and when we are caught in the net of these organizations, whether political or so-called spiritual, we are more concerned, are we not, with what we believe than with how we live our life. What matters, surely, is not to find out what is the ideal way of living but rather to discover for ourselves the pattern of behavior in which the mind is caught and to see the true significance of such behavior.

Righteousness has nothing whatever to do with organized conduct because organized conduct, which is social morality, has produced this great confusion and chaos in the world. Society accepts envy, greed, ambition, cruelty, the ruthless pursuit of one's own fulfillment; it admits and justifies the possibility of killing on a large scale. The soldier who kills more than the others in battle is a hero in the eyes of society, and when a society professing a particular religion sanctions killing on a vast and inhuman scale, then obviously the religion which it professes has failed.

To understand righteousness it is necessary to step out of the pattern of society. By society I do not mean the organized means of communication, of supplying food, clothing, shelter, and so on, but the whole psychological or moral issue which is involved in society. A person who seeks to inquire into what is true religion obviously cannot belong to a society which accepts greed, envy, the pursuit of personal ambition, the search for power, fame, and all the rest of it. To belong to a society based on cruelty and the pursuits of self-interest, and still be religious, is obviously impossible. Yet organized religions throughout the world have condoned such a society. Organized religions do not insist that you step out of greed, envy, ruthlessness. They are far more concerned with what you believe, with ritual, organization, property, and all the rest of the confusion, paraphernalia, and rigmarole that exist in and around every organized religion.

So a man who would inquire into what is true religion must lay the foundation of righteousness by being without envy, without ambition, without the greed for power. This is an actual possibility, I am not being idealistic. Ideals and actuality are incompatible. A man who pursues the ideal of nonviolence is indulging in violence. He is concerned, not with ceasing to be violent, but with ultimately arriving at a state which he calls nonviolence. Being violent, the mind has an ideal of nonviolence which is over there in the distance; it will take time to achieve that state, and in the meantime the mind can continue to be violent. Such a mind is not concerned with getting rid of violence but with slowly trying to become nonviolent. The two states are entirely different, and I think it is very important to understand this fact. The ending of a quality such as violence or greed is not a matter of time, and it does not come about through ideals; it has to be done immediately, not through time. We get caught up in the gradualism of ideals when we are concerned with time.

Please do not jump to conclusions or say, "Without ideals I shall be lost," but rather listen to what is being said. I know all the arguments, all the justifications of ideals. Just listen, if you kindly will, without a conclusion, and try to understand what the speaker is talking about; do not block your understanding by saying, "I must have ideals."

Ideals have existed for centuries. Various religious teachers have talked of ideals, but they may all be wrong and probably are. To adhere to an ideal is obviously to postpone freeing the mind from violence, greed, envy, ambition, and the desire for power. If one is concerned, as one should be, with righteousness, which is the foundation upon which rests all true inquiry into what religion is, then one must investigate the possibility of ridding the mind of violence, of greed, of envy, of acquisitiveness, not at some time in the distant future, but now. It is entirely possible for the mind to be free immediately of these and all the related qualities that society has imposed on us—or rather, that we have cultivated in our relationship with each other, which is society.

Righteousness or behavior is not something to be gained, to be arrived at, but it must be understood from moment to moment in the actuality of daily living. That is why it is important to have self-knowledge, to know how you think, how you feel, how you act, how you respond to another. All that indicates the manner of your approach to life, and therein lies the foundation of righteousness, not in some utopia, ideal, or organized belief. The actual foundation must be laid in our daily living. But most of us are not concerned with that; we are concerned with the label which we call religion.

If you and I as individuals really put our minds to this, we shall see that change does not come about through ideals, through time, through pressure and convenience, or through any form of political activity, but only through being deeply concerned with bringing about a radical transformation in ourselves. Then we shall discover that it is possible to free the mind from violence, greed, and all the rest of it, not in time, but outside of time, because virtue or righteousness is not an end in itself. If virtue is an end in itself, it becomes a self-centered activity leading to mere respectability, and a mind that is merely respectable is imitative; it conforms to a pattern and is therefore not free.

Virtue is merely a matter of putting the mind in order, like putting a house in order, and nothing more than that. When the mind is in order, when it has clarity and is without confusion, without conflict, then it is possible to go further. But for a man who is seeking power, who is burning inwardly with ambition, greed, envy, cruelty, and all the rest of it—for such a man to talk about religion and God, is errant nonsense; it has no meaning. His God is only the God of respectability.

That is why it is important to lay the foundation of righteousness, which is to step out of the present society. Stepping out of society does not mean becoming a hermit, a monk, or a sannyasi, but being without greed, without envy, without violence, without the desire for position and power. The moment you are without those things, you are out of time, out of the society which is made up of them.

So the real revolution is religious; it is this stepping out of the present society, not remaining within the field of society and trying to modify it. Most revolutions are concerned with the modification of society, but to me that is not revolution at all; it is merely the perpetuation of the past in another form. The religious revolution is the only revolution, which is individually to step out of this complex society based on envy, greed, power, anger, violence, and brutality in the relationship between human beings.

It is only when the mind is free from violence, and from all this business of trying to cultivate virtue, that it is capable of inquiring into what is truth, what is God—if there is God. It does not assume anything. When the mind is capable of such inquiry, that inquiry is devotion. Devotion is not attachment to some idol, to some picture, person, or symbol. But when the mind has freed itself from envy and greed, when it has put its own house in order, which is virtue, and is therefore capable of inquiring to find out what is true and whether there is something beyond the measure of the mind—then that inquiry, that perseverance is true devotion, without which there is irreverence and disrespect.

So the man who would be religious cannot belong to any organized belief, which only conditions the mind, but must be concerned with behavior, which is righteousness—his own behavior, not that of others. Most of us are so eager to reform others and so little concerned with the transformation of ourselves. What matters is not how others behave—your friend, your wife, or your husband—but how you behave.

If you consider this matter really seriously, you will find that education comes to have quite a different significance. What we call education now is merely a process of being trained to earn a livelihood as a lawyer, a doctor, a soldier, a businessman, a scientist, or what you will, and that is all most of us are concerned with. Such education is obviously very superficial, and so our lives are equally superficial. But if we understand this inquiry into what is true religion, into what is reality, God, then we shall help the children, the coming generation, to grow in freedom so that they do not become machines in the routine of an office, or mere breadwinners, but are able to throw off the tyranny of organized belief, the tyranny of governments, and thereby to reshape the world. Then the whole structure, not only of our education, but of our culture, of our behavior, of our relationship, will be entirely different. Again, this is not an ideal, a thing to be vaguely hoped for in the future.

So it seems to me very important that those of us who are serious—and I hope there are some who are serious—should be concerned with the understanding of ourselves. This is not a self-centered activity. It becomes a self-centered activity only when you are concerned with the understanding of yourself in order to arrive somewhere—in order to achieve freedom, to find God, not to be jealous, and so on. If you are concerned with God, or with sex, or with the attainment of power, your mind is occupied; and an occupied mind is obviously self-centered, though it may be occupied with God. You have to understand the whole process of self-knowledge, that is, you have to know yourself; and you cannot know yourself if you are not aware, observant, conscious of your words, of your gestures, of your manner of speech in relationship with another. To be aware in your relationship with another is to observe the way you talk to women, the way you talk to your wife, to your children, to the bus conductor, to the policeman; it is to see how respectful you are to the governor, and how contemptuous you are of the servant. To be aware is to be conscious of the operation of your own mind, but you cannot be aware if you condemn what you discover.

You will find that out of this self-knowledge comes a well-ordered mind—which is being virtuous, not becoming virtuous. Such a mind is capable of stillness because it is no longer in contradiction with itself, it is no longer driven or riven by desire. To be still requires a great deal of energy, and energy is depleted when the mind is self-contradictory, when it is not aware of its own operation, which means there is no self-knowledge. There is the depletion of energy as long as desire pulls in different directions, but such depletion of energy ceases when there is total self-knowledge. Then you will find that the mind, being full of energy, is capable of being completely still, and a still mind can receive that which is eternal.

Many questions have been sent in—questions about sex, about organized belief, about what kind of education the serious parent should give to his children, and so on. It is obviously impossible to answer all of them because each question is very complex and cannot just be answered yes or no. Life has no yes or no answers. However, during these talks, representative questions have been dealt with, and if you care to go into what has already been said, I think you will find the answer to your particular question. Books have been printed, and you may be interested in them—or you may not. That is your affair. But if you have sufficiently paid attention to what has been said, I think you will answer your questions for yourself. To find the right solution to a problem, no effort is required. Effort denies the understanding of the problem. Whereas, if you are really serious about inquiring into the problem, then you will find that the problem resolves itself.

Question: Religions have prescribed certain practices in meditation for one's spiritual growth. What practice do you advocate? Can right meditation be helpful in one's daily life?

KRISHNAMURTI: Meditation is a very complex and serious problem, and I shall go into it step by step. Without meditation, life is merely a matter of environment, of circumstances, of pressures and influences, and therefore has very little significance. Without meditation, there is no perfume to life. Without meditation, there is no compassion, no love, and life is then merely a thing of sensation. And without meditation, the mind is not capable of finding out what is true.

Before we ask how to meditate, or what practice is necessary in order to meditate, must we not first find out what meditation is? And the very inquiry into what is meditation is meditation. Please listen to what I am saying, if you will, because this is very important. As I said, a mind that is incapable of meditation is incapable of understanding life. It is because we do not know what meditation is that our life is so stupid, superficial, made up of mere achievements, failures, successes, misery.

So, to find out what is meditation, is meditation; and this evening you and I are going to inquire into it together. To ask how to meditate when you do not know what meditation is, is too immature. How can you practice what you do not know? The books, the priests, the teachers will tell you what meditation is—and they may all be mistaken because they are all interpreters. An interpreter is a traitor. Please listen, sirs, don't laugh it off. An interpreter is a traitor because he is interpreting according to his conditioning. Truth does not want any interpretation. There can be no interpreter of what is true because it is you who have to find out what is true. We are now going to find out together the truth about meditation, but if you do not follow step by step, giving your whole attention to it, you will not understand what meditation is. I am not saying this dogmatically, but you will have to see the truth of it for yourself.

Prayer which is a supplication, a petition, either conscious or unconscious, is not meditation, even though such prayer may be answered. The mechanism by which prayer is answered is something which we won't go into now because it is too complex and would require another half-hour to explain. But you can see that prayer which is a supplication, a petition, a demand, a begging, is not meditation because you are asking something for yourself or for somebody else.

Then you will find also that the process of controlling the mind is not meditation. Please listen to this; don't throw it out and say, "What nonsense!" We are inquiring.

Now, what is the way of concentration in so-called meditation? You try to fix your mind on an idea, on a thought, on a sentence, on a picture or an idol made by the hand or by the mind, but other thoughts constantly creep in. You spend your time fighting them off, until after years of practice in controlling the mind, you are able to suppress all ideas except one, and you think you have achieved something. What you have achieved is the technique of suppressing, sublimating, or substituting one idea for another, one desire for another, but in that process is involved conflict; there is a division between the maker of effort and the object he hopes to achieve through effort. This effort to control the mind in order to achieve a result—peace, bliss, nirvana, or whatever it be—is self-centered activity and nothing more; therefore, it is not meditation. This does not mean that in meditation the mind is allowed to wander as it likes. Let us go into this slowly.

We see the truth that a mind which is merely concerned with control, with discipline, with suppressing its own thoughts, is making itself narrow; it is an exclusive mind, and such a mind is incapable of understanding what is meditation. A mind that suppresses part of itself and concentrates on the idea of peace, on an image made by the hand or by the mind, is obviously afraid of its own desires, its own ambitions, its own feelings of envy, greed, and so on, and in suppressing them, such a mind is not meditating; though it may repeat a thousand mantras, or sit silent and alone in some dark forest or mountain cave, it is incapable of understanding meditation.

So, having discovered that control is not meditation, you begin to ask yourself what are these jumbling thoughts that precipitate themselves one on top of another, that wander all over the place like monkeys, or flutter after each other like butterflies. There is now no question of controlling them because you see that you are the various thoughts and contradictory desires which are endlessly pursuing each other. These thoughts, these contradictions, these desires are part of you; you are not different from them, any more than the qualities of the diamond are different from the diamond itself. Remove the qualities of the diamond, and there is no diamond; remove the qualities, the thoughts of the mind, and there is no mind. So meditation is obviously not a matter of control.

But if you do not control your thoughts, then what? Then you begin to inquire into your thoughts. Do you understand, sirs? The mind is no longer suppressing thought, but inquiring into the motive, the background of its thought, and you will find that this inquiry into its own thought has an extraordinary effect on the mind. Then the mind ceases to manufacture thought. Please do understand this. When you begin to inquire into the whole process of thinking without suppressing, condemning, or justifying anything, without trying to concentrate on one thought by excluding all other thoughts, then you will find that the mind is no longer manufacturing thought. Please do listen. The mind manufactures thought through sensation, through memory, through the object which it wants to achieve; but the moment it begins to inquire into the process of thinking, it ceases to produce thought because then the mind is beginning to free itself from that whole process. In this free movement of the mind as it inquires into its own pursuits and sorrows, the mind begins to understand itself, and that understanding comes from self-knowledge.

So you have seen that prayer—which involves conditioning, demand, petition, fear, and so on—is not meditation. Nor is there meditation when one part of the mind, which you call the lower self, is dominated by another part of the mind, which you call the higher self, or the atma. This contradiction in the mind is caused by the fact that one desire is controlling another, and that is obviously not meditation. Nor is it meditation to sit in front of a picture and repeat *japams,* mantras. What happens when you sit quietly and repeat certain phrases? Your mind becomes hypnotized, does it not? Your mind gradually goes to sleep, and you think that you have attained bliss, a marvelous peace! It is only in your daily life that you can find out what meditation is, not in the repetition of certain words and phrases.

Now, if praying, chanting, sitting in front of a picture, controlling thought, is not meditation, then what is meditation? The mind has moved away from the false because it has seen the truth in the false. Do you understand, sirs? The mind has seen the truth that control is false, and this truth has liberated it from the desire to control. Therefore the mind is free to inquire into the process of thinking, which leads to self-knowledge. That is, the mind begins to understand itself when it is just watching its own operation without condemnation, judgment, or evaluation, and then you will find that the mind becomes very quiet; it is not made quiet. Generally you try to make the mind quiet; all your religious books, your priests, tell you to train the mind to be quiet, to practice quietness. The mind that has practiced quietness, that has trained itself to be still, is like a monkey that has learned a trick. You cannot have stillness through desire. You have to understand desire, not escape from or suppress it. Because desire is always contradictory, you have to understand it; and in the process of understanding desire, you will find that the mind becomes completely still—the totality of the mind, not just the superficial layer which is occupied with your daily living. Do you understand, sirs? To have ambition, envy, greed, the desire for power, and yet talk about meditation, is to be in a state of illusion. These two are incompatible, they don't go together.

It is only when there is self-knowledge, which is to have an understanding of your daily living, your daily relationships, that the mind becomes quiet without being forced or disciplined to be quiet. Then you will find that the mind is completely still—the totality of it, the unconscious as well as the conscious. The unconscious, which is the sum total of all your traditions, your memories, your motives, your ambitions, your greed, is far more conservative than the conscious mind, far more effective in its desires and pursuits; and it can be understood only through self-knowledge. When through self-knowledge the mind is completely still, in that stillness you will find there is no experiencer to experience because the experiencer and the experienced are the same. To realize this requires a great deal of attention, inquiry, discovery. The observer and the observed, the watcher and the watched are one, they are not two separate entities. The thinker is not different from the thought; the two are essentially the same, though for various reasons—convenience, security, permanency, and so on—thought has made the thinker separate and permanent.

So, if you have followed this inquiry into what is meditation, and have understood the whole process of thinking, you will find that the mind is completely still. In that total stillness of the mind, there is no watcher, no observer, and therefore no experiencer at all; there is no entity who is gathering experience, which is the activity of a self-centered mind. Don't say, "That is *samadhi*"—which is all nonsense, because you have only read of it in some book and have not discovered it for yourself. There is a vast difference between the word and the thing. The word is not the thing; the word *door* is not the door.

So, to meditate is to purge the mind of its self-centered activity. And if you have come this far in meditation, you will find there is silence, a total emptiness. The mind is uncontaminated by society; it is no longer subject to any influence, to the pressure of any desire. It is completely alone, and being alone, untouched, it is innocent. Therefore there is a possibility for that which is timeless, eternal, to come into being.

This whole process is meditation.

January 27, 1957

Bombay, India, 1957

First Talk in Bombay

There is a great deal of difference between learning and being taught, and it seems to me that it is very important to understand the distinction between the two. To learn there must be great humility, for learning is a very arduous process, and the mind is disinclined to learn. Most of us are merely taught, and the man who is merely taught is incapable of learning. In learning, which is a constant process, there is not the division of the teacher and the taught, the guru and the disciple; there is only learning.

There is no learning when the mind is waiting to be taught and merely accumulates knowledge as memory. In the process of being taught, which requires no effort and is only the cultivation of memory, there is the teacher and the disciple, the one who knows and the one who does not know; and that distinction is maintained throughout life. I think it would be wise if we both understood from the very beginning the falseness of that distinction, and established between us the true relationship in which there is neither the teacher nor the taught, but only learning; and to learn we need great humility. A man who says, "I know," actually does not know. He knows only that which is past, that which is dead. But for the man who is learning every day, and not merely accumulating knowledge, there is neither the teacher nor the taught; there is only the understanding of reality from moment to moment.

So, you and I should understand that we are taking a journey together, a journey on which to look, to listen, and to learn; for if we understand that, we shall be able to learn from everything around us, and not just from a particular book, teacher, or religion. The whole process of living is religion, as we shall discover for ourselves if we really begin to understand what it means to learn. But it is very difficult for most of us to comprehend this because most of us want to be taught, for then we have no responsibility, no struggle—you know and I do not know, you teach me and I merely accept. In being taught there is a sense of security; there is no investigation, no inquiry, no search, and it would be a mistake if you listened to these talks with the attitude that you are being taught by me, or that I am going to reveal something miraculous or extraordinary. But if both of us with real humility begin to understand the whole process of living, then in that very understanding there is the miracle of change.

After all, that is what we must be concerned with, is it not? We must be concerned with this one question: How to bring about a radical change within ourselves that will affect not only our social relationships but also our thought, our emotions, our creative expression, and our daily living. If a radical change does not take place within the individual, surely any reform from the outside will merely force him to adjust to the new pattern and is therefore no change at all. A change brought about through compulsion, through influence, through sociological pressure, through various forms of legislation, is not a real change but merely a modified continuity of what has been. Change within the field of time is no change—time being the process of thought, of compulsion, of imitation, of gradual adjustment.

Now, is there a fundamental change which is not brought about by any pressure, by any conformity to an ideological pattern? Is there a change which is totally from within and not the result of any pressure from outside? We do change superficially through various forms of compulsion, through reward and punishment, through external pressure, through being influenced by the books we read, and so on; but it seems to me that such change takes place only on the surface, which is no real change at all. Yet that is what most of us are doing with our life. The conscious mind adjusts to a new social, economic, or legislative pattern, but that does not transform the individual fundamentally. So, if we are at all serious, the question must inevitably arise: Is it possible for the individual to change radically so that he approaches life not partially, fragmentarily, but as a whole entity, a total human being?

Most of us react to reward and punishment, to some form of compulsion, and that is what we call action in our daily life. If you observe, you will see that your action, religiously and in other ways, is partial, fragmentary; it is not the total action of your whole being. And it seems to me imperative, in the present crisis of the world, that each one of us should find out for himself if it is possible to act not in mere conformity to patterns, whether ideological, governmental, or self-imposed, but as a total human being, with all one's body, mind, and heart. Is it possible to act in such a complete manner? Fundamentally, I think that is the only problem that confronts man.

We see what is happening in the world; we see the tyranny, the appalling cruelty that is going on, the various miseries that we all go through, the compulsions, the uniformity of thinking as a nationalist, a socialist, an imperialist, or whatever it be. In this process there is no total action on the part of the individual, no action in which his mind and heart are one, his whole being completely integrated. And it seems to me, if we are at all serious and thoughtful, that it must be our chief concern to bring about this total action on the part of the individual because as long as our action is merely fragmentary, either of the mind alone, or of the feelings alone, or merely of the senses, such action must be contradictory and will invariably create confusion.

Now, is there a desire, a longing, a wish, a will, that can act as a total being? Or is desire always contradictory? And is it possible for the mind to understand the totality of itself, the conscious as well as the unconscious, and act, not partially or fragmentarily, but as an integrated human being, without self-contradiction? To me such action is the only righteous action because all other forms of action must create conflict both within and without.

So, how is this change to be brought about? How is the mind to act as a total entity, undivided within itself? I do not know if you have ever thought about this problem at all. If you have, you probably think that the mind's contradictory desires can be harmonized, and that this harmony comes through effort, through ideological pursuits and various forms of discipline. But is it possible to harmonize contradictory desires, as most of us are trying to do? I am violent, and

I want to be nonviolent; I want to be an artist in the true sense of the word, and yet the whole tendency of my mind is that of ambition, of greed and envy, which prevents this creative effort. So there is always a contradiction going on within ourselves. These conflicting desires do produce certain activities, but they also are contradictory in themselves, as we can see every day of our life. And is it possible for the mind to come to that understanding of the totality of itself in which action is no longer a matter of imitation, of compulsion, of fear, or the desire for reward?

You see, it is incredibly difficult to communicate in words something which we all feel—that there must be an action which is not put together by the mind, an action which is not the result of fragmentary thinking, an action which is the response of our whole being. We feel this, but we do not know how to get at it. We may turn to religion, hoping to find an action which will not be contradictory, which will be complete, but religion for most of us is rather vague and superficial; it is a matter of belief and has no validity in our daily life. We pay lip service to what we call religion, but it is without fundamental significance and merely becomes another factor of contradiction in our life. We think we ought to love, but we do not. We want to seek God, and at the same time we are caught up in worldly pursuits, so we are torn between the two. Yet it seems to me that the real understanding of what religion is, is the only solution to all our problems. What matters, surely, is that each one of us should directly experience reality, and in the very process of experiencing reality, there is an action of reality. It is not a question of experiencing truth and then acting, but rather there is an action of truth in the very process of experiencing and understanding truth. Then it is the truth that acts, not the person who understands the truth.

That is why it is very important to understand what it means to learn. Can I learn anything if I start from a conclusion, if I already have a definition of what God is, what truth is, or what religion is? To start thinking from a conclusion, surely, is not to think at all; it prevents the mind from going further. To start thinking from a conclusion is vanity, which means there is no humility. When there is humility the mind says, "I do not know"; therefore, it is willing to learn, to inquire, to suffer, to find out. But most of us do not want to do that; we want to be told because in being told, there is a sense of safety, security, and that is all we seek. We want to be made secure, comfortable, and such a mind is obviously incapable of learning.

Truth cannot be taught; you have to discover it for yourself, and you cannot possibly discover it if you start with the assumption that there is truth or no truth, that there is God or no God. You can find out whether there is truth or not only if you begin to learn, if you begin to search, if you begin to inquire, and there is no inquiry when you start with a conclusion, with an assumption.

If you watch your own mind, you will see how extraordinarily difficult it is to be free of conclusions. After all, what you know is a series of conclusions made up of what you have been taught, what you have learned from books, or what you have found in your own reactions, and you start to think, to build the house of thought on that foundation. But surely a mind that wants to find out what truth or God is must start without any assumption, without any conclusion, so that it is free to inquire. And if you observe your own mind, you will see that it is not free. It is full of conclusions, burdened with the knowledge of many thousands of yesterdays; it thinks in terms of what the Gita says, or what the Bible or the Koran says, or what some teacher has said, and it begins by assuming that to be the truth, and if it already knows what truth is, obviously it need not seek truth. I think it is very important to see the significance of this.

The people of this country are under pressure from the West. The dynamic scientific revolt that is going on in Europe and America is influencing your thinking here and changing the ways of your life, but only superficially. You are merely conforming to a new pattern, a new way of living, so you are going to have extraordinary contradictions within yourselves, great suffering, until you understand individually how to think out all the problems anew.

To think anew, each one of us must start as though he knew nothing; he must begin to inquire, and that requires great humility. But humility is not to be cultivated because the moment you cultivate it, it is no longer humility; it is a form of arrogance. Whereas, if you begin to learn about yourself, to be aware of your contradictions, to observe your own thoughts and feelings without condemnation or approval—which is to start without any assumption—then you will find that through self-knowledge there comes an action which is not fragmentary, which is total. Such a man is the truly religious human being, not he who goes to the temple and quotes the Gita. The religious man is one who is on a journey of self-discovery. You cannot know yourself if you start with the assumption that you are this or that, and it is extraordinarily difficult to be free of assumptions because tradition through centuries has imprinted certain ideas on the mind. An old tradition may be broken and wiped away, and a new tradition, a new set of ideas implanted, but action from any assumption, either old or new, must create a contradiction in our life, and such a contradiction invariably produces sorrow both within and without.

To see all this, surely you must ask yourself if there is a way of living which is the action of your whole being. At present you do not know what your whole being is because you are broken up, divided, and your action is fragmentary; but when you realize that you are broken up, that your action is divided, fragmentary, when you are fully aware of this conflict, then you will discover for yourself that beyond it there is love, a state of mind which is whole, not fragmentary, a state of mind which is not put together by desire, which is not the result of discipline, of conformity, pressure. This discovery is the real source of action independent of your fragmentary wants and purposes, and that is why it is very important to understand yourself, to know your own contradictory nature without trying to force what you are to fit the pattern of a certain ideal or ideology. And I assure you, there is a great joy in knowing yourself, in seeing all that you are, both the ugly and the beautiful, the insensitivity as well as the extreme sensitivity of the mind. Out of that full awareness there comes a mind which knows total action, and it is only such a mind that can create a new relationship, a new world.

At each of these meetings there will be questions and answers—or rather, there will be questions, but I am afraid there will be no answers. Life has no answer. Life is to be lived, it is not a thing to be concluded. Most of us seek an answer, a conclusion, something which the mind can cling to; and when it is found, it sets the pattern for the rest of our life. We put a question in order to find an answer, but there is no answer, and if we can really understand that, then questions become extraordinarily significant, full of meaning, because then the mind is concerned with the problem itself and not with the answer, which means that we have to give our complete attention to the problem.

At present you approach your problem, whatever it be, with the desire to find an answer, a solution, or you try to make the problem conform to what you think is the right answer, so your problem remains and multiplies. Whereas, if you see that an answer offers no way out of the problem, but only increases it, then your desire to find an answer will drop away, and you will give your whole mind to the problem—and that is the beauty, the challenge of a problem.

When you suffer inwardly, not physically, but psychologically, your immediate reaction is to seek an answer; you want to know why you suffer, and you say it is karma, or you accept some other explanation, which only smothers the problem. The problem of suffering is still there. What is important is to begin to inquire into the problem itself, which means that you cannot cling to any hypothesis, to any conclusion, to any hope. Then sorrow has an extraordinary meaning, the problem has vitality.

So, if I may, I am going to discuss the question with you. We are going to take a journey into the problem together, and if you don't pay attention to the problem, you will not understand what I am talking about. But if you really begin to inquire into the problem, then you will find that you have an extraordinary vitality to pursue it to the end. Most of us have no vitality except that of routine—going to the office, living according to established habits, repeating a particular set of words, and so on, all of which has a certain vitality. But I am talking of a different kind of vitality, that tremendous energy which arises when you are confronted with a problem that demands your whole attention.

I do not know if you have ever given your whole attention to something. I doubt it because complete attention is an astonishing thing. To give complete attention to a flower, to a bird, to a tree, to a child, to somebody's face, means that there must be no naming of the thing. When you look at a flower and say, "It is a rose, how beautiful it is," your attention has already wandered. To give your complete attention to something, there can be no verbalization, no communication, no describing it to another; you must be completely with it.

In the same way, if you can give complete attention to a problem, whatever it may be, you will find that there is not only the resolution of that particular problem, but that you have the capacity to deal with every problem, and therefore there is no fear. It is fear that dissipates energy and destroys complete attention.

So, if we can together go into these questions with complete attention, then we shall find that they have extraordinary significance; but if you merely rely on my description and do not observe your own reactions to what is being said, you will have no vitality to discover the truth of the problem. So please follow the problem for yourself. Do not wait for me to take the journey and then come back and tell you what that journey should mean to you, but let us take the journey together.

Question: All religions teach the need of curbing the senses. Are the senses a hindrance to the discovery of truth?

KRISHNAMURTI: Let us find out the truth of the matter and not rely on what the various teachers and books have said, or on what your local guru has implanted in your mind.

We know the extraordinary sensitivity of the senses—the sense of touch, of hearing, of seeing, tasting, and smelling. To see a flower completely, to be aware of its color, of its delicate perfume and beauty, you have to have senses. It is when you see a beautiful man or woman, or a fine car, that the trouble begins, for then desire comes in. Let us go slowly.

You see a beautiful car. There is perception or seeing, sensation, contact, and finally desire. That is how desire comes into being. Then desire says, "It would be marvelous to own that car, I must have it," so you spend your life and energy in getting money to buy the car. But religion says, "It is very bad, it is evil to be worldly. Your senses will lead you astray, so you must subjugate, control them. Don't look at a woman, or don't look at a man; discipline yourself, sublimate your desire." So you begin to curb your senses, which is the cultivation of insensitivity. Or seeing around you the ugliness, the dirt, all the squalor and misery, you shut it out and say, "That is evil; I must find God, truth." On the one hand you are suppressing, making the senses insensitive, and on the other you are trying to become sensitive to God; so your whole being is becoming insensitive. Do you understand, sirs? If you suppress desire in any form, your mind is obviously made insensitive, though you may be seeking God.

So the problem is to understand desire and not to be a slave to it, which means being totally sensitive with your body, with your mind and heart—sensitive to beauty and to ugliness, to the sky, to the flowers, to birds on the wing, to the sunset on the water, to the faces around you, to hypocrisy, and to the falseness of your own illusions. To be sensitive to all that is what matters, and not merely to cultivate sensitivity towards truth and beauty while denying everything else. The very denial of everything else brings about insensitivity.

If you consider it, you will see that to suppress the senses, to make them insensitive to that which is tempestuous, contradictory, conflicting, sorrowful, as all the swamis, yogis, and religions insist, is to deny the whole depth and beauty and glory of existence. To understand the truth, you must have complete sensitivity. Do you understand, sirs? Reality demands your whole being; you must come to it with your body, mind, and heart, as a total human being, not with a mind paralyzed and made insensitive through discipline. Then you will find that you need not be frightened of the senses because you will know how to deal with them, and they will not lead you astray. You will understand the senses, love them, see their whole significance, and then you will no longer torture yourself with suppression, control. Don't you see that, sirs?

Love is not divine love or married love or brotherly love—you know all the labels. Love is just love, without giving it a meaning of your own. When you love a flower with your whole being, which is not just to say, "How beautiful," and walk by, or when you love a human being completely, with all your mind, heart, and body, then you will find there is no desire in it, and therefore no conflict, no contradiction. It is desire that creates contradiction, misery, the conflict between *what is* and 'what should be', the ideal. The man who has suppressed his senses and made himself insensitive does not know what love is; therefore, though he may meditate for the next ten thousand years, he will not find God. It is only when your whole being is made sensitive to everything—to the depth of your feelings, to all the extraordinary intricacies of your mind—and not just to what you call God, that desire ceases to be contradictory. Then there is an altogether different process taking place, which is not the process of desire. Love is its own eternity, and it has its own action.

Question: When you talk of freedom from the past, do you mean that an individual's past, with all its experiences, memories, sorrows and joys, can be wiped away totally? Can the mind then have an existence without the past?

KRISHNAMURTI: This is really a very complex question, and I hope you will pay attention to it. To pay attention is not merely to hear my words or my description, but as you are sitting and listening, actually to be aware of your own mind—the mind that is thinking, struggling, reacting, that is looking over there and over here. Just watch that mind, and you will find the answer for yourself.

Now, can the mind wipe away the past, the thousand yesterdays? That is what is involved in this question. The yesterdays of pleasure and pain, of recognition or fame, the things you have learned, and the things that you hope to do tomorrow, the qualities that you have gathered through many years and which are consciously as well as unconsciously urging you to think in a certain direction—all that is the past, with its extraordinary vitality. The past is not only the content of the conscious mind, which has learned the technique of modern living and acquired a specialized capacity by which to earn a livelihood; the past is also made up of the things that lie hidden in the unconscious, the motives of which you are not aware, the impressions of what the centuries have told you and of what your ancestors have left behind. All that is the past.

Now the question is: Can the mind free itself from all this, disentangle itself from the total content of the past? Don't translate it into karma. I am purposely not using that word because you have certain reactions to it which would cause you easily to step by and so miss the significance of this question.

The mind is the conscious as well as the unconscious. The conscious has the capacity to adjust itself to the present environment. The unconscious, on the other hand, is the residue of many yesterdays; it is conservative, heavy to move; it does not want to conform to the modern, to the immediate. All that is the past. And the questioner asks: Can the mind free itself from the past?

What is the mind? Surely, the mind is made up, put together by the past, that is, by time. Please listen to this, and you will see how simple it is. The mind is the result of time, time being memory, knowledge, the experience of many yesterdays. All that is the past, and why do you want to be free of it? Why does your mind say, "I must be free of the past"? Do you understand, sirs? Are you making this into an artificial problem for yourself because I have said that the mind must be free of the past? Or do you say, "Life is something new to be lived, to be completely fathomed every minute, and I cannot do that if I meet life with my prejudices, with my nationalism, with my gods, with my dogmas, and beliefs, that is, if I come to it with my past"? Surely there is a difference, is there not? Does the problem arise because of me, or because you want to understand life for yourself?

So, is it possible for the mind to free itself from the past? Is it possible for the mind to have no causation of any kind, no motive, no thought which is the result of the past? Please, sirs, listen to this with the same intensity that you would feel in seeking a new job if you had lost your present one. Is it possible for the mind to be without a causation, without a motive, without the past? You don't know the answer. Some say yes and others say no, but leave those people aside. They have no direct experience; it is merely an assumption. You will have to find out for yourself.

Now, how are you going to find out? Do you understand the problem? The problem is this. Your mind is the result of time, of tradition, of memory; it is the result of what it has been taught as a Hindu, a Christian, or what you will, and is it possible for such a mind to be without this background, without this immense pressure of the past? If the mind is not capable of being without the dead weight of the past, it can never be free.

You may talk about freedom, you may talk about God, but it has no meaning at all until the mind can free itself from the past.

So you have to find out for yourself what thinking is. Do you understand? If you do not know what thinking is, you will not know what the past is. Surely all your thinking is the result of the past. You think as a Hindu, as a Christian, as a communist, as this or that, because you have been trained to think in those terms. So the problem is: Can the mind see and free itself from all thinking which is based on the past? Can it be completely still, without any movement of thought?

Now, don't close your eyes and go into a trance, thinking you are meditating, for you will only be hypnotizing yourself. Just see that all thinking is based on a cause; it is the reaction of a particular background, and put this question to yourself: Can the mind exist without thinking, or is it the very nature of the mind to think? Do you understand, sirs? You have to find out. It is no use my telling you. You have to find out for yourself whether it is possible for the mind to be without thought. And you can find that out only if you understand the whole process of thinking, which means that you must know what thinking is.

Very simply, what we call thinking is the reaction of memory. Memory is the cause and thinking is the effect. And is it possible for a mind which is always thinking, thinking, thinking, going round and round in circles, worrying, wanting, suppressing itself, being envious, greedy, and all that—is it possible for such a mind to bring that whole pattern to an end? That is, can the experiencer cease to experience? Again, you will find out only if you begin to inquire seriously into the whole process of thinking, of memory; and if you pay attention to your memories, to the operation of your own mind, it is really extraordinarily simple. Then, in spite of all the books, in spite of all the people who say it is possible or impossible, you will find out for yourself that the mind can be totally free from the past—which does not mean that you don't recognize the past or that you forget your address. That would be silly; it would be a state of amnesia. But you will find that it is possible for the mind to be totally empty, and you will also find that a mind which is totally empty is the really creative mind, not the mind which is cluttered up with memory because being empty, it is always capable of receiving that which is truth. It is like a cup, which is useful only when it is empty. A mind that is full of memory, that is burdened with associations, knowledge, can never understand what truth is.

So you must begin to understand the whole process of the past, and you can do that only by pursuing it, by being aware of it every day in whatever you are doing. Then you will find that there is a state of mind totally dissociated from the past, and in that totality of dissociation from the past, you will know that which is eternal.

February 6, 1957

Second Talk in Bombay

I think most of us are easily satisfied with explanations, and we do not seem able to go beyond mere words and directly experience something original for ourselves. We are always repeating like gramophone records, merely following some authority who promises a certain result.

Now, it seems to me that religion is something entirely different. It is not this worship of words, nor is it the projection of symbols and the experiencing of those symbols. Religion is the experiencing of that which lies beyond the measure of the mind, but to experience that state, to realize the immensity of it, one really has to understand the process of one's own thinking. Most of us are indifferent to the impressions, to the pressures, to the vitality of existence; we are easily satisfied, and some of us dare not even look at the problems about us and within ourselves.

So I think it would be worthwhile if we could, this evening, look at our problems, not theoretically or abstractly, but actually, and see what our problems really are. Not that we are going to resolve the problem of war, or put an end to the butchery that is going on in Hungary, and so on; but we are easily led away by the very enormity of these issues, and there is not that clarity of thinking which can come into being only when we begin with ourselves, not with somebody or something else. The world problem is our problem because we are the world. What we think does affect the world; what we do does affect society. The individual problem is directly related to the world problem, and I do not think we are giving sufficient importance to the power of individual thinking and action. Historically I am sure you will find that it is always individuals who produce the great movements that are brought about.

So we have to look first and foremost at our own problems because they are directly related to world problems, and if you and I can spend the whole of this hour in doing that, then perhaps we shall come out of it with a different outlook, a fresh impulse, an explosive vitality.

Now, what is our basic problem? As students, or businessmen, as politicians, engineers, or so-called seekers of the truth, whatever that may be, what fundamentally is our problem?

First of all, it seems to me that the world is rapidly changing and that the Western civilization, with its mechanization, its industrialization, its scientific discoveries, its tyranny, parliamentarianism, capital investment, and so on, has left a tremendous imprint on our minds. And we have created through the centuries a society of which we are a part and which says that we must be moral, righteous, virtuous, that we must conduct ourselves in accordance with a certain pattern of thought which promises the eventual achievement of reality, God, or truth.

So there is a contradiction in us, is there not? We live in this world of greed, envy, and sexual appetites, of emotional pressures, mechanization, and conformity, with the government efficiently controlling our various demands, and at the same time we want to find something greater than mere physical satisfaction. There is an urge to find reality, God, as well as to live in this world. We want to bring that reality into this world. We say that to live in this world we have to earn money, that society demands that we be acquisitive, envious, competitive, ambitious; and yet, living in this world, we want to bring the other thing into being. We may have all our physical needs provided, the government may bring about a state in which we have a great measure of outward security, but inwardly we are starving. So we want the state which we call religion, this reality which brings a new impulse, an explosive vitality to action.

Surely, that is my problem, that is your problem. How are we to live in this world, where living implies competition, acquisitiveness, ambition, the aggressive pursuit of our own fulfillment, and also bring into being the perfume of something which is beyond? Is such a thing possible? Can we live in this world and yet have the other? This world is becoming more and more mechanized; the thoughts and actions of the individual are increasingly controlled by the state. The individual is being specialized, educated in a certain pattern to follow a daily routine. There is compulsion in every direction, and living in such a world, can we bring into being that which is neither outward nor inward, but which has a movement of its own and requires a mind that is astonishingly swift, a mind that is capable of intense feeling, intense inquiry? Is that possible? Unless we are neurotic, unless we are mentally peculiar, surely that is our problem.

Now, any intelligent man can see that going to temples, doing puja, and all the other nonsense that goes on in the name of religion is not religion at all; it is merely a social convenience, a pattern which we have been taught to follow. Man is educated to conform to a pattern, not to doubt, not to inquire; and our problem is how to live in this world of envy, greed, conformity, and the pursuit of personal ambition, and at the same time to experience that which is beyond the mind, call it God, truth, or what you will. I am not talking about the God of the temples, of the books, of the gurus, but of something far more intense, vital, immense, something which is immeasurable.

So, living in this world with all these problems, how am I to capture the other? Is that possible? Obviously not. I cannot be envious and yet find out what God or truth is; the two are contradictory, incompatible. But that is what most of us are trying to do. We are envious, we are carried along by the old momentum, and at the same time we dream of finding out whether there is God, whether there is love, truth, beauty, a timeless state. If you observe your own thinking, if you are at all aware of the operation of your own mind, you will see that you want to have one foot in this world and one foot in that other world, whatever it may be. But the two are incompatible, they cannot be mixed. Then what is one to do?

Do you understand, sirs? I realize that I cannot mix reality with something which has no reality. How can a mind that is agitated by envy, that is living in the field of ambition, greed, understand something which is completely still and which has a movement of its own in that stillness? As an intelligent human being, I see the impossibility of such a thing. I also see that my problem is not to find God because I do not know what that means. I may have read innumerable books on the subject, but such books are merely explanations, words, theories which have no actuality for a person who has not experienced that which is beyond the mind. And the interpreter is always a traitor; it does not matter who that interpreter is.

My problem, then, is not to find truth, God, because my mind is incapable of it. How can a stupid, petty mind find the immeasurable? Such a mind can talk about the immeasurable, write books about it; it can fashion a symbol of truth and garland the symbol, but that is all on the verbal level. So, being intelligent and aware of this fact, I say, "I must begin with what I actually am, not with what I should be. I am envious, that is all I know."

Now, is it possible for me, while living in this society, to be free of envy? To say it is or is not possible is an assumption, and therefore has no value. To find out if one can do it requires intensity of inquiry. Most of you will say it is impossible to live in this world without envy, without greed. Our whole social structure, our code of morality is based on envy, so you assume it is not possible and that is the end of it. Whereas, a man who says, "I don't know if there is a reality or not, but I want to find out; and to find out my mind must obviously be free of envy, not just in patches, but totally, because envy is a movement of agitation"—it is only such a man who is capable of real inquiry. We shall go into that presently.

So my problem is not to inquire into reality, but to find out whether, living in this world, I can be free of envy. Envy is not mere jealousy, though jealousy is part of it, nor is it merely being concerned because someone else has more than I. Envy is the state of a mind which is demanding more and more all the time—more power, more position, more money, more experience, more knowledge. And demanding the 'more' is the activity of a mind which is self-centered.

Now, can I live in this world and be free of self-centered activity? Can I cease to compare myself with somebody else? Being ugly, I want to be beautiful; being violent, I want to be nonviolent. Wanting to be different, to be 'more', is the beginning of envy—which does not mean that I blindly accept what I am. But this desire to be different is always in relation to something which is comparatively greater, more beautiful, more this or more that, and we are educated to compare in this way. It is our daily craving to compete, to surpass, and we are satisfied with being envious, not only consciously but also unconsciously.

You feel that you must become somebody in this world, a great man or a rich man, and if you are fortunate, you say it is because you have done good in the past—all that nonsense about karma, and so on. Inwardly also you want to become somebody—a saint, a virtuous man—and if you observe this whole movement of becoming, this pursuit of the 'more', both outwardly and inwardly, you will see that it is essentially based on envy. In this movement of envy your mind is held, and with such a mind, can you discover the real? Or is that an impossibility? Surely, to discover the real, your mind must be completely free of envy; there can be no demand for the 'more', either openly or in the hidden recesses of the unconscious. And if you have ever observed it, you will know that your mind is always pursuing the 'more'. You had a certain experience yesterday, and you want more of it today; or being violent, you want to be nonviolent, and so on. These are all the activities of a mind which is concerned with itself.

Now, is it possible for the mind to be free from this whole process? That is my inquiry, not whether there is or there is not God. For an envious mind to seek God is such a waste of time; it has no meaning except theoretically, intellectually, as an amusement. If I really want to find out whether there is God or not, I must begin with myself; that is, the mind must be totally free from envy, and I can assure you, that is an enormous task. It is not just a matter of playing with words.

But you see, most of us are not concerned with that; we do not say, "I will free my mind from envy." We are concerned with the world, with what is happening in Europe, with the mechanization of industry—anything to get away from the central point, which is that I cannot help to bring about a different world until I as an individual have changed fundamentally. To see that one must begin with oneself is to realize an enormous truth, but most of us overlook it; we easily brush it aside because we are concerned with the collective, with changing the social order, with trying to bring about peace and harmony in the world.

Few people are concerned with themselves except in the sense of achieving success. I do not mean that kind of concern. I mean being concerned with the transformation of oneself. But first of all, most of us do not see the importance, the truth of change; and secondly, we do not know how to change, how to bring about this astonishing, explosive transformation within ourselves. Changing in mediocrity, which is to change from one pattern to another, is no change at all.

This explosive transformation is the result of all one's energy coming together to solve the fundamental problem of envy. I am taking that as the central issue, though there are many other things involved in it. Have I the capacity, the intensity, the intelligence, the swiftness to pursue the ways of envy, and not just say, "I must not be envious"? We have been saying that for centuries, and it has no meaning. We have also said, "I must follow the ideal of nonenvy," which is equally absurd because we project the ideal of nonenvy and are envious in the meantime.

Please observe this process. The fact is that you are envious, while the ideal is the state of nonenvy, and there is a gap between the two that has to be filled through time. You say, "Eventually I shall be free of envy"—which is an impossibility because it has to happen now or never. You cannot set some future date on which you will be nonenvious.

So, is it possible for me to have the capacity to inquire into and be totally free from envy? How does that capacity arise? Does it arise through any method or practice? Do I become an artist by practicing a particular technique day after day? Obviously not. So please do listen to this for two minutes, not with the desire to have something, but to find out how the capacity in question comes into being. Do you understand, sirs? The desire to have that capacity is a selfish movement of the mind, whereas if I do not try to cultivate it but begin to inquire into the whole process of envy, then the means of totally dissolving envy is already there.

Now, in what manner do I inquire into the process of envy? What is the motive behind that inquiry? Do I want to be free of envy in order to be a great man, in order to be like Buddha, Christ, and so on? If I inquire with that intention, with that motive, such inquiry projects its own answer, all of which will only perpetuate the monstrous world which we have now. But if I begin to inquire with humility, that is, not with a desire to achieve success, then an entirely different process is taking place. I realize that I have not got the capacity to be free of envy, so I say, "I shall find out"—which means that there is humility from the very beginning. And the moment one is humble, one has the capacity to be free of envy. But the man who says, "I must have that capacity, and I am going to get it through these methods, through this system"—such a man is lost, and it is such people who have created this ugly, treacherous world.

A mind that is really humble has an immense capacity for inquiry, whereas the mind that is under the burden of knowledge, that is crippled with experience, with its own conditioning, can never really inquire. A humble mind says, "I do not know, I shall find out"—which means that finding out is never a process of accumulation. Not to accumulate, you must die every day, and then you will find, because you are fundamentally, deeply humble, that this capacity to inquire comes of itself, it is not a thing that you have acquired. Humility cannot be practiced, but because there is humility, your mind has the capacity to inquire into envy, and such a mind is no longer envious.

Do you understand, sirs? A mind which says, "I do not know," and which does not want to become something has totally ceased to be envious. Then you will find that righteousness has quite a different meaning. Righteousness is not respectability, it is not conformity, it has nothing to do with social morality, which is mere convenience, a manner of living made respectable through centuries of compulsion, conformity, pressure, and fear. A mind that is really humble, in the sense I have explained, will create its own righteousness, which is not the righteousness of a pattern. It is the righteousness of living from humility and discovering from moment to moment what is truth.

So your problem is not the world of newspapers, ideas, and politicians; it is the world within yourself—but you have to realize, to feel the truth of this, and not merely agree because the Gita or some bearded gentleman says it is so. If you are aware of that inner world and are watching yourself without condemnation or justification from day to day, from moment to moment, then in that awareness you will find there is a tremendous vitality. The mind that is accumulating is frightened to die, and such a mind can never discover what is truth. But to a mind that is dying every minute to everything that it has experienced, there comes an astonishing vitality because every moment is new; and only then is the mind capable of discovery.

Sirs, it is good to be serious, and we are very rarely serious in our life. I do not mean just listening to somebody who is serious, or being serious about something, but having the feeling of seriousness in ourselves. We know very well what it is to be gay, flippant, but very few of us know the feeling of being deeply serious without an object to make us serious—that state in which the mind approaches every situation, however gay, happy, or exciting, with serious intent. So it is good to spend an hour together in this way, being serious in our inquiry, because life for most of us is very superficial, a routine relationship of work, sex, worship, and so on. The mind is always on the surface, and to go below the surface seems to be an enormously difficult task. What is necessary is the state of explosiveness, which is real revolution in the religious sense, because it is only when the mind is explosive that it is capable of discovering or creating something original, new.

Question: I have done something wrong and sinful, and it has left me with a terrible feeling of guilt. How am I to get over this feeling?

KRISHNAMURTI: Sir, what do you mean by sin? The Christians have a concept of sin which you have not, but you do feel guilty when you have more money, when you have a bigger house than somebody else—at least you should. (Laughter) When you are riding in a comfortable car and you see a queue of people one mile long waiting to catch a bus, it does something to you—either you have what is called a feeling of guilt, or you want to transform something radically, not in the stupid economic sense, but in the religious sense, so that these things cannot happen in the world. Or you may feel guilty because you realize that you have a certain capacity, an insight which others have not. But strangely we never feel guilty about such things; we feel guilty only about worldly things—having more money, a better social position, and so on.

Now, what is this sense of guilt, and when are you aware of it? Is it a form of pity? Most of us are occupied with ourselves in different ways from morning till night, and consciously or unconsciously we move along in that stream. When there is a sudden challenge, that movement of self-occupation is disturbed, and then we feel guilty; we feel that we are doing something wrong or that we have not done something right, but that feeling is still within the stream of self-centered activity, is it not? I do not know if you are all following this.

Why should you feel guilty? If you are living intensely with your whole being, if you are fully aware of everything about you and within yourself, the unconscious as well as the conscious, where is there room for guilt? It is the man who lives in fragments, who is divided within himself, that feels guilty. One part of him is good, the other part corrupt; one part is trying to be noble, and the other is ignoble; one part is ambitious, ruthless, and the other part talks about peace, love. Such people feel guilty because they are still within the pattern of their own making. As long as there is self-centered activity, you cannot get over the feeling of guilt; it is impossible. That feeling disappears only when you approach life totally, with your whole being, that is, when there is no self-fulfillment of any kind. Then you will find that the sense of guilt does not exist at all because you are not thinking about yourself. There is no self-centered activity.

Sirs, if you are listening and are not acting, it is like a man who is always tilling and never sowing. It is better not to listen to a truth than to listen without acting, for then it becomes a poison. Whether you approve or disapprove of the details of what is said here is irrelevant; what matters is to see the truth that as long as you function within the field of self-centered activity you are bound to have various kinds of sorrow and frustration. Sorrow and frustration cease only when you are living totally, with the intensity of your whole being, of your mind, heart, and body; and you cannot live with that completeness, with that intensity, if you are concerned about your own virtue. You may be free from the feeling of guilt today, but it will arise in another form tomorrow or the day after tomorrow.

Just try this, sirs: try a little bit to live intensely every day, with all your mind, heart, and body, with all your capacity, feeling, energy. Desire is contradictory in itself, but if you love intensely with your body, mind, and heart, with everything that you have, then you will find there is no contradiction, there is no sin. It is desire, envy, ambition, that creates contradiction, and the mind caught in contradiction can never find that which is real.

Question: How can I be sensitive when I am tortured by desire?

KRISHNAMURTI: Why are we tortured by desire? Why have we made desire into a torturous thing? There is desire for power, desire for position, desire for fame, sexual desire, the desire to have money, to have a car, and so on. What do you mean by that word *desire?* And why is it wrong? Why do we say we must suppress or sublimate desire, do something about it? We are trying to find out. Don't just listen to me, but go into it with me and find out for yourself.

What is wrong with desire? You have suppressed it, have you not? Most of you have suppressed desire for various reasons—because it is not convenient, not satisfactory, or because you think it is not moral, or because the religious books say that to find God you must be without desire, and so on. Tradition says you must suppress, control, dominate desire, so you spend your time and energy in disciplining yourself.

Now, let us first see what happens to a mind that is always controlling itself, suppressing, sublimating desire. Such a mind, being occupied with itself, becomes insensitive. Though it may talk about sensitivity, goodness, though it may say that we must be brotherly, we must produce a marvelous world, and all the rest of the nonsense that people talk about who suppress desire—such a mind is insensitive because it does not understand that which it has suppressed. Whether you suppress or yield to desire, it is essentially the same because the desire is still there. You may suppress the desire for a woman, for a car, for position; but the very urge not to have these things, which makes you suppress the desire for them, is itself a form of desire. So, being caught in desire, you have to understand it, and not say it is right or wrong.

Now, what is desire? When I see a tree swaying in the wind, it is a lovely thing to watch, and what is wrong with that? What is wrong in watching the beautiful motion of a bird on the wing? What is wrong in looking at a new car, marvelously built and highly polished? And what is wrong in seeing a nice person with a symmetrical face, a face that shows good sense, intelligence, quality?

But desire does not stop there. Your perception is not just perception, but with it comes sensation. With the arising of sensation, you want to touch, to contact, and then comes the urge to possess. You say, "This is beautiful, I must have it," and so begins the turmoil of desire.

Now, is it possible to see, to observe, to be aware of the beautiful and the ugly things of life, and not say, "I must have," or "I must not have"? Have you ever just observed anything? Do you understand, sirs? Have you ever observed your wife, your children, your friends, just looked at them? Have you ever looked at a flower without calling it a rose, without wanting to put it in your buttonhole, or take it home and give it to somebody? If you are capable of so observing, without all the values attributed by the mind, then you will find that desire is not such a monstrous thing. You can look at a car, see the beauty of it, and not be caught in the turmoil or contradiction of desire. But that requires an immense intensity of observation, not just a casual glance. It is not that you have no desire, but simply that the mind is capable of looking without describing. It can look at the moon and not immediately say, "That is the moon—how beautiful it is," so there is no chattering of the mind coming in between. If you can do this, you will find that in the intensity of observation, of feeling, of real affection, love has its own action, which is not the contradictory action of desire.

Experiment with this and you will see how difficult it is for the mind to observe without chattering about what it observes. But surely, love is of that nature, is it not? How can you love if your mind is never silent, if you are always thinking about yourself? To love a person with your whole being, with your mind, heart, and body, requires great intensity; and when love is intense, desire soon disappears. But most of us have never had this intensity about anything, except about our own profit, conscious or unconscious; we never feel for anything without seeking something else out of it. But only the mind that has this intense energy is capable of following the swift movement of truth. Truth is not static, it is swifter than thought, and the mind cannot possibly conceive of it. To understand truth, there must be this immense energy, which cannot be conserved or cultivated. This energy does not come through self-denial, through suppression. On the contrary, it demands complete abandonment, and you cannot abandon yourself, or abandon everything that you have, if you merely want a result.

It is possible to live without envy in this world which is based on envy, on acquisitiveness, and the pursuit of power, position; but that requires an extraordinary intensity, a clarity of thought, of understanding. You cannot be free of envy without understanding yourself, so the beginning is here, not somewhere else. Unless you begin with yourself, do what you will, you will never find the end of sorrow. The purification of the mind is meditation—the purification of the mind which is concerned with itself. You have to understand yourself, and you can play with it a little bit every day. A man who plays with the understanding of himself will perceive far more than he who preaches to others.

February 10, 1957

Third Talk in Bombay

When religion becomes universal, it ceases to be religion. When religion is a matter of belief, of conversion, of belonging to a group which subscribes to certain ideas, then the seed of religion has gone out of it. For religion is something that must be understood by each individual in the process of living, in the activities of our daily life, and it has therefore nothing to do with educating the mind to function in a particular pattern of thought.

So it seems very important to understand the function of the individual in a society which is merely the mechanism of a collection of ideas, and where what we call morality is a matter of staying within a particular pattern of behavior. But righteousness is not the following of a pattern; it is the action of a mind which understands its own relationship with another. If I am moral merely in the social sense, such morality, though it is socially convenient, has nothing whatsoever to do with religion. Surely, to find out what truth is, what reality or God is, the mind must be free from social morality because social morality leads to respectability, to conformity, and the mind that merely conforms to an ethical or moral pattern obviously can never find out what is true.

Virtue is really the ordering of the mind, and our problem is how to bring about virtue without the cultivation of virtue, is it not? If I cultivate virtue, it ceases to be virtue, and yet without virtue there is no order. Virtue is really a disciplining of the mind without an end in view; it is like putting a room in order. Virtue is not an end in itself; it merely makes the mind clear, free, uncontaminated by society.

So the problem is, is it not, how can one's mind, one's whole being, be virtuous immediately, and not go through the process of becoming virtuous? Because the struggle to become virtuous only strengthens narrowness, the self-centered activity of the mind. I think that is fairly clear—that when I try to become virtuous, I am really emphasizing the activity of my own egotism, and therefore it is no longer virtue.

Virtue frees the mind, and the mind is not free as long as there is no virtue. But the so-called virtue on which most of us base our behavior is merely a social convenience, and society, being rooted in acquisitiveness, in competition, egotism, envy, cannot possibly understand the virtue of being and not becoming.

If we do not understand what it is to be virtuous, the mind will never be free to inquire, to find out what reality is. Virtue is essential as conduct, as behavior, but behavior which is based on compulsion, on conformity, fear, is no longer the action of a virtuous mind. So we must find out what it is to be virtuous, without the cultivation of virtue. I think the two things lead in entirely different directions. A man who cultivates virtue is all the time thinking about himself; he is everlastingly concerned about his own progress, his personal improvement, which is still the activity of the 'me', the self, the ego; and this activity obviously has nothing whatever to do with virtue, which is a state of being and not becoming.

Now, how can a mind whose whole social and moral conditioning has been to cultivate virtue by using time as a means of becoming virtuous—how can such a mind free itself of that sense of becoming, and be in a state of virtue? I do not know if you have ever thought of the problem in this way. To understand it, I think we have to find out what it means to discipline the mind.

Most of us use discipline to achieve a result. Being angry, I say I must not be angry, so I discipline myself, control, suppress, dominate my anger, which means that I conform to an ideological pattern. That is what we are used to: a constant struggle to adjust what we are to what we think we should be. In order to become what we should be, we go through certain practices; we discipline ourselves day after day, month after month, year in and year out, hoping to arrive at a stage which we think is right. So in discipline there is involved not only suppression but also conformity, narrowing the mind down to a particular pattern. Please understand, sirs, that I am not condemning discipline. We are examining the whole process involved in conduct that is based on discipline.

If I can understand the present process of discipline, which is the process that most of us know, and see the falseness or the truth of it, then I shall have a totally different feeling of discipline, a discipline which has no relation to fear, and such a feeling of true discipline is essential. But the discipline that we practice is based on fear and conformity, on the struggle to become something through substitution, identification, or sublimation. All these things are involved in the practice of discipline by a mind which is in confusion, and obviously such discipline, being based on fear, has no relationship to reality. If I discipline myself because my neighbor or society or the priest or some sacred book has told me it is the right thing to do, then such discipline is obviously immature, infantile; it has no meaning at all, and any conduct based on that pattern only leads to respectability, which has nothing whatsoever to do with reality.

Now, if I understand that mere conformity to a pattern through fear is not discipline, then what is discipline? The mind must function without disorder; it must be free of confusion, and virtue is obviously the ordering of the mind so that it can fly straight and not crooked, without the distortion of its own ambitions, envies, and desires. But to fly straight, there must be a discipline which is not related to the discipline of conformity, sublimation, or suppression, that is, a discipline in which no struggle is involved, no effort to become something. And how is such a discipline to come about without violation, without the action of will?—because after all, will is the apex of desire. Is it possible for the mind to be disciplined without the coming into being of the entity who desires to discipline it? Do you follow?

I think this is an important issue, and may I suggest that one should listen to it, not with antagonism because one's mind habitually functions in the old discipline and therefore rejects the other, but rather to find out what the other discipline is. The ordinary discipline, though it may look noble, is essentially based on fear; and our inquiry is to find out if there is a discipline which is not based on fear, which is not a result of the action of will.

We can see that the action of will does produce a result. If I desire something very ardently, if I patiently pursue it, I will get it. But that is the functioning of will, and will is essentially a process of resistance, and a mind whose discipline is merely a process of resistance cannot possibly understand the other.

So, how is the individual mind, yours and mine, to come to the state of discipline without disciplining itself? After all, virtue—which is being virtuous, not becoming virtuous—is a state of discipline not based on self-centered activity. And how is the mind to free itself from the self-centered activity which it now calls discipline? Such discipline can produce certain results, which may be noble or ignoble; but self-centered activity in any form, with its will, with its fears, can never be virtuous. And is it possible for my mind to be free of all self-centered activity without disciplining itself? That is the real issue in conduct, in behavior. When I use the words *my mind*, it is merely a way of speaking; it is not *my* mind, it is *the* mind.

Now, this mind, as far as I can see, functions only in self-centered activity; whether it meditates on God, or pursues sexual gratification, or practices the ideal of nonviolence, or plunges into social reform, its activity is essentially self-centered, that is, within the area of time, within the field of its own thought. And is it possible for the mind to free itself from that self-centered activity without compulsion, without the discipline which is conformity to a pattern?

Why does one put this question? Most of us discipline ourselves in the ordinary sense. Being envious, we say that we must not be envious, we must be strict with ourselves. We have not understood, but we say, "If I can progress through discipline, I will eventually understand." We do not look at the significance of such a discipline, we never question this process of discipline itself.

Now, by questioning, by inquiring into it, you will see that such discipline has no value at all, except socially, and it cannot possibly lead to reality. Reality is to be understood only when there is complete abandonment, and you cannot abandon yourself as long as there is any form of self-centered activity. You cannot be austere when austerity is cultivated, for then the mind is seeking a result. There is a different kind of austerity which has nothing whatever to do with giving up one thing in order to arrive at something else, and it can never be known as long as the mind forces, controls, suppresses itself. The austerity of suppression does bring a sense of power, of domination over oneself, and in that there is a great pleasure, a great vitality, but it does not lead in the direction of reality. On the contrary, it is merely a perpetuation of self-centered activity away from the world. It is like having all the treasures of the world in a different direction. So, is it possible for the mind to be austere as long as there is the entity who is seeking to be austere?

Sirs, this is not something metaphysical, mystical, or vague. If you really pursue it, think it out, if you really look in the direction I am pointing, you will discover for yourself that out of this inquiry a discipline comes which has nothing whatsoever to do with the self-centered activity of seeking a result. The discipline you are used to is utterly false; it may have value in the social sense, but it has no relationship to the inquiry after reality. Yet there must be virtue in order to find reality, so what is one to do?

Now, when my mind seeks, not out of the desire for a result, but out of the sheer necessity of seeking because it sees the falseness of what it has been doing, then that very process of inquiry is discipline which has nothing whatsoever to do with self-achievement. I am inquiring, and to inquire, the mind must be completely uncontaminated, free of all pressures. A mind that is tethered to worry, to ambition, to greed, to envy, to passion, is obviously incapable of inquiry. Truth has to be found, not believed in, and to find it the mind must be free. The moment I see the truth of that, my mind is freeing itself from the false, and therefore there is true discipline; there is no entity who disciplines, but the very perception of what is false makes the mind understand the nature of true discipline.

So virtue is essential to the understanding of reality, and virtue is not respectability. Being virtuous, and not trying to become virtuous, demands enormous inquiry, clear thinking, and you cannot possibly think clearly if there is any form of fear. Therefore there must be the understanding of fear without asking how to overcome fear; there must be the understanding of violence without trying to become nonviolent. Then you will find that there is a discipline which is unrelated to the discipline of social morality, a discipline which is essential because it makes the mind capable of pursuing with extraordinary rapidity the swift movement of truth. If you would watch a bird in flight, you must give your whole attention to it, and that very attention is discipline. The reality of the books, of the priests, of society is no reality at all; it is mere propaganda, and therefore not true. If you want to understand what is reality, if you want to find out what is truth, your mind must be capable of astonishing clarity, of silence and swiftness;

and the mind is not clear, it is not silent, it is not swift as long as it is tethered to any form of discipline as expressed in the morality of society. When you understand all this, you will find there is a discipline, an austerity which is not the result of self-centered activity, and it is this discipline which is essential if the mind is to follow the swift movement of truth.

You see, the difficulty for most of us is that we have had a pleasurable experience, and we discipline ourselves because we want the pleasurable experience to continue. I have had a moment of clarity, of joy, of extraordinary perception of something beyond the measure of words, and it has left an imprint on my mind; and because I want more of it, I control myself, I practice virtue, and so on. That is a form of envy, is it not? Envy breeds discipline, but that is not freedom.

Now, a mind that seeks reality finds in that very search a process of discipline in which there is no experiencing on the part of the experiencer. For the experiencer not to have experience demands tremendous clarity, an astonishing steadiness of thought, of understanding; and out of this understanding of the totality of the mind, which is self-knowledge, there comes a discipline, a conduct, a behavior which brings about the austerity that is essential to abandonment. Only through the abandonment which is the outcome of austerity is there beauty. Only the mind that abandons itself completely is really austere, and it is such a mind that is capable of understanding that which is truth, that which is reality.

Question: Thought is the seed which contains within it the beginning and the ending, the totality of time. This seed quickens and germinates in the darkness of the mind. What action is possible to burn away this seed?

KRISHNAMURTI: There is only one action, which is the action of silence. But first of all, I hope you have understood the question. The questioner says that the seed of thought, which is the totality of time, matures in the dark womb of the mind, and he asks how this seed of thought, this result of time, this product of the past, is to be completely burned out—but not through a process, not through a method or a system, which implies time, and therefore we are back again in the darkness where the germination and continuity of thought is taking place. So the question is: How is thought, which is the totality of time, to end?

Now, before I begin to find out, I must inquire into what thinking is, must I not? And in asking that question, I have given myself a challenge to which there is a response according to my memory. When I say, "What is thinking?" the mechanism of memory is set going—the memory of my experiences, of my knowledge, of what I have learned or been told about thinking. So my mind is delving into memory to find an answer to the question, which is the challenge. This delving into memory for an answer, and the verbal communication of it to you, is what we call thinking, which is the process of time.

I hope I am making myself clear because it is really very important to understand this. It is only when you understand the process of your own thinking that you will find out what it is to have a mind that is totally still. For the mind to be still, there must be complete energy—energy which is not dissipated, which is total, in which there is the vitality of your whole being. To have that total energy which brings silence to the mind, one must inquire into what is thinking; and we see that thinking is the response of memory, which is fairly simple. If I ask you where you live, you reply quickly because that is something you are familiar with. If I ask you a more complicated question, you hesitate;

there is a gap between my question and your answer; in that gap the mind is thinking, looking into memory. If I ask you a still more complicated question, the gap is longer. The mind is searching, groping after the answer, and if it does not find the answer it says, "I do not know." But when it says, "I do not know," it is in a state of wanting to know, and therefore it is still caught up in the process of thinking.

We see, then, what thinking is. The question that sets the mind in motion may be simple or very complex, but it is always the mechanism of memory which responds, whether that memory be of something which is in the extremely recent past, in the past of yesterday, or in the past of a century ago. So the whole process of thinking is the response of memory. It is this process of thinking which says, "I must discipline myself, I must free myself from fear, from greed, from envy, I must find God"; it is this process of thinking which has a belief in God, or which says, "There is no God," but it is still within the field of time because thinking itself is the totality of time.

Now, for a man who would find reality, or who would seek the understanding that will uncover reality, thinking must cease—thinking in the sense of the totality of time. And how is thinking to cease?—but not through any form of practice, discipline, control, suppression, which is all within the field of thought, and therefore within the area of time. The mind which says, "I must inquire into something which is not of time"—that very mind, which is the process of thinking, of time, must come to an end. Is it not so?

I hope you are not merely listening to my words because words are ashes; they have no meaning except on the verbal level, but if you are capable of pursuing the significance of that which lies beyond the words, then you will understand the extraordinary beauty and depth of a mind that frees itself from the process of time. In time there is no depth, in time there is no virtue, in time there is only the germinating and maturing of thought—thought which is always conditioned, thought which can never be free. There is no such thing as "free" thought, that is sheer nonsense. Thinking is only thinking, and when you see what the significance of thinking is, you will never talk about "free" thought.

So our question is: Is it possible for thought, which is the result of the past, the totality of time, to cease immediately? I say it is possible only when the mind is completely still. If you ask, "How is the mind to be completely still?" the "how" is the demand for a method, so you are again caught in time. But there is a "how" which is not of time because it is not the demand for a method. Do you follow what I am saying, sirs? You can ask "how," meaning "Teach me the method that will in time put an end to thinking," and such a "how" is merely the continuation of thinking by which you hope to come to a state where there is no thinking—which is an obvious impossibility. But if you see the falseness of that process, then the "how" has a different significance altogether.

Please pay attention to this, for if you understand it, you will know immediately for yourself what it is to have a still mind; nobody will have to teach you, and you will not want a guru. The "how" which implies a method involves time, and therefore the continuation of thought which is conditioned, in which there is no freedom. That "how" has no validity when you are inquiring into what is truth because to inquire into what is truth, there must be freedom—freedom from thought.

Now, the moment you see that the "how" which demands a method is merely the continuation of time, what happens to your mind? I hope you are watching your own mind and are not just listening to my words.

What happens to your mind when you see that the "how" which demands a method is not the way to free the mind? You are left with a "how" which is inquiry, are you not? And to inquire you must start with complete silence because you know nothing. Do you understand?

A mind that is inquiring has no accumulation; its inquiry is not additive, it has no gatherings of knowledge. Do you understand, sirs? If I am inquiring into what love is, I cannot say that love is spiritual, divine, or the outcome of karma, and all that, which is merely a process of thinking. I will never find out what love is through thinking because thought is conditioned, thought is the result of time. Thought projects ideas about love, but what it projects is not love. To inquire into what love is, the mind must be free of information, of ideas, of thought. When I see the truth of that, my mind becomes completely still; I do not have to ask how to make it still. What is important is right inquiry, which is to inquire so that the mind is free from the knowledge accumulated through experience by the experiencer.

Thought, which is the totality of time, germinates in the dark recesses of the mind, for the mind is the result of time, of many thousands of yesterdays. The mere continuance of thought, however noble, however erudite, however dignified, is still within the field of time, and such a mind is incapable of finding out what is beyond the measure of itself.

What matters, then, is for the mind which is the result of time to begin to inquire into itself, and not speculate about the state of a mind which is free from time. It is only when the mind begins to inquire into itself that it is aware of its own processes and the significance of its thinking. You can be totally and immediately aware of all the dark corners of the mind where thought is functioning only when you realize that thought can never lead the mind to freedom. If you really understand this, then you will find that the mind becomes completely still, not only the conscious mind, but also the unconscious, with all its racial inheritance, its motives, dogmas, and hidden fears. But there is that total stillness of the mind only when there is the tremendous energy of self-knowledge. It is self-knowledge that brings this energy, not your abstinence from sex, from alcohol, from this or that—which is again a form of self-centered activity. This total energy is essential, and the intensity, the fullness, the vitality of it can come only when there is self-knowledge.

But self-knowledge is not cumulative; it is the discovery of what you are from moment to moment, and total energy exists only when there is this intensity of self-knowledge. Then the mind is completely still, and in that stillness there is great beauty of which you do not know; in that stillness there is an astonishing movement which destroys the germination of the mind. That silence has its own activity, its own operation on society, and it will produce an action irrespective of the particular social pattern. But the mind that is merely caught up in social reform, in bringing about equality through legislation, and all the rest of it, will never know this other action which operates on the totality. That is why it is very important to understand yourself. Out of that understanding, which is total self-knowledge, there is real abandonment, and only then is there this extraordinary sense of silence.

I do not know if you have ever sat quietly in the early morning, when the mind is not active, and watched the still sky, the brilliant stars, the trees, the birds. Try it sometime, not to meditate—for then it is the self-centered activity of the meditator—but just for the fun of it. Then you will find there is a silence which has no relationship to knowledge. It is not the end of noise, or the opposite of noise. It is a silence which is really the creativity of all things, the beginning of all things. But you will never find it if you do not have this total knowledge of yourself. The understanding of yourself is the beginning of freedom.

February 17, 1957

Fourth Talk in Bombay

I wonder what most of us are seeking. And when we do find what we seek, is it totally satisfactory, or is there always the shadow of frustration in that which we have sought out? And is it possible to learn from everything, from our sorrows and joys, so that our minds are made fresh and are capable of learning infinitely more?

Most of us listen to be told what to do or to conform to a new pattern, or we listen merely to gather further information. If we are here with any such attitude, then the process of listening will have very little significance in what we are trying to do in these talks. And I am afraid most of us are only concerned with that—we want to be told, we are listening in order to be taught, and a mind that merely wants to be told is obviously incapable of learning.

I think there is a process of learning which is not related to wanting to be taught. Being confused, most of us want to find someone who will help us not to be confused, and therefore we are merely learning or acquiring knowledge in order to conform to a particular pattern; and it seems to me that all such forms of learning must invariably lead not only to further confusion but also to deterioration of the mind. I think there is a different kind of learning, a learning which is an inquiry into ourselves and in which there is no teacher and no taught, neither the disciple nor the guru. When you begin to inquire into the operation of your own mind, when you observe your own thinking, your daily activities and feelings, you cannot be taught because there is no one to teach you. You cannot base your inquiry on any authority, on any assumption, on any previous knowledge. If you do, then you are merely conforming to the pattern of what you already know, and therefore you are no longer learning about yourself.

I think it is very important to learn about oneself because it is only then that the mind can be emptied of the old, and unless the mind is emptied of the old, there can be no new impulse. It is this new, creative impulse that is essential if the individual is to bring about a different world, a different relationship, a different structure of morality. And it is only through totally emptying the mind of the old that the new impulse can come into being, give it whatever name you like—the impulse of reality, the grace of God, the feeling of something completely new, unpremeditated, something which has never been thought of, which has not been put together by the mind. Without that extraordinarily creative impulse of reality, do what you will to clear up the confusion and bring order in the social structure, it can only lead to further misery. I think this is fairly obvious when one observes the political and social events that are taking place in the world.

So it is important, it seems to me, that the mind be emptied of all knowledge because knowledge is invariably of the past; and as long as the mind is burdened with the residue of the past, of our personal or collective experiences, there can be no learning.

There is a learning which begins with self-knowledge, a learning which comes with awareness of your everyday activities—what you do, what you think, what your relationship with another is, how your mind responds to every incident and challenge of your daily life. If you are not aware of your response to every challenge in life, there is no self-knowledge. You can know yourself as you are only in relation to something, in relation to people, to ideas, and to things. If you assume anything about yourself, if you postulate that you are the atma, or the higher self, for example, and start from that, which is obviously a form of conclusion, your mind is incapable of learning.

When the mind is burdened with a conclusion, a formulation, there is the cessation of inquiry. And it is essential to inquire, not merely as it is being done by certain specialists in the scientific or psychological field, but to inquire into oneself and to know the totality of one's being, the operation of one's own mind at the conscious and also at the unconscious level in all the activities of one's daily existence—how one functions, what one's responses are when one goes to the office, rides in the bus, when one talks with one's children, with one's wife or husband, and so on. Unless the mind is aware of the totality of itself—not as it should be, but as it actually is—unless it is aware of its conclusions, its assumptions, its ideals, its conformity, there is no possibility of the coming into being of this new, creative impulse of reality.

You may know the superficial layers of your mind, but to know the unconscious motives, drives, fears, the hidden residue of tradition, of racial inheritance—to be aware of all that and to give it close attention is very hard work; it demands a great deal of energy. Most of us are unwilling to give close attention to these things; we have not the patience to go into ourselves step by step, inch by inch, so that we begin to know all the subtleties, the intricate movements of the mind. But it is only the mind which has understood itself in its totality and is therefore incapable of self-deception—it is only such a mind that can free itself of its past and go beyond its own movements within the field of time. This is not very difficult, but it requires a great deal of hard work.

You work a great deal when you go to the office; you have to work to earn your livelihood, or to do anything else in life. You have been trained to work hard in the commercial world, and you are also willing to work hard in the so-called spiritual world if there is a reward at the end of it. It you are promised a seat in heaven, or if you believe that you can achieve bliss, an everlasting peace, you will work hard to get it, but that is merely an action of greed.

Now, there is a different way of working, which is to inquire into ourselves and to know exactly what is going on within the field of the mind, not in order to gain some reward, but for the very simple reason that there can obviously be no end to misery in the world as long as the mind does not understand itself. And after all, the world in which we live is not the enormous world of political activities, of scientific research, and so on; it is the little world of the family, the world of relationship between two people at home or in the office, between husband and wife, parents and children, teacher and pupil, lawyer and client, policeman and citizen. That is the little world we all live in, but we want to escape from that world of relationship and go out into an extraordinary world which we have imagined and which does not really exist at all. If we do not understand the world of relationship and bring about a fundamental transformation there, we cannot possibly create a new culture, a different civilization, a peaceful world. So it must start with ourselves. The world demands an immense, a radical change, but it must begin with you and me; and we cannot bring about a real change in ourselves if we do not know the totality of our world of thoughts, of feelings, of actions, if we are not aware of ourselves from moment to moment. And you will see, if you are so aware, that the mind begins to free itself from all influences of the past. After all, the mind is now the result of the past, and all thinking is a projection of the past; it is simply a response of the past to challenge, so merely to think of creating a new world will never bring a new world into being.

Most people, when they are confused, disturbed, want to return to the past; they seek to revive the old religion, to reestablish the ancient customs, to bring back the form of worship practiced by their ancestors, and all the rest of it. But what is necessary, surely, is to find out whether the mind that is the result of the past, the mind that is confused, disturbed, groping, seeking—whether such a mind can learn without turning to a guru, whether it can undertake the journey on which there is no guide. Because it is possible to go on this journey only when there is the light which comes through the understanding of yourself, and that light cannot be given to you by another; no Master, no guru can give it to you, nor will you find it in the Gita, or in any other book. You have to find that light within yourself, which means that you must inquire into yourself, and this inquiry is hard work. No one can lead you, no one can teach you how to inquire into yourself. One can point out that such inquiry is essential, but the actual process of inquiring must begin with your own self-observation.

A mind that would understand that which is true, that which is real, that which is good, or that which is beyond the measure of the mind—give it whatever name you like—must be empty, but not be aware that it is empty. I hope you see the difference between the two. If I am aware that I am virtuous, I am no longer virtuous; if I am aware that I am humble, humility has ceased. Surely that is obvious. In the same way, if the mind is aware that it is empty, it is no longer empty because there is always the observer who is experiencing emptiness.

So, is it possible for the mind to be free of the observer, of the censor? After all, the observer, the censor, the watcher, the thinker, is the self, the 'me' that is always wanting more and more experience. I have had all the experiences that this world can give me, with its pleasure and pain, its ambition, greed, envy, and I am dissatisfied, frustrated, shallow. So I want further experience on another level which I call the spiritual world, but the experiencer continues, the watcher remains. The watcher, the thinker, the experiencer may cultivate virtue; he may discipline himself and try to lead what he considers to be a moral life, but he remains. And can that experiencer, that self, totally cease? Because only then is it possible for the mind to empty itself and for the new, the truth, the creative reality to come into being.

To put it very simply, is it possible for me to forget myself? Don't say yes or no. We do not know what it means. The sacred books say so-and-so, but all that is mere words, and words are not reality. What is important is for the mind to find out whether that which has been put together—the experiencer, the thinker, the watcher, the 'I'—can disappear, dissolve itself. There must be no other entity who dissolves it. I hope I am making myself clear. If the mind says, "The 'I' must be dissolved in order to arrive at that extraordinary state which the sacred books promise," then there is the action of will; there is an entity who wants to arrive, so the 'I' still remains.

Now, is it possible for the mind to free itself of the observer, of the watcher, of the experiencer, without any motive? Obviously, if there is a motive, that very motive is the essence of the 'me', of the experiencer. Can you forget yourself entirely without any compulsion, without any desire for reward or fear of punishment—just forget yourself? I do not know if you have tried it. Has such a thought even occurred to you, has it ever come to your mind? And when such a thought does arise, you immediately say, "If I forget myself, how can I live in this world, where everybody is struggling to push me aside and get ahead?" To have a right answer to that question, you must first know how to live without the 'me', without the experiencer, without the self-centered activity which is the creator of sorrow, the very essence of confusion and misery. So is it possible, while living in this world with all its complex relationships, with all its travail, to abandon oneself completely and be free of the things which go to make up the 'me'?

You see, sirs and ladies, this is an inquiry, it is not an answer from me. You will have to find out for yourself, and that requires enormous investigation, hard work—much harder work than earning a livelihood, which is mere routine. It requires astonishing vigilance, constant watchfulness, a ceaseless inquiry into every movement of thought. And the moment you begin to inquire into the process of thinking, which is to isolate each thought and think it through to the end, you will see how arduous it is; it is not a lazy man's pleasure. And it is essential to do this because it is only the mind that has emptied itself of all its old recognitions, its old distractions, its conflicts and self-contradictions—it is only such a mind that has the new, the creative impulse of reality. The mind then creates its own action; it brings into being a different activity altogether, without which mere social reform, however necessary, however beneficial, cannot possibly bring about a peaceful and happy world.

As human beings we are all capable of inquiry, of discovery, and this whole process is meditation. Meditation is inquiry into the very being of the meditator. You cannot meditate without self-knowledge, without being aware of the ways of your own mind, from the superficial responses to the most complex subtleties of thought. I am sure it is not really difficult to know, to be aware of oneself; but it is difficult for most of us because we are so afraid to inquire, to grope, to search out. Our fear is not of the unknown but of letting go of the known. It is only when the mind allows the known to fade away that there is complete freedom from the known, and only then is it possible for the new impulse to come into being.

Question: In your last talk you finally conceded the essential need of discipline, but you complicated the issue by saying that this necessary discipline was the discipline of total attention. Please explain.

KRISHNAMURTI: I was pointing out in my last talk, if I remember rightly, that the discipline of suppression, sublimation, or substitution is no discipline at all; it is merely conformity to a pattern, a mechanical process based essentially on fear and respectability. I was also pointing out that there is an altogether different kind of discipline which is not related to fear at all, a discipline of total attention.

Now, what do we mean by attention? Do we ever attend to anything? Please, sirs, follow this a little bit. Do we ever attend to anything, listen to anything, observe anything? Or is our attention, our observation, our listening merely a process of resistance? I hear that crow, and I resist it in order to listen to something else; I resist the shouting of those children because I want to listen to what is being said. This resistance is partial attention, and partial attention is no attention at all. Surely that is obvious, is it not? What is the state of my mind when it is resisting a noise because it wants to listen to something? There is a conflict going on within the mind, the conflict which invariably arises through resistance; and where there is conflict, there is no attention. I think that is fairly clear. Where there is any form of resistance, there is conflict, and a mind in conflict is incapable of paying attention.

Now, is it possible for the mind to be free of resistance, of conflict? How does conflict arise? It arises when one desire is opposed by another, when there is tension between two desires. That again is fairly clear.

Please, sirs, I am explaining, and if you are merely listening to the explanations, then you are missing the whole significance of what is being said. But if, as you listen, you watch your own mind, observe your own ways of thinking, then you will see it all very clearly, and that very clarity of perception will bring about attention, you will not have to make an effort to attend. The moment you make an effort to attend, that effort implies resistance, and there can be no attention when there is resistance. Resistance, conflict, arises when there are opposing desires, the tension of wanting and not wanting. So the mind has to understand the whole process of desire, and not identify itself with one desire in opposition to another, or try to make one desire conform to another, however noble, significant, or worthwhile it may be. All desire is contradictory in itself, and therefore desire is the very root of resistance.

So, can the mind understand desire? Does the mind know what desire is? The mind knows desire for something, desire for a woman, desire for a man; it knows desire in terms of wanting this or rejecting that. Now, I am asking you a question: Does the mind know what desire is? Is the mind aware of its own state when it is desiring? And is there desire without the object of desire, without the thing that creates desire?

I see something beautiful, and there is sensation, contact, from which arises the desire to possess; so desire is a reaction. And is there desire which is not a reaction? Can the mind experience what desire is in itself? I hope you are following this.

Look, sirs, does the mind know what it is to love? Do you know the quality, the sense of love—not what you love, not the object, but the feeling itself? Or is that feeling always associated with the object? And if there is no object, does the feeling exist independent of the object? If the feeling is dependent on the object, if it arises only through awareness of the object, then, though we call it love, it is obviously not love but merely the sensation which that object produces, and therefore a source of conflict.

Now, please inquire with me, think with me, feel with me. Is it possible for the mind to have the feeling of love without the object, or independent of the object? Is it possible for the mind to attend without the object of attention?

I am afraid I am making this a little bit complicated, but the thing itself is complicated, and if you do not follow it, I am sorry. You will have to inquire into all this for yourself, and not just say, "Discipline is discipline; why do you bother so much about it?" The discipline you have known is merely a mechanical habit, it has no vitality, it is destructive, disintegrating. And that is what is happening to most of you—through so-called discipline you are destroying the vitality of thought, of independent inquiry, of full attention.

I say there is a discipline which is not related to this horror of conformity, and that is the discipline of attention. But there is no attention when there is resistance, conflict. And can the mind be free of conflict? To inquire into that, the mind has to find out what creates conflict. The cause of conflict is the desire for an object—that is, when it is the object which creates the desire. That is fairly clear. What do we do when the object creates the desire? We discipline ourselves against the object, do we not? We become hermits, sannyasis; we resist, suppress, control, which only creates more and more conflict. And that is what we call being austere—which is a most immature way of thinking.

The next question is: Is it possible for the mind to see the object without the arising of desire? Can it just look at the object and not suppress its own reaction? Because the whole of living is reaction, is it not? To see the beauty of a tree, of the earth, of the clear sky, of the sea, of a bird on the wing, to see the faces which smile and the tears of sorrow—to see and feel all that is living, and to shut yourself off from any of it through discipline, through resistance, is to make life very shallow, dull, and stupid.

So, is it possible for the mind to see everything, the beautiful and the ugly, without the arising of desire? And when the mind is not caught up with the object of desire, is there no feeling? Please inquire for yourself. Is there no feeling without the object? Is there no love without the object? Is there no listening without the speaker? And if your mind can so listen, can so love, can so feel, then you will find that an extraordinary freedom from the past comes into being which is total attention. Then you don't have to make an effort to discipline yourself because that total attention is its own discipline.

I do not know if you have noticed that when the mind gives its whole attention to something, the watcher is not, the experiencer does not exist. Do you understand, sirs? If I listen to those crows totally, without resistance, if I listen with full attention, in that attention there is no watcher, no experiencer, no entity who is listening; there is only complete attention, complete listening, complete life without a shadow. Such attention brings its own discipline which is much more subtle, much more arduous, and much more strict than the stupid discipline of fear and conformity.

The state of complete attention is austerity, and it is only in that state that the mind can abandon itself, and only then is it possible for the mind to receive the creative impulse of reality. Merely to resist a desire only tortures the mind and creates the conflict of duality with all its philosophical speculations about reality. Whereas, if your mind is capable of giving total attention to something—to your children, to your wife or husband, to a bird, to a tree, to your everyday tasks—then you will find that there is no contradiction, no resistance. Resistance arises, contradiction comes into being only when there is the entity who is watching, evaluating, judging, condemning, and that entity is the self, the 'me'.

Conformity at any time is not moral, but there is a discipline which is not the outcome of fear, of respectability, of conformity to social morality, and this discipline comes when the mind is capable of giving total attention in which there is no contradiction or distraction. It is not a question of how the mind is to avoid being distracted because in giving total attention, there is no distraction.

Sirs, you all do as every child does when he plays with a toy. The child is completely lost in the toy; it is absorbing him, but that is not attention because the toy is important. Similarly, you sit in front of a picture and let the picture absorb you—which is what you call meditation. The image, the chant, the *shloka*, the mantra absorbs you, but that is not attention. In that there is conflict because the image, the word, or the symbol becomes all-important. If you see the truth of this, you will find that an attention comes which has no object. Such attention is not a gift; it is merely attention without effort, without an object, and therefore without a shadow. It is the object of attention that casts the shadow of contradiction in the mind which is attending. Attention without an object is a state of complete emptiness; the mind is capable of listening completely because it is not resisting.

Question: Day follows day, with old age and death coming inexorably nearer. I listen to you, but the anguish of the approaching end does not diminish. Teach me to face old age and death with equanimity.

KRISHNAMURTI: What do you mean by old age? Going bald, losing one's teeth? The physical organism inevitably wears itself out through long use. Is that old age? Or is old age the deterioration of the mind? You may be very young, healthy, strong, and yet be old because your mind is already on the path of deterioration.

So what do we mean by old age? Surely we are not talking of the gradual wearing out of the body through use and decay. We do not mean that. We mean the state of the mind which has grown old because it has no innocence. Do you understand, sir? The mind is old when it is not fresh, when it is always thinking in terms of the past and using the present as a passage to the future. It is such a mind that is not young. And can such a mind be made new, innocent, fresh? Can it renew itself from moment to moment so that it never grows old? Surely that is our problem, not how to stop the aging of the body, which is of course impossible. New drugs may be invented which will keep you going fifty years longer, but then what? However young you may be, the process of deterioration already exists in the functioning of the mind. So is it possible for the mind not to deteriorate?

What are the factors of deterioration? That is the problem. And can the mind be kept fresh, innocent? It is only the innocent mind that can learn, not the mind that is burdened with knowledge and is therefore already old. So, how is the mind to be made new, fresh, innocent? Do you understand, sir?

This mind is the result of time, of many yesterdays, of all the conflicts, impressions, contradictions, hopes, and fears of the past; it is the outcome of innumerable wants, of pleasure and pain, of vital ambitions, and fearful frustrations. And how is this mind—which has been put together through time, through experience, through conditioning—to be made new?

Whether the physical organism is young or old, the mind is old because it is already fixed, molded; it functions in a routine, in a wheel of fear, and how is such a mind to be made new, innocent? Surely, only by dying to the past, to everything it has known. Do you understand, sir? Is it possible to die to "my house," "my family," "my God," "my nationality," "my belief," "my tradition," to all the impressions, compulsions, influences that have made me, and yet be aware of my family, of the beauty of a tree, the beauty of a flower, of the sunset, of the sky?

After all, what are you? You are the memories of your joy, of your ambitions and frustrations, of the little property you own; you are the memory or recognition of your wife or husband, of your children, and the anticipation of what you are going to achieve; you are a bundle of tensions, of contradictions, of innumerable impressions. All that is the 'you'. Whether you believe in God or in no-God, it is still within the field of memory, of the known, of thought. And is it possible to die to all that immediately? To wait for death to come and then ask, "Is there life after death?" is merely to continue the mind which has grown old.

So, is it possible for the mind to cease, to put an end without any cause to the deteriorating factor, which is conflict, the process of recognition as "mine" and "yours"? Sir, try it. Live for one day, one hour, as though you were going to die, actually going to die the next hour. If you knew you were about to die, what would you do? You would gather your family together, put your money, your little property in order, and draw up a will; and then, as death approached, you would have to understand all that you had been. If you were merely frightened because you were dying, you would be dying for nothing; but you would not be frightened if you said, "I have lived a dull, ambitious, envious, stupid life, and now I am going to wipe all that totally from my memory, I am going to forget the past and live in this hour completely." Sir, if you can live one hour as completely as that, you can live completely for the rest of your life. But to die is hard work—not to die through disease and old age, that is not hard work at all. That is inevitable; it is what we are all going to do, and you cushion yourself against it in innumerable ways. But if you die so that you are living fully in this hour, you will find there is an enormous vitality, a tremendous attention to everything because this is the only hour you are living. You look at this spring of life because you will never see it again; you see the smile, the tears, you feel the earth, you feel the quality of a tree, you feel the love that has no continuity and no object. Then you will find that in this total attention the 'me' is not, and that the mind, being empty, can renew itself. Then the mind is fresh, innocent, and such a mind lives eternally beyond time.

February 20, 1957

Fifth Talk in Bombay

As life is so complicated, it seems to me that one must approach it with great simplicity. Life is a vast complex of struggle, of misery, of passing joys and, perhaps for some, the pleasurable continuity of a satisfaction they have known. Confronted with this extraordinarily intricate process which we call existence, surely we must approach it very simply because it is the simple mind that really understands the problem, not the sophisticated mind, not the mind that is burdened with knowledge. If we want to understand something very complex, we must approach it very simply, and therein lies our difficulty because we always approach our problems with assertions, with assumptions or conclusions, and so we are never free to approach them with the humility they demand.

And may I point out that this talk will be utterly futile if we listen to what is being said merely on the verbal or intellectual level because mere verbal or intellectual listening has no significance when we are confronted with immense problems. So let us try to listen, for the time being at least, not just on the verbal level, or with certain conclusions at which the mind may have arrived, but with a sense of humility so that you and I can explore together this whole problem of knowledge.

The undoing of knowledge is the fundamental revolution; the undoing of knowledge is the beginning of humility. Only the mind that is humble can understand what is true and what is false, and is therefore capable of eschewing the false and pursuing that which is true. But most of us approach life with knowledge—knowledge being what we have learned, what we have been taught, and what we have gathered in the incidents and accidents of life. This knowledge becomes our background, our conditioning; it shapes our thoughts, it makes us conform to the pattern of what has been. If we would understand anything, we must approach it with humility, and it is knowledge that makes us unhumble. I wonder if you have noticed that when you know, you have ceased to examine *what is*. When you already know, you are not living at all. It is the mind that is undoing what it has gathered that is actually and not merely intellectually dissipating what it has known—it is only such a mind that is capable of understanding. And for most of us knowledge becomes the authority, the guide which keeps us within the sanctuary of society, within the frontiers of respectability. Knowledge is the center from which we judge, evaluate, from which we condemn, accept, or reject.

Now, is it possible for the mind to free itself from knowledge? Can that self-center, which is essentially the accumulation of knowledge, be dissolved so that the mind is really humble, innocent, and therefore capable of perceiving what is truth?

After all, what is it that we know? We know only facts, or what we have been taught about facts. When I examine and ask myself, "What is it that I really know?" I see that I actually know only what has been taught me, a technique, a profession, plus the information which I have acquired in the everyday relationship of challenge and response. Apart from that, what do I know, what do you know? What we know is obviously what we have been taught, or what we have gathered from books and from environmental influences. This accumulation of what we have acquired or have been taught reacts to the environment, thereby further strengthening the background of what we call knowledge.

So, can the mind, which has been put together through knowledge, undo what it has gathered and thereby remove authority altogether? Because it is the authority of knowledge that gives us arrogance, vanity, and there is humility only when that authority is removed, not theoretically but actually, so that I can approach this whole complex process of existence with a mind that does not know. And is it possible for the mind to free itself from that which it has known?

We can see that there is a great deal of tyranny in the world, and that tyranny is spreading; there is compulsion, there is misery, both physically and inwardly, and the constant threat of war, and with such a world there must obviously be some kind of radical change in our thinking. But most of us regard action as more important than thought; we want to know what to do about all these complex problems, and we are more concerned with right action than with the process of thinking which will produce right action.

Now, the process of thinking obviously cannot be made new as long as one starts thinking from any assumption, from any conclusion. So I must ask myself, as you must ask yourself, whether it is possible for the mind to undo the knowledge it has gathered because knowledge becomes authority, which produces arrogance, and with that arrogance and vanity we consciously or unconsciously look at life, and therefore we never approach anything with humility.

I know because I have learned, I have experienced, I have gathered, or I guide my thought and activity in terms of some ideology to which I conform. So gradually I build up this whole process of authority in myself—the authority of the experiencer, of the one who knows. And my problem is: Can I who have gathered so much knowledge, who have learned so much, who have had so many experiences—can I undo all that? Because there is no possibility of a radical change without the undoing of knowledge. The very undoing of knowledge is the beginning of such a change, is it not?

What do we mean by "change"? Is change merely a movement from the knowledge I have accumulated to other fields of knowing, to new assumptions and ideologies projected from the past? This is generally what we mean by "change," is it not? When I say I must change, I think in terms of changing to something I already know. When I say I must be good, I have an idea, a formulation, a concept of what it is to be good. But that is not the flowering of goodness. The flowering of goodness comes only when I understand the process and the accumulation of knowledge, and in the undoing of what I know. Then there is the possibility of a revolution, a radical change. But merely to move from the known to the known is no change at all.

I hope I am making myself clear because you and I do need to change radically, in a tremendous, revolutionary way. It is an obvious fact that we cannot go on as we are. The crisis and the appalling things that are taking place in the world demand that the individual approach all these problems from a totally different point of view, with a totally different heart and mind. That is why I must understand how to bring about in myself this radical change. And I see that I can change only when I am undoing what I have known. The disentangling of the mind from knowledge is in itself a radical change, because then the mind is humble; and that very humility brings about an action which is totally new. As long as the mind is acquiring, comparing, thinking in terms of the 'more', it is obviously incapable of action which is new. And can I who am envious, acquisitive, change completely, so that my mind is no longer acquiring, comparing, competing? To put it differently, can my mind empty itself, and in that very process of emptying itself discover the action which is new?

So, is it possible to bring about a fundamental change which is not the outcome of an action of will, which is not merely the result of influence, pressure? Change based on influence, pressure, on an action of will, is no change at all. That is obvious if you go into it. And if I feel the necessity of a complete, radical change within myself, I must surely inquire into the process of knowledge, which forms the center from which all experience takes place. Do you understand? There is a center in each one of us which is the result of experience, of knowledge, of memory, and according to that center we act, we "change"; and the very undoing of that center, the very dissolution of that 'me', of that self, of that process of accumulation, brings about a radical change. But that demands the hard work which is involved in self-knowledge.

I must know myself as I am, not as I think I should be; I must know myself as the center from which I am acting, from which I am thinking, the center which is made up of accumulated knowledge, of assumptions, of past experience, all of which is preventing an inward revolution, a radical transformation of myself. And as we have so many complexities in the world at the present time, with so many superficial changes going on, it is necessary that there should be this radical change in the individual, for it is only the individual, and not the collective, that can bring about a new world.

Looking at all this, is it possible for you and me as two individuals to change, not superficially, but radically, so that there is the dissolution of that center from which all vanity, all sense of authority springs, that center which actively accumulates, that center which is made up of knowledge, experience, memory?

This is a question that cannot be answered verbally. I put it only in order to awaken your thinking, your inquiry, so that you will start on the journey alone. Because you cannot start on this journey with the help of another, you cannot have a guru to tell you what to do, what to seek. If you are told, then you are no longer on this journey. But can you not start on this journey of inquiry alone, without the accumulation of knowledge which prevents further inquiry? In order to inquire, the mind must be free of knowledge. If there is any pressure behind the inquiry, then the inquiry is not straight, it becomes crooked, and that is why it is so essential to have a mind that is really humble, a mind that says, "I do not know, I will inquire," and that never gathers in the process of inquiring. The moment you gather, you have a center, and that center always influences your inquiry.

So, can the mind inquire without accumulating, without gathering, without emphasizing the center through the authority of knowledge? And if it can, then what is the state of such a mind? Do you understand? What is the state of the mind that is really inquiring? Surely, its state is that of emptiness.

I do not know if you have ever experienced what it is to be completely alone, without any pressure, without any motive or influence, without the idea of the past and the future. To be completely alone is entirely different from loneliness. There is loneliness when the center of accumulation feels cut off in its relations with another. I am not talking of that feeling of loneliness. I am talking of the aloneness in which the mind is not contaminated because it has understood the process of contamination, which is accumulation. And when the mind is totally alone because through self-knowledge it has understood the center of accumulation, then you will find that, being empty, uninfluenced, the mind is capable of action which is not related to ambition, to envy, or to any of the conflicts that we know. Such a mind, being indifferent in the sense that it is not seeking a result, is capable of living with compassion. But such a state of mind is not to be acquired, it is not to be developed. It comes into being through self-knowledge, through knowing yourself—not some enormous, greater self, but the little self that is envious, greedy, petty, angry, vicious. What is necessary is to know the whole of the mind which is your little self. To go very far, you must begin very near, and the near is you, the 'you' that you must understand. And as you begin to understand, you will see that there is a dissolution of knowledge so that the mind becomes totally alert, aware, empty, without that center, and only such a mind is capable of receiving that which is truth.

Question: I am a student. Before I heard you, I was keen about my studies and making a good career for myself. But now it all seems so futile, and I have completely lost interest in my studies and in a career. What you say seems very attractive, but it is impossible to attain. All this has left me very confused. What am I to do?

KRISHNAMURTI: Sir, have I made you confused? Have I made you see that what you are doing is futile? If I have been the cause of your confusion, then you are not confused because when I go away, you will revert to your former confusion or your clarity. But if this questioner is serious, then what has actually taken place is that by listening to what has been said here he has awakened himself to his own activities; he now sees that what he is doing, studying to build up a career for the future, is rather empty, without much significance. So he says, "What am I to do?" He is confused, not because I have made him confused, but because by listening he has become aware of the world situation, and of his own condition and relationship with the world. He has become aware of the futility, the uselessness of all this business of building up a future career. He has become aware of it; I have not made him aware.

Sir, I think this is the first thing to realize: that by listening, by watching, by observing your own activities, you have made this discovery for yourself; therefore, it is yours, not mine. If it were mine, I would take it away with me when I go. But this is something that cannot be taken away by another because it has been realized by you. You have watched yourself in action, you have observed your own life, and you now see that to build up a career for the future is a futile thing. So, being confused, you say, "What am I to do?"

What are you to do, actually? You have to go on with your studies, have you not? That is obvious, because you have to have some kind of profession, a right means of livelihood. Do you understand? Please do listen to this, sirs. You have to earn a livelihood through a right means. And law is obviously not a right means because it maintains society as it is—a society which is based on acquisitiveness, on greed, on envy, on authority and exploitation, and which is therefore in turmoil within itself. So law is not the profession for a man who is at all serious in religious matters, nor can he become a policeman or a soldier. Soldiering is obviously a profession of killing, and there is no difference between defense and offense. A soldier is prepared to kill, and the function of a general is to prepare for war.

So, if those three are not right professions, then what are you to do? You have to think it out, have you not? You have to find out for yourself what you really want to do, and not rely on your father, on your grandmother, on some professor, or on anybody else to tell you what to do. And what does it mean to find out what you really want to do? It means finding out what you love to do, does it not? When you love what you are doing, you are not ambitious, you are not greedy, you are not seeking fame because that very love of what you are doing is totally sufficient in itself. In that love there is no frustration because you are no longer seeking fulfillment.

But you see, all this demands a great deal of thinking, a great deal of inquiry, meditation, and unfortunately the pressure of the world is very strong—the world being your parents, your grandparents, the society around you. They all want you to be a successful man, they want you to fit into the established pattern, so they educate you to conform. But the whole structure of society is based on acquisitiveness, on envy, on ruthless self-assertion, on the aggressive activity of each one of us; and if you see for yourself, actually and not theoretically, that such a society must inevitably rot from within, then you will find your own way of action through doing what you love to do. It may produce a conflict with the present society—and why not? A religious man, or the man who is seeking truth, is in revolt against the society which is based essentially on respectability, acquisitiveness, and the ambitious search for power. He is not in conflict with society, but society is in conflict with him. Society can never accept him. Society can only make him a saint and worship him—and thereby destroy him.

So the student who has been listening is now confused. But if he does not escape from that confusion by running off to the cinema, by going to a temple, by reading a book, or by turning to a guru, and realizes how his confusion has arisen; if he faces that confusion and in the process of inquiry does not conform to the pattern of society, then he will be a truly religious man. And such religious men are necessary, for it is they who will bring about a new world.

Question: To you the observation of thought or feeling within consciousness seems to be a state of complete objectivity. How is this possible? Can you separate a thought or a feeling from the matrix of thought?

KRISHNAMURTI: Let me explain the question as far as I understand it. Thought is part of consciousness; thinking, feeling, is part of the mind. What we think and feel—the contradictions, the tensions, the ambitions, the greed, the aspirations, the desire to be powerful, the fulfillment and frustration—is all within the field which we call consciousness.

Consciousness is like a single piece of cloth, and the questioner asks me, "How can you separate one thought or one feeling from this complex field of consciousness and examine it objectively, go right to the end of it without any distortion? Is that possible?"

Now, you will find out whether it is possible or not by listening to what I am going to explain. The explanation is merely verbal, but we are going into the problem together, and this is meditation, real meditation, and therefore it is hard work. It requires enormous attention to separate one thought, or one feeling, and pursue it until it is understood, dissolved, without letting any other thought or feeling, any other pressure interfere. And can we do it? It is like following a single thread in a large piece of cloth from the beginning right through to the end of it. Have you ever tried it? To follow that thread demands not only visual attention but the attention of your mind and heart, of your whole being; otherwise, you will lose it. And what we are now going to do is like that; it requires hard work, close attention—not the attention of narrowness, not the concentration which is exclusion, but an objectivity of following in which there is an awareness of everything. I do not know if you follow all this. No, I am afraid you don't.

Sirs, I am going to approach it in another way. There is a feeling, and a feeling is a thought as well as a desire. Desire, feeling, and thought are not separate units, they are interrelated, and therefore they are extraordinarily vital. They are a living thing, and my attention must be equally living, vital, to follow them.

So, can I look at a desire, at a thought, at a feeling, and go to the very end of it? Let us take the desire, the feeling, the thought which we term *envy*. Envy is not merely the jealousy you feel because your neighbor is more beautiful than you are, or has a bigger house. That is only part of envy. Envy is the desire for the 'more', for more knowledge, more experience; it is the sense of comparison which says, "I am this and I must become that." Envy is the feeling of 'becoming': becoming virtuous, becoming noble, becoming a saint, achieving enlightenment. All that is envy.

Now, we are going to follow envy as you would follow a thread in the cloth. Envy is in operation; it is a living thing, so I must pay complete attention, not only at the superficial, conscious level, but also at the unconscious level, because the unconscious, with all its traditional and racial inheritance, is based on envy. I have been taught to achieve, to fulfill, to become, and all that is part of envy. So, can I follow envy step by step in myself, objectively, and see what its relationship is to the whole? And can I also examine it by itself?

I hope this is not too difficult or abstract. It is not, really, because if the mind is to be free of envy, it has to go through all this. And the mind must be free of envy because if it is envious, there can be no understanding of truth. The understanding of truth requires humility, and as long as the mind is envious, as long as it wants to become a governor, an executive, a banker, a Master, or what you will, it is not humble.

So, can your mind, which is the matrix in which all thought-feeling is held, separate the one feeling of envy and pursue it? You know what it is to be envious. I have described it, and it is what you are. Though you may not acknowledge it, though you may find excuses for it, you are envious. That is obvious. And can you pursue that feeling of envy right to the end? We are going to do it as I talk, so please follow this.

I am fully conversant with the fact that I am envious; there is no excuse. I do not justify or condemn it. There it is. It is as factual as this microphone and is observed as objectively. So my mind has separated that feeling, that desire which it has termed envy, and is capable of watching it in action. That is, my mind is aware of its envy when it sees a car, or a beautiful person, or a man who is erudite; therefore, it is able to observe the absurdity of becoming and follow all the implications of envy.

Now, can my mind be without comparison? Can it function without the thought of the 'more' and yet not vegetate? Most of us say, "If I do not compete, learn, struggle to become something, I shall vegetate, I shall go to pieces, disintegrate." But my question now is: Can my mind be without envy, without the struggle to become something, and yet be extraordinarily active, very alert?

I see how my mind has always operated on this thought, this feeling, this desire which it calls envy. My mind invariably approaches it with condemnation or justification. But I now see that if I want to understand something, there must be no condemnation, no justification; so condemnation and justification have ceased. I also see that by naming the feeling, giving it the term envy, I am condemning it, because that very word envy is condemnatory.

So, can my mind separate the word from the feeling? Is that possible? Because the moment the mind has a feeling, that feeling is immediately named. If you observe, you will see that the feeling and the naming are almost simultaneous. And the real part of meditation is for the mind to separate the word from the feeling—which is hard work, it demands close attention—so that the feeling remains without the verbalization.

You verbalize a feeling in order to recognize it, and for various other reasons. Naming it establishes the feeling in the mind, which is the process of recognition; therefore, by recognition, the new feeling has become the old feeling. A feeling is always new, but we verbalize it in order to establish it in the old, in order to recollect and communicate it. But we won't go into all that now.

So I now have the feeling, the desire, the thought which is called envy, separated from the matrix of all thoughts. I see the implications of envy, both inwardly and socially. Then I see how extraordinarily difficult it is for the mind to free the naming from the feeling because they are practically simultaneous. So, is it possible for the mind to separate the word from the feeling? And if it is, then what happens to the feeling when this is done? If the mind no longer identifies that feeling with a word, the feeling does not remain; then there is a totally different kind of movement in that feeling.

Most of us know a feeling only through the process of verbalization and recognition. By recognition we either put an end to that feeling, or we give it a continuity. If it is a pleasurable feeling we say, "How nice, I want more of it," but if it is ugly, we condemn it. Whereas, if we do not name either the pleasurable feeling or the ugly feeling, then there is only the feeling—and that is essential because it is by pursuing the pleasurable and denying the ugly that the mind becomes insensitive, incapable of feeling. And it is this feeling, this impulse which is not related to verbalization, that is new.

I wonder if you have ever noticed that every feeling is new if you do not term it. It is the naming of the feeling that makes the feeling old, and then you have destroyed the impulse. The impulse is the new, but it is made old by recognizing, by naming.

Sirs, as I said, this is a very difficult thing to do. When you go home, experiment by taking a piece of cloth and seeing if you can follow one thread to the end; follow it not merely visually, but with all your attention. Try it and you will see how very difficult it is.

Similarly, it is extraordinarily hard work for the mind to follow one thought, one feeling, one desire right to the end without distortion, without any deviation because, as I was explaining earlier in the talk, it is knowledge as the word that destroys the new. The word, which is knowledge, is the old; and the moment you recognize a feeling, you have already made it into the old because to recognize is to name it. You cannot recognize something unless you have already known it. When there is a feeling, the mind immediately labels it, and so makes that feeling into the old. But if you do not name it—and not to name a feeling is astonishingly difficult, it is really hard work and demands great attention, meditation, tremendous alertness—then you will see that the feeling is entirely new; it is not to be recognized, and a feeling which is new has its own movement, its own activity. So the mind is capable of separating one thought, one feeling, one desire from the matrix of consciousness.

February 24, 1957

Sixth Talk in Bombay

I think it would be a waste of time and utterly futile if we merely listened to all these talks either to refute or to accept intellectually any statements that are made. But if we can directly experience what is being said, that is, if one is able to follow the operations of one's own mind, then I think these talks will be really worthwhile. Because we are concerned not with abstractions and idealizations but with ordinary daily living, with all its sorrows, pains, and pleasures; and it seems to me that what is important is to bring about, sanely and rationally, a radical change in our daily existence, and that merely to cling to theories, to ideologies, or make intellectual assertions is utterly futile and has no value at all in a world that demands on the part of each individual a direct, responsible action. To bring about a radical change in our daily living, we must surely understand the whole process of 'becoming' as distinct from 'being'.

All our thinking and activity is based on becoming, is it not? I am using that word *becoming* very simply, not philosophically, but in the ordinary sense of wanting to become something either in this world or in the so-called spiritual world. If we can understand this process of wanting to become something, then I think we shall have understood what sorrow is, because it is the desire to become that gives to the mind the soil in which sorrow can grow. And as our lives, with rare moments of happiness, are filled with anguish, sorrow, pain, fear, with every form of conscious and unconscious conflict, I think it is important to understand this whole issue of 'becoming'.

In our desire to become, we give importance to secondary things like politics, social reform, ideologies, and to the various forms of organized religion which offer comfort through the process of 'becoming'. After all, that is what we are doing, is it not? We are struggling to become something, either politically or socially, outwardly or inwardly. We have never a moment when there is no 'becoming' and only 'being'—that 'being' which is nothing. But that 'being' which is nothing cannot possibly be understood if we do not fully grasp the significance of 'becoming'.

All comparative thinking is a form of 'becoming'. Envy, ambition, and the various kinds of fulfillment with their frustrations, are essentially a process of 'becoming', through which sorrow takes root in the mind. Again, the word *sorrow* is not a philosophical term but one which we all understand, and we cannot be free of sorrow until we understand this process of 'becoming'.

All of us are trying in different ways to become something: more noble, less greedy, nonviolent; we are trying to fulfill ourselves through work, through God, through family, through property, through identification with an idea, and so on. In innumerable ways we are trying to become something, to fulfill ourselves, and I think in this process lies the whole web of sorrow. Being caught in that web we say, "How am I to get rid of sorrow?" We are only concerned with getting rid of sorrow, and we do not understand the process of 'becoming'.

Now, why is it that all of us in different ways have persisted through centuries in this path of 'becoming'? Why does each one of us want to be something? If I am ugly, I want to be beautiful; if I am stupid, I want to be clever; if I am envious, I want to be free from envy. So there is a constant battle between what I am and what I think I should be. The 'should be' is the aim of every person who wants to become, and in this process there is infinite struggle, pain, fear, frustration. And seeing this process, being aware that my mind is caught in the web of sorrow, how am I to be free from sorrow?

When we put that question to ourselves, most of us say, "I must discipline myself against desire, against envy." We don't see that resistance is another form of 'becoming', and that through resistance we are giving importance to secondary issues. That is, being in sorrow, I try in various ways to escape from the pain of sorrow, and in escaping I give importance to secondary issues. The escape, which is the secondary issue, offers a means of fulfillment without eradicating sorrow.

Look at what is happening in the world. Secondary issues—like politics, like social reform, or the identification of oneself with a particular reformatory movement—are assuming primary values in our life. Why? Is it not because they offer to the individual a means of fulfilling himself? That is, they offer a way in which I can become something, though I continue to create sorrow around me and in myself. The urge to become something, this egotistic desire to expand, is so strong, so vital, that it must find ways and means of expressing itself, and that is why the secondary issues dominate our present-day existence.

Every morning the newspapers are full of these secondary issues, and the noise they make drowns out the whisper of the primary, which is something totally different. The primary is the understanding of the not-becoming, of the 'being' which is nothing—that nothing in which truth, reality, God, or what you will, shows itself in its totality. But the mind that is seeking in different ways to become, to fulfill—through memory, through identification with the family, with the country, with an ideology—can never find the other; and without the other, all ideologies, political activities, and reformatory movements only breed further sorrow, further confusion. We don't seem to realize this because we are always concerned with the immediate satisfaction, the immediate fulfillment of ourselves through secondary issues.

So, if we are at all aware of ourselves, we will see how important in our lives certain movements, certain activities, certain ideologies and economic theories have become. And it is important to understand these things as secondary values, for then perhaps we shall approach them with a different feeling, that is, without the desire to become.

There is a religious revolution which takes place in the individual when there is no 'becoming' of any kind, that is, when I inwardly see the fact of what I am without any form of distortion—the fact that I am envious, acquisitive, utterly lacking in humility. If I am aware of the fact of what I am and do not approach it with an opinion, with a judgment, with an evaluation—because opinion, judgment, and evaluation are based on the intention of transforming the fact, which is the desire to become something—then that fact itself brings about a transformation in which there is no 'becoming' at all. To be aware of the fact that one is envious without condemning it is extraordinarily difficult because the very word *envy* has a condemnatory significance. But if you can free the mind from that condemnatory evaluation, if you can be aware of the feeling without identifying the feeling with the word, then you will find that there is no longer the urge to change it into something else. A feeling without verbalization, without evaluation, has no quality of 'becoming'. And you will also find that when there is a feeling without verbalization, there is no desire for its fulfillment. There is a desire for the fulfillment of a feeling only when there is identification of that feeling with a word, with an evaluation.

So it is 'becoming' that gives soil to the root of sorrow, and if you go into it very deeply, really think it out so that the mind frees itself from the whole process of 'becoming', then you will find that you have eliminated sorrow altogether. It is only such a mind that is concerned with the primary, which is reality, and because it is concerned with the primary, its action on the secondary will have its own significance.

Merely to be concerned with the secondary will never lead to the primary. It is like putting a room in order, cleaning and decorating the room, all of which is essential, but it has no meaning without that which comes into the room. Similarly, virtue is essential. A mind that is virtuous, austere, has put itself in order; and the mind must have order, it must have clarity. But order, clarity, humility, austerity, have no significance in themselves; they have significance only because the mind that has them is capable of proceeding without the experiencer who is gathering further experience, and therefore there is no 'becoming' but only 'being'. That is, the mind is completely empty of all ideas based on the experiencer, on the thinker, on the observer who is always 'becoming'. It is only in emptying the mind of this whole process of 'becoming' that there is 'being', which has its own movement unrelated to 'becoming'; and a man who, while 'becoming', seeks that state of 'being', will never find it. The man who is pursuing ambition, fulfillment, who desires to become something, will never find reality, God. He may read all the sacred books, do puja every day, go to all the temples in the world, but sorrow will be his shadow.

So it seems to me very important to understand in oneself this process of 'becoming'—and such understanding is essentially self-knowledge. Self-knowledge is the understanding of 'becoming', which is the 'me'; and without that understanding, the mind can never be empty and hence free to understand the real, which is something totally different. But when there is understanding of the real, then you will find that our social activities, our political actions, our everyday relationships with each other, have an entirely different quality. Then they will not be the soil in which sorrow can grow and flourish.

It is very important, then, for a religious man to understand himself, the 'himself' who is always pursuing the path of 'becoming'; and when, through self-knowledge, 'becoming' ceases—there is within him a religious revolution. This is the only revolution that can bring about a different world in every way—economically, politically, and in our social relationships.

To understand reality, effort is not necessary. Effort exists only when there is a 'becoming', that is, when I use discipline as a means of attainment, of reaching happiness, and hence there is a struggle to achieve, to fulfill, which is a process of resistance. All that is the path of 'becoming', in which there is sorrow; and a man who would understand reality must be free of this path of 'becoming', not verbally or ideologically, but actually. He must understand this whole problem through self-knowledge. When the mind is free from 'becoming', you will find that it has an extraordinary activity of its own, an activity which cannot be verbalized, which cannot be described or communicated to another; and that activity is reality, it is the movement of creation itself.

There are three questions this evening, and as I have explained, I am not going to answer these questions because life has no answers. Life must be lived, and a man who merely sits on the bank wanting to swim, who only asks a question in order to receive an answer, is not living. But if you are living, you will find the answer at every step, and that is why it is very important to understand the problem itself and not seek an answer, a solution to the problem.

Question: Reality has been defined as satyam, shivam, sundaram, *or truth, goodness, and beauty. All religious teachers have stressed truth and goodness. What place has beauty in the experiencing of reality?*

KRISHNAMURTI: Is there a difference between goodness, truth, and beauty? Are they three different things, or really one thing which can be called by these three different names? To understand truth, goodness, or beauty, we have tried to suppress desire, to discipline, control, or find a substitute for desire. Finding that desire is tremendously active, volcanic in its operation, and that it brings extraordinary sorrow, pain, and joy, we say we must be free of desire. That is what all religions have maintained, that we must be free of desire in order to find truth, beauty, goodness; so for centuries we have proceeded to suppress desire; and in the very suppression of desire we have lost sensitivity to goodness, to truth, to beauty.

What is beauty? It is really a very complex question, and books have been written about it. But if you and I, who are simple people, not erudite or scholarly, want to find out what beaufy is, how are we to set about it? How am I to find out what beauty is, not verbally or theoretically, but actually to experience the feeling of that extraordinary thing called beauty?

Most of us know only the beauty that has been made up or put together, do we not? For most of us, beauty is a reaction, a response. And I am asking myself: Is there a feeling which may be termed beauty, goodness, or truth, and which is not a response, not merely a reaction?

I see that tree and I say, "How lovely it is." The tree is something that has been created, and I respond to it. I say it is beautiful and pass by. Similarly, I see that building, which again is something that has been put together, and I say, "How ugly it is." That also is a response. And is beauty merely a response, a reaction to something which has been created? Or is there a state of mind which may be called beauty and which is not the result of a reaction?

After all, our minds are the result of reaction, of challenge and inadequate response to challenge, and therefore there is struggle, there is pain. On this whole process the mind is based, extensively or very narrowly; and when I see a tree, a bird, a nice-looking person, a child, or when I see poverty, squalor, ugly buildings, I say, "How beautiful!" or "How ugly!" depending on my reaction and on the kind of attention I give. When I am fully attentive, in that full attention is there a reaction? And is there attention when there is an object of attention? Do you understand, sirs, or is this too complex? I don't think it is complex if you follow it carefully.

As I have said, attention with an object is no attention at all because the object absorbs you. But if I am fully attentive, with the totality of my being, then in that state is there a reaction? In that state is there what is called the beautiful and the ugly?

After all, there is ideological beauty, the beauty laid down by the ideal, and there is the beauty of experience, the essence of experience. Now, I am asking myself—and I think it is a legitimate question—is there a state in which the mind is fully aware of and understands its own reaction to beauty as well as to ugliness, and does not call it beautiful or ugly because it is giving that complete attention in which there is the totality of experience? And in that state of total attention, is there an entity who says, "I have experienced beauty," or "I have experienced ugliness," or is there only a feeling, an experiencing which is not a reaction, not the result of a cause?

So, can the mind—without losing its sensitivity to the ugliness and to the beauty created by man in a building or in a statue—experience that totality of attention in which it does not create the beautiful and the ugly? Do you understand? Surely, it is only the mind that is in conflict, that is caught up in its own desires, in its own fulfillments and frustrations—it is only such a mind that creates what is called the beautiful and the ugly.

Sirs, as I said, this is a very complex question, and to understand really, not merely verbally, what is beauty or goodness or truth, the mind must be empty of the word and its reaction to that word. Then you will find that there is a totality of experience, and not an experiencer who is experiencing the totality. In that state there is a creativeness which has nothing to do with the creations of the contradictory mind which must find a release through building, through architecture, through the writing of poems, essays, and so on. Listening to all this, you may say, "Are you not talking in order to find release, in order to fulfill?" I don't think so because the truly religious man is not seeking fulfillment. As I explained, fulfillment is the soil in which sorrow grows.

Question: To you, love is the solvent of all human problems. I have no love, and yet I have to live. But love can never be cultivated. Does this mean that my problems can never be solved?

KRISHNAMURTI: We will come to the feeling of what love is if we understand how we live. Most of us want a definition of love, or we seek that state of love which we call universal, cosmic, godly, and all the rest of it, without understanding our daily existence. Don't we know in our daily living any kind of friendliness, kindliness, gentleness? Are we never generous, compassionate? Have we never the feeling of being good to another without motive; have we never a sense of great humility? Are not these the expressions of love? And when you love another, is there not a total feeling in which the 'I' is nonexistent?

What generally happens is that we identify ourselves with another, or with a family, with a nation, with a party or an ideology, and in this identification of ourselves with something, there is an intensity of feeling, of action, but we have not really forgotten ourselves. On the contrary, through identification we have expanded ourselves. The movement, the party, the ideology, the church, or whatever it be with which the mind has identified itself is an extension of the 'I'. The man who has consciously or unconsciously identified himself with something has no love, though he may talk of love. When you talk about loving your country, you don't love the country, which is made up of people, human beings; what you love is the idea of the country with which you have identified yourself, and for which you are willing to kill, to die.

So, when the mind consciously or unconsciously identifies itself with something—with a movement, with a party, with an ideology, with a family, with a religion, with a guru—such a mind is incapable of loving, and I think it is very important to understand this because good people get lost through identification, and they don't see the falseness of it. And if the identification which we call love is not love, then what is love?

Surely, love is the state of mind in which the 'me' has no importance. To love is to be friendly. Do you understand, sirs? When you love, you have no enmity, you cause no enmity. And you do cause enmity when you belong to religions, to countries, to political parties. When you have a great deal of land, immense wealth, while others have little or nothing, you cause enmity, though you may go to temples, or build temples with your wealth. You have no friendliness when you are seeking position, power, prestige.

Yes, you will all nod your heads and agree with me, but you are going to pursue your ancient ways; and the tragedy is not that you have no love but that you have no understanding of the ways of your own life; you do not see the significance of the way you are actually living. If you understood that, really felt it, then you would be generous. Surely, the generosity of the hand and of the heart is the beginning of friendliness, and where there is friendliness, there is no need for justice by law. Where there is friendliness, there is goodness, a compassion without motive. You have been friendly occasionally, when you were not thinking about yourself, when you were not so concerned about your own country, your own problems. And when you go beyond all that, there comes something entirely different—a state in which the mind is compassionate and yet indifferent.

We know indifference in the sense of detachment, which is the result of calculation; it is an act thought out by the mind in order to protect itself from pain. We also know the indifference of a mind which says, "I have been through a great deal of pain, misery, and now I am going to be indifferent." Again, that is an action of will. But I am talking of an indifference which is totally unrelated to the intellectual indifference brought about by a mind that wishes to resist pain. There is an indifference which is the outcome of compassion; the mind is compassionate, and yet indifferent. Have you ever felt that way? When you see something in pain, you help it, and yet you are indifferent in the very process of helping. But what is it that we generally do? We feel compassionate because we see suffering, and we want to change things, bring about a reform, so we are full of action; but the mind is so bent on producing a result that it loses the sense of compassion.

So, if you observe yourself, the functioning of your own mind, you will find that all these things exist in your daily life. You know moments of compassion, moments of love, of generosity, but they are very rare. All our calculated actions are based on this process of becoming something important, and only the mind that is free from 'becoming' can know that love which is the solvent of our many problems.

Question: If, as you say, God or reality is beyond the mind, then has God any relationship to my everyday life?

KRISHNAMURTI: Sir, what is our everyday life, not theoretically or ideologically, but actually? It is confused, miserable, ambitious, envious, stupid, is it not? We quote a lot of books containing the experiences of others about which we know nothing; we repeat what we have been taught; we struggle, suffer, and occasionally there is a movement of joy which is gone before we can feel the depth of it. That is our life: a vain process of lying, cheating, trying to become something important, struggling to dominate, to suppress. And do you think such a life has anything to do with reality, with goodness, with beauty, with God, with something which is not man-made? Yet, knowing what our daily life is, we want to bring that reality into it, so we go to temples, we read the sacred books, we talk about God, we say that we are seeking salvation, and so on. We want to bring that immensity, that which is measureless, into the measurable. And is such a thing possible?

Do you see how the mind deceives itself? Can you bring the unknown, that which cannot be experienced, into the conditioned, into the realm of the known? Obviously not. So don't try it. Don't try to find God, truth, for it has no meaning. All you can do is to observe the operation of your own mind, which is the area of conflict, misery, suffering, ambition, fulfillment, frustration. That you can understand, and its narrow borders can be broken down. But you are not interested in that. You want to capture God and put Him in the cage of what you know, the cage you call the temple, the book, the guru, the system, and with that you are satisfied. By doing that you think you are becoming very religious. You are not. You are just hypocrites, robbing, cheating, lying within the cage.

So, a man who is aware of all this is not concerned with reality, with the immeasurable, the unknowable; he is concerned with the ending of envy, with the ending of sorrow, with the ending of this whole process of 'becoming'. That you can do—you can do it every day by being alert to your envy, watchful of the way you talk, the way you show respect which is no respect, the way you acquire, accumulate. Through self-knowledge the mind can liberate itself from its limitations, its conditioning, and this liberating of itself from conditioning is meditation. Do not try to meditate on reality because you cannot; that is an impossibility. Meditation on God has no meaning. How can a mind which is conditioned, small, petty, envious, meditate on something unknowable? All the mind can do is to free itself from the known—the known of everything that you have been taught, of your ambitions, your identifications, your greeds. Freeing the mind from the memory of all this is meditation. And when the mind is free, then you will find that there comes an extraordinary quietness, a stillness in which there is no experiencer who is always measuring, remembering, calculating, desiring. Then the mind is aware of something totally different, a state which is in itself a blessing, which has within itself a movement that has no center and therefore no beginning and no ending. A mind that is capable of this total attention without the entity who is experiencing what is taking place will find there is a reality, a goodness, a beauty which is not a reaction, which is not an opposite, which is without a cause, and is therefore something in itself. But the realization of that immensity cannot come about unless the mind is totally empty of the known.

March 3, 1957

Questions

Stockholm, 1956

1. We Swedes do not as a rule like to tackle the problems of life only with the mind, leaving the emotions aside. Is it possible to solve any problem only with the mind, or only by the emotions? 4
2. Juvenile delinquency is increasing. What is the reason and what is the remedy? 4
3. Can one live in the world without ambition? Does it not isolate us to be without ambition? 5
4. Does suffering ultimately lead one to inward peace and awareness? 8
5. Why do you go about the world giving talks? Is it for self-fulfillment, or is it because you think you can help people in that way? 8
6. I have read an American book which certainly seems to prove through hypnosis that reincarnation is a fact. What comment will you make on this? 9
7. Can we reach an understanding of ourselves other than by conscious effort? 13
8. Is it possible for any of us, who are living in this particular society, to bring about the change of which you are talking? 13
9. A man has a right to go his own way, and if he does so, will not this change come about? 13
10. You say that in order to bring about a change we must understand the background. Do you mean by this that we must understand reincarnation and karma? 14
11. I think it is rather important to know what we mean by seeing and watching. You have said that there is no motive or center, but only a process. How can a process watch another process? 14
12. If anyone wishes to find freedom along the lines you have spoken of, is it not also necessary for that person to renounce the church or whatever other religious organizations he is taking an interest in? 15
13. Can you tell us more clearly what it is you mean by consciousness? 18
14. Is it possible for the ordinary person to come to this freedom without special training and knowledge? 18
15. One finds that one makes the same mistakes repeatedly. Are there those who have been able to break this pattern? 19
16. Would you kindly explain what you mean by negative thinking? 19

17. Would you please give us some practical way of getting free from our conditioned minds? You say that any particular training, such as yoga or other spiritual exercises, only makes us slaves, but I still think we have to use some kind of method. You say that to have this freedom, we must devote our lives to it, but how are we to do this without a method or a system? 19
18. To observe is to be free already, and to understand is also to be free—if I have understood you rightly. So it seems to be a real problem to know how to begin. 21
19. Experience which is in the deepest conformity with our innermost wishes will, I think, help us to free our minds. I personally have found that fasting and the vegetarian way of living are helping me to free my mind. When the stomach is empty, the mind is set free. Should one give up such experience? 22
20. I think that, living in this world of time and space, it is impossible to escape from experience. If we fight against our experiences, or cling to them, then they leave a hardened residue in the mind. But I think it is possible to go through experiences and still keep oneself absolutely free. I have done something like this myself. If one does not fix one's position in an experience but just allows it to pass over one like a wave, then something happens—one will be changed and one will be free. 22
21. It seems fairly clear that when we are caught in a certain experience, the mind is not free. But when we live, as it were, in the dance of experience, then experience brings us to a point where we look at things differently and the mind has a chance to be free. 23
22. I can follow you to the extent of seeing that it is a hindrance to accumulate knowledge for the sake of knowledge, and I also see the futility of disciplines, methods, and of striving for more and more sensation. But I cannot understand why you say we must not collect any experiences. You yourself must have had many experiences, for you have traveled and given lectures for over thirty years. You say we should free ourselves from religions, dogmas, and conventional biases. To do that we must know the structure of society, and we cannot get to know that structure without a great deal of penetrating personal experience, such as you certainly have had. 23
23. But without a center which accumulates memories, I would be lost; I would not even know where I lived. Surely it is right to remember and store up memories; otherwise, how can I live? 24
24. If we can reason freely, we may be able to find a way of freeing our minds from the conclusions which lead us in the wrong direction. The fact that we have flags shows that we are on the wrong path; we think as Swedes instead of as human beings. Perhaps it will free us if we can ask; will this deed, which is the result of my thinking, benefit those among whom I live, or will it not? 25
25. All that I can do with a conclusion is to become aware of it, to question it; and when I do that, I find that I do not know. 25
26. I think one must begin by discovering a means. 26
27. One can learn to accept oneself. 27
28. Truth will make us free. 27
29. We must be able to conquer envy by some sort of feeling of brotherhood. 27
30. If we understand our envy, we see how it inhibits us. 27

31. We must try to look at envy very calmly when it comes into our minds, and not hope too much to get rid of it. 28

32. Is this not the main difficulty, that we never really meet envy? We are envious, but we do not see our envy, actually. We can help our children to be free of it. 28

33. How would it be if one studied one's needs and tried to reduce them? 28

34. I think we must accept envy and give it its right place in our lives. If we can see, without condemning it, that envy does not lead anywhere, we shall get rid of it. Perhaps envy is based on fear. If we could believe in ourselves as individuals, then we would not have to be envious. 28

35. If I dwell in the self, it is not possible. But by meditating every day I can find out that the self has no value, and be free from envy. If we could live in the now, we should not be attracted by what happened yesterday or what will happen tomorrow. We must know that we are envious and live with it, feel it in every cell, and then this envy will absorb itself and something will suddenly happen. 28

36. Who are we that we should think we can get rid of envy? After all, life has made us envious. We can try to be a little less envious, but even if we do not achieve that aim, life will still go on for many more years. 28

37. When you speak of the mind being free, what do you mean by *mind?* 29

38. If I know I am envious and I look at it without any condemnation, would that not be a way to be free of it? We tried to find out yesterday how to be free of experience and of conclusions. Can we leave envy for a moment and go into the question of what it is to be free? If there is a center, what is it? Is it a spark of God? And is not God free? What does it mean to be free? 29

Brussels, 1956

1. Is not authority helpful in this world of chaos and confusion? 35

2. Will you please tell us what freedom is? Is this not an illusion which we are all pursuing? 36

3. Is there such a thing as real happiness? Can anyone ever find it, or is our pursuit of it an illusion? 40

4. You seem to deny yoga. Do you think it has no value at all? 41

5. How is it possible to live in this world without any kind of security? 42

6. Although what you say seems to be of the highest religious quality, you do not lay down any mode of conduct. Why don't you do this? Most of us definitely need one. 48

7. What is the fundamental difference between the materialistic and the religious concept of life? 49

8. How is it possible to free oneself from psychological dependence on others? 52

9. Does awareness mean a state of freedom, or merely a process of observation? 53

10. When we dream, do we enter the collective unconscious? Are the dreams symbolic of our psychological state and therefore a useful guide? 54

11. You talked yesterday of mediocrity. I realize my own mediocrity, but how am I to break through it? 58

12. How are we to put an end to man's cruelty towards animals in the form of vivisection, slaughterhouses, and so on? 59

13. What is death, and why is there such fear of it? 60
14. What are your ideas about education? 64
15. What is the meaning of existence? What is it all about? 65
16. Do you believe in God? 66

Hamburg, 1956

1. We are full of memories of the last war, with all its terror. Can we ever free our minds of the past and start anew? 72
2. We have had enough of war. We want peace. How can we prevent a new war? 73
3. You said yesterday that authority is evil. Why is it evil? 77
4. Why do you put so much emphasis on self-knowledge? We know very well what we are. 78
5. You say that true religion is neither belief nor dogma nor ceremonies. What then is true religion? 79
6. Crime among young people is spreading everywhere. What can we do about it? 83
7. If we transform ourselves and become peaceful, while others do not transform themselves but remain aggressive and brutal, are we not inviting them to attack and violate us as helpless victims? 83
8. You say the mind must be quiet, but it is always busy, night and day. How can I change it? 84
9. Are yogic exercises helpful in any way to human beings? 88
10. A well-known author has written a great deal about the use of certain drugs which enable man to arrive at some visionary experience of union with the divine ground. Are those experiences helpful in finding that state of which you speak? 89
11. Is our life predetermined, or is the way of life to be freely chosen? 90
12. Will awareness free us, as you suggest, from our undesirable qualities? 90
13. Most of us are caught up in and are bored with the routine of our work, but our livelihood depends on it. Why can we not be happy in our work? 95
14. You reject discipline and outward order and suggest that we should act only by inner impulse. Will this not add to the great instability of people and encourage the following of irresponsible urges, especially among the youth of our time, who only want to enjoy themselves and are already drifting? 96
15. What happens after death? And do you believe in reincarnation? 97
16. You talk so much against the church and organized religion. Have they not done a lot of good in this world? 102
17. Will self-knowledge put an end to suffering, which apparently necessitates the soul taking birth over and over again? 103
18. Is it possible to influence the thinking of mankind in the right direction by suitable thoughts and meditation? 104

Athens, 1956

1. What makes up a problem? And is any problem solved by dissecting it and finding its cause? 110

2. Psychoanalysts offer the panacea of analysis, asserting that by just knowing what it is all about, one is cured, but this does not always hold true. What is one to do when in spite of knowing the cause of one's trouble, one is still unable to get rid of it? 114
3. What would happen to the world if all men and women were to arrive at a state so far removed from attachment to a definite person that marriage and love affairs became unnecessary? 115
4. How is one to deal with a very small child if one is to avoid influencing him in any way? 115
5. Is it possible to live without any attachment? 116
6. In what way can self-knowledge help to solve the many pressing problems of the world—for instance, starvation? 118
7. If a man has no ambition, how is he to live in this world of competition? 119
8. What is the real meaning of brotherhood? 119
9. Should one give any importance to one's dreams or not? 119

New Delhi, 1956

1. I read in the newspaper today your statement that to solve man's problems, what is needed is not an economic or social revolution but a religious revolution. What do you mean by religious revolution? 125
2. You seem to be against the very essence of authority. Is not the acceptance of authority inevitable in our individual lives? Without it would not society be reduced to chaos? 126
3. People well versed in the Hindu scriptures say that *sadhana* is essential for *mukti.* Vinoba Bhaveji has said that what you speak of as freedom cannot be the same as *mukti* because you do not seem to believe in *sadhana.* 131
4. What is habit? There are certain needs which are fundamental, and others which are based on the psychological memory of pleasure. Does this mean that one should indulge, or not indulge, depending on whether the need is fundamental or based on memory? 133
5. You often use the term *understanding* in connection with the dissolution of problems. What exactly do you mean by understanding? 138
6. You said the other day that one has to see the totality of a problem to comprehend it. What is it that enables one to see the problem in its entirety? 139
7. In the process of thinking, one has to draw on one's knowledge and experience. Are you not doing the same? Then why do you condemn knowledge and experience? 144
8. We find the need for discipline even in our daily living. Is not discipline necessary for the proper education of the young? 146
9. Sleep is a period of rest for both the mind and the body. What is it that actuates dreams? 150
10. We all have moments of inward clarity, but we seem unable to relate these glimpses of light to our personal, national, and international problems. Unless we can establish a relationship between clarity and action, of what value is this clarity? 152

11. Our most constant fear throughout life is the fear of death. Are we afraid of dying because we do not want to part with life, or because we do not know what lies beyond? 153
12. I entirely agree with you that it is necessary to uncondition one's mind. But how can a conditioned mind uncondition itself? 157
13. How can I experience God, which will give a meaning to my weary life? Without that experience, what is the purpose of living? 159
14. I have practiced meditation most earnestly for twenty-five years, and I am still unable to go beyond a certain point. How am I to proceed further? 160

Madras, 1956

1. Though political leaders, social reformers, and the various holy men are everlastingly denouncing it, exploitation continues to exist in human affairs, from the topmost government official to the illiterate drudge of the village. You too have preached against it for thirty years. How do you envisage action in which there is no exploitation? 167
2. There is action as legislation at the governmental level; there is action as reform at the level of Gandhiji and Vinobaji, and there is action according to the various types of religious teachers. It seems to me that all these forms of action are pulling in different directions, and that the individual, being enticed by the promises which each one offers, is caught in conflict within himself. What do you consider to be right action, which will not produce this contradiction? 173
3. Is not a certain amount of disciplinary training necessary to understand what you are teaching? 180
4. Most of us seem to be after so many things—sex, position, power, and so on—which promise a sense of happiness and fulfillment, but which bring with them all kinds of frustration and suffering. Is this inevitable? 181
5. Is friendship prevented by spreading justice, which is to organize society on an equitable basis? Can the organization of a society with equal opportunities for all lead to that sense of compassion which will ultimately put an end to governmental intermeddling in our personal lives? 187
6. Tradition, ideals, and a certain sense of social morality used to keep mediocre people like me occupied in a righteous manner, but such things no longer have any meaning to most of us. How are we to break through our mediocrity? 189
7. You were born in a village of very poor environment, and you say that you have never studied the scriptures. What good karma has brought you to this liberation? 190
8. My son and others who have been abroad seem to have had the moral fiber knocked out of them. How does this happen, and what can we do to develop their character? 195

Colombo, 1957

1. Like many of my valued friends, I am an ardently religious Sinhalese Buddhist, and I feel intensely for our religion and our culture. But unfortunately, in furthering our religion and our culture, I see that we are unconsciously getting divided into opposing parties. What would you advise me to do? 200
2. In Ceylon we have various religions, but some priests incite their followers to hate those belonging to other religions, which creates serious trouble among the people in general. What is the true function of a priest? 201
3. What is the religious life? Is it compatible with the struggle for existence which most of us have to face? Is the religious life necessary at all? 206
4. To me the greatest fear is the fear of death. How am I to get over this fear? 208
5. You say that the mind will be free when the thinking process ceases. Hinduism and Buddhism advocate various practices towards this end. What method do you advocate? 213
6. You say that the conditioning of the mind, with which we approach all our problems, breeds conflict and prevents the understanding of truth. How can the mind be unconditioned? 215
7. Is it not desirable to revive the great religions and the glorious cultures associated with them, since in their pure form they have helped many people towards the spiritual life? 216
8. What is understanding? Is it awareness? Is it right thinking? If understanding does not come about through the functioning of the mind, then what is the function of the mind? 219
9. According to the theory of karma, in which many of us believe, our actions and circumstances in this life are largely governed by what we did in our past lives. Do you deny that we are governed by our karma? What about our duties and responsibilities? 221
10. Religions have prescribed certain practices in meditation for one's spiritual growth. What practice do you advocate? Can right meditation be helpful in one's daily life? 227

Bombay, 1957

1. All religions teach the need of curbing the senses. Are the senses a hindrance to the discovery of truth? 235
2. When you talk of freedom from the past, do you mean that an individual's past with all its experiences, memories, sorrows, and joys, can be wiped away totally? Can the mind then have an existence without the past? 236
3. I have done something wrong and sinful, and it has left me with a terrible feeling of guilt. How am I to get over this feeling? 243
4. How can I be sensitive when I am tortured by desire? 244
5. Thought is the seed which contains within it the beginning and the ending, the totality of time. This seed quickens and germinates in the darkness of the mind. What action is possible to burn away this seed? 249

6. In your last talk you finally conceded the essential need of discipline, but you complicated the issue by saying that this necessary discipline was the discipline of total attention. Please explain. 255
7. Day follows day, with old age and death coming inexorably nearer. I listen to you, but the anguish of the approaching end does not diminish. Teach me to face old age and death with equanimity. 258
8. I am a student. Before I heard you I was keen about my studies and making a good career for myself. But now it all seems so futile, and I have completely lost interest in my studies and in a career. What you say seems very attractive, but it is impossible to attain. All this has left me very confused. What am I to do? 262
9. To you the observation of thought or feeling within consciousness seems to be a state of complete objectivity. How is this possible? Can you separate a thought or a feeling from the matrix of thought? 263
10. Reality has been defined as *satyam, shivam, sundaram,* or truth, goodness, and beauty. All religious teachers have stressed truth and goodness. What place has beauty in the experiencing of reality? 269
11. To you, love is the solvent of all human problems. I have no love, and yet I have to live. But love can never be cultivated. Does this mean that my problems can never be solved? 270
12. If, as you say, God or reality is beyond the mind, then has God any relationship to my everyday life? 271

Index

Abandonment: and reality, 249; and self-knowledge, 251
Accumulation: and awareness, 53; and the center, 23–24; and the creation of patterns, 64; and emptiness, 30; and experience, 51; and exploitation, 168–69; as hindrance to learning, 212; and knowledge, 172–73, 260–62; as memory, 21; and the petty mind, 157; and security, 87; and self-knowledge, 59; versus the sensitive mind, 152; versus truth, 243. *See also* Mind; Past
Acquisitiveness: and career, 263; as hindrance to truth, 3. *See also* Ambition; 'Becoming'
Action: and cause and effect, 222; and the center, 178–80; and change, 137; and comparison, 188; and the desire to do "good", 46; as fragmentary, 232–33, 234; and thinking, 221; as thought, 260. *See also* Total action
Active of will: as desire, 57–58; and discipline, 247
Activity: divisions of, 174
Actual. *See* Fact
Adjustment: and change, 135–36. *See also* Conformity; Discipline
Agreement: understanding, 157–58
Aloneness: and discovery of the truth, 171, 173; and experiencing reality,130; and the free mind, 114, 167; as incorruptible, 109; versus isolated, 5; versus loneliness, 262. *See also* Occupied mind; Quiet mind
Ambition: as compassionless, 202; and the contradiction of religion, 239–41; and daily life, 207; as destructive, 116; effects of, 5–6; and fear, 132–33; and the feeling of nothingness, 119; freedom from, 8; as hindrance to freedom, 126; and identity, 45; and the need for change, 46; as path to war, 45; and society, 130; and war, 74. *See also* 'Becoming'; Comparison; Envy; 'More'
Americans. *See* Conditioning; Divisions; Ideology; Nationalism; Society; War
Analysis: and the free mind, 26–27
Analyzer and the analyzed: as one, 114. *See also* Thinker and the thought
Animals: cruelty to, 59–60
Answers: futility of search for, 35, 199; as hindrance to the problem, 173; and the problem, 124. *See also* Listening
Assumptions: as hindrance, 166–67; and the occupied mind, 157. *See also* Comparison
Atma: and conditioning, 158; and 'me', 140; as oversoul, 142, 143
Attachment: freedom from, 116; versus freedom from possessiveness, 115
Attention: and achieving understanding, 85; as approach to problems, 72; versus discipline, 181, 248; as divided, 117; and the hindrance of effort, 139–40; meaning of, 255–57; and the meaning of words, 112; and the perception of confusion, 36; to problems, 35, 167, 200; the process of, 235; and reaction, 269–70; and self-knowledge, 181; and separation of feeling and thought, 264, 266; and the still mind, 111–12; and total action, 175; as total good, 33; and the unoccupied mind, 189. *See also* Concentration; Listening; Meditation
Austerity, 248–49; as complete attention, 257; and sensitivity, 134–35
Authority, 204–6; acceptance of factual, 126–27; and anarchy, 70; versus comparison, 188–89; and conformity, 138; and confusion, 35–36; and the control of thought, 99–101; and the disciple, 127–28; and discipline, 96; and education, 65, 147; evil of, 70, 77–78; freedom from, 99–101; versus the free mind, 172–73; as futile, 71; as hindrance, 21 as hindrance to discovery, 122–24; as hindrance to religion, 181; as hindrance to self-inquiry, 254; as hindrance to self-knowledge, 48; as hindrance to truth, 109–10, 165; as hindrance to understanding, 33 as immoral, 198; and the interpretation of dreams, 120; and knowledge, 260–61; and the known, 87; and the meaning of life, 66; need to abandon, 131–32; and religion, 125; and righteousness, 184; search for, 2–3, 205–6; and the search for life's meaning, 63; and the search for security, 36; versus self-discovery, 179; spiritual, 204–5; types of, 205–6
Awareness: and acceptance, 59; of attachment, 116; and beauty, 270; and the cessation of dreams, 120; choiceless, 16, 36; versus concentration, 161; of conditioning, 108, 122–23; and desire, 245; and dreams, 55; of emptiness, 30; and the end of 'becoming', 272; and experience, 145–46; and ex-

ploitation, 169; and freedom from conditioning, 158–59; and freedom from dreams, 151–52; and freedom from influences, 115–16; and freedom from the past, 209–10; and guilt, 243–44; and habit, 19; and learning, 173; of life and death, 60–61; of loneliness, 52–53; meaning of, 53–54; and mediocrity, 59; and the mind, 20; as moment to moment, 111; need for, 64; process of understanding, 90–92; and self-knowledge, 9, 34, 199; and suffering, 58; and the thinker, 15; and total attention, 140; and total change, 184; of totality, 253; understanding, 17; and violence, 82–83. *See also* Quiet mind; Reality

Background: and conditioning, 20–21; defining, 11–12; need to understand, 11–12, 14; and thinking, 214, 219–20. *See also* Environment; Society
Beauty: defining, 269–70; goodness and truth as one, 269
'Becoming': versus 'being', 266–69; and the desire for 'more', 241; and the effort of self-denial, 75; and envy, 241–42; and exploitation, 169; freedom from, 246–47; as hindrance to total comprehension, 87–88; process of, 266–69; as secondary, 267–68; and sorrow, 57–58; and thought, 113. *See also* Ambition
Behavior: as righteousness, 223–26
'Being': versus 'becoming', 266–69; as nothing, 266, 268; as primary, 267–68. *See also What is*
Belief: and conditioning, 66-67, 108–9, 221–23; and death, 97; and escape, 7; freedom from, 24; and freedom from conditioning, 26; as hindrance to search, 170; as hindrance to truth, 32; and organizations, 15–16; organized, 223–25. *See also* Religion; Tradition
Believer and nonbeliever: and conditioning, 34; as same, 102–3
Beyond the mind, 141–42. *See also* Quiet mind; Reality; Truth
Bondage: and the struggle to be free, 36–37
Books: futility of sacred, 146; and permanence, 179; versus self-knowledge, 176. *See also* Authority; Conditioning
Boredom: and society, 95
Brotherhood: meaning of, 119
Buddhism. *See* Authority; Conditioning; Conformity; Organized religion; Religion

Capacity: to go beyond virtue, 62–63
Capitalism. *See* Authority; Conformity; Divisions; Ideology; Society; War
Career: futility of, 262. *See also* Work
Cause and effect: process of, 221–22
Center: and the accumulative process, 178–79; and action, 178–80; and change, 44, 46; conditioned, 26; defining, 23–24; and experience, 16–17, 261-62; and knowledge, 260–61; as limiting, 21; as 'me', 15; and moment to moment, 218–19; and permanence and impermanence, 178–79; and thought, 14–15. *See also* Self
Certainty: search for, 86. *See also* Permanence
Challenge: and conflict, 25; new, 197; as renewal, 187; and response, 157; and the responsive mind, 149
Challenge and response: and conditioning, 205
Change: achieving, 109, 114; achieving fundamental, 10–12; affecting the collectivist, 193; defining, 11; desire to avoid, 99–100; and the dying of the mind, 118; and feeling, 185; as fundamental problem, 116–18; as gradual, 117; how to achieve, 231–33; and 'I', 44–45; and the individual, 13; individual and societal, 155; and mediocrity, 59; motives for, 44; movement of, 190–95; possibilities for, 44–45; resistance of the mind to, 216–18; without self-centered action, 82; without self-interest, 80; and self-knowledge, 210; and the thinker and the thought as one, 83; understanding, 13; and will, 13–14. *See also* Religion; Revolution; Transformation; True Religion
Character: development of, 195–96
Children: conditioning of, 194; and discipline, 146–47; and education, 5; and envy, 28; influencing, 115–16; and the significance of education, 64–65; as social sacrifice, 59–60. *See also* Authority; Conformity
Choice: negates freedom, 90
Christianity: and the belief in damnation, 202; and conditioning, 22. *See also* Authority; Conditioning; Conformity; Divisions; Organized religion
Church: tyranny of, 77. *See also* Religion
Civilization: and increasing complexity, 155. *See also* Problems; Society; World Problems
Clarification: versus confusion, 66
Clarity: achieving, 152–53. *See also* Confusion
Collective: and belief, 54–55; growth of, 79–80; and individual, 38–39; versus individual action, 204; versus individual thought, 176; and religion, 217–18. *See also* Conformity; Society
Collective response: as valueless, 176–77
Comfort: and the need for authority, 48. *See also* Security
Communication: without conclusions, 169–70; and words, 37, 112, 144, 146. *See also* Verbalization
Communism: influence of, 104. *See also* Authority; Conformity; Divisions; Ideology; Society; War
Comparison: and ambition, 241; and condemnation, 110–11; and conflict, 30; versus the free mind, 17; futility of, 52–53; as hindrance to listening, 91; as hindrance to understanding, 34; and the mind, 265
Compassion, 191–95; and compulsion, 191–92; versus divisions, 201; importance of, 188–89; and indifference, 217; loss of, 60; transmitting, 192; and war, 74. *See also* Love
Complexity: versus simplicity, 259. *See also* Problems: Society
Compulsion: and change, 135, 185, 232–33; and the conforming mind, 100–101; as hindrance, 192–93; and superficial change, 232. *See also* Conformity; Discipline; Tradition
Concentration: versus attention, 140, 175; versus meditation, 105, 160–61, 227–28
Conclusion: versus creativity, 122; and experience, 22–24; as hindrance to communication, 169–70; as

hindrance to thought, 121, 123, 206; and learning, 233–34; as repetition, 166. *See also* Conditioning
Condemnation: and conditioning, 215; and emptiness, 94; and envy, 28–29, 91, 265, 268; and hindrance to self-knowledge, 33–34; as hindrance to understanding, 110–11, 139; and understanding, 13
Conditioned mind, 215; versus the alert mind, 161–62; conscious and unconscious, 151–52; freedom from, 19–20; as hindrance to freedom, 108–9; versus religion, 107–9; as shackled, 165–66. *See also* Conditioning, Conformity
Conditioning: achieving freedom from, 26; "bad" and "good", 104; and the basic problem of existence, 122, 124; and belief, 26, 102; and belief in God, 66–67; and change, 11–12; of children, 146–47; and the collective, 31–32, 54–55, 177–78; and the desire for permanence, 7–8; and dreams, 150-52; and environment, 221–22; and experience, 22, 24; factors of, 37–38; freedom from, 22, 24, 37–39, 71, 157–58; versus the free individual, 39; and the free mind, 18, 130; as hindrance to discovery, 170–71, 173; as hindrance to understanding, 86, 198–99; and the individual, 90; and influence of symbols, 115; versus inquiry, 242; and method, 213–14; and the mind, 78, 142–43; and the mind of man, 98–101; on national levels, 163–64; and the past, 205; and the problem of existence, 48–50; and problems, 121–24, 197; and the process of thinking, 50–51; and religion, 202; and response, 145-46; and right action, 221; and the self, 34; and the shaping of the mind, 2–3; and thought, 113–14, 250–51; understanding, 25
Conflict: to challenge and response, 25; and change, 11, 14; through choice, 90; between the conscious and the unconscious, 120; of contradictory desires, 110; creation of, 116–17; versus the creative, 17; and desire, 27; and the division of memories, 73; and effort, 144; and emptiness, 30; and envy, 29–30; and the fragmentary outlook, 148–49; versus freedom, 29, 58; and habit, 134–35; and ideology, 74; and leaders, 173–75; and patterns, 99; and resistance, 255–56; and response, 51; and the search for happiness, 41; and society, 43–44; and sorrow, 56–58; and the thinker and the thought, 85, 115; and will, 26–27. *See also* Confusion
Conflict of duality: and comparison, 221; and resistance, 257; and the thinker and the thought, 41
Conformity: and change, 135, 137–38; and character, 195-96; and discipline, 96–97, 146–47, 247; and the education of children, 65; and experience, 51; and juvenile delinquency, 4–5; and method, 213–14. *See also* Compulsion; Method; Patterns; Tradition
Confusion, 203–6; and the absence of clarity, 152; and conclusions, 206; and the creation of leaders, 77; and the fragmentation of life, 128; freedom from, 66; freedom from authority, 35–36; and intellectual acceptance, 126; and the meaning of existence, 65–66; and the petty mind, 100–101; and the search for guidance, 204–6; and self-understanding, 35; and *what is,* 4. *See also* Conflict
Conscious: and adjustment, 232; and daily life, 141; as dreamless, 151–52; as the educated mind, 211; and the environment, 54; and the free mind, 3; function of, 237. *See also* Conditioning; Knowledge; Mind; Unconscious
Conscious and unconscious, 33, 34; and conditioning, 39; and hindrance of the past, 108–9; and time, 113
Conscious mind: capability of, 63–64
Consciousness: and change, 45–46; 136; and daily activity, 120; defining, 18, 136–37; and experience, 21; process of, 263–64; and self-knowledge, 34; and thought, 113; as the totality of experience, 50–51. *See also* 'Me'; Mind; Self; Self-centered activity
Continuance: and identification, 76
Continuity: desire for, 154–55, 208–9; and desire for the known, 43; and the fear of death, 60–61; and reincarnation, 9–10; and suffering, 103. *See also* Religion
Contradiction: and action, 232–34; in a complex world, 239–40; and conflict, 10; and identification, 76; and the self, 174–75
Control: versus meditation, 227–28. *See also* Discipline
Conversion: and conflict, 202–3
Corruption: and authority, 184
Creation: and attention, 189; versus certainty, 209; and the mind, 190
Creative: and dreams, 120; and the free mind, 131, 164–66; as the limitless mind, 155; versus memory, 219; and a new world, 17; versus the past, 87; and reality, 223
Creative effort: and contradiction, 233
Creative mind: as uncluttered, 238. *See also* Empty mind
Creativeness: and the individual, 37, 40; and the mind, 3; state of, 8
Creative reality: and the cessation of the self, 254. *See also* Awareness
Creative stillness: achieving, 17. *See also* Quiet mind
Creativity: versus continuity, 61
Crime: as revolt within society, 83
Cruelty: social base of, 59–60
Culture: meaning of, 200

Daily life: action in, 232; and God, 271–72; and love, 270–71; and the relationship to God, 271–72; understanding, 207. *See also* Conscious; Consciousness
Dead mind: versus the still mind, 84. *See also* Occupied mind; Petty mind
Death: awareness of, 61; and continuity of the 'me', 10; fear of, 60–61, 153–55, 208–10; and reincarnation, 97–98; and the unknowable, 97–98. *See also* Desire; Escape; Knowledge
Death and life: as one, 97–98
Delinquency, 4–5; as social revolt, 65. *See also* Children; Conformity

Democracies: and conditioning, 163. *See also* Governments
Dependence: and attachment, 115; and compassion, 189; as corrupter, 92; and fear, 9; freedom from psychological, 52–53; problem of, 92–93; reasons for, 93; and reform, 210; and sorrow, 194
Dependent mind: and freedom, 109
Desire: without condemnation, 221; and conflict, 27, 233–34; and contradiction, 110; versus meditation, 229; and the mind, 256–57; and the senses, 236; and sorrow, 56–58; suppression of, 244, 269; understanding, 157; and will, 26–27; as will, 13–14
Desire, feeling, and thought: as one, 164–66
Deterioration: individual and societal, 148–49; and the mind, 258. *See also* Conflict; Confusion; World problems
Devotion: and inquiry, 225
Discipline: of attention, 255–57; without coercion, 96–97; and creating conflict, 180–81; examining, 246–49; and experience, 16; versus the free mind, 131–32; and going beyond the mind, 141–42; of suppression, 255; versus transformation, 118; types of, 146. *See also* Conformity; Method; Tradition
Discontent: and change, 45; and envy, 29–30, 47; versus illusions, 32; and the religious man, 34; and the search for contentment, 182–83 and the search for satisfaction, 217. *See also* Ambition
Discovery: versus distraction, 61–62; and the free mind, 41–42
Distraction: versus attention, 140; and dependence, 52. *See also* Concentration; Meditation
Disturbance: and change, 216–17
Divisions: between analyzer and analyzed, 174; and conflict, 117; in daily and religious life, 207–8; economic reasons for, 201; of life and death, 98; of living and dying, 153–55; between people, 24; and religion, 200–201, 219; and security, 42–43; between spiritual and worldly, 123; versus total action, 175. *See also* also Thinker and the thought; Totality; Whole
Dogma: and the desire for security, 15–16; freedom from, 79; versus religion, 72; and the shallow mind, 32. *See also* Belief; Conditioning; Tradition
"Doing good": and the free mind, 25. *See also* Reform
Domination: and the mind, 117
Doubt: and inquiry, 157
Dreams, 119–20; cause of, 150–52; and the conscious and unconscious, 54–55; interpreting, 150–52; process of, 150–52
Drugs: and experiencing, 89
Duality: conflict of, 160; versus fundamental change, 138
Dying: daily, 208–9, 242–43; and living fully, 259; meaning of, 153–55; to the past, 258. *See also* Continuity; Fear; Religion

East: and scientific change, 234; and West, 1; and world problems, 44. *See also* Technology
Economic security: and inward insecurity, 3
Education, 64–65; as accumulation of knowledge, 86; and competition, 60; and conformity, 83; and the demands of society, 95; and discipline, 146–47; and juvenile delinquency, 5; and livelihood, 226; meaning of, 65; purpose of, 5. *See also* Authority; Children
Effort: and attention, 256–57; to become, 75; and 'becoming', 268; and change, 136–38; and conditioning, 101; and conflict, 41; futility of, 92, 111, 143–44; as hindrance to change, 117, 159; process of, 57–58; and suffering, 57; versus understanding, 13. *See also* Quiet mind; Reality
Ego. *See* Center; Consciousness; 'Me'; Self-centered activity
Egotism. *See* Ego
Emotions: and the mind, 4. *See also* Feeling
Emptiness: acceptance of, 30; and discontent, 30; and dogma, 15–16; escape from, 52–53; and envy, 30; and fear, 93–94; and identification, 76; and identity, 7–8. *See also* Aloneness
Empty mind: and awareness, 254; and the word, 270. *See also* Petty mind; Quiet mind
End: of the center, 179–80; fear of, 154–55, 209; of thought, 179–80, 213-14, 249–50;. *See also* Continuity; Death; Truth
Energy: and attention, 111, 235; and self-knowledge, 251; and the silent mind, 249; and the still mind, 213, 226
English. *See* Conditioning; Divisions; Ideology; Nationalism; Society; War
Enlightened: conditioning, 190; defining, 194; and tradition, 194
Entity: and the process of thought, 142
Environment: and creation of patterns, 38; and the education of children, 65. *See also* Background; Conditioning; Society
Envy: attempt to be free of, 46; as basis for life, 207–8; and the desire for 'more', 264; experiencing, 47–48; freedom from, 27–30, 240–42, 245, 268; freeing the mind of, 132; process of, 264–65; as social and religious base, 91; and transformation, 241–42; understanding, 27–30; and will, 26–27. *See also* Ambition; 'Becoming'; Comparison; Condemnation
Equality and inequality: and learning, 173
Escape: from boredom, 95; and confusion, 7; and dependence through drugs, 89; from emptiness, 94; freedom from the desire to, 8; futility of, 30; through God, 159; from loneliness, 52-53; from self-knowledge, 124; from sorrow, 56–58; from uncertainty, 15; understanding, 52–53
Evil: of authority, 77–78
Exclusiveness: and concentration, 160–61
Existence, 65–66; problem of, 86; totality of, 129
Experience, 16–17; and the center, 23–24; collective and individual, 144–45; and conclusions, 22–24; as conditioned and conditioning, 20–21, 22, 26, 39, 205; as endless process, 25–26; and the futility of search for, 89; as help or hindrance, 21; as limitation, 21; and the meaning of life,

159–60; as mind conditioner, 51; and the past, 218; and the self, 40, 76; as transforming, 71
Experiencer and the experience: and 'becoming', 268; as one, 67, 229; and violence, 81-83. *See also* Thinker and the thought
Experiencing: directly, 74; envy, 47; versus escape, 7–8; and the free mind, 66–67; versus listening to words, 115; versus past experience, 145–46; reality, 233; religion, 186; sorrow, 56; thought, 112–14
Exploitation, 167–69; and authority, 36, 78; and the state of inquiry, 35; and the totalitarian spirit, 9; types of, 168. *See also* Society
Exploiter: and the need for authority, 48

Fact: versus idea, 124; and the importance of awareness, 59; versus opinion, 52, 157–58; and truth, 30; and word, 123. *See also What is*
Factual knowledge, 218–19. *See also* Technology
Faith: as cultivated, 63
Fear: and continuation, 208–9; of death, 258–59; of death as an end, 60–61; and discipline, 247; and envy, 28, 30; examining, 37; facing, 93–94; freedom from, 213; and the free mind, 109; and the futility of escape, 52; of the known, 255; and the need for dependence, 93; need to understand, 132; of not-being, 97–98; and reincarnation, 153–55; and religion, 34; as root of activity, 93–94; and virtue, 248
Feeling: versus action, 188; versus intellect, 185; and mediocrity, 189; without thought, 185; without verbalization, 268; and the word, 92; without word conditioning, 47–48
Feeling, desire, and thought: as one, 264–66
Few: versus the understanding of the many, 62. *See also* Collective; Individual
Fixed point: as hindrance to observation, 53; meaning of, 25; versus reality, 131
Follow: desire to, 99–100
Followers, 174; and confusion, 77; and the desire for authority, 78; as hindrance to truth, 123–24; and leaders, 8–9; as stupid, 198. *See also* Conformity
Following: as unrighteous, 184
Fragmentation: and guilt, 243–44; of problems, 148–49. *See also* Divisions
Freedom: from160 accumulation, 21; achieving, 3, 15; from ambition, 5–6; from authority, 78, 99, 109–10, 138; from background, 12; as a beginning, 18; versus bondage, 36–37; from conclusions, 24, 121–24; from conditioning, 90, 101–2, 108–9, 145–46, 157–59, 164–67, 198; and the craving for experience, 16; difficulty of achieving, 164–65; from dreams, 55, 151–52; from envy, 91–92, 207–8, 264–65; from exploitation, 169; fear of, 97; from fear of death, 209–10; from ideas, 49; from knowledge, 260–62; from the known, 160; meaning of, 22, 29; from method, 213; of the mind, 220; and moral character, 195–96; versus the need to seek, 6; from the past, 222–23, 236–38; from the petty mind, 157; and the process of thinking, 19; as the religious revolution, 126; versus security, 7–8; through the self, 38; and silent awareness, 30; from social conditioning, 32; from society, 12; state of, 20; from suffering, 56, 58; versus thinking, 214; from time, 250–51; from violence, 80–81, 84; within ourselves, 116
Freedom from conditioning: process of, 215
Freedom from fear: and the still mind, 213
Free mind: achieving, 3–4, 18, 47, 114, 165–67, 219, 251; defining, 3; and discipline, 131–32; and discovering the true, 165; and the discovery of God, 70; and the discovery of the new, 38; and "doing good", 25; and effort, 143–44; and individuality, 177–80; and inquiry into thought, 229; versus the need for permanence, 43; as path to God, 172; and the search for God, 32; as social danger, 164; and stillness, 272; and transformation, 225; and truth, 107–9
Fresh mind: and problems, 170–72. *See also* New; Quiet mind
Friendliness: as motiveless, 271
Friendship: and justice, 187–88
Frustration: and dissatisfaction, 181–83. *See also* Conflict; Confusion; Fulfillment
Fulfillment: and frustration, 194; and the mind, 37, 185
Fundamental revolution: and true religion, 186. *See also* Change; Religion; Religious revolution; Revolution; Transformation

Generosity: and friendliness, 271
Germans. *See* Conditioning; Divisions; Ideology; Nationalism; Society; War
God: approach to, 41–42; and belief, 66–67, 102; and conditioning, 125; as escape from life, 159–60; and experience, 16; and the fixed point, 127; and freedom from envy, 241–42; freedom to discover, 3; futility of search for, 272; and illusion, 125; and permanence, 10; as a state of constant renewal, 37; as static, 201; and the unknown, 118. *See also* Reality; Truth
Godless: and God-fearing, 66
Good life, 62
Goodness: versus conformity, 176; development of, 195–96
Goodness, truth, and beauty: as one, 269
Government: action by, 173–74; and conformity, 201; and conditioning, 163–64; as powerful, 188; tyranny of, 77. *See also* Authority; Society
Grace: futility of search for, 63
Gradualism: as hindrance to change, 203; *See also* Revolution
Guilt: feelings of, 243–44
Guru. *See* Authority

Habit, 213; as adjustment, 5; freedom from, 38; and the free mind, 42, 49; and self-awareness, 19; understanding the types of, 133. *See also* Belief; Conditioning; Patterns
Happiness: and the absence of self, 75; futility of pursuit, 40–41; futility of search for, 183; and search for, 31–32. *See also* God; Reality
Hatred: cause of, 110
Hindrances: to understanding problems, 1

Hinduism: and conditioning, 22. *Se also* Authority; Conditioning; Conformity; Divisions; Organized religion
"How": and conditioning, 109; as the continuation of thought, 250–51; and the fragmentary outlook, 149. *See also* Discipline; Method; Patterns
Humility: and freedom from envy, 242–43; and the new, 234; and sensitivity, 176; unconscious, 64; and understanding, 259–60. *See also* Virtue

'I': and the collective, 178; as the conscious mind, 18; as memory, 208; as product of society, 44–45. *See also* Center; Consciousness; 'Me'; Mind; Self
Idealist: and conformity, 96; as self-centered, 81
Ideals: versus actuality, 224–25; and change, 137–38; as distraction, 117–18; as hindrance to change, 11, 80, 83; and violence, 80–81. *See also* Fact
Ideas: as hindrance, 121–23; and psychological security, 32. *See also* Belief; Conditioning; Tradition
Identification: and the absence of love, 270–71; as false solution, 62; and fragmentation, 206; and 'I', 270–71; and ideology, 125; living without, 76; and psychological security, 7; and time, 98. *See also* Continuity
Ideology: and the approach to problems, 197; and conformity, 260; and world problems, 163–64. *See also* Conditioning; Method
Ignorance: and awareness, 9; as cause of suffering, 8, 103–4
Illusion: and drugs, 89; and the pursuit of happiness, 41
Immeasurable: experiencing, 71; futility of search, 187; and self-awareness, 102. *See also* God; Reality; Truth
Immortality, 153–54. *See also* Continuity; Reality
India, 196. *See also* Conditioning
Indians. *See* Conformity; Divisions; Ideology; Nationalism; Society; War
Indifference: and compassion, 271; as escape from pain, 271
Individual: and change, 5, 232–33; versus the collective, 79; as collective entity, 54; and collective influences, 38–39; and conflict, 174; and the creative, 171; and freedom, 90; and freedom from authority, 206; and freedom from society, 171; and freedom from the collective, 164, 166–67; and freedom from violence, 81; without identification, 75–76; importance of, 239, 241–43; and for inward change, 191–92; and the new world, 261; and peace, 84; and religion, 217–18, 267-68; and self-transformation, 107–10, 116–18; and society, 13; as society, 129–30; and total action, 232–34; as the true religious man, 39; understanding, 246; as the world, 118
Individual action: as effective, 204, 206. *See also* Individual
Individual creativity: and creativeness, 37; defining, 54, 176–77; importance of, 20
Individuality: versus the individual, 177
Individual problems: as the world problems, 70, 85
Individual thinking: and collective thinking, 176

Industrialization: and world change, 239–40, 241. *See also* Technology
Influence: on conscious thought, 113; desire to, 104; problems of, 115–16; social, 147
Inner revolution. *See* Change; Revolution
Innocence: futility of cultivating, 64
Innocent mind: achieving, 43. *See also* Mind; New
Inquiry: and conclusion, 233–34; as a constant need, 37; difficulty of, 168–69; and discipline, 248; and discontent, 217; and envy, 242; and escape, 130; and freedom of the self, 40; and the free mind, 32, 33, 261–62; and God, 102–3; as good, 125; without judgment, 179–80; as meditation, 40; as motiveless, 39; and the mind, 251; need for inner, 253–55; versus the petty mind, 157; and religion, 223–25; and the resolution of problems, 35; and righteousness, 224–25; and thought, 228–29; and uncertainty, 43; and understanding, 220
Insensitivity: and the conscious mind, 151–52; cultivating, 134; and suppressing, 236. *See also* Compassion; Conformity; Sensitivity
Integrated mind, 152; and problems, 121
Intellectuals, 175–76
Interpreter: versus truth, 227. *See also* Authority
Irreligious: and ritual, 164. *See also* Religion; Tradition
Isolation: fear of, 5–6; as nonexistent, 148. *See also* Aloneness; Loneliness
Interpreters: versus original experiencers, 161. *See also* Authority

Judgement: as hindrance to understanding, 3. *See also* Comparison; Condemnation; Envy
Justice: as legislation, 201. *See also* Law
Juvenile delinquency: roots of, 4–5. *See also* Children

Karma, 14, 190; and cause and effect, 221–23; freedom from, 222–23
Knowledge: and acting, 46; as burden, 9; and destruction of the new, 266; and experience, 23, 144–45, 218–19; exploring, 259–62; freedom from, 21, 252, 261–62; versus the fresh mind, 86; as hindrance to free thought, 19; as hindrance to perception, 86–87; as hindrance to religion, 186; as hindrance to truth, 2–3; and identification, 76; and learning, 172–73, 212–13; as past experience, 205; and thinking, 219. *See also* Accumulation; Memory; Past
Known: and change, 137–38; defining, 98; and fear of death, 61; freedom from, 87; as hindrance to change, 138; and ideal, 118; and learning, 212; and the mind, 43; and the search for God, 159–60; versus the unknowable, 51; and the unknown, 272

Labels: as cause of conflict, 202; freedom from, 201. *See also* Naming; Words
Law: and friendliness, 188; versus right profession, 263
Leaders: and conflict, 173–75; as escape, 7; and exploitation, 168; and followers, 8–9. *See also* Authority
Learning: versus being taught, 231, 233; without division, 197–98; versus ideology, 197; process

of, 172–73, 212–13, 252–53. *See also* Education; Knowledge; Listening
Life: and the absence of answers, 167, 234; approach to understanding, 170–71; awareness of, 61; as beautiful and ugly, 134; as complicated, 259; as constant movement, 69; as fragmented, 128; free from exploitation, 168; giving meaning to, 159–60; as movement, 14, 86; the need to view as a whole, 86–88; purpose of, 65–66; as simple and complex, 54; as superficial, 40; understanding, 125. *See also* Death
Life and death: and continuity, 97-98; as one, 60–61
Listening: as an art, 185; and awareness, 262; and awareness of conditioning, 122; without comparison, 136, 203–4; without conclusions, 169–70; and the desire to be taught, 252; and the discovery of truth, 211; with humility, 259; versus interest, 180–81; without interpretation, 33; without judgement, 1–2; as part of awareness, 91; and the quiet mind, 88; ways of, 112, 113. *See also* Attention
Livelihood: and education, 226; as necessity, 262–63. *See also* Work
Living: defining, 159; as process of dying, 98: as reaction, 257; as religion, 231; as religious process, 231; understanding, 153–55. *See also* Death
Loneliness: and accumulation, 262; and the search for sensation, 16. *See also* Aloneness; Emptiness; Happiness
Love: and action, 195; versus ambition, 5, 116; approach to problem, 156; and attachment, 115; of children, 147; communicating, 146; and complete attention, 175; and demand, 60; and desire, 245; and education, 95; and the free mind, 47; and habit, 134–35; and the loss of compassion, 60; meaning of, 236; as nonidentification, 155; as not of the mind, 150; and the object of attention, 256–57; and the process of thought, 113; of profession, 263; as reality, 202; as religious, 216; versus sentimentality, 95; and sin, 244; and total action, 175–76; as total attention, 117–18; understanding, 270–71

Mass: and fear, 84. *See also* Collective
Materialism: versus religion, 49
'Me': and ambition, 130; and attention, 140; as the center, 15; and the desire for continuity, 154; effect of cessation of, 74; and effort, 57; and experiencing, 67; and knowledge, 76; and memory, 218–19; and need for permanence, 10; and the root of fear, 93–94; and self-forgetfulness, 255; as source of sorrow, 57; and suffering, 56; and violence, 81. *See also* Consciousness; Mind; Self; Self-centered activity
Mediocre mind: defining, 189; and the desire to improve, 59. *See also* Petty mind
Mediocrity: and the need for permanence, 43; and tradition, 49, 51
Meditation, 227–29; and achieving peace, 84; as attention, 264; defining, 161; and freedom from conditioning, 272; as inquiry, 40; and listening, 136; and motiveless inquiry, 77; need for, 104–5; and self-knowledge, 179, 255; understanding, 160–62. *See also* Concentration; Mind
Memories: and the center, 24; collective and individual, 143; pleasant and unpleasant, 73.
Memory, 72–73; companions of, 171; and continuity, 208–10; and dividing the thinker from the thought, 114; and experience, 21, 144–45; and the fear of death, 61; and habit, 133–34; and knowledge, 144–45, 218–19, 249; painful and pleasurable, 17; and positive thinking, 19; and the process of thought, 84–85, 214; purpose of, 51; and thinking, 250; and tradition, 49–51; and 'you', 258–59. *See also* Accumulation; Mind
Method: function of, 213–14; as hindrance, 41–42; as hindrance to change, 109; as hindrance to freedom, 18; as hindrance to the free mind, 131; versus right meditation, 160. *See also* Conditioning; Conformity; Discipline; "How"
Mind: and the ability to discover, 43; achieving freedom of, 164–67; and achieving the religious life, 62–63; and achieving truth, 20; and approach to problems, 155–56; attempt to capture, 98–101; attempt to mold, 163–64; and authority, 35–36; and awareness, 15; and awareness of conditioning, 78; and awareness of thinking, 53–54; beyond the measure of, 198; cessation of, 258; collective and individual, 54–55; and conclusions, 253; and condemnation, 110–11; as conditioned, 11–12, 157–58; conditioned to problems, 121–24; conditioned versus the free, 12; and conditioning, 37–39, 222; and the conflict of choice, 90; and confusion, 65–66; conscious and unconscious, 151–52, 237; as creative, 16–17; as creator of materialism and religion, 49; and the cultivation of virtue, 246–48; and death, 209–10; and desire, 257; and the desire for security, 42; and direct experience, 71; and discipline, 96–97, 247–49; divided, 113; and domination of, 117; and dreams, 55; and emotion, 4; and emptiness, 30, 94; as envious, 207–8; and envy, 46–47; and escape from uncertainty, 15–16; or eternal, 33; and experience, 9, 22–24; and experiencing the unknown, 66–67; and fear, 52; and feeling, 185; and formation of habits, 38; and freedom, 21; and freedom from 'becoming', 268–69; and freedom from conditioning, 108–9, 122–24, 170–72; and freedom from fragmentation, 148–49; and freedom from the center, 26; and freedom from the known, 51; and freedom from the past, 87, 127–28; and freedom from violence, 81; and freedom from words, 47–48; and freedom from worship, 49; freedom of, 206; free from conclusions, 170–71; free from conflict, 256; free from dependence, 93; free from fear, 20; and free inquiry, 33; free of the collective, 177–80; free of the observer, 254–55; function of, 220–21; and habit, 47, 133–35; and the hindrance of conclusions, 24; and the hindrance of conformity, 146–47; and the hindrance of systems, 41–42; as humble, 259–61;

without identification, 76; and independent thought, 130; influence on, 198; and inquiry, 43, 233–34; as instrument of inquiry, 217–18; and inward revolution, 63; as the known, 98; lazy, 222–23; and learning, 212–13; limiting, 16–17; and love, 216, 271; and memory, 73, 219–20, 249–50; and method, 213; and the need for certainty, 132; and the need for change, 46; and the need for radical transformation, 203; new, 258; as observant, 17; as old, 258; and the past, 254; and permanence, 179; poverty of, 37; process of, 269; and the process of desire, 58; and relationship, 71–72; as the result of time, 43; and righteousness, 184; and self-deception, 272; and self-knowledge, 141-44, 221; and self-understanding, 118; and the state of not-knowing, 19, 50; and suffering, 58; and suppression, 244; and truth, 34; as uncreative, 3; understanding, 1–4; and understanding death, 61; understanding the process of, 223; and understanding the totality, 140–41; as unprejudiced, 69; and will, 26–27

Mind control, 227–28

Mode of conduct: and the desire for authority, 48

Moment to moment: versus accumulation, 127–28; and awareness, 51, 53–54, 242–43, 254; and the awareness of death, 61; and the free mind, 206; and the new mind, 258; and observation, 176; and righteousness, 225; and self-knowledge, 251; and truth, 218

Moral fiber: disintegration of, 195

Morality: defining, 184

'More': and envy, 47, 132; freedom from, 172–73; pursuit of, 241. *See also* Accumulation; Ambition; 'Becoming'

Motive: versus attention, 175; and change, 100–101; and the desire to be secure, 79; and effort, 75; freedom from, 39; and freedom from envy, 242; and frustration, 182–83; as hindrance to change, 45–46; and 'me', 254–55; and search, 217

Movement: without causation, 183; without center, 180; and change, 137; and truth, 198

Mukti: as freedom, 131

Naming: and envy, 91–92; as hindrance to awareness, 140. *See also* Labels; Verbalization; Words

Nationalism: as a cause of war, 70; and the desire for permanence, 7; as hindrance to love, 178; and religion, 201; as road to war, 24, 73, 84. *See also* Conditioning; Divisions; Government; Society

National symbols: and conditioning, 115

Negative: and experience, 16

Negative thinking: defining, 19

New: achieving, 33; and approach to problems, 197; and challenge, 157; and change, 138; and the difficulty of listening, 204; discovery of, 145–46; and the dying, 53; experiencing, 71; feeling, 265–66; and the hindrance of memory, 214; and living, 154–55; versus memory, 50; need for, 252–55; versus the past, 73; as religious revolution, 186; and the state of not-knowing, 50; and the totality approach, 149; understanding, 130. *See also* Fresh mind; Truth

New society: versus reformation, 166

New thinking: and self-knowledge, 234

New world: achieving, 101–2, 128; and freedom from authority, 101; and freedom from conditioning, 177–78; need for, 107; and the next generation, 194; and a religious revolution, 95–96; and understanding authority, 99, 101

Nonviolence, 80–81. *See also* Violence; War

Not-knowing: as the highest form of thinking, 19. *See also* Awareness; Reality

Observation: and awareness, 53–54; and desire, 245. *See also* Attention

Observer and the observed: and the quiet mind, 142–44. *See also* Thinker and the thought

Occident: and Orient, 31–32. *See also* East; West

Occupied mind: defining, 156–57; and mediocrity, 189; and self-centeredness, 226. *See also* Conscious; Petty mind; Quiet mind

Old age: meaning of, 258

Order: without tradition, 146

Organizations: versus freedom, 15–16; and path to love, 188–89

Organized religion: and the absence of self, 75; and the mind of man, 98–99; versus religion, 199; and the search for God, 102–3; versus the true religion, 34; and universal morality, 80. *See also* Authority; Conditioning

Orient: and Occident, 31–32. *See also* East; West

"Ought to be": versus what I am, 70

Pain: and experience, 17; and pleasure of living, 159. *See also* Sorrow; Suffering

Parents: and the desire to have children conform, 14; and the education of children, 65. *See also* Authority

Past: and consciousness, 50, 54; defining, 54, 237–38; desire for, 254; desire to erase, 73; and experience, 145–46; freedom from, 50, 123, 149, 237–38; as hindrance to learning, 252–53; as hindrance to the timeless, 87; influences of, 223; as knowledge, 97–98; need to be free of, 203; and the old mind, 258; and thinking, 214. *See also* Accumulation; Knowledge; Memory; Mind

Past, present, and future: and conditioning, 26

Patriotism, 115

Patterns: attempt to be free of, 99; and change, 11–12; creating new, 45; need to be free of, 171; of thinking, 38. *See also* Discipline; Method

Peace: achieving, 79; acquiring, 9; futility of pursuit, 40; need for, 116–17; as vulnerable to attack, 83–84. *See also* War

Perception: versus knowledge, 86–87

Permanence: and the center, 178–79; and impermanence, 178–79; search for, 7, 10, 42–43. *See also* Continuity; Death; Security

Petty mind: and ambition, 153; and approach to problems, 155–57; as basic problem, 100–101; defining, 156–57; versus the new, 179; versus

the unknown, 214. *See also* Conscious Mind; Occupied mind; Quiet mind
Physical interdependence: versus psychological dependence, 92
Physical security: need for, 42; versus psychological security, 3. *See also* Continuity; Escape
Planned economy: versus freedom, 174
Pleasure: and discipline, 249; and experience, 17; and memory, 133–34. *See also* Pain
Policeman: versus right profession, 263
Politicians: and control, 163–64. *See also* Authority; Government
Positive thinking: defining, 19, 139
Prayer, 227, 228
Predeterminism: and the loss of freedom, 90
Prejudice: as hindrance to thinking, 2–3
Priest: function of, 202
Problem of existence: as basic problem, 122, 124
Problem of life: understanding, 85–86, 88
Problems: and answers, 167, 180, 235; without answers, 35; approach to, 1–2, 4, 72, 199–200, 240, 242–43; awareness of, 173; basic, 239–41; of change, 116–18; collective and individual, 148–49; complexity of, 128; of conflict, 29; of envy, 29–30; and feeling versus thinking, 123; and the futility of seeking solutions, 150; growing complexity of, 155, 197; and the hindrance of conditioning, 170–71; importance of approach to, 155–56; inquiry into, 35; interrelation of, 128; new approach to, 121–24; and the process of thought, 112–13; psychological, 187; separation from, 139; versus solutions, 54; and the thinker and the thought as one, 114–15; understanding, 110; as universal, 1–2, 31, 69; as a whole, 139–41
Process: as centerless, 14–15; of thought and conditioning, 101–2
Profession: finding the right, 263. *See also* Work
Progress: and the mind, 143
Propaganda: and technology, 192
Property: and religions, 202
Psychoanalysis: futility of, 114
Psychological dependence: and freedom from, 92–93; reasons for, 52–53
Psychological memory: as knowledge, 219
Psychological security: desire for, 42; versus the free mind, 32; versus physical security, 3
Psychology: of conflict, 41; and political thought control, 163

Questions: and the absence of clarity, 4; approach to, 199–200; asking the right ones, 152–53; significance of, 234–35. *See also* Answers; Listening; Problems
Quiet mind: and the absence of conflict, 41; and the absence of fear, 94; achieving, 8, 72, 84–85, 120, 161–62; and achieving creativity, 39–40; and the full life, 3; and self-knowledge, 144, 229; and the true, 109

Radical change: achieving, 100–102, 135–38; and effort, 111; need for, 43–44, 185–86. *See also* Change; Religion; Revolution; Transformation; True religion
Reality: achieving, 40, 67, 77; without assumptions, 166–67; and the cessation of thought, 250; discovery of, 2; as effortless, 269; experiencing, 62; futility of seeking, 20; and the limitations of thought, 39; as living, 146; as pathless, 20, 202; and the priest, 202; and the religious revolutionary, 12; through revolutionary change, 135–36; and security, 72; versus self-centered activity, 248–49; understanding, 190; and virtue, 248–49. *See also* God; Truth
Reform, 175–76; and acquisitiveness, 45; and change, 210; as endless process, 63; as hindrance to change, 83; and revolution, 108. *See also* Reformation
Reformation, 184; as hindrance to religion, 186–87; versus the new society, 166. *See also* Reform; Revolution
Reincarnation, 9–10; and belief, 97; and continuance, 154–55; as escape from death, 14; and the fear of death, 60, 208
Relationship: without authority, 165; between the compassionate and the collectivist, 193; without condemnation, 71, 119; and conditioning, 18; defining, 53; without dogma, 43; without evaluation, 34; of the individual to society, 172–73; and the little world, 253; between problems, 85–86; and the psychological world, 98–99; and the search for permanence, 42; and self-awareness, 102; and self-knowledge, 124; and society, 192; understanding, 181
Religion, 223–26; and authority, 48, 99; as commercial, 202; and the conditioned mind, 163–64; and contradiction, 233, 239–40; defining, 125, 216; without dependence, 210; as dogma, 43, 124, 177, 179–80; free from tradition, 107; as fundamental necessity, 107–8; as individual discovery, 216–18; versus materialism, 49; without the 'me', 7; meaning of, 43, 62, 200; as more than dogma, 70–71; organized, 15–16; and the path to God, 149; quality of true, 203; versus religious society, 34; reviving, 216; versus romanticism, 63; and the senses, 236; as social convenience, 240; and suppression, 244; understanding, 186. *See also* Belief; Change; Revolution; True Revolution
Religious institutions: and illusions, 32
Religious life, 62–64, 206–8
Religious man: and the cessation of 'becoming', 268; defining, 234; and freedom from dogma, 39–40; and social rejection, 263; as the true revolutionary, 34, 48
Religious mind: defining, 72; and freedom from envy, 48
Religious organizations: as conditioners, 179–80; and control, 164; divisions among, 201–2
Religious person: and freedom from dependence, 92
Religious problem: and the complex society, 69
Religious revolution: and the absence of 'becoming', 267–69; achieving, 3, 128; and freedom from dogma, 199; meaning of, 125–26; need for, 95;

as outside of society, 83; as salvation, 79. *See also* Change; Religion; True religion
Renewal: and ending, 155, 209
Repetition: and continuity, 154; versus meditation, 228
Resistance: and attention, 255–56; and 'becoming', 267; and the 'me', 257; to the new, 216
Respectability: and ambition, 5; and social morality, 246–47. *See also* Conformity; Discipline
Response: and background, 219–20; and conflict, 25
Revival: of religions, 216
Revolt: as uncreative, 83
Revolution: without dependence, 210; individual, 116; as inward transformation, 44; need for religious, 124; and questioning authority, 131; and religion, 225; religious, 3, 108–110; and superficial reform, 108; in thinking, 63; as the true religious mind, 107–9; through understanding, 118; and understanding patterns. *See also* Change
Revolutionary: as the religious man, 34
Right action, 173–74. *See also* "Right thinking"
Righteous action: defining, 232
Righteous mind: defining, 184
Righteousness, 184, 223–26; and humility, 242; versus the traditional, 189
Right relationship: versus guru and disciple, 122; and love, 195. *See also* Authority; Relationship
"Right thinking": and the desire to influence, 104; understanding, 219–21. *See also* Right action
Ritual: and religion, 210. *See also* Belief; Habit
Russians. *See* Conditioning; Divisions; Ideology; Nationalism; Society; War

Sacred: versus sentimental, 187
Sadhana: as method, 131–32
Safety: and technology, 192
Satisfaction: and religion, 217; and the superficial, 61
Science: and change, 12. *See also* Technology
Search: awareness of, 32; and conditioning, 31–32; as contradiction, 33; for happiness, 31; importance of, 217–18; motiveless, 182–83; motives for, 161. *See also* Security
Secondary issues: and 'becoming', 267–68
Security: through authority, 36; and being taught, 231; and the creation of authority, 77–78; and the demand for permanence, 42; and discipline, 96; and knowledge, 87; versus learning, 233; and the need for a leader, 127; and organizations, 15; and politics, 164; and psychological dependence, 92–93; search for, 2–3, 206; search for, inward and outward, 7; understanding motives for, 6–7. *See also* Search
Self: absence of, 75; achieving understanding of, 33; cessation of, 254; versus creativity, 17; ending of, 76; and envy, 28; and experience, 16; and mediocrity, 189; as society, 44–45. *See also* Center; Consciousness; 'Me'
Self-awareness: available to all, 190; and 'becoming', 267–68; characterizing, 211; of conditioning, 101–2; and confusion, 262; and total action, 234. *See also* Awareness; Mind; Self-knowledge
Self-centered: and the quiet mind, 84; and violence, 81–82
Self-centered activity: and accumulation, 168–69; as the central problem, 54; and change, 100–101; and cultivation, 223, 226; and discipline, 247–49; freedom from, 241; and guilt, 243–44; and meditation. *See also* Consciousness; 'Me'; Tradition
Self-concern: and sorrow, 56
Self-conscious: and struggle, 63
Self-contradiction: and confusion, 204
Self-discipline: versus social discipline, 96
Self-fulfillment: as endless process, 6–7; futility of search for, 182; and guilt, 243–44
Self-importance: absence of, 169
Self-knowledge: achieving, 110, 199; without authority, 69–70; and awareness, 53–54, 221; and 'becoming', 268–69; and the beginning of meditation, 105; and clarity, 205–6; and compassion, 262; and conclusions, 25; versus condemnation, 179; and conditioning, 215; versus confusion, 36, 66; difficulty of achieving, 78–79; and discipline, 249; and the end of thought, 214; and energy, 251; and freedom from conditioning, 125–26, 199; freedom from fear, 213; and the free mind, 228–29, 272; without illusion, 76; importance of total, 71–72; and love, 176; and meditation, 161–62; as moment to moment, 127–28; versus the need for authority, 181; and the new, 50–51, 252–53; and the problem, 124; and reality, 9; and relationship, 144; and religion, 187; and revolution, 210; versus self-centered activity, 88–89; versus self-concern, 55; versus the shallow life, 87; and sorrow, 56–57; and suffering, 103–104; and the timeless, 203; and total action, 211; and transformation, 129–30; and truth, 34; and the unconscious, 51; and understanding, 2–3; and understanding the mind, 32–33; and the well-ordered mind, 226; and wisdom, 16, 33; and world problems, 118–19
Self-observation: and the process of relationship, 181
Self-occupation: and dreams, 55
Self-understanding: defining, 3–4
Sensation: and the desire to possess, 245; and drugs, 89; as experience, 16–17
Senses, 235–36
Sensitivity: and the aware mind, 151–52; and habit, 134–35; and the individual, 190; as love, 176; need for, 236
Sentimentality: versus emotion, 4
Separation: and religion, 125. *See also* Divisions
Serious: and danger, 64; state of being, 243
Shallow mind: and knowledge, 3. *See also* Petty mind
Shallowness: and the sense of power, 95; and social formulas, 12
'Should be': and 'becoming', 267. *See also* Ambition; *What is*
Silence: and creativity, 251–52. *See also* Quiet mind; Silent mind
Silent mind: and the absence of ambition, 135; achieving, 251; and the cessation of thought, 250–51;

and energy, 249; and exploitation, 169; and happiness, 127; and individual action, 180; as intense, 85. *See also* Empty mind; Occupied mind; Quiet mind
Simplicity: as approach to life, 259
Sin: and guilt, 243–44
Sleep: and the sensitive mind, 152
Social complexity: and social justice, 188
Socialism. *See* Authority; Conformity; Divisions; Ideology; Society; War
Social justice: and friendship, 187–88
Social morality: and religion, 224–25, 246, 249
Social order: and mind control, 163–64, 166
Social patterns: renunciation of, 201
Social problem: and the individual problem as one, 107–10
Social structure: and psychological conflict, 63
Society: achieving freedom from, 45; and authority, 99–101; and career pressures, 263; and character, 196; characterizing, 171–72; as competitive, 119; as conditioner, 37–38, 174; as conditioner of the individual, 129–30; and conditioning, 31–32, 34; as corrupt, 65; defining, 45; and education, 146–47; freedom from, 12, 172; and friendship, 187–88; as hindrance to freedom, 40; and individual change, 192; and juvenile delinquency, 4–5; and outward security, 7; and the pattern of war, 84; and predetermination, 90; rejection of, 126; and relationship, 180; as relationship between people, 70; and religious revolution, 95; understanding, 12; and violence, 59–60, 80; and world conflict, 43–44. *See also* Collective; Government; Individual
Soldier: versus right profession, 263
Solutions: and desire, 157
Sorrow, 56–58; creating, 57; and the desire to become, 266–68; freedom from, 194; and living totally, 244; as problem of life, 124. *See also* Pain, Suffering
Soul: belief in, 10
Specialists: as authority, 77. *See also* Leaders
Spiritual: achieving, 49; and divisions, 123. *See also* Religion
Spiritual authority: defining, 127
Spontaneity: and awareness, 54
State. *See* Government; Society
Still mind, 4; achieving, 111–12, 199; awareness, 221; through change, 138; without contradiction, 221; and freedom, 30; and freedom from belief, 114; and freedom from envy, 48; and timelessness, 17. *See also* Happiness; Quiet mind; Revolution
Striving: and envy, 29–30
Student: and freedom, 193. *See also* Children
Struggle: and the growth of self, 75
Success: and conflict, 5–7; results of search for, 64; worship of, 116. *See also* Ambition; 'Becoming'
Suffering: defining, 8; escape from, 35; problems of, 235; and rebirth, 103. *See also* Sorrow
Superficial: and the search for satisfaction, 211. *See also* Petty mind; Shallowness
Suppression: and conformity, 246; and the insensitive mind, 244; and the senses, 236. *See also* Discipline; Method
Systems. *See* Discipline; Method; Patterns

Teacher: and change, 193; and follower, 18; as stupid, 198. *See also* Authority; Education
Teacher and disciple: division between, 231
Teaching: and discipline, 180–81. *See also* Authority
Technical knowledge, 9. *See also* Technology
Technique: as hindrance to meditation, 104–5. *See also* Discipline; "How"; Patterns
Technology: advance of, 191–92; effects of, 192
Thinker and the thought, 142; and the conflict of duality, 41; and meditation, 105; as one, 14–15, 67, 82–83, 114–15; and the quiet mind, 85; and violence, 82–83. *See also* Mind
Thinking: and awareness of the process, 39; and conclusions, 23–24; without condemnation, 228–29; and conditioning, 40; consciousness of, 54; ending, 179–80; ending the process of, 213–14; experiencing the process of, 112–14; and influences of conditioning, 198; and inquiry, 139; as limited, 113; as memory response, 219; negative and positive, 19; process of, 19, 50, 143, 214, 220, 238, 249–50, 260; as product of tradition, 50; suppositional, 22; understanding, 112–14; understanding the process of, 59. *See also* Mind
Thought: coming to an end, 84–85; and conditioning, 104; and continuity, 10; as endless, 84; field of, 142. *See also* Mind; Thinking
Thought control: government, 163–64
Thought, desire, and feeling: as one, 264–66
Time: and change, 193–94, 232; and experience, 51; versus the free mind, 127; and gradual change, 117–18; and the mind, 113, 142, 237, 258; revolution of, 170; and the role of religion, 118; and the struggle to become, 87–88; and thinking, 250–51; versus transformation, 102. *See also* Continuity
Timeless: as basic, 232–34; and the creative, 10; and freedom from fear, 209–10
Total action: and the free mind, 210–11; understanding, 174–76
Total attention: and the cessation of 'me', 259; and discipline, 257; and reality, 272. *See also* Meditation
Total change. *See* Change; Religion; Revolution; Transformation; True Religion
Totality: of approach to problems, 4; awareness of, 253; defining, 129; versus the detail of thought, 64; versus the fragmentary, 148–49; the need to understand, 85–88; of problems, 139–41
Totality of life: versus the fragmentary, 148–49
Totality of mind: conscious and unconscious, 141, 143–44
Total mind: and the hindrance of ideas, 111
Total revolution: versus authority, 205–6; and the free mind, 130. *See also* Change; Religion; Religious revolution, Revolution
Tradition: versus change, 69; and contradiction, 234; freedom from, 109, 178; as hindrance to God,

71; and mediocrity, 11–12, 26, 59; and memory, 51; versus new relationships, 192; and time, 127; versus true religion, 186. *See also* Accumulation; Conformity: Discipline; Memory
Training: versus the free mind, 18; as hindrance, 19–20. *See also* Method
Transformation: versus accumulation, 157; achieving, 102; and conflict, 117–18; and the experiencer and the experience as one, 83; as personal action, 253; and the self, 241; of society, through the individual, 129–30. *See also* Change; Religion; Revolution; True Religion
True: and the cessation of influence, 104; and the cessation of thought, 113; and freedom from fear, 133; and the free mind, 164–67; and the hindrance of belief, 107–9; and understanding the mind, 142–43. *See also* Reality
True religion; meaning of, 79; need for, 63; versus society, 224–25. *See also* Change; Religious revolution; Revolution
True revolution: and religion without security, 79
Truth: achieving, 165–67; approach to, 170–73; attempt to achieve, 240–43; versus authority, 205–6; versus the collective, 79; versus conditioning, 2, 8; as constant renewal, 131; and discontent, 32; discovery of, 233–34; and energy, 245; and fact, 30; and freedom, 27; and freedom from the known, 212; and the free mind, 12, 54, 123; futility of search for, 162; and humility, 264; and the individual, 70; and liberation, 40, 211; and the limitless mind, 20; versus organized religion, 200–201; as pathless, 201; perception of, 64; and religion, 217–18; and sentimentality, 236. *See also* God; Reality
Truth, beauty, and goodness: as one, 269
Tyranny: and control, 172; versus the spiritual life, 205; as the unknowable, 89–90, 197–98; and yoga, 41–42. *See also* God; Reality

Ugly: and beautiful, 269–70
Uncertainty: and the creation of reality, 35–56. *See also* Confusion
Unconditioned mind: and change, 195. *See also* Conditioning; Quiet mind
Unconscious: and awareness, 253; and challenge, 220; and conditioning, 38–39; describing the function of, 211–12; and dreams, 120, 151–52; and the free mind, 3; function of, 237; and the mind, 55; and motives, 39; and the power of thinking, 141–43; and self-knowledge, 51; and suppression, 146; and the unknown, 61
Understanding: attachment, 116; 'becoming', 266–69; and the capability of the many, 62; without comparison, 34; concentration, 160–61, 227–28; without condemnation, 13; conditioning, 215; conflict, 41; conscious mind, 211–12; consciousness, 18; dependence, 92–93; desire, 58, 221, 244–45; discipline, 146–47, 246–49; discontent, 183; envy, 27–30, 264–65; escape, 52–53; fear, 37, 93–94, 132; habit, 133–35; individuality, 176–77; influence, 116; karma, 221–23; knowledge, 259–62; learning, 231, 233; and listening, 112; love, 270–71; meditation, 160–62, 227–29; mind, 141–44, 237; need to seek, 6–7; oneness of living and dying, 154–55; past, 237; patterns, 11–12; problems, 110, 121, 124–25, 150, 173; process of, 139; and the process of the mind, 220–21; religion, 186; religious inquiry, 223–24; religious life, 207–8; righteousness, 223–25; right thinking, 220–21; the self, 33; thinking, 238, 249–51; thought process, 112–14; total action, 175–76; totality, 129; totality of life, 86–88; unconscious, 211–12; violence, 81; virtue, 246–48
Universal: as false, 80
Universal religions: and belief, 217; as contradiction, 245
Unknown: and change, 137; versus the conditioned, 272; fear of, 97–98; versus the known, 160; and self-knowledge, 212. *See also* God; Reality; Truth
Utopia: and conformity, 137–38

Vegetarianism: and freedom, 22
Verbal: world as, 141
Verbalization: as process of condemnation, 94. *See also* Conditioning; Naming; Words
Violence, 80–83; and change, 137; freedom from, 224–25; understanding, 80. *See also* War
Virtue: and awareness, 9; and the clever mind, 225; cultivation of, 246–48; and the ordered mind, 268; as respectability, 63; spontaneous versus cultivated, 62. *See also* Humility
Virtuous life: going beyond, 62
Visions: as conditioned, 161

War: causes of, 73–74; creating, 116; versus love of children, 59; and organized religion, 103; separation as cause of, 115; and the social structure, 45. *See also* Divisions; Government; Society; Violence
Watcher and the watched: as one, 14–15. *See also* Analyzer and the analyzed; Observer and the observed; Thinker and the thought
Wealth: as societal motivator, 45
Welfare state, 174; and need for physical security, 42. *See also* Government; Security
West: and East, 1; and influence on the East, 234, 239; and world problems, 44. *See also* Technology
What is: escape from, 4, 8, 52; versus ideals, 117; and knowledge, 259–60; and truth, 132; versus 'what should be', 11, 137; and will, 13–14. *See also* Fact; 'What should be'
'What should be': and idealism, 96
Whole: and living and dying, 154–55; versus the particular, 128–29. *See also* Divisions; Totality
Will: and the creation of conflict, 46; defining, 13–14; examining, 26–27; and the free mind, 26–27
Wisdom: and awareness, 20; beginning of, 119; and self-knowledge, 124, 167; and understanding discontent, 183
Words: as communication, 144–46; as conditioned, 47–48, 112, 114; freedom from, 185; as knowledge, 266; as memory, 144–46; and problems, 123; ver-

sus the thing, 229. *See also* Naming; Verbalization
Work: dissatisfaction with, 95; inquiry as, 253, 255. *See also* Livelihood; Profession
World: conflicts in, 107; and need for change, 203; as personal relationships, 252; physical and psychological problems of, 10. *See also* Collective; Divisions; Individual
World change: and contradiction, 239–40
Worldly: and divisions, 123
World problems: and change, 260; and deterioration, 183; East and West, 44; and human relationship, 43–44; and individual change, 118–19; as individual problems, 239–41, 242; and the search for truth, 36; and self-knowledge, 70, 124

Yoga: and the search for God, 41–42; and value of exercise, 88–89
'You': and the cessation of knowledge, 262; defining, 258. *See also* Self

www.ingramcontent.com/pod-product-compliance
Lightning Source LLC
Chambersburg PA
CBHW080429140626
46572CB00003B/7
9781934989432